Everyman, I will go with thee,
and be thy guide

Gerard Manley Hopkins

POETRY AND PROSE

Edited by
WALFORD DAVIES

EVERYMAN
J. M. DENT · LONDON
CHARLES E. TUTTLE
VERMONT

This edition first published in Everyman Paperbacks in 1998

Revised 2002

J. M. Dent
Orion Publishing Group
Orion House
5 Upper St Martin's Lane,
London WC2H 9EA
and
Charles E. Tuttle Co., Inc.
28 South Main Street,
Rutland, Vermont 05701, USA

Printed in Great Britain by
Clays Ltd, St Ives plc

British Library Cataloguing-in-Publication Data
is available on request

ISBN 0 460 87714 3

CONTENTS

Note on the Author and Editor x
Chronology of Hopkins's Life and Times xii
Dedication xxiv
Introduction xxv

POEMS 3

1   The Escorial 3
2   Winter with the Gulf Stream 7
3   Spring and Death 8
4   New Readings 9
5   Heaven-Haven 9
6   'I must hunt down the prize' 10
7   'Why should their foolish bands, their hopeless
    hearses' 10
8   'It was a hard thing to undo this knot' 10
9   'Miss Story's character! too much you ask' 11
10 Io 12
11 To Oxford 13
    'New-dated from the terms that reappear' 13
    'Thus, I come underneath this chapel side' 13
12 The Alchemist in the City 14
13 To Oxford 15
    'As Devonshire letters, earlier in the year' 15
14 'Myself unholy, from myself unholy' 16

15 'See how Spring opens with disabling cold' 16

16 'My prayers must meet a brazen heaven' 17

17 Shakspere 17

18 'Let me be to Thee as the circling bird' 18

19 The Half-way House 18

20 A Complaint 19

21 'Moonless darkness stands between' 20

22 'The earth and heaven, so little known' 20

23 'The stars were packed so close that night' 21

24 The Nightingale 22

25 The Habit of Perfection 23

26 Nondum 24

27 Lines for a Picture of St Dorothea 26

28 Horace: *Persicos odi, puer, apparatus* 27

29 Horace: *Odi profanum volgus et arceo* 28

30 The Elopement 29

31 The Wreck of the Deutschland 31

32 Moonrise 40

33 The Silver Jubilee 41

34 The Woodlark 41

35 Penmaen Pool 43

36 God's Grandeur 44

37 The Starlight Night 45

38 Spring 45

39 In the Valley of the Elwy 46

40 The Sea and the Skylark 46

41 The Windhover 47

42 Pied Beauty 48

43 Hurrahing in Harvest 48

44 The Caged Skylark 49

45 The Lantern out of Doors 49

46 The Loss of the Eurydice 50
47 The May Magnificat 53
48 'Denis, whose motionable, alert, most vaulting wit' 55
49 'The furl of fresh-leaved dogrose down' 55
50 'He mightbe slow and something feckless first' 56
51 'What being in rank-old nature should earlier have that breath been' 56
52 Binsey Poplars 57
53 Duns Scotus's Oxford 58
54 Henry Purcell 58
55 'Repeat that, repeat' 59
56 The Candle Indoors 60
57 The Handsome Heart 60
58 'How all's to one thing wrought!' 61
59 Cheery Beggar 62
60 The Bugler's First Communion 62
61 Morning, Midday, and Evening Sacrifice 64
62 Andromeda 65
63 Peace 65
64 At the Wedding March 66
65 Felix Randal 67
66 Brothers 67
67 Spring and Fall 69
68 Inversnaid 69
69 'As kingfishers catch fire, dragonflies draw flame' 70
70 Ribblesdale 70
71 A Trio of Triolets 71
72 The Leaden Echo and the Golden Echo 72
73 *from* St Winefred's Well 74
74 The Blessed Virgin compared to the Air we Breathe 80

75 'The times are nightfall, look, their light grows less' 83

76 'Not of all my eyes see, wandering on the world' 84

77 'To seem the stranger lies my lot, my life' 84

78 'I wake and feel the fell of dark, not day' 85

79 'Strike, churl; hurl, cheerless wind, then' 86

80 'No worst, there is none. Pitched past pitch of grief' 86

81 To what serves Mortal Beauty? 87

82 'Not, I'll not, carrion comfort, Despair, not feast on thee' 87

83 'Yes. Why do we all, seeing of a soldier, bless him?' 88

84 'Thee, God, I come from, to thee go' 89

85 'Patience, hard thing! the hard thing but to pray' 89

86 'My own heart let me more have pity on' 90

87 To his Watch 91

88 Spelt from Sibyl's Leaves 91

89 On the Portrait of Two Beautiful Young People 92

90 Harry Ploughman 93

91 Tom's Garland 94

92 Epithalamion 95

93 'The sea took pity: it interposed with doom' 97

94 That Nature is a Heraclitean Fire and of the comfort of the Resurrection 97

95 In honour of St Alphonsus Rodriguez 98

96 'Thou art indeed just, Lord, if I contend' 99

97 'The shepherd's brow, fronting forked lightning' 99

98 To R. B. 100

SELECTED PROSE 101

Early Diaries and Journals 101

Letters 129

Devotional Writings 160

Modern Critical Views 185
Explanatory Notes to the Poems 248
Suggestions for Further Reading 313
Note on the Text 316
Acknowledgements 317
Index of Titles and First Lines (Poetry) 319

NOTE ON THE AUTHOR AND EDITOR

GERARD MANLEY HOPKINS was born on 28 July 1844 at Stratford, Essex, the first of eight children in a devout but moderate Anglican family of wide talents in the arts. The family moved from Stratford to Hampstead in 1852. The poet's father, a marine adjuster, was later Consul-General for Hawaii and their Chargé d'Affaires for Great Britain. After attending Highgate School as a boarder (1854–62), where he won most of the poetry prizes, Hopkins gained a classics exhibition to Balliol College, which he entered in April 1863. An outstanding student, he achieved a First in both Honour Moderations and Greats. A year before graduating he converted to Roman Catholicism and was received into that church by Cardinal Henry Newman in October 1866. In 1868, on deciding to become a Jesuit priest, he burned his early poems.

The eight years of training leading to his full ordination in September 1877 included periods in the Jesuit Novitiate at Manresa House, Roehampton, at the St Mary's Hall seminary at Stonyhurst in Lancashire, and at St Beuno's College in the Vale of Clwyd in North Wales, where he learned a good deal of the Welsh language. At St Beuno's he also resumed the writing of poetry at a new enhanced stage with 'The Wreck of the Deutschland', inspired by the death in that wreck of five Franciscan nuns, refugees from the anti-clerical Falk Laws in Germany. The poem was the first fully to employ the metrics Hopkins called 'sprung rhythm' and to adapt effects learned from strict-metre Welsh poetry. Thereafter followed a continuous body of poems, small in number but in many ways ahead of their time, and now recognised as major. The poems, however, were produced in virtual obscurity. Only a few correspondents had the privilege of reading them, pre-eminently an Oxford friend, Robert Bridges, who in 1918 published *Poems of Gerard Manley Hopkins*, twenty-nine years after Hopkins's death.

Beyond the crucial North Wales period, from 1877 onwards Hopkins's career as a Jesuit priest took the form of various teaching and ministering posts: in Lancashire, London, Oxford, Bedford Leigh near Manchester, Liverpool, Glasgow, and back at Roehampton and Stonyhurst again. Finally, in 1884, he was appointed Fellow in Classics and Professor of Greek and Latin Literature at the new University College, Dublin. Heavy teaching and examining duties took their toll of the poet's always frail constitution, and he succumbed to typhoid fever. He died on 8 June 1889, and is buried in the Jesuit plot in Glasnevin Cemetery, Dublin.

WALFORD DAVIES, formerly Senior Lecturer in English Literature at St Anne's College, Oxford, holds a personal chair in English Literature at the University of Wales, and is currently Visiting Professor in English Literature at Wheaton College, Illinois.

He is the author of two critical studies of Dylan Thomas (*Dylan Thomas*, Open University Press, 1986, and *Dylan Thomas*, University of Wales Press, 1990). Amongst other volumes by and about Dylan Thomas that he has edited for Dent are *Early Prose Writings* (1971), *New Critical Essays* (1972), *The Collected Stories* (1983), *Selected Poems* (1993) and, with Ralph Maud, *Collected Poems 1934–1953* (1988) and *Under Milk Wood* (1995). Other editions include *Wordsworth: Selected Poems* (Dent, 1974), *Gerard Manley Hopkins: The Major Poems* (Dent, 1979), *Thomas Hardy: Selected Poems* (Dent, 1982), *Deaths and Entrances* (Gregynog Press 1984), *Under Milk Wood* (Penguin, 2000) and *Dylan Thomas: Selected Poems* (Penguin 2000).

CHRONOLOGY OF HOPKINS'S LIFE

Hopkins, too, was keen on recording dates and headlines from year to year. In his private Journal *for 1870 and 1871, for example, he listed many events taken from* Whitaker's Almanack. *Amongst major European events of Roman Catholic import, and others of more local British interest, he recorded the loss of the turret-ship* H.M.S. Captain *in a storm off Cape Finisterre on 7 September 1870, with the loss of some 500 lives. Amongst the drowned was a Catholic convert, whose children would now have to be brought up as Protestants. The event, and its significance for Hopkins, obviously prefigured the loss, five years later, of the* Deutschland.

Year	Age	Life
1843		Manley Hopkins and Kate Smith (parents) marry. Manley publishes *The Philosopher's Stone and Other Poems*
1844 (28 July)		Gerard Manley Hopkins born Stratford, Essex; eldest of five brothers, three sisters
1849	4	Poet's father (and uncle) publish *Pietas Metrica* (poems)

CHRONOLOGY OF HIS TIMES

Year	Literary Context	Historical Events
1833	Keble, Assize Sermon – 'On the National Apostasy'	Oxford Movement begins
1837	Carlyle, French Revolution	Accession of Queen Victoria
1839	Carlyle, Chartism	Chartist riots
1840	Browning, Sordello Darwin, Voyage of the Beagle	Queen Victoria marries Prince Albert
1841	Carlyle, Heroes and Hero-Worship	Peel (Conservative) becomes Prime Minister; Edward VII born
1842	Tennyson, Poems Wordsworth, Poems Chiefly of Early and Late Years	Mines Act Chartist riots
1843	Carlyle, Past and Present Ruskin, Modern Painters I	Wordsworth made Poet Laureate on Southey's death
1844	Barnes, Poems of Rural Life	Factory Act, restricting working hours
1845	Browning, Dramatic Romances	Newman converted to Roman Catholicism; Irish potato famine
1846	Keble, Lyra Innocentium Lear, Book of Nonsense George Eliot, translation of Strauss's Life of Jesus	Repeal of the Corn Laws Pius IX becomes Pope
1847	Tennyson, The Princess	Communist League founded
1848	Newman, Loss and Gain. Communist Manifesto	Pre-Raphaelite Brotherhood founded; democratic revolutions in France, Germany, Austria, Poland and Italy
1849	Arnold, Strayed Reveller and Other Poems Froude, The Nemesis of Faith Ruskin, Seven Lamps of Architecture	

Year	Age	Life
1851	6	Poet's father reviews Tennyson's *In Memoriam* in *The Times*
1852	7	Family moves to Oak Hill, Hampstead. Attends day school at Hampstead
1854–63	10–18	Boarder at Highgate School, near Hampstead. R. W. Dixon (later correspondent) taught there 1861; School Poetry Prize (1860) for 'The Escorial'; Governors' Gold Medal for Latin verse (1862)
1856 (Feb)	12	Poet's father appointed consul-general for Hawaii in London
1857	13	Poet's father publishes *A Handbook of Average*, on shipping insurance. Visits Belgium and Rhineland
1860	16	Touring south Germany with his father
1862	18	Poet's father publishes *History of Hawaii*, praising Catholic missionaries there

Year	Literary Context	Historical Events
1850	Tennyson, *In Memoriam* Browning, *Christmas Eve and Easter Day* Wordsworth, *The Prelude*	Tennyson made Poet Laureate on Wordsworth's death; restoration of the Roman Catholic hierarchy in England
1851	Ruskin, *Pre-Raphaelitism* and (–1853) *The Stones of Venice I*	The Great Exhibition in London
1852	Arnold, *Empedocles on Etna* Newman, *Scope and Nature of University Education*	Derby (Conservative) becomes Prime Minister; death of Wellington
1853	Arnold, *Poems*	
1854	Tennyson, *The Charge of the Light Brigade* George Eliot, translation of Feuerbach's *Essence of Christianity*	Crimean War (–1856); Dogma of the Immaculate Conception of Mary declared by Pope Pius IX
1855	Browning, *Men and Women* Tennyson, *Maud and Other Poems* Arnold, *Poems*, second series	Palmerston (Liberal) becomes Prime Minister
1856	Newman, *Callista*	
1857	Ruskin, *The Political Economy of Art*	Indian Mutiny (–1859)
1858	Clough, *Amours de Voyage*	Derby (Conservative) becomes Prime Minister
1859	Tennyson, *Idylls of the King* Darwin, *Origin of Species* Mill, *On Liberty*	Palmerston (Whig-Liberal) becomes Prime Minister
1860	Wilson and others, *Essays and Reviews*	Wilberforce and Huxley debate at Oxford meeting of British Association; Lincoln elected President of USA
1861	Palgrave, *Golden Treasury* Mill: *Utilitarianism*	Prince Albert dies; American Civil War (–1865)
1862	Clough, *Collected Poems* Meredith, *Modern Love* Ruskin, *Unto this Last*	Bismarck elected German Prime Minister, devoted to uniting Germany under Prussian (Protestant) leadership

Year	Age	Life
1863 (April)– 67 (June)	19–23	Classics exhibitioner, Balliol College, Oxford; friendship with Mowbray Baillie and Robert Bridges (later correspondents); 1864: First in 'mods'; 1863–66: keeps Diaries – descriptions of nature, drawings, word-lists, drafts of early poems. 1866 (May): starts private Journal [to 1875 (Feb)] – descriptions of nature, theory of 'inscape' and 'instress'
1865 (March)	21	Begins daily spiritual notes
1866 (Oct)	22	Received by Newman into Roman Catholic Church
1867 (June) (July)	22 22	First class degree in 'Greats' Visits Paris
1867 (Sept)– 68 (April)	23	Resident schoolmaster, Oratory School, Birmingham, under Cardinal Newman. Decides 2 May 1868 to become a Jesuit priest. Decides 11 May 1868 to burn his early poems 1863–65. July: walking tour of Switzerland
1868 (Sept)– 70 (Sept)	24–6	'Novitiate' period as candidate for Jesuit ministry at Manresa House, Roehampton. Sept 1870: takes vows of poverty, chastity and obedience
1870 (Sept)– 73 (Aug)	26–9	'Philosophate' three-year period of study at St Mary's Hall, Stonyhurst, Lancashire. Summer 1872: first reads Duns Scotus

Year	Literary Context	Historical Events
1863	Huxley, *Man's Place in Nature* Lyell, *Geological Evidence of the Antiquity of Man*	
1864	Newman, *Apologia Pro Vita Sua* Browning, *Dramatis Personae* Tennyson, *Idylls of the Hearth (Enoch Arden)*	Pius IX's *Syllabus of Errors*, condemning Socialism, Pantheism, civil marriage and religious indifferentism; in Germany, Bismarck requires civil marriage of all
1865	Newman, *Dream of Gerontius* Arnold, *Essays in Criticism*, first series Whitman, *Drum-Taps* & *Sequel to Drum-Taps* Carroll, *Alice's Adventures in Wonderland*	Russell (Whig-Liberal) becomes Prime Minister; President Lincoln assassinated
1866	Swinburne, *Poems and Ballads* Ruskin, *Ethics of the Dust*	Derby (Conservative) becomes Prime Minister
1867	Arnold, *New Poems* Ruskin, *Time and Tide* Marx, *Das Kapital, I*	Second British Reform Act; women's suffrage societies launched
1868	Browning, *The Ring and the Book*	Disraeli (Conservative) becomes Prime Minister (Feb); Gladstone (Liberal) becomes Prime Minister (Dec)
1869	Arnold, *Collected Poems* and *Culture and Anarchy*	
1870	Newman, *Grammar of Assent* Rossetti, *Poems* Huxley, *Lay Sermons*	Declaration of Papal Infallibility; Forster's Education Act; Franco-Prussian War (–1871)

Year	Age	Life
1873 (Aug)–74 (Aug)	29–30	Teaching Rhetoric at Manresa House, Roehampton, including 'Poetry and Verse'
1874 (Aug)–1877 (Oct)	30–33	The final period of training (theological study) at St Beuno's College, Flintshire, North Wales
1875 (6 Dec)	31	The wreck of the *Deutschland* leads to the resumption of poetic career
1877 (April)	32	Real start of correspondence with Robert Bridges. 23 September 1877: final ordination as Jesuit priest
1877 (Oct)–78 (May)	33	At Mount St Mary's College, Chesterfield: administration and classics teaching
1878 (May–June)	33	Stonyhurst again, preparing senior students in classics for London University examinations. Correspondence with Canon Dixon begins
1878 (July–Nov)	34	Acting curate at the Jesuit church of Farm Street, Mayfair
1878 (Dec)–79 (Octoer)	34–5	Assistant priest at the new parish church of St Aloysius, Oxford; chaplain to Cowley barracks
1879 (Oct–Dec)	35	Curate at St Joseph's, Bedford Leigh, near Manchester

Year	Literary Context	Historical Events
1871	Carroll, *Through the Looking Glass* Darwin, *The Descent of Man* Lear, *Nonsense Songs and Stories* Whitman, *Democratic Vistas* and *Passage to India*	Oxford and Cambridge end religious tests; legalisation of trades unions. Early 1970s, Bismarck, now Chancellor, legislates against Catholics, banishes Jesuits from Germany
1873	Bridges, *Poems* Arnold, *Literature and Dogma* Pater, *Studies in the Renaissance*	(May) Falk Laws in Prussia make the Catholic Church subject to state control
1874		Disraeli (Conservative) becomes Prime Minister; Factory Act
1875		German Catholic clergy jailed under Falk Laws; (5 Dec) five nuns embark in the *Deutschland* for America
1876	Bridges, *The Growth of Love*	Queen Victoria proclaimed Empress of India
1877	Arnold, *Collected Poems*	
1878	Swinburne, *Poems and Ballads*, series II	Leo XIII becomes Pope; (–1880) Bismarck repeals most of the Falk Laws
1879	Barnes, *Poems of Rural Life* (dialect poems) Browning, *Dramatic Idyls*, first series Bridges, *Poems* Tennyson, *The Lover's Tale*	

Year	Age	Life
1879 (Dec)–81 (Aug)	35–7	Select Preacher at St Francis Xavier's, Liverpool. In 1880 Bridges considers first collection of Hopkins's poems
1881 (Sept–Oct)	37	Temporary parish priest, St Joseph's, Glasgow
1881 (Oct)–82 (Sept)	37–8	'Tertianship' or 'Second Novitiate' period at Manresa House, Roehampton – study, prayer and physical work. Writes notes on the Spiritual Exercises. August 1882: takes final vows in the Society of Jesus
1882 (Sept)–84 (Feb)	38–9	At Stonyhurst again, teaching classics to senior students. Coventry Patmore visits Stonyhurst August 1883 – start of correspondence. August: in Holland with his parents. Bridges starts his second collection of Hopkins's poems.
1884 (Feb)–89 (June)	39–44	The final period: in Dublin as Fellow of the Royal University of Ireland and Professor of Greek and Latin Literature at University College. Lecturing and heavy examining duties. Increasing sense of physical and spiritual collapse, expressed in the 'terrible sonnets' of 1885
1886 (May)	41	Holiday in England: meets Bridges again
1887 (Aug)	43	Holiday in England. Poet's father publishes *The Cardinal Numbers*, acknowledging Hopkins's help in the volume
1888 (Aug)	44	Holiday in Scotland

Year	Literary Context	Historical Events
1880	Bridges, *Poems* Browning, *Dramatic Idyls*, second series Swinburne, *Studies in Songs* Tennyson, *Ballads and Other Poems*	Gladstone (Liberal) becomes Prime Minister
1881	Wilde, *Poems*	
1882	Scott, *A Poet's Harvest* Swinburne, *Tristram of Lyonesse and Other Poems* Whitman, *Specimen Days in America*	(May) Phoenix Park murders in Dublin
1883	Bridges, *Prometheus the Fire-Giver* Carroll, *Rhyme? and Reason?*	
1884	*The Oxford English Dictionary* (–1928) Ruskin, *The Art of England*, *The Pleasures of England* and *The Storm Cloud of the Nineteenth Century*	Third Reform Act
1885	Bridges, *Eros and Psyche* Tennyson, *Tiresias and Other Poems* Pater, *Marius the Epicurean* Ruskin, *Praeterita. Dictionary of National Biography* started	Salisbury (Conservative) becomes Prime Minister; fall of Khartoum; unemployment demonstrations in London; Irish Home Rule Bill defeated
1886	Tennyson, *Locksley Hall Sixty Years After* and *Promise of May and Other Poems*	Gladstone (Liberal) becomes Prime Minister (Feb); Salisbury (Conservative) becomes Prime Minister (Aug)
1887	Pater, *Imaginary Portraits*	Golden Jubilee of Queen Victoria
1888	Arnold, *Essays in Criticism*, second series	Kaiser Wilhelm II comes to power in Germany

Year	Age	Life
1889 (8 June)	44	Dies of typhoid at the age of forty-four; buried in the Society of Jesus part of Glasnevin cemetery, Dublin
1893		Bridges publishes eleven poems by Hopkins in A. H. Miles's *Poets and Poetry of the Century*
1915		Bridges publishes six poems by Hopkins in *The Spirit of Man*
1918		Bridges (ed.), *Poems of Gerard Manley Hopkins*

Year	Literary Context	Historical Events
1889	Pater, *Appreciations* Swinburne, *Poems and Ballads*, third series	Birth of Adolf Hitler
1890	Emily Dickinson, *Poems*	Death of Tennyson and Newman; (March) Bismarck resigns
1901		Death of Queen Victoria; accession of Edward VII
1914		(July) Outbreak of First World War
1918		(Nov) End of First World War

Hazel's

It Is Rhyme We Like, Not Echo

(1)

> The nearer hills, the other side of the valley, shewed a hard and
> beautifully detached and glimmering brim against the light, which
> was lifting there. All the length of the valley the skyline of hills
> was flowingly written all along upon the sky. A blue bloom, a
> sort of meal, seemed to have spread upon the distant south,
> enclosed by a basin of hills. Looking all around but most in
> looking far up the valley I felt an instress and charm of Wales.[1]

Thus a private journal entry of 6 September 1874. The thirty-
year-old Gerard Manley Hopkins had newly arrived at St
Beuno's College in Flintshire, North Wales. There, during the
next three years, he completed the final period of training
leading to his ordination as a Jesuit priest. It was there that so
much that shapes the poetry came most fully home to him. So it
is useful to look both backward and forward from that point.

The previous ten years had been a period of momentous
decisions radiating from his conversion to Roman Catholicism
in 1866 as a classics undergraduate at Oxford where Pusey had
dubbed him 'the star of Balliol'.[2] The Oxford of that period was
torn by intense religious debate, with Anglican loyalties under
pressure from two opposing forces, the general liberalising tendency of the age and the claims of tradition. In the face of
increasing secularisation, the Broad Church position minimised
dogma in order to reconcile Christianity with developments in
modern thought, while the Low or Evangelical Church reacted
by urging all the more literally the strict authority of scripture.
Neither view questioned the historical authenticity of the Church
of England as such, and within that church there still remained
a third option for a conservative young man making a decision
at that time. This was the High Church or 'Tractarian' position,
headed at Oxford by leaders like Pusey and Liddon. It was a
position to which Hopkins had given his natural allegiance. Ever

since the Oxford Movement of the 1830s, when *Tracts for the Times* was published, 'Tractarian' thought had urged an Anglo-Catholic stand against the levelling tendencies within the church. It insisted that the Church of England was itself Catholic, and that its bishops represented a true Apostolic succession. It also satisfied the young Hopkins's taste for ritual. But the 'Tractarians' did not accept the Roman doctrine of papal infallibility, which is what saved a belief in 'transubstantiation' (that in the Eucharist the consecrated elements become literally the body and blood of Christ) from the charge of superstition. It was this that proved the stumbling-block for Hopkins, as two decades earlier it had been for John Henry Newman, whose account of his own conversion to Roman Catholicism in his *Apologia Pro Vita Sua* (1864) was published during Hopkins's second year at Oxford. It prevented Hopkins from continuing in a church which otherwise, both aesthetically and dogmatically, he deeply loved and lamented leaving.

An equal trauma was the break from the moderate High Anglican traditions of his family and from his parents' expectations for their eldest child. It remained as painful at the end of his life as initially it had been bitter. His father had sought to prevent the conversion, and this filial break was compounded in being a break also with the very order of things in England. In Catholic Ireland at the end of his life, Hopkins's profound patriotic love for Anglican England ('wife/ To my creating thought') darkened into love-in-estrangement:

> To seem the stranger lies my lot, my life
> Among strangers. Father and mother dear,
> Brothers and sisters are in Christ not near . . .
>
> I am in Ireland now; now I am at a third
> Remove.[3]

His decision in 1868 to go all the way and become a Jesuit priest placed the separation beyond private belief or personal discomfort. As a follower of St Ignatius Loyola, founder of the Counter-Reformation order of the Jesuits, he was now dedicating himself to a disciplined *exploration* of his faith, and to the reconversion of Britain to Roman Catholicism. It was no merely notional aim. Only this ultimate vision even begins to explain the relentless self-sacrifice that marks his career from there on. In all he did after 1868 there is a refusal to accept anything merely 'notion-ally', and a determination to write as if in a permanent state of emergency. The very tone of the poetry – 'Buy then! bid then!', 'Have, get, before it cloy', 'After-comers cannot guess the beauty been'[4] – manifests the zeal of the convert.

Intellectually equipped to have been the leading Catholic apologist of his generation, Hopkins's fate after the North Wales period (1874–7) was to serve in posts for which, temper-amentally and physically, he was just not suited. More congenial intellectual projects had simply to be abandoned. His fate was as teacher at various Jesuit colleges, with periods as assistant priest at churches in London, Oxford, Manchester, Liverpool and Glasgow. The sordid urban conditions in Liverpool and Glasgow, and the ruinous inroads that industry made every-where into the world of nature, were to appall the sensibility of one who saw nature as a norm, not a luxury. In this he was always to remember the years in North Wales. Even at Rhyl in 1874 the sound of the sea and of a skylark off-land seemed to him to shame that 'shallow and frail town' in its surrender to the beginnings of the tourist boom.[5]

In 1884, he was to be appointed Professor of Greek at University College, Dublin, and Fellow of the Royal University of Ireland. This was the former Catholic University of Ireland, whose rectorship John Henry Newman had left thirty years before, having failed to persuade the Irish bishops that higher education should be something wider and deeper than sectari-anism. Hopkins had reached the right post at the wrong time. In 1884 the Royal University of Ireland was only a cobbled federation of institutions at Dublin, Galway, Cork and Belfast. It was little more than an examinations body – what Matthew Arnold called 'the grand name without the grand thing'. The contrast with Oxford could not have been greater. Hopkins's often over-detailed lectures and sermons had always shown a weak grasp of the needs of an actual audience. In Dublin over-scrupulous concern in the colossal burden of five years of examination-marking ('it is killing work to examine a nation') increased the danger. In this subjection to discipline, well beyond the demands of his order, he was his own worst enemy where health and a sense of personal deservingness were con-cerned. It was bound to bring about physical as well as spiritual collapse, precipitated in the end by the rat-infested conditions of the house in St Stephen's Green in which he had to live. He died of typhoid, at the age of forty-four, on 8 June 1889, the vigil of Pentecost.

(2)

But Hopkins survives, not because of the outward career. He was also a poet. *That* is what is shown by the journal entry of 1874 with which we started. The immediately preceding image shows the same wonderfully focused writing:

> The cleave in which Bodfari and Caerwys lie was close below. It was a leaden sky, braided or roped with cloud, and the earth in dead colours, grave but distinct.

Hopkins's real biography is in the 'rehearsal of own, of abrupt self'[6] that this particular kind of writing makes possible. It is a poetry more accessible to our own time than it ever could have been to Victorian readers, despite the deeply Victorian nature of so much of its interests. Robert Bridges – the Oxford friend who, along with one or two other correspondents, was Hopkins's only audience during his lifetime – judged happily when he delayed publication of the poems until 1918, twenty-nine years after Hopkins's death. Like Thomas Wentworth Higginson's reaction to Emily Dickinson in America around the same time, even Bridges' admiration was held back by a deep period-resistance to the originality of the poems.

Five years before arriving at St Beuno's College in 1874 Hopkins had already made another momentous decision – to destroy his undergraduate poems. The journal entry recording the fact – the 'Slaughter of the innocents'[7] – reflects the agony. Earlier journal entries show the same pain: 'On this day by God's grace I resolved to give up all beauty until I had His leave for it'.[8] And later entries echo the hope that one day the poet as well as the priest in him could be officially blessed. He told R. W. Dixon in 1878 that he had resolved 'to write no more, as not belonging to my profession, unless it were by the wish of my superiors'.[9] That permission came in the wake of a tragic event of 7 December 1875. The *Deutschland*, a ship bound from Bremen to New York, was wrecked in the mouth of the Thames. Among the drowned were five Franciscan nuns, refugees from the anti-clerical Falk Laws in Germany. The fact that there were no attempts at early rescue, although the ship took over twenty-four hours to sink, made the tragedy also a national scandal, reported in graphic detail in *The Times*, and the *Illustrated London News*. But it was the death of the nuns that focused Hopkins's attention. In response to a casual remark by his superior, that someone should commemorate the event, he wrote 'The Wreck of the Deutschland'.

Since 1868 he had written only 'two or three little presentation pieces'.[10] And now an opportunity to embark on a major poem had come unsought. It salved his fear that poetry was an unpriestly luxury, a fear that reflected a deep personal modesty. After all, poetry, painting and music were talents encouraged even in his own devoutly religious family. The wreck of the *Deutschland*, like the beauty of the Vale of Clwyd, challenged not only his imagination but also his belief. It called for praise and obedience, not just art. Poetry would be a luxury only if it failed to reflect this, an indulgence only if its language failed to be singular and inevitable. In the end, feelings of guilt at being a poet were to prove less oppressive than feelings of loss at having to be a secret one. Although the Jesuit priest always modestly accepted his personal obscurity, he also knew that a certain measure of feed-back was necessary to the creative process. The late sonnet 'Thou art indeed just, Lord, if I contend with thee' (p. 99) springs not from guilt at being a poet, but from a fear that the poetry is failing through being ignored. The notion of an absent audience merges with that of an absent God: the poems are 'cries like dead letters sent/To dearest him that lives alas! away'.[11] And yet isolation from the growing audience for literature in Victorian England worked ultimately to Hopkins's advantage. It enabled him to be eccentric (free of the centre) without the ridicule that that freedom would have entailed in public.

The path of obscurity also suited the convert in him, but it was certainly not smooth. The refusal of the Jesuit journal *The Month* to publish 'The Wreck of the Deutschland' in 1875 was a forecast of the critical blankness felt by even Robert Bridges in the face of the poetry's technical risks. But such a strong impulse to create was given rich sustenance at St Beuno's, quite apart from the dogmatic opportunity presented by the *Deutschland*'s tragedy. The North Wales landscape stimulated the idea that what the individuating powers of language do is complement the endless detail of the created world itself. Facing Snowdon across the broad Vale of Clwyd and overlooking beautiful smaller valleys such as that of the Elwy, dappled and river-run, the setting provided rich emblems for all that he had intellectually decided on. It called freshly, in another country, 'away in the loveable West', to his natural capacity for Praise. The Catholic 'Wreck of the Deutschland' has the same motive as the Protestant *Paradise Lost* – to 'justify the ways of God to men'. But Hopkins takes his power of advocacy, not from abstract dogma, but from concrete natural images – mountain waters, stars, river, wild fruit and 'pied and peeled May', counterpointed by their opposite in the murdering snow-storm that wrecked the ship. One stanza in particular distils the sharp insight that marks also the shorter poems of those three creative years in Wales:

> I kiss my hand
>   To the stars, lovely-asunder
> Starlight, wafting him out of it; and
>   Glow, glory in thunder;
> Kiss my hand to the dappled-with-damson west:
> Since, tho' he is under the world's spelndour and wonder,
>   His mystery must be instressed, stressed;
> For I greet him the days I meet him, and bless when I understand.

Stanza 5

All the hallmarks of the career are already there. The expressive, yet strenuously structured, form. The relish for the natural world, but salted and sobered by the conjoining of lovely *starlight* and challenging *thunder*. The relationship between outer-natural image and inner-religious significance, calling not only for unique inner perception ('instressed' – that word again) but also for tense outward proclamation ('stressed'). And, conveniently expressing everyone's experience on first reading Hopkins, 'I greet him the days I meet him, and bless when I understand'.

(3)

Robert Bridges said that 'The Wreck of the Deutschland' stood at the entrance to the poems 'like a great dragon folded in the gate to forbid all entrance'.[12] It is certainly true that works of smaller compass allow easier access. Towards the end of his life Hopkins lamented that he had 'no inspiration of longer jet than makes a sonnet'.[13] But the sonnet was in fact his ideal form, carrying a verbal resourcefulness unique in English poetry since Shakespeare. The long folds of 'The Wreck of the Deutschland' are powerfully epitomised in the shorter poems. A new reader does well therefore to start with the sonnets of 1877, Hopkins's third year in North Wales. These include 'God's Grandeur', 'The Starlight Night', 'Pied Beauty' and 'Hurrahing in Harvest'. They distil the disciplined joy that marked Hopkins's resumption of his career as a poet, and out of which arose his positive response even to the tragedy of the *Deutschland*. The number of these shorter poems would have been greater had Hopkins been granted what he himself earnestly wished, an extra fourth year of study at St Beuno's College.

A good point of departure in characterising the nature of the poetry is the most celebrated of those shorter poems of the St Beuno's period, 'The Windhover', which the poet at one stage described as 'the best thing I ever wrote'. In it, we can see distilled the main features of Hopkins's art:

THE WINDHOVER
to Christ our Lord

I caught this morning morning's minion, king-
   dom of daylight's dauphin, dapple-dawn-drawn Falcon, in
      his riding
Of the rolling level underneath him steady air, and striding
High there, how he rung upon the rein of a wimpling wing
In his ecstasy! then off, off forth on swing,
   As a skate's heel sweeps smooth on a bow-bend: the hurl
      and gliding
   Rebuffed the big wind. My heart in hiding
Stirred for a bird, – the achieve of, the mastery of the thing!

Brute beauty and valour and act, oh, air, pride, plume, here
   Buckle! AND the fire that breaks from thee then, a billion
Times told lovelier, more dangerous, O my chevalier!

   No wonder of it: sheer plod makes plough down sillion
Shine, and blue-bleak embers, ah my dear,
   Fall, gall themselves, and gash gold-vermilion.

The first point concerns the irreducible integrity of the immediate subject. The sub-title dedication – 'to Christ our Lord' –

disposes us to expect indirect meanings beyond the apparent, but the poem remains decisively a minutely observed description of this particular falcon's flight. A comment of Ezra Pound's comes to mind: 'I believe that the proper and perfect symbol is the natural object, that if a man uses "symbols" he must so use them that their symbolic function does not obtrude; so that *a* sense, and the poetic quality of the passage, is not lost to those who do not understand the symbol as such, to whom, for instance, a hawk is a hawk.'[14] Even in 1918, the year of Bridges' first edition, Pound was not thinking of Hopkins's poem, but the comment is wonderfully relevant. For Hopkins, the solid reality of the world is not to be quenched in metaphor. This is so despite the fact that everything in 'The Windhover' is charged and refracted through analogies. Objects are viewed in a highly elaborate way, but they do not disappear as subjects. They do not just 'stand for' something else. Indeed, they are less compromised by Hopkins's ornate renderings, and his theology, than they are in more typically Victorian poets by symbolic landscapes, dream atmosphere, medieval allegory, classical myth, and 'poetic' properties generally. In this sense, the classical symbolism of Hopkins's sonnet 'Andromeda' (1879), an allegory of the Victorian church beset by its enemies, is uncharacteristic of him:

> All while her patience, morselled into pangs,
> Mounts; then to alight disarming, no one dreams,
> With Gorgon's gear and barebill/thongs and fangs. (p. 65)

Yet, even there, the irresistible concreteness still respects the independent reality of things, even things within metaphors.

'Thing' or 'things' is a big word in Hopkins: 'These things, these things were here and but the beholder/Wanting' ('Hurrahing in Harvest'), 'Each mortal thing does one thing and the same' ('As kingfishers catch fire'), 'the achieve of, the mastery of the thing!' in 'The Windhover'. But that denaturing word 'thing' only puts into relief Hopkins's aim to raise 'things' to the level of phenomena. 'No wonder of it': what the last three lines of 'The Windhover' realise is the ability of even ordinary things (a kestrel, a plough, dead embers falling from the bottom of a grate) to reflect a glory normally associated with agents higher up the scale of creation. This directs us to recognise the hierarchy as a whole: the embers, the plough, the windhover in masterful flight, the suddenly ecstatic human perceiver, and then

'Christ our Lord'. Sadly, the twenty-first-century reader may no longer know even the 'things' themselves, because they are vanished or fast vanishing – hand-tended hayfields, plough-shares, kingfishers, dragonflies, kestrels.

But it is more complex than that. The idea of a hierarchy that sanctions the humble by association, but still *remains* a hier-archy, sprang naturally from Hopkins's Roman Catholicism. It finds its most poignant expression in the sonnet to St Alphonsus Rodriguez who was for forty years a simple hall-porter at the College of Palma in Majorca, a man whose 'honour' was not 'flashed off exploit' like the windhover's but a quiet 'conquest' in a 'world without event' (p. 98). The same hierarchy informs the political view of society in 'Tom's Garland: upon the Unemployed' (p. 94). But it should be remembered that the way that poem sees the body politic as a naturally ordained hierarchy of parts is not just Victorian. It recalls Menenius's speech in Shakespeare's *Coriolanus*; and in a letter to Bridges, Hopkins evoked St Paul, Plato and Hobbes.[15] It is also worth remember-ing writers only a few generations back from Hopkins who, like him, justify social stratification by an appeal to the world of nature. For example, here is Hazlitt paraphrasing Burke:

> The inequality of the different orders of society did not destroy the unity and harmony of the whole. The health and well-being of the moral world was to be promoted by the same means as the beauty of the natural world; by contrast, by change, by light and shade, by variety of parts . . . To think of reducing all mankind to the same insipid level, seemed to him the same absurdity as to destroy the inequalities of surface in a country for the benefit of agriculture and commerce.[16]

That pleasure in seeing 'inequalities of surface in a country' matches Hopkins's delight in 'Landscape plotted and pieced – fold, fallow, and plough' (p. 48). Better than 'Catholic' or 'Vic-torian', therefore, might be simply 'English'. Even Hopkins's respect for the serving forces in 'The Bugler's First Communion' (p. 62) and in the sonnet beginning 'Yes. Why do we all, seeing of a soldier, bless him? bless/ Our redcoats, our tars?' (p. 88) is not just 'Victorian'. The very question that opens that sonnet has its natural answer in Dr Johnson's view that 'Every man thinks meanly of himself for not having been a soldier, or not having been to sea'. Hopkins's views, though certainly not exactly Johnsonian, are just as deeply English. There is obviously more than one sense in which this Jesuit celebrates belonging to an order.

But we need to get closer to the texture, the inner activity, of the poetry itself. If we are to see both the poet's 'heart in hiding' and 'Christ our Lord' reflected in the windhover then all three are to be identified as being addressed in these lines:

> AND the fire that breaks from thee then, a billion
> Times told lovelier, more dangerous, O my chevalier!

If the bird is beautiful, how beautiful too must be the act of ecstatic recognition in a human perceiver, and how much more beautiful must Christ be. But an even deeper meaning is at work. What the images of plough and embers share is the paradox that it is in being resisted and broken that they are made to shine. It is the harrowing encounter with the hard earth that makes the plough (and the earth) shine; and it is the *fall*, *gall*, and *gash* of disintegration that cause the blue-bleak embers to break into vermilion flame. This sense of breakage then retrospectively activates the challenge of the sonnet as a whole, throwing us back on that word 'Buckle!'. The poet has in fact seen two aspects of the bird in flight. On one view, its controlling mastery; on another, the bird 'buckled', spreadeagled, crucified on the wind. It is that latter moment that is 'a billion times told lovelier, more dangerous'. Of course, the martial imagery, the zeal of the new Jesuit, gives other meanings to that word 'Buckle': the sense of 'buckling on armour', for example, or 'buckling down' to a deed. But the deepest emphasis of the sestet is that sense of buckling under stress and being broken. The full meaning, therefore, makes Christ present not only in princely aggrandisement but in the paradox of his suffering on the cross. *That* is the realisation that explodes in the pain ('gall'), the spear-wound ('gash'), and the blood ('vermilion') of the final line.

The word 'explode' is Hopkins's own. 'One of two kinds of clearness one should have,' he wrote, 'either the meaning to be felt without effort as fast as one reads or else, if dark at first reading, when once made out *to explode*'.[17] Pent-up meanings are all the more forceful when they finally dawn on us ('No wonder of it!'). In 'The Windhover', what explodes is the poem's main meaning. But local images and a series of otherwise quite innocent words can also flare up. When, in 'God's Grandeur' (p. 44), Hopkins says

> Oh, morning, at the brown brink eastward, springs

the appropriateness of 'springs' is not immediately apparent. Dawn is not usually thought of as 'springing', even though the Biblical 'dayspring' (Luke 1:78) is relevant here. A more ordinary force in the word 'springs' was released in the rhyming line two lines back:

> There lives the dearest freshness deep down things.

That 'dearest freshness' is now linked to literal 'springs' of water. We need to reconsider what we normally mean by rhyme. Deeper than any simple chiming of 'springs' with 'things' is the subtle filament from the springing of light to the springing of water, both miraculous.

Or take the tension that 'The Lantern out of Doors' sets up between two uses of the word 'interest', at the beginning and at the end of the poem:

> Sometimes a lantern moves along the night,
>   That interests our eyes . . .

> Christ minds: Christ's interest, what to avow or amend
>   There . . .   (p. 49–50)

The movement from something that only idly 'interests our eyes' to something much less idle – 'Christ's interest' – is achieved by deepening the very word 'interest' into its financial-redemptive meaning via other words of cost such as 'rare', 'rich' and 'buys':

> Men go by me whom either beauty bright
>   In mould or mind or what not else makes rare:
>   They rain against our much-thick and marsh air
> Rich beams, till death or distance buys them quite.

The poems zealously 'explode' extra meanings in the most ordinary words. Language is constantly directed inwards to create new meanings rather than, as in so much other Victorian poetry, outwards to create atmosphere. It is the difference between a 'Shakespearean' and a 'Spenserian' use of language. The contrast is also with the decorative side of Keats, an influence to which Hopkins's own early poems had fallen prey. In the mature Hopkins each single word (or its omission) has a stringent part to play in the creation of meaning. In the phrase 'dapple-dawn-drawn Falcon' in 'The Windhover' the bird is attracted by the dawn, certainly, but is also pictorially 'drawn', outlined vividly against the dawn light. It is the poet as visual artist who here claims to have 'caught' the shape, the mood, the moment of the bird's flight. And it is this inward precision that makes 'explosion' possible. In that sense, 'implosion' might be a better term. But the word 'implosion' had not been coined in Hopkins's day. It would have taken Hopkins to coin it.

That notion of hitting off the inner *reality* of a thing is what it is all about. The verb 'Buckle!' in 'The Windhover' culminates a series of six nouns:

> Brute beauty and valour and act, oh, air, pride, plume, here
> Buckle!

These qualities of the bird's flight come together to make one unique event. The way they do so is at the heart of what Hopkins means by 'inscape' and 'instress', the major concepts that matured in his mind on resuming his poetry in North Wales in 1875. The early diaries (1863–6) and journals (1866–75) are full of descriptions and drawings that seek to understand the intricate *composition* of things – cloud formations, church architecture, the action of water coming through a lock, a particular sunrise or sunset, an individual plant or tree or flower. In a letter of 1863 he wrote:

> for a certain time I am astonished at the beauty of a tree, shape, effect etc, then when the passion, so to speak, has subsided, it is consigned to my treasury of explored beauty, and acknowledged with admiration and interest ever after, while something new takes its place in my enthusiasm. The present fury is the ash, and perhaps barley and two shapes of growth in leaves and one in tree boughs and also a formation of fine-weather cloud.

Details are isolated from context. Everything is a landscape in itself. It is worth remembering that close botanical interest came to a fine flowering in Victorian England, often as the hobby of country clerics. But Hopkins's enterprise is not just antiquarian. Nor is his sense of detail that of the Pre-Raphaelites. One cannot forget Ezra Pound's witty joke about the Pre-Raphaelite painter who, engaged in depicting a twilight scene, rowed across the river in daylight to record more minutely the shape of the leaves on the further bank. Closer to Hopkins's purpose was Ruskin's attention in *Modern Painters* (1843) to the 'laws' governing the distinctive configurations of things such as fronds or clouds, the shapes of trees, or the symmetry of a chestnut fan. Seeking to understand the 'laws' of detail is different from simply *using* detail. In this way Hopkins shares also in that 'urge to know' that we see in Leonardo da Vinci's drawings. A scientific curiosity is always part of an artist's attempt to understand the patterns of physical reality. It is the natural interest that caused Hopkins to write four letters to *Nature*, detailing for example the colour changes he had observed in the phenomenal sunsets caused by the Krakatoa eruption of 1883.[19]

But what such fingerprints reveal for Hopkins is the nature of the Creator. It is clear already from 'The Windhover' that important concepts ('beauty', 'valour', 'act', 'pride') combine with physical qualities in creating that particular moment in which things 'buckle' together. What is fired by the bird's flight is an act of recognition beyond the ability of science to explain, or explain away. A reader with knowledge of the 'spots of time' in Wordsworth's *Prelude*, of Joyce's 'epiphanies', or Eliot's 'timeless moments' in *Four Quartets* ('the intersection of the timeless with time'), will be at home with the kind of experience Hopkins is describing. But the exact nature of the experience remains individual enough for him to have had to coin the words 'inscape' and 'instress' to describe it.

From its first use in a notebook of 1868, the word 'inscape' (coined by analogy with 'landscape') varies in its implications. But its main meaning is distinctive pattern, the relationship between parts that creates the integrity of the whole, which in turn is different at different times. 'All the world is full of inscape and chance left free to act falls into an order as well as purpose.'[20] So there is pattern even in natural accident. When W. B. Yeats in 'Among Schoolchildren' asks

> O chestnut tree, great-rooted blossomer,
> Are you the leaf, the blossom or the bole?

he is saying that no living ('rooted') thing is ever a mere aggregate of its parts. That celebration of irreducible completeness ('How can we know the dancer from the dance?') is Hopkinsian, but Hopkins pursues it much more strenuously. He takes it, for example, into the realm of language and individual personality as well as of 'things'. The sense of outrage at the injury done to nature by industrialism in 'God's Grandeur'(p. 44) or 'The Sea

and the Skylark' (p. 46) was something he shared with more
public contemporaries like Matthew Arnold and William Morris.
But Hopkins's focus cannot be shifted from particular to general
loss. When the 'Binsey Poplars' were felled, what the 'strokes of
havoc' did was *'unselve'* a 'sweet *especial* scene' (p. 57). Nor can
Hopkins's message be shifted from individual to public responsibility. At Roehampton, six years earlier, an ash tree had been
felled: 'I heard the sound and looking out and seeing it maimed
there came at that moment a great pang and I wished to die and
not see the inscapes of the world destroyed any more'.[21] No two
things, if properly seen, are identical. Individuality is irreplaceable. The key-note of 'inscape' is therefore not just pattern, but
unique pattern. In a Victorian culture already based on industrial
mass-production, this resistance to replaceability is itself an
irreplaceable part of Hopkins.

'Instress' is what explains why 'inscape' is no simple conser-
vationist matter. 'Instress' is the active energy that binds parts
into the 'inscape' of the whole, and for Hopkins it is the creative
energy of God himself, at work in the world. We could see its
opposite as 'distress', the notion of falling apart, of incoherence.
In his first use of the word in the journals, describing the
philosophy of Parmenides, Hopkins writes that 'all things are
upheld by instress and are meaningless without it'.[22] But it is
also a faculty of the human mind when it brings things into
creative relationship. It demands an act of pure attention, and
sometimes of solitary meditation, for 'with a companion the eye
and the ear are for the most part shut and instress cannot
come'.[23] Just as the prefix *in* emphasises the inwardness
involved, the word *stress* emphasises the tension (what Hopkins
elsewhere calls the 'stalling'[24]) that holds things in that distinctive relationship which comprises the 'inscape' of the whole.

Ideas regarding pattern and harmony, relayed through medieval philosophy from the views of Plato and Aristotle, are
central to Western aesthetic thought. Thus Thomas Aquinas,
whose teaching the Jesuits were meant to follow, speaks of three
aspects of beauty: *integritas*, the object as an entity discrete
from other entities; *consonantia*, the harmony of the related
parts constituting the object; and *claritas*, the brightness or
radiance of the object. But Hopkins diverges from Aquinas. We
can approach the divergence through James Joyce's analysis of
Aquinas's terms in Stephen Dedalus's words in *Stephen Hero*:

Now for the third quality. For a long time I couldn't make out what Aquinas meant. He uses a figurative word (a very unusual thing for him) but I have solved it. *Claritas* is *quidditas*. After the analysis which discovers the second quality [the *consonantia*] the mind makes the only logically possible synthesis and discovers the third quality. This is the moment which I call epiphany. First we recognize that the object is *one* integral thing, then we recognize that it is an organized composite structure, a *thing* in fact: finally, when the relation of the parts is exquisite, when the parts are adjusted to the special point, we recognize that it is *that* thing which it is. Its soul, its whatness, leaps to us from the vestment of its appearance. The soul of the commonest object, the structure of which is so adjusted, seems to us radiant. The object achieves its epiphany.

'When the parts are adjusted to the special point, we recognize that it is *that* thing which it is': this comes close to defining, respectively, 'instress' and 'inscape'. Stephen's excited emphasis on individuality is closer to Hopkins than it is to Aquinas. In fact, it would find its validation, not in Aquinas, but in the British medieval philosopher and Franciscan Friar, Duns Scotus. In Scotus, Hopkins found support for something already natural in his own way of seeing the world. At St Mary's seminary at Stonyhurst in 1872, six years after starting his journal and three years before restarting his poetry, a journal entry reads: 'At this time I had first begun to get hold of the copy of Scotus on the Sentences in the Baddely [Badeley] library and was flush with a new stroke of enthusiasm. It may come to nothing or it may be a mercy from God. But just then when I took in any inscape of the sky or sea I thought of Scotus.'[25] Hopkins also shared Scotus's belief in the Immaculate Conception of Mary and the belief that Christ's Incarnation was predestined irrespective of any reparation for human sin. But it was Scotus's theory of knowledge that caused this 'new stroke of enthusiasm'. Aquinas, and the Schoolmen generally, emphasised those aspects of a thing that related it to a universal category. Although all knowledge starts in the senses, what we recognised were the general classes of reality to which all individual things belonged. It was therefore generic classes alone that allowed us to make intellectual sense of particulars ('*particulare sentitur*; *universale intelligitur*'). But Duns Scotus believed that it is already a feature of the generic category to make the individual thing distinctive.

Our knowledge is therefore of the 'haecceitas', the *thisness* of a thing – not simply the 'quidditas' or *whatness* of its universal category. Everything reveals its ideal self *because*, not in spite of, its particularity. Hopkins seized on the emphasis. It legitimised his enjoyment of the endless detail of the created world. The poet's note at the head of his sonnet to Henry Purcell (p. 58) praises Purcell because he 'uttered in notes the very make and species of man as created both in him and in all men generally'. Beyond the distinctive beauties of the natural world in sonnets such as 'Pied Beauty', 'As kingfishers catch fire' and 'Duns Scotus's Oxford', the distinctiveness of an individual human being then becomes even more important, because the distinctiveness reflected in man is that incarnate in Christ himself.

(4)

For every Jesuit the pattern for realising the unique example of Christ was the sixteenth-century *Spiritual Exercises* of St Ignatius Loyola. Its four parts or 'Weeks' (purgation of past sins; contemplation of the Life of Christ and an Election to follow God's will; meditation on Christ's Passion; and on the Resurrection) had been central to Hopkins's formal training since his novitiate period in September 1868, and it remained the model for study, meditation and practice throughout his career. The inscaping of Christ's glory-through-suffering in the windhover's flight ('Buckle! AND the fire that breaks from thee then . . .') and in the wreck of the *Deutschland* has the disciplined meditation of the *Spiritual Exercises* behind it. The aim is to bring home the individual reality of Christ to the individual mind of man, along with the unique identities of nature, and the discriminations made possible by language. Hopkins reflects this discipline by showing that the sensational world of unique things is experienced by unique *perceivers*. Thus, in his uncompleted commentary on the *Spiritual Exercises*, started in 1880, the most relevant part for a study of the poetry is that on the 'First Principle and Foundation', which precedes the first 'Week'. St Ignatius's opening injunction, 'Man was created to praise', underlines everything. But in his commentary Hopkins halts with '*Homo creatus est*' – 'Man was created'. And his thoughts on the evidence that man *is* a created being, not an accident, turn on what he calls a 'feeling of myself, that taste of myself,

of *I* and *me* above and in all things'. Since human nature is unusually distinctive even in a distinctive world, it cannot have been arbitrarily 'evolved, condensed, from the vastness of the world': each human can have been created only by 'one of finer or higher pitch and determination than itself'. It is here that Hopkins's naturally individuating, Scotist, tendency fuses with his religious, Loyolan, duties as a Jesuit – in recognising that his own individual sensibility is at the service of proof and praise. 'I find myself both as man and as myself something most determined and distinctive, at pitch, more distinctive and higher pitched than anything else I see'.[26]

Determined, distinctive, at pitch: nothing better illustrates this feel-of-self than the irresistible need also to find an exact language for it. This involved, for Hopkins, considering anew the very resources of language: 'as air, melody, is what strikes me most of all in music and design in painting, so design, pattern or what I am in the habit of calling "inscape" is what I above all aim at in poetry'.[27] Just as God's instress is what brings inscapes into focus in nature, what activates them in Hopkins's poetry is the special kind of pressured movement that he developed for his verse. He called it 'sprung rhythm'. Its individual power will already have been felt in the reader's experience of 'The Windhover'. It had its first and fullest manifestation in 'The Wreck of the Deutschland': 'I had long had haunting my ear the echo of a new rhythm which I now realized on paper.'[28] The lectures on problems of rhythm, metre and prosody that Hopkins delivered during his year's teaching at Manresa House, Roehampton, directly before he went to St Beuno's in 1874, gave depth to what could be done with the stress, measure and movement of his own verse.

The common rhythm of traditional English poetry – what Hopkins called 'standard' or 'running' rhythm – is measured in feet of either two or three syllables. Those of two syllables can be either iambic ($\smile$ –) or trochaic (– $\smile$); those of three syllables either anapaestic ($\smile\smile$ –) or dactylic (– $\smile\smile$). But of course irregular effects can happen at the beginning or the end of lines, either before the main pattern has got into its stride or after it has already been established. Hopkins also drew attention to unusual metrical units even in standard rhythm, in which feet can appear to be paired, thus allowing double or composite feet to arise. Anyway, any poem with real rhythmic life will always cloud its basic pattern from time to time, not just in variations but also in the natural variations of the spoken voice. A counterpoint therefore develops, between the basic pattern and the deviations.

So regularity leaves room for the irregular. But sprung rhythm is not simply a capitalisation on that fact. Hopkins himself often adopts a standard rhythm (the iambic pentameter of the sonnet, for example) and then counterpoints it:

> The world is charged with the grandeur of God.
>> It will flame out, like shining from shook foil;
>> It gathers to a greatness, like the ooze of oil
> Crushed. Why do men then now not reck his rod?
> Generations have trod, have trod, have trod . . .

Here, the basic iambic pentameter is perceptible as a ghost-presence underneath the variations mounted on it, or counter-pointed to it, by the freer spoken voice. Variations could of course be so numerous that the underlying pattern isn't per-ceived at all and we hear, not counterpoint, but uncompromised natural speech. Some of the poems of John Donne would be good examples. But neither case is a case of sprung rhythm. Donne, for example, like Hopkins in 'God's Grandeur', accepts a regular count of syllables per line. And the first thing that sprung rhythm is, is a rejection of *that* principle.

'To speak shortly, it consists in scanning by accents or stress alone, without any account of the number of syllables, so that a foot may be one strong syllable, or it may be many light and one strong.'[29] In such a scheme, a foot can vary from one to four syllables, which is not the case in standard rhythm. And Hopkins went further. He allowed himself the freedom to add to any foot what he calls 'hangers' or 'outriders'. These are one, two, or three syllables not counted in the official metre: 'not part of it, not being counted, but part of it by producing a calculated effect which tells in the general success'.[30] For particu-lar rhythmic effects sprung rhythm allows, more freely than common rhythm, the use of any number of slack syllables, predetermined only by the poet's ear. The two principles at the heart of sprung rhythm are therefore as follows. First, the complete removal of any traditional metrical pattern we might call 'iambic' or 'trochaic' etc. Then its freedom (limited only by the ear) to decide the number of syllables per line. Another aspect is what Hopkins calls 'over-reaving' – the effect whereby the scansion of one line continues that of the preceding line. So 'if the first has one or more syllables at its end the other must have so many the less at its beginning; and in fact the scanning runs on without break from the beginning, say, of a stanza to the end and all the stanza is one long strain, though written in lines asunder'.[31] The opening lines of 'The Wind-hover' are a good example. In sprung rhythm the metrical unit is not any individual line or section but the movement of the whole.

And in the whole effect, the aim was an enthusiastic 'abrupt-ness'. Hopkins said that by 'sprung' he meant 'abrupt'. The attraction was not the luxury of extra syllables but this sharp collision of stresses. 'For why,' he asked, 'if it is forcible in prose to say "lashed: rod", am I obliged to weaken this in verse, which ought to be stronger, not weaker, into "láshed birch-ród" or something?'[32] Hopkins knew better than anyone that English is naturally a stressed language. The sheer expressiveness of sprung rhythm had precedents in a variety of sources from Greek drama to the Hebrew Psalms, from Old English allitera-tive verse to nursery rhymes. But, to explain the nature of his music, Hopkins had to add a varied complement of markings to denote unusual stresses, elisions, or pauses. (At one stage he even contemplated adding signs to distinguish subject, verb and object, to reveal the general grammatical construction to the eye.) But, even with metrical markings, few would feel confident in scanning the poetry; and even Hopkins granted that metre is not an exact science. 'Do you think all had best be left to the reader?' he once asked.[33] It was a wise hesitation. Increasing familiarity with Hopkins's poems convinces us that metrical aids are not called for. Sprung rhythm, like any other, depends for one thing on an individual's pronunciation of the words. The length of Hopkins's lines may sometimes surprise, but none is such a rhythmic monstrosity as to need the rationalisation of hindsight. Hopkins has, throughout, the power he once attrib-uted to Dryden – that of 'the naked thew and sinew of the English language'.[34] Why, then, should sprung rhythm be worth describing at all?

The answer is that it is the corner-stone of the *kind* of poet Hopkins is. He is a paradox. He chose to question inherited rules, and yet no poet was ever a more strenuous formalist. The priest and the poet were at one in feeling that rules are a test of strength, that they produce greater deliverance the more you deliver. On questions of prosody, as nowhere else in the disciplines he was subject to, he could bend some of the rules, but never without deferring to the genius of the language itself. The emphasis therefore still falls on *discipline*. Bridges once compared 'The Leaden Echo and the Golden Echo' to the poetry of Walt Whitman, but Hopkins refused the comparison with the free-wheeling verse of the American: 'For that piece of mine is very highly wrought,' he replied. 'The long lines are not rhythm run to seed: everything is weighed and timed in them.'[35] Severe calculation underlies the most spontaneous-seeming effects. A good example is 'The Starlight Night':

> Look **a**t the stars! look, look up **a**t the skies!
>   O look **a**t **a**ll the fire-folk sitting in the **a**ir!
>   The **b**right **b**oroughs, the **c**ircle-**c**itadels there!
> **D**own in **d**im woods the **d**iamond **d**elves! the **e**lves'-**e**yes!
> The **g**rey lawns cold where **g**old, where quick**g**old lies!
>   **W**ind-beat **w**hitebeam! airy abeles set on a flare!
>   **F**lake-doves sent **f**loating **f**orth at a **f**armyard scare! (p. 45)

The images have clearly been arranged alphabetically – **a** to **g**, but with **f** and **g** reversed, just to add to the challenge. Or consider the always meticulous play with vowels. For example, in 'The Sea and the Skylark'

> Left hand, off land, I hear the lark ascend (p. 46)

and in 'To R.B.'

> The roll, the rise, the carol, the creation. (p. 100)

The vowels are run up a scale determined by their pronunciation in the mouth.

(5)

At a crucial moment, residence in North Wales had been a major determining factor. It had brought the poet into relationship with the strict-metre tradition of Welsh-language verse. An alphabetical arrangement of images – known as *cymeriad* – is only one of many ways in which that tradition delights in pattern and hard craft. Under the tutorship of a local woman, Susannah Jones,

Hopkins actually learned Welsh, and to a standard that impressed no less a scholar than Sir John Rhys, Oxford's first Professor of Celtic. Hopkins even wrote two poems in Welsh, one in the ultra-strict form of the *cywydd*.[36] A picture is also now emerging of different manuscript sources he had to hand, enabling him to test his Welsh by tasting classic pre-1500 Welsh strict-metre poetry in the original. For example, a manuscript anthology of 1630, which includes Tudur Aled, a poet Hopkins says that he read, was probably in the library of St Beuno's College during his period there.[37] Similarly, Dafydd ap Gwilym's '*Cywydd y Ser*' ('Poem on the Stars') was available, along with an English translation, in a volume of 1873.[38] The gifted linguist in Hopkins would always have taken advantage of such availability. '*Cywydd y Ser*' was only one poem in which he could have sampled a technique so congenial to him – that of '*dyfalu*' ('likening' or 'comparison'). This is when images are accumulated in a riddling exercise that seeks to evoke the object in terms of what it is not. It is a kind of peppering of the target, where the whole board of analogies is as interesting as the bull's-eye itself. It is how Dafydd ap Gwilym, like Hopkins, describes the starlight night. Here is Dafydd ap Gwilyn describing mist by the same means:

Cnu tewlwyd gwynllwyd gwanllaes	An opaque, pale-grey limply-trailing fleece
Cyfliw â mwg, cwfl y maes.	Smoke-coloured, cowl of the plain.
Coetgae glaw er lluddiaw lles,	A field of rain against progress,
Codarmur cawad ormes	Coat-armour of an oppressive shower.[39]

George Herbert's 'Prayer' and Henry Vaughan's 'Son-dayes' would be good examples of how this Welsh technique first entered major English poetry. It creates extra space in a little room. Hopkins's favourite form, it will be remembered, is that of the sonnet.

Such techniques also answered to his belief that 'in art we strive to realise not only unity, permanence of law, likeness, but also, with it, difference, variety, contrast: it is rhyme we like, not echo, and not unison but harmony'.[40] This is true even of *cynghanedd*, the most basic technique he learned from classic Welsh poetry. This chiming of consonants within strict patterns is the epitome of how difference can co-exist with sameness, allowing consonants to agree without forcing vowels to do so:

> It dates from day
> Of his going in Galilee;
> Warm-laid grave of a womb-life grey (p. 32)

Hopkins's own use of *cynghanedd* shows that he understood better even than most Welsh poets of his time the particular purpose of the device in early Welsh poetry – that of highlighting stress. This muscular verse pressure is exactly what made Saunders Lewis compare Hopkins to Tudur Aled, one of the greatest early Welsh poets that Hopkins read.

Another Welsh technique for creating extra room within the narrow walls of a sonnet or stanza creates it within the syntax itself. It is the device called *sangiad*. This is when the syntax is broken into by material that is at a tangent to the main thought but without interrupting the main run of the grammar:

> How to kéep – is there any ány, is there none such, nowhere
> known some, bow or brooch or braid or brace, láce, latch or
> catch or key to keep
> Back beauty, keep it, beauty, beauty, beauty . . . from vanishing
> away? (p. 72)

The main clause here is '*How to keep . . . Back beauty . . . from vanishing away*'. And here is a brief example of the device in Welsh:

***Gwae ni**, hil eiddil Addaf,*	**Woe to us**, Adam's feeble race,
*Fordwy rhad, **fyrred yr***	A surge of blessing, **that**
haf!	**summer is so short!**

The diversions suit Hopkins's need, not just for extra syllables, but also for extra thought. A contracted form of *sangiad* is called *trychiad*, which interrupts even a single word in midstream. An appropriate Welsh example would be the splicing of the Welsh name for St Winefred, a saint about whom Hopkins also wrote:

*Chwaer i **Wen**-gymen,*	Sister to **Wine**-perfected, gold-
gemaur	gem,
*-**frewi** a'i gwallt o frig aur*	**-fred** with her hair a crown of
	gold.

Interrupted in the same way is Harry Ploughman's hair:

> in a wind lifted, windlaced –
> See his wind-lilylocks-laced . . . (p. 94)

The paradox whereby sudden ventilation conveys the sense of crowded-in thought is a model for some of Hopkins's most brilliant 'asides':

> That night, that year
> Of now done darkness I wretch lay wrestling with (my God!) my God.
> (p. 88)

Later poets have often copied such devices without knowing their origins. Harold Bloom has said that 'the later poet opens himself to what he believes to be a power in the parent-poem that does not belong to the parent proper but to a range of being just beyond the precursor'.[41] In Hopkins's case, one 'range of being just beyond the precursor' is the adopted Welshness of his craft.

But it answered also to a deep Englishness. The way in which the alliteration of *cynghanedd* stresses key words was akin to the muscular beat of Old English alliterative verse, and the Welsh technique *dyfalu* matched the riddling delight of the Old English device called 'variation'. In this way, the Welsh influence allowed Hopkins to rejoin his own native English tradition, at a point before it took a different turn in the French-influenced poetry of Chaucer. And it would have pleased Hopkins that the Welsh examples came from the Catholic centuries of Wales before Anglicanism and Nonconformity took over. But another help was the fact that Welsh poetic forms were much more intricate than anything in English. Hard craft that was such hard graft helped lessen his feeling of guilt in writing poetry at all. It reconciled the poet with the priest. So when we pay the poetry the praise he himself gave to Purcell's music – that 'it is the rehearsal/Of own, of abrupt self there so thrusts on, so throngs the ear' (p. 58) – we salute not only the 'abrupt' expressiveness but also the disciplined 'rehearsal' that sets it all unchangeably in order. 'No wonder of it,' one might say, 'sheer plod makes plough down sillion shine'.

(6)

In a letter of 1864, Hopkins wrote that the language of poetry can be divided into three kinds.[42] The third and lowest ('Delphic') – that which defines verse as distinct from prose – he only briefly mentions. His first two categories, however, show the logic behind the distinctiveness that he himself attempts. The second category, defining the threshold of excellence, he terms 'Parnassian':

> It can only be spoken by poets, but it is not in the highest sense poetry. It does not require the mood of mind in which the poetry of inspiration is written. It is spoken *on and from the level* of a poet's mind, not, as in the other case, when the inspiration which is the gift of genius, raises him above himself . . . Great men, poets I mean, have each their own dialect as it were of Parnassian, formed generally as they go on writing, and at last – this is the point to be marked, – they can see things in this Parnassian way and describe them in this Parnassian tongue, without further effort of inspiration. In a poet's particular kind of Parnassian lies most of his style, of his manner, of his mannerism if you like.

The other thing about Parnassian is that the reader can imagine himself writing it. Of course, whether he *could* write it is another matter, but the possibility of imagining it is what causes a poet to pall on us, as Wordsworth sometimes palls ('We seem to have found out his secret'), or as Tennyson sometimes seems merely 'Tennysonian'. Hopkins defines an extra category – 'Castalian' – 'a higher sort of Parnassian'. The point about Castalian is that one cannot conceive having written it, but it remains nevertheless too 'characteristic' of the poet, 'too so-and-so-all-overish'. One might reply that refining the highly 'characteristic' is exactly what Hopkins himself does, and that, when not at his best, he more than anyone appears 'too so-and-so-all-overish'.

But if we are not to leave it at that, much depends on his definition of his highest category:

> The first and highest is poetry proper, the language of inspiration. The word inspiration need cause no difficulty. I mean by it a mood of great, abnormal in fact, mental acuteness, either energetic or receptive, according as the thoughts which arise in it seem generated by a stress and action of the brain, or to strike into it unasked . . . In a fine piece of inspiration every beauty takes you as it were by surprise . . . every fresh beauty could not in any way be predicted or accounted for by what one has already read.

This Keatsian notion of 'loading every rift with ore', this tireless love of inscapes, is an overstatement of the way in which poetry actually works. It belies the incremental way in which any 'style' is actually created. It is the slow accumulation of related effects that makes a work individual. There is also something precious about phrases like 'a fine piece of inspiration', 'every beauty', 'every fresh beauty'. Just as, within Parnassian, Hopkins would anthologise, looking for the stroke of 'inspiration', so within even the poetry of 'inspiration' he would anthologise further, claiming for every surprise, every fresh beauty, a quality that could 'not in any way be predicted or accounted for by what one has already read'. This is putting sudden effects at too high a premium. Even Hardy, a poet four years his senior, would not have recognised the rationale of such verse. Yeats – a poet only twenty years his junior, who had had himself to come out from under the exquisite influence of Pre-Raphaelite verse – said that he 'could not focus on Hopkins's poetry for more than a few minutes at a time'.[43] And even Coleridge had said that 'a poem of any length neither can be, or ought to be, all poetry'.[44] For Coleridge, Hardy and Yeats, Parnassian would simply be that lower level of style which acts as vehicle for the greater intensities of what Hopkins calls 'poetry proper, the language of inspiration'. And yet, if any work challenges Coleridge's belief that no 'poem of any length' can be full of poetry, in this sense of consistent intensity, it must be 'The Wreck of the Deutschland'. (Another would be Eliot's *The Waste Land*, but more because of its lacunae than its texture.) But we would also have to add that Hopkins never again attempted anything as long. He was content thereafter to 'explode' space within short sonnets.

His craving for endless intensity may have been the result of his unpublished obscurity. It is as if the excitement which published poems normally create in their audience had in his case to be prefigured in the verse itself. Apart from Robert Bridges, there just wasn't going to be any other feed-back. The output was not in any ordinary sense 'put out'. And having told Bridges that 'You *are* my public', he proceeded, in the main, to ignore even Bridges's advice as to what poetry can or cannot do. To borrow an expression from Auden, Hopkins had to *become* his admirers.[45] Backing this need for self-sanction was his Christian belief in the Incarnation, in the idea of infinite riches in a little room – within the world, within man, within language, within the sonnet, within the image, within the word, within even the single sound. Given this rich containment, the smallness of his output just doesn't matter.

But the question still arises whether such verbal implosions are, in Donald Davie's words, 'self-expression at its most relentless', a means 'for the individual will to impose itself on time', producing in the end 'a muscle-bound monstrosity'.[46] Davie's verdict would have seriously shocked Hopkins's natural modesty. He already knew that 'it is the virtue of design, pattern, or inscape to be distinctive' and that 'it is the vice of distinctiveness to become queer'.[47] But if the poetry leaves us only with a sense of imposed will, it remains deadlocked in the personal, where it would be useless as poetry of praise. The final court of appeal is each reader's experience of the poems. But it is clear that Hopkins himself aimed at impersonality – 'a mood of great, abnormal in fact, mental acuteness, either energetic or receptive, according as the thoughts which arise in it seem generated by a stress and action of the brain, or to strike into it unasked'. The poetry came out of highly individual states of emotion. It also involved taking highly individual possession of the language. But an impersonality still inheres in so actively 'fetching out', as he put it, the language's own potentials. It is a view of language, not as mere vehicle, but as one of the realities of the external world:

> Poetry is speech framed for contemplation of the mind by the way of hearing or speech framed to be heard for its own sake and interest even over and above its interest of meaning. Some matter and meaning is essential to it but only as an element necessary to support and employ the shape which is contemplated for its own sake.[48]

Modern criticism, which places more emphasis on a poem's negotiable relationship to the reader ('framed for contemplation') than on its confessional source in the poet will like that last statement. But, even without an audience, Hopkins still had something more seriously communicative in mind than the 'art for art's sake' or 'French *symboliste*' ideas of the late nineteenth century in which he died. He would certainly have resisted the theorist notion of 'the death of the author' that our own age has thrown up.

(7)

Hopkins's poetry is always claimed to have been ahead of its time. An ordinary literalness underlies the claim. Only 'ahead of its time', belatedly in 1918, twenty-nine years after his death, was he even read. The compliment is also ironic, given that so much in Hopkins's theology and language went *back* in time. And then there is so much that marks the man as being clearly of his *own* time. Commenting on the battle of Majuba Hill in the war with the Boers in 1881, he lamented what he saw as British cowardice in the face of an outnumbered enemy: 'The effect will, I am afraid, be felt all over the empire.'[49] (In his sadness at the agitation for Home Rule in Ireland in the 1880s his characteristic imperial Englishness even separated him from his fellow Jesuits.) And, in any case, the irreplaceable part played by the world of nature in the language of his sensibility reminds us how deeply Hopkins as a Victorian shared the nineteenth century with the Romantics, whereas so much twentieth-century Modernist poetry cut off that appeal to nature, partly in reaction against the sentimentality of its survival in the Georgian poets. Again, to the first and second Modernist generation alike (that of Eliot and that of Auden), Hopkins's vision would have seemed alien. Yeats and Eliot wrote out of the disintegration of the Christian world-view that stood, conservatively complete, at the centre of Hopkins's verse. As it happened, it was only after the first inroads of Modernism in English poetry had already been made that Hopkins was published, late enough for his influence to count, not with Eliot and Pound or the late Yeats, but with the young poets of the 1930s. And the political and social preoccupations of that generation meant that Hopkins's influence was isolated in technical effects, at a remove from the real character and concerns of the 1930s. Again, the altering of expression in our time is the result of an anti-poetical impulse that has created a new poetic out of the prosaic, the ironic and the understated. It has also involved 'the breaking of forms' in ways that Hopkins wouldn't even have countenanced. Any low-key note in Hopkins (carrier pigeons in the third stanza of the 'Deutschland', for example, or tram rails in 'The Candle Indoors', or the outrageous rhymes of 'The Loss of the Eurydice' and 'The Bugler's First Communion') are levelled upwards by the sheer formal energy of the verse. He remains, *par excellence*, the poet of high-definition performance.

So our feeling that we read him as we read the Moderns must come from other things. In any explanation, his religion cannot be simply set aside. It is interesting, for example, that Hopkins's dogmatic emphasis caused Eliot to call him a 'devotional' rather than a 'religious' poet.[50] For Eliot, a religious poet works on a wider range of human experience than was open to Hopkins. But Eliot also implies that 'religious' denotes a more modern, tentative sense of mystery, in the face of which even language loses its confidence. In this sense, Eliot's agnostic *The Waste Land* is no less 'religious' than his Anglo-Catholic *Four Quartets*. Nearer Hopkins's own themes, a poet like Edward Thomas is also instructive, reflecting a sensibility that seems of our own time even without the technical hallmarks of Modernist verse. Thomas's experience in 'Old Man' –

> I see and I hear nothing;
> Yet seem, too, to be listening, lying in wait
> For what I should, yet never can, remember

– might be called religious, even though not concerned with matters of belief in the usual sense. But Hopkins would have come back at this widened view of what 'religious' means from a specifically Catholic, not just a Christian, position. He wrote to Bridges: 'You do not mean by mystery what a Catholic does. You mean an interesting uncertainty: the uncertainty ceasing interest ceases also. This happens in some things; to you in religion. But a Catholic by mystery means an incomprehensible certainty.'[51] Even so, a modern reader who doesn't already share Hopkins's Catholicism is likely to recognise himself more in Edward Thomas's reticence than in Hopkins's certainty.

A bold assurance supplements Victorian poetry even when it does not have Hopkins's faith. It divides a modern, demoralised Edward Thomas not only from Hopkins but also from the Arnold of 'Dover Beach' and the Tennyson of 'In Memoriam'. Even in 1912–13 Thomas Hardy's poems on the memory of his first wife are still the other side of a divide from Edward Thomas. Hardy recovers lost scenes with confident clarity ('Even to the original air-blue gown!'), whereas the very point about 'Old Man' is the existential unreality created by time. The point is that the 'incomprehensible certainty' of Hopkins's theology parallels a more ordinary kind of certainty: for him the natural world is very tangibly *there*, always available for description. The way in which he takes possession of it makes Edward Thomas again an instructive contrast. In his poem 'The Glory' Thomas asks a question that Hopkins himself might have asked:

> Shall I now this day
> Begin to seek as far as heaven, as hell,
> Wisdom or strength to match this beauty?

But for Thomas an inner blankness cuts him off. He sees, but cannot *feel*, how beautiful things are: 'I cannot bite the day to the core'. In turn, that very metaphor of appetite and taste is pure Hopkins. In 'Hurrahing in Harvest' he is seen to 'down all that glory in the heavens to glean our Saviour', and in the 'Deutschland' he conveys his recognition of Christ's presence in that very image of biting to the core:

> How a lush-kept plush-capped sloe
>   Will, mouthed to flesh-burst,
> Gush! – flush the man, the being with it, sour or sweet. (Stanza 8)

It is a relish that obviously helps him animate all the objects of his praise, whether in the natural world, in his pastoral duty or in his celebration of heroes. Everything comes down to the way in which he uses language. He refuses to see words as merely referential tools, as signs which stand over against things, merely pointing to them. In Hopkins, words *become* things. Compared even to the heavy tangibility of Keats and Tennyson ('The long light shakes across the lakes', 'The moan of doves in immemorial elms'), Hopkins's concern with the thinginess of language is extreme. But it is also wonderfully adaptable. His physical use of language is at its best when it mimes, not only things, but the *movement* of things through time:

> Never ask if meaning it, wanting it, warned of it – men go
> ('The Wreck of the Deutschland')

> Evening strains to be time's vast, womb-of-all, home-of-all,
>   hearse-of-all night
> ('Spelt from Sibyl's Leaves')

> Squandering ooze to squeezed dough, crust, dust
> ('That Nature is a Heraclitean Fire').

It is a technique that embodies even the movement of thought itself. Consider 'Felix Randal', by no means the densest of the poems:

This seeing the sick endears them to us, us too it endears.
My tongue had taught thee comfort, touch had quenched thy tears,
Thy tears that touched my heart, child, Felix, poor Felix Randal.

An ordinary compassion ('endears them to us') momentarily gives way to a priestly pride in ministering to the sick ('my tongue had taught thee comfort') and then returns again to a more selfless love ('child, Felix, poor Felix Randal'). But the reciprocity of feeling is in the reciprocity of the sounds themselves: '*endears them to us . . . us too it endears . . . taught thee comfort . . . touch had quenched . . . touched my heart*'.

Without such impressive effects, endless alliteration or onomatopoeia ('As tumbled over rim in roundy wells/Stones ring', p. 70) would seem too often a case of killing one bird with two stones, and would deserve Robert Graves's reprimand in 'The Cool Web':

> There's a cool web of language winds us in,
> Retreat from too much joy or too much fear.

Language, Graves says, is what releases us from, not embroils us in, experience. If we let our tongues lose self-possession, 'we shall go mad no doubt and die that way'. But everything about Hopkins lives close to possession. He thrives on detail and relentless empathy. A congenital taste for the 'exquisite' was boosted by the aesthetic climate of his undergraduate days at Oxford. And his own frail constitution would have sharpened this delight in physical things, the attraction of opposites: the masterful windhover, a world *charged* with the grandeur of God, the muscular Harry Ploughman and the massive Felix Randal before 'sickness broke him'. The small-limbed Hopkins is at his best on dynamic subjects. But this love of explosive concreteness was also a tribute to his belief that God's Word became the world. Praise of a solid world in solid words was praise of God.

Yet this power of empathy is exactly what made more terrible the pressure of his own sense of himself ('The keener the consciousness the greater the pain . . . the higher the nature the greater the penalty'). It is that very ability to *taste* that makes him so devastating on the one experience that our own period is most able to identify with – the experience of psychic collapse:

> I am gall, I am heartburn. God's most deep decree
> Bitter would have me taste: my taste was me.

The final Irish sonnets release a terrible sense of pain and wastage. The super-sensitivity is in the broad tradition of Romantic poetry. Even withdrawal from the condition becomes a theme for poems, in the form of Keats's Indolence, Coleridge's Dejection, or Wordsworth's belief that he had moved from absolute oneness with nature to the more detached moral experience of 'the still sad music of humanity'. But Hopkins's availability to experience was even more extreme. For him, withdrawal from the edge was a matter, not of the better conduct of his poetic career, but of the retention of sanity itself. The plea in one of his late sonnets is that he might 'live to my sad self hereafter kind,/ Charitable; not live this tormented mind/ With this tormented mind tormenting yet' (p. 90). Because of the unpublished status of the poems, we are here in the presence of a more nakedly confessional pain than any public readership before our own time was ever used to. That the late sonnets still impose order on such pain ('if ever anything was written in blood, one of these was') is the greatest sign we have of the line between neurosis and art.

For the truth is that poems are never written in blood. Words in Hopkins 'become things' in a special sense. What they most fully become is themselves. Ultimately, poetry doesn't so much kill the gap between words and things as open the connection between words and other words. Hopkins's language doesn't so much mime external reality as compound it, by making language *part* of that reality. More frequent than those moments when the language is simply miming things—

> as a skate's heel sweeps smooth on a bow bend
> ('The Windhover')

– is where the 'thinginess' of language seems enough on its own. The actual referent in the real world is often supplied only with difficulty. For example, the skylark's song in 'The Sea and the Skylark':

> His rash-fresh re-winded new-skeinèd score
> In crisps of curl off wild winch whirl

or the effect of light through eyelashes in 'The Candle Indoors':

to-fro tender trambeams truckle at the eye.

It is not that the referent is slighted. Quite the opposite – it is given a new order of attention, made possible not only by the world but by language-and-world together. The difference between small-time mimetic effects and this fuller verbal life can be gauged by comparing with Hopkins these lines from W. H. Auden's 'Seaside',

> Here at the small field's ending pause
> When the chalk wall falls to the foam and its tall ledges
> Oppose the pluck
> And knock of the tide,
> And the shingle scrambles after the suck-
>   ing surf.

Here is stanza 32 of 'The Wreck of the Deutschland':

> The recurb and the recovery of the gulf's sides,
>   The girth of it and the wharf of it and the wall;
> Stanching, quenching ocean of a motionable mind;
> Ground of being, and granite of it: past all
>   Grasp God, throned behind
> Death with a sovereignty that heeds but hides, bodes but abides.

In his philological examination of the common roots of now distinct words in his early diaries, Hopkins's main interest is in words that share onomatopoeic explanations:

> the derivation of *granum*, *grain* may be referred to the head
>   Grind, gride, gird, grit, groat, grate, greet, κϱονϵιν, crush, crash, κϱοτϵῖν, etc.
>   Original meaning to *strike*, *rub*, particularly *together*. That which is produced by such means is the *grit*, the *groats* or crumbs, like *fragmentum* from *frangere*, *bit* from *bite*. *Crumb*, *crumble* perhaps akin.

It is this relationship between words themselves that brings their relationship to the world into the poems. Thus in the 'Deutschland' stanza just quoted, the shared sounds of 'Stanching', 'quenching' and 'ocean' bring the same sound to life in 'motionable' and make it mime the reality. But far deeper is the reconciliation of conceptual opposites in the shared sounds of 'heeds but hides, bodes but abides'. Even more radical is the reconciliation of opposites in that one word 'Ground' – that which supports is also that which grinds! And the sanction for that reading comes not just from the physicality that links *ground* and *grind* to the world but from the question with which the immediately preceding stanza had ended:

> is the shipwrack then a harvest,
> does tempest carry the *grain* for thee?

The whole effect shares in the onomatopoeic interest of the philological notes in the diaries. But it is still dominated by the paradox at the very opening of the poem – that of being 'at the wall/Fast' though 'mined with a motion'. In this way the words solidly face one another (often across many pages) as well as vertiginously facing the world. They dramatise moral paradoxes just as effectively as they do realistic reproductions. 'It is rhyme we like, not echo.'

Most relevant of all to our empathy with Hopkins's condition in the second half of the nineteenth century is not our post-Freudian, post-Modernist receptiveness to the literature of extremes, but something that was even more basic in everything he wrote. His poetry stood out against Victorian England in a deeper way than by abstractly challenging its theology, lamenting the industrial ruination of its landscapes, or simply seeking to be 'ahead of its time'. Others, aloud in their own time, were doing that. An even deeper instinct was driving Hopkins. He invaded the innermost particularities of the English language itself. A view of poetry as 'shape which is contemplated for its own sake' may seem surprising coming from a Jesuit, whose official duty, after all, was to teach, persuade and convert. But when Hopkins resumed his poetry in 1875 he was calling to his side in that duty the very language itself. The medium itself as message gave him a posture for combat within the gates. This is the ultimate paradox in his 'outsiderness' as a Roman Catholic, an intensely individual sensibility, and a poet without an audience. But he took possession of the language, not as a national outsider like Joyce or Eliot or Dylan Thomas, consciously changing its cultural feel, and wreaking vengeance on it, but as one who was himself deeply English. Though uniquely advantaged by having crossed so many national and regional boundaries within the British Isles, the possibility of his poetry falling out of a recognisably *English* idiom was his fear, not his boast.

Following the language back to its roots, avoiding the standard familiarities that had overlain its basic character, was his way of countering the official Anglicanism that had overlain his own essentially sixteenth-century Catholicism. The irreducibility of the poems, their power of simultaneous rather than serial suggestiveness, means that, even without sharing the exact nature of his faith, we *become* Hopkins as we read. His endless insistence to Bridges that his poems should be read aloud was aimed at completing that connection between voice and faith.

It was as if this grappling with the inner realities of the language was a way of defending the integrity of inward, individual life, whatever its faith might be. The contemporaneity we share with him is that which we share with all great creative writers of the last two centuries of industrial civilisation, centuries in which echo and easy reproduction have threatened to replace rhyme and relationship. His contemporaneity comes from his respect for a life lived individually and according to a sense of values. Early on, he had imagined survival in a hostile world in terms of elected silence and retreat:

> And I have asked to be
> Where no storms come,
> Where the green swell is in the havens dumb,
> And out of the swing of the sea. (p. 9)

But his best retreat was into the secret places of language, which, when opened up and opened out, have their own storms, their own swells and swings, but still remain the very means by which we think.

WALFORD DAVIES

References

1 *The Journals and Papers of Gerard Manley Hopkins*, ed. H. House and G. Storey, 1959, p. 258.
2 The ascription of the phrase to Pusey ('Father *Gerard Hopkins*, styled by Dr Pusey "the star of Balliol"') is in *Letters and Notices*, April 1910, p. 39, part of a private series of Jesuit reminiscences of noviceship days.
3 'To seem the stranger lies my lot, my life' (p. 84).

4 'The Starlight Night' (p. 45); 'Spring' (p. 45); 'Binsey Poplars' (p. 57).

5 'The Sea and the Skylark' (p. 46).

6 'Henry Purcell' (p. 58).

7 *The Journals and Papers of Gerard Manley Hopkins*, p. 165.

8 Ibid., p. 71.

9 *Correspondence of Gerard Manley Hopkins and R. W. Dixon*, ed. C. C. Abbott, 1956, p. 14.

10 Ibid.

11 'I wake and feel the fell of dark, not day' (p. 85).

12 Notes, *The Poems of Gerard Manley Hopkins*, 1st edn., ed. R. Bridges, 1918.

13 *Letters of Gerard Manley Hopkins to Robert Bridges*, ed. C. C. Abbott, 1955, p. 270.

14 'A Retrospect', *Pavannes and Divisions*, 1918, p. 9.

15 *Letters of Gerard Manley Hopkins to Robert Bridges*, p. 272.

16 Hazlitt, 'Character of Mr Burke', *The Complete Works of William Hazlitt*, ed. P. P. Howe, 1930–4, p. 307.

17 *Letters of Gerard Manley Hopkins to Robert Bridges*, p. 90.

18 *Further Letters of Gerard Manley Hopkins*, ed. C. C. Abbott, 1956, p. 202.

19 The titles of his four contributions to *Nature* between 1882 and 1884 were: 'A Curious Halo', 'Shadow-beams in the East at Sunset', 'The Remarkable Sunsets' (the Krakatoa eruptions) and 'The Red Light Round the Sun – the Sun Blue or Green at Setting'.

20 *The Journals and Papers of Gerard Manley Hopkins*, p. 230.

21 Ibid.

22 Ibid., p. 127.

23 Ibid., p. 228.

24 Ibid., p. 196.

25 Ibid., p. 221. The edition of Duns Scotus referred to is the *Scriptum Oxoniense super Sententiis*, 2 vols., Venice, 1514.

26 *The Sermons and Devotional Writings of Gerard Manley Hopkins*, ed. C. Devlin S. J., 1959, pp. 122–30.

27 *Letters of Gerard Manley Hopkins to Robert Bridges*, p. 66.

28 *Correspondence of Gerard Manley Hopkins and R. W. Dixon*, p. 14.

29 Ibid.

30 *Letters of Gerard Manley Hopkins to Robert Bridges*, p. 45.

31 'Author's Preface': Hopkins's own description of sprung rhythm, published in Bridges's first edition of the poems, 1918.

32 *Letters of Gerard Manley Hopkins to Robert Bridges*, p. 46.

33 The question was written by Hopkins on an autograph copy of 'The Leaden Echo and the Golden Echo' sent to Bridges. He had commented that 'with the degree of stress so perpetually varying no marking is satisfactory'.

34 *Letters of Gerard Manley Hopkins to Robert Bridges*, pp. 267–8: 'he is the most masculine of our poets; his style and his rhythms lay the strongest stress of all our literature on the naked thew and sinew of the English language . . .'

35 *Letters of Gerard Manley Hopkins to Robert Bridges*, p. 157.

36 A *cywydd* is one of the main metrical forms of Welsh prosody. Its most frequent pattern today would be a rhyming couplet, with seven syllables to the line, within the consonantal rules of *cynghanedd*, and with the accent falling alternately on the last and the penultimate syllable of the line.

37 See Geraint Gruffydd, 'Llawysgrif Heythrop a Brân Maenefa', *Y Faner*, 6 March 1981, p. 8.

38 Edited by Cynddelw (Robert Ellis), Liverpool 1873.

39 Dafydd ap Gwilym, 'Y Niwl' ['The Mist'], *Gwaith Dafydd ap Gwilym*, ed. T. Parry, 1952, p. 184

40 *The Journals and Papers of Gerard Manley Hopkins*, p. 83.

41 Harold Bloom, *The Anxiety of Influence*, 1973, p. 15.

42 *Further Letters of Gerard Manley Hopkins*, pp. 215–20, 221–2.

43 *Hopkins Among the Poets*, ed. R. F. Giles, The International Hopkins Association Monograph Series, 1985, p. 8.

44 *Biographia Literaria*, ch. XIV.

45 'He became his admirers' – Auden's comment on Yeats's death in 'In Memory of W. B. Yeats'.

46 'Hopkins as a Decadent Critic', *Purity of Diction in English Verse*, 1952, pp. 160–82.

47 *Letters of Gerard Manley Hopkins to Robert Bridges*, p. 66.

48 'Poetry and Verse' (lecture notes), *The Journals and Papers of Gerard Manley Hopkins*, p. 289.

49 *Further Letters of Gerard Manley Hopkins*, p. 158.

50 'A Note on Hopkins', *After Strange Gods*, 1934.

51 *Letters of Gerard Manley Hopkins to Robert Bridges*, p. 187.

POEMS

I

The Escorial

Βάτραχος δὲ ποτ᾽ ἀκρίδας ὥς τις ἐρίσδω

1

There is a massy pile above the waste
Amongst Castilian barrens mountain-bound;
A sombre length of grey; four towers placed
At corners flank the stretching compass round;
A pious work with threefold purpose crown'd –   5
A cloister'd convent first, the proudest home
Of those who strove God's gospel to confound
With barren rigour and a frigid gloom –
Hard by a royal palace and a royal tomb.

2

They tell its story thus; amidst the heat   10
Of battle once upon St Lawrence' day
Philip took oath, while glory or defeat
Hung in the swaying of the fierce melée,
'So I am victor now, I swear to pay
The richest gift St Lawrence ever bore,   15
When chiefs and monarchs came their gifts to lay
Upon his altar, and with rarest store
To deck and make most lordly evermore.'

3

For that staunch saint still prais'd his Master's name
While his crack'd flesh lay hissing on the grate;   20
Then fail'd the tongue; the poor collapsing frame,
Hung like a wreck that flames not billows beat –
So, grown fantastic in his piety,
Philip, supposing that the gift most meet,
The sculptur'd image of such faith would be,   25
Uprais'd an emblem of that fiery constancy.

4

He rais'd the convent as a monstrous grate;
The cloisters cross'd with equal courts betwixt

Formed bars of stone; Beyond in stiffen'd state
The stretching palace lay as handle fix'd.   30
Then laver'd founts and postur'd stone he mix'd.
– Before the sepulchre there stood a gate,
A faithful guard of inner darkness fix'd –
But open'd twice, in life and death, to state,
To newborn prince, and royal corse inanimate.   35

5

While from the pulpit in a heretic land
Ranters scream'd rank rebellion, this should be
A fortress of true faith, and central stand
Whence with the scourge of ready piety
Legates might rush, zeal-rampant, fiery,   40
Upon the stubborn Fleming; and the rod
Of forc'd persuasion issue o'er the free. –
For, where the martyr's bones were thickest trod,
They shrive themselves and cry, 'Good service to our
    God.'

6

No finish'd proof was this of Gothic grace   45
With flowing tracery engemming rays
Of colour in high casements face to face;
And foliag'd crownals (pointing how the ways
Of art best follow nature) in a maze
Of finish'd diapers, that fills the eye   50
And scarcely traces where on beauty strays
And melts amidst another; ciel'd on high
With blazoned groins, and crowned with hues of majesty.

7

This was no classic temple order'd round
With massy pillars of the Doric mood   55
Broad-fluted, nor with shafts acanthus-crown'd,
Pourtray'd along the frieze with Titan's brood
That battled Gods for heaven; brilliant-hued,
With golden fillets and rich blazonry,
Wherein beneath the cornice, horsemen rode   60
With form divine, a fiery chivalry –
Triumph of airy grace and perfect harmony.

8

Fair relics too the changeful Moor had left
Splendid with phantasies aerial,
Of mazy shape and hue, but now bereft   65
By conqu'rors rude of honor; and not all
Unmindful of their grace, the Escorial
Arose in gloom, a solemn mockery
Of those gilt webs that languish'd in a fall.
This to remotest ages was to be   70
The pride of faith, and home of sternest piety.

9

.   .   .   .

10

He rang'd long corridors and cornic'd halls,
And damasqu'd arms and foliag'd carving piled. –
With painting gleam'd the rich pilaster'd walls – .
Here play'd the virgin mother with her Child   75
In some broad palmy mead, and saintly smiled,
And held a cross of flowers, in purple bloom;
He, where the crownals droop'd, himself reviled
And bleeding saw. – Thus hung from room to room
The skill of dreamy Claude, and Titian's mellow gloom.   80

11

Here in some darken'd landscape Paris fair
Stretches the envied fruit with fatal smile
To golden-girdled Cypris; – Ceres there
Raves through Sicilian pastures many a mile;
But, hapless youth, Antinous the while   85
Gazes aslant his shoulder, viewing nigh
Where Phoebus weeps for him whom Zephyr's guile
Chang'd to a flower; and there, with placid eye
Apollo views the smitten Python writhe and die.

.   .   .   .

12

Then through the afternoon the summer beam   90
Slop'd on the galleries; upon the wall
Rich Titians faded; in the straying gleam
The motes in ceaseless eddy shine and fall
Into the cooling gloom; till slowly all

Dimm'd in the long accumulated dust;   95
Pendant in formal line from cornice tall
Blades of Milan in circles rang'd, grew rust
And silver damasqu'd plates obscur'd in age's crust.

13

But from the mountain glens in autumn late
Adown the clattering gullies swept the rain;   100
The driving storm at hour of vespers beat
Upon the mould'ring terraces amain;
The Altar-tapers flar'd in gusts; in vain
Louder the monks dron'd out Gregorians slow;
Afar in corridors with painèd strain   105
Doors slamm'd to the blasts continually; more low,
Then pass'd the wind, and sobb'd with mountain-echo'd
    woe.

14

Next morn a peasant from the mountain side
Came midst the drizzle telling how last night
Two mazèd shepherds perish'd in the tide;   110
But further down the valley, left and right,
Down-splinter'd rocks crush'd cottages. – Drear sight,
An endless round of dead'ning solitude:
Till, (fearing ravage worse than in his flight,
What time the baffled Frank swept back pursu'd   115
Fell on the palace, and the lust of rabble rude,)

15

Since trampled Spain by royal discord torn
Lay bleeding, to Madrid the last they bore,
The choicest remnants thence; – such home forlorn
The monks left long ago: Since which no more   120
Eighth wonder of the earth, in size, in store
And art and beauty: Title now too full –
More wondrous to have borne such hope before
It seems; for grandeur barren left and dull
Than changeful pomp of courts is aye more wonderful.

2

Winter with the Gulf Stream

The boughs, the boughs are bare enough
But earth has never felt the snow.
Frost-furred our ivies are and rough

With bills of rime the brambles shew.
The hoarse leaves crawl on hissing ground   5
Because the sighing wind is low.

But if the rain-blasts be unbound
And from dank feathers wring the drops
The clogged brook runs with choking sound

Kneading the mounded mire that stops   10
His channel under clammy coats
Of foliage fallen in the copse.

A simple passage of weak notes
Is all the winter bird dare try.
The bugle moon by daylight floats   15

So glassy white about the sky,
So like a berg of hyaline,
And pencilled blue so daintily,

I never saw her so divine.
But through black branches, rarely drest   20
In scarves of silky shot and shine,

The webbed and the watery west
Where yonder crimson fireball sits
Looks laid for feasting and for rest.

I see long reefs of violets   25
In beryl-covered fens so dim,
A gold-water Pactolus frets

Its brindled wharves and yellow brim,
The waxen colours weep and run,
And slendering to his burning rim   30

Into the flat blue mist the sun
Drops out and all our day is done.

3
Spring and Death

I had a dream. A wondrous thing:
It seem'd an evening in the Spring;
– A little sickness in the air
From too much fragrance everywhere: –
As I walk'd a stilly wood,   5
Sudden, Death before me stood:
In a hollow lush and damp,
He seem'd a dismal mirky stamp
On the flowers that were seen
His charnelhouse-grate ribs between,   10
And with coffin-black he barr'd the green.
'Death,' said I, 'what do you here
At this Spring season of the year?'
'I mark the flowers ere the prime
Which I may tell at Autumn-time.'   15
Ere I had further question made
Death was vanish'd from the glade.
Then I saw that he had bound
Many trees and flowers round
With a subtle web of black,   20
And that such a sable track
Lay along the grasses green
From the spot where he had been.
  But the Spring-tide pass'd the same;
Summer was as full of flame;   25
Autumn-time no earlier came.
And the flowers that he had tied,
As I mark'd, not always died
Sooner than their mates; and yet
Their fall was fuller of regret;   30
It seem'd so hard and dismal thing,
Death, to mark them in the Spring.

4
New Readings

Although the letter said
On thistles that men look not grapes to gather,
   I read the story rather
How soldiers platting thorns around CHRIST'S Head
   Grapes grew and drops of wine were shed.   5

   Though when the sower sowed,
The wingèd fowls took part, part fell in thorn
   And never turned to corn,
Part found no root upon the flinty road, –
   CHRIST at all hazards fruit hath shewed.   10

   From wastes of rock He brings
Food for five thousand: on the thorns He shed
   Grains from His drooping Head;
And would not have that legion of winged things
   Bear Him to heaven on easeful wings.   15

5

Heaven-Haven

A nun takes the veil

   I have desired to go
     Where springs not fail,
To fields where flies no sharp and sided hail
    And a few lilies blow.

   And I have asked to be   5
     Where no storms come,
Where the green swell is in the havens dumb,
    And out of the swing of the sea.

6

'I must hunt down the prize'

I must hunt down the prize
   Where my heart lists.
Must see the eagle's bulk, render'd in mists,
   Hang of a treble size.

Must see the waters roll
   Where the seas set
Towards wastes where round the ice-blocks tilt and fret
   Not so far from the pole.

7

'Why should their foolish bands, their hopeless hearses'

Why should their foolish bands, their hopeless hearses
Blot the perpetual festival of day?
Ravens for prosperously-boded curses
Returning thanks, might offer such array.
Heaven comfort sends, but harry it away,
Gather the sooty plumage from Death's wings
And the poor corse impale with it and fray
Far from its head an angel's hoverings.
And count the rosy cross with bann'd disastrous things.

8

'It was a hard thing to undo this knot'

It was a hard thing to undo this knot.
The rainbow shines, but only in the thought

Of him that looks. Yet not in that alone,
For who makes rainbows by invention?
And many standing round a waterfall   5
See one bow each, yet not the same to all,
But each a hand's breadth further than the next.
The sun on falling waters writes the text
Which yet is in the eye or in the thought.
It was a hard thing to undo this knot.   10

9

'Miss Story's character!
too much you ask'

Miss Story's character! too much you ask,
When 'tis the confidante that sets the task.
How dare I paint Miss Story to Miss May?
And what if she my confidence betray!
What if my Subject, seeing this, resent   5
What were worth nothing if all compliment!
No: shewn to her it cannot but offend;
But candour never hurt the dearest *friend*,
Miss Story has a moderate power of will,
But, having that, believes it greater still: 10
And, hide it though she does, one may divine
She inly nourishes a wish to shine;
Is very capable of strong affection
Tho' apt to throw it in a strange direction;
Is fond of flattery, as any she,   15
But has not learnt to take it gracefully;
Things that she likes seems often to despise,
And loves – a fatal fault – to patronise;
Has wit enough, but less than female tact,
Sees the right thing to do, and does not act;   20
About herself she is most sensitive,
Talks of self-sacrifice, yet can't forgive;
She's framed to triumph in adversity;

Prudence she has, but wise she'll never be;
Her character she does not realise, 25
And cannot see at all with others' eyes;
(And, well supplied with virtues on the whole,
Is slightly selfish in her inmost soul)
Believes herself religious, and is not;
And, thinking that she thinks, has never thought; 30
Married, will make a sweet and matchless wife,
But single, lead a misdirected life.

10

Io

Forward she leans, with hollowing back, stock-still,
Her white weed-bathèd knees are shut together,
Her silky coat is sheeny, like a hill,
Gem-fleeced at morn, so brilliant is the weather.
Her nostril glistens; and her wet black eye 5
Her lids half-meshing shelter from the sky.

Her finger-long new horns are capp'd with black;
In hollows of her form the shadow clings;
Her milk-white throat and folded dew-lap slack
Are still; her neck is creased in close-ply rings; 10
Her hue's a various brown with creamy lakes,
Like a cupp'd chestnut damask'd with dark breaks.

Backward are laid her pretty black-fleeced ears;
The knot of feathery locks upon her head
Plays to the breeze; where now are fled her fears, 15
Her jailor with his vigil-organ dead?
Morn does not now new-basilisk his stare,
Nor night is blown with flame-rings everywhere.

II
To Oxford

(i)

New-dated from the terms that reappear,
More sweet-familiar grows my love to thee,
And still thou bind'st me to fresh fealty
With long-superfluous ties, for nothing here
Nor elsewhere can thy sweetness unendear.   5
This is my park, my pleasuance; this to me
As public is my greater privacy,
All mine, yet common to my every peer.
Those charms accepted of my inmost thought,
The towers musical, quiet-walled grove,   10
The window-circles, these may all be sought
By other eyes, and other suitors move,
And all like me may boast, impeached not,
Their special-general title to thy love.

(ii)

Thus, I come underneath this chapel-side,
So that the mason's levels, courses, all
The vigorous horizontals, each way fall
In bows above my head, as falsified
By visual compulsion, till I hide   5
The steep-up roof at last behind the small
Eclipsing parapet; yet above the wall
The sumptuous ridge-crest leave to poise and ride.
None besides me this bye-ways beauty try.
Or if they try it, I am happier then: 10
The shapen flags and drillèd holes of sky,
Just seen, may be so many unknown men
The one peculiar of their pleasured eye,
And I have only set the same to pen.

12

The Alchemist in the City

My window shows the travelling clouds,
Leaves spent, new seasons, alter'd sky,
The making and the melting crowds:
The whole world passes; I stand by.

They do not waste their meted hours,   5
But men and masters plan and build:
I see the crowning of their towers,
And happy promises fulfill'd.

And I – perhaps if my intent
Could count on prediluvian age,   10
The labours I should then have spent
Might so attain their heritage,

But now before the pot can glow
With not to be discover'd gold,
At length the bellows shall not blow,   15
The furnace shall at last be cold.

Yet it is now too late to heal
The incapable and cumbrous shame
Which makes me when with men I deal
More powerless than the blind or lame.   20

No, I should love the city less
Even than this my thankless lore;
But I desire the wilderness
Or weeded landslips of the shore.

I walk my breezy belvedere   25
To watch the low or levant sun,
I see the city pigeons veer,
I mark the tower swallows run

Between the tower-top and the ground
Below me in the bearing air;   30
Then find in the horizon-round
One spot and hunger to be there.

And then I hate the most that lore
That holds no promise of success;
Then sweetness seems the houseless shore,   35
Then free and kind the wilderness.

Or ancient mounds that cover bones,
Or rocks where rockdoves do repair.
And trees of terebinth and stones
And silence and a gulf of air.   40

There on a long and squarèd height
After the sunset I would lie,
And pierce the yellow waxen light
With free long looking, ere I die.

13

To Oxford

As Devonshire letters, earlier in the year
Than we in the East dare look for buds, disclose
Smells that are sweeter-memoried than the rose,
And pressèd violets in the folds appear,
So is it with my friends, I note, to hear   5
News from Belleisle, even such a sweetness blows
(I know it, knowing not) across from those
Meadows to them inexplicably dear.
'As when a soul laments, which hath been blest' –
I'll cite no further what the initiate know.   10
I never saw those fields whereon their best
And undivulgèd love does overflow.

14
'Myself unholy, from myself unholy'

Myself unholy, from myself unholy
To the sweet living of my friends I look –
Eye-greeting doves bright-counter to the rook,
Fresh brooks to salt sand-teasing waters shoaly: –
And they are purer, but alas! not solely   5
The unquestion'd readings of a blotless book.
And so my trust, confusèd, struck, and shook
Yields to the sultry siege of melancholy.
He has a sin of mine, he its near brother;
Knowing them well I can but see the fall.   10
This fault in one I found, that in another:
And so, though each have one while I have all,
No *better* serves me now, save *best*; no other
Save Christ: to Christ I look, on Christ I call.

15
'See how Spring opens with disabling cold'

See how Spring opens with disabling cold,
And hunting winds and the long-lying snow.
Is it a wonder if the buds are slow?
Or where is strength to make the leaf unfold?
Chilling remembrance of my days of old   5
Afflicts no less, what yet I hope may blow,
That seed which the good sower once did sow,
So loading with obstruction that threshold
Which should ere now have led my feet to the field.
It is the waste done in unreticent youth   10
Which makes so small the promise that yield
That I may win with late-learnt skill uncouth
From furrows of the poor and stinting weald.
Therefore how bitter, and learnt how late, the truth!

16

'My prayers must meet a brazen heaven'

My prayers must meet a brazen heaven
And fail or scatter all away.
Unclean and seeming unforgiven
My prayers I scarcely call to pray.
I cannot buoy my heart above;   5
Above it cannot entrance win.
I reckon precedents of love,
But feel the long success of sin.

My heaven is brass and iron my earth:
Yea iron is mingled with my clay,   10
So harden'd is it in this dearth
Which praying fails to do away.
Nor tears, nor tears this clay uncouth
Could mould, if any tears there were.
A warfare of my lips in truth,   15
Battling with God, is now my prayer.

17

Shakspere

In the lodges of the perishable souls
He has his portion. God, who stretch'd apart
Doomsday and death – whose dateless thought must chart
All time at once and span the distant goals,
Sees what his place is; but for us the rolls   5
Are shut against the canvassing of art.
Something we guess or know: some spirits start
Upwards at once and win their aureoles.

  .   .   .   .

18

'Let me be to Thee as the circling bird'

Let me be to Thee as the circling bird,
Or bat with tender and air-crisping wings
That shapes in half-light his departing rings,
From both of whom a changeless note is heard.
I have found my music in a common word,   5
Trying each pleasurable throat that sings
And every praisèd sequence of sweet strings,
And know infallibly which I preferred.
The authentic cadence was discovered late
Which ends those only strains that I approve,   10
And other science all gone out of date
And minor sweetness scarce made mention of:
I have found the dominant of my range and state –
Love, O my God, to call Thee Love and Love.

19

The Half-way House

Love I was shewn upon the mountain-side
And bid to catch Him ere the drop of day.
See, Love, I creep and Thou on wings dost ride:
Love, it is evening now and Thou away;
Love, it grows darker here and Thou art above;   5
Love, come down to me if Thy name be Love.

My national old Egyptian reed gave way;
I took of vine a cross-barred rod or rood.
Then next I hungered: Love when here, they say,
Or once or never took Love's proper food;   10
But I must yield the chase, or rest and eat. –
Peace and food cheered me where four rough ways meet.

Hear yet my paradox: Love, when all is given,
To see Thee I must see Thee, to love, love;
I must o'ertake Thee at once and under heaven 15
If I shall overtake Thee at last above.
You have your wish; enter these walls, one said:
He is with you in the breaking of the bread.

20

A Complaint

I thought that you would have written: my birthday came and went,
And with the last post over I knew no letter was sent.
And if you write at last, it never can be the same:
What *would* be a birthday letter that after the birthday came?

I know what you will tell me – neglectful that you were not 5
But is not that my grievance – you promised and you forgot?
It's the day that makes the charm; no after-words could succeed
Though they took till the seventeenth of next October to read.

Think this, my birthday falls in saddening time of year;
Only the dahlias blow, and all is Autumn here. 10
Hampstead was never bright; and whatever Miss Cully's charms
It is hardly a proper treat for a birthday to rest in her arms.

Our sex should be born in April perhaps or the lily-time;
But the lily is past, as I say, and the rose is not in its prime:
What I did ask then was a circle of rose-red sealing-wax 15

And a few leaves not lily-white but charactered over with
   blacks.

But late is better than never: you see you have managed so,
You have made me quote almost the dismalest proverb I
   know:
For a letter comes at last: (shall I say before Christmas is
   come?)
And I must take your amends, cry Pardon, and then be
   dumb.   20

21

'Moonless darkness stands between'

Moonless darkness stands between.
Past, the Past, no more be seen!
But the Bethlehem star may lead me
To the sight of Him Who freed me
From the self that I have been.   5
Make me pure, Lord: Thou art holy;
Make me meek, Lord: Thou wert lowly;
Now beginning, and alway:
Now begin, on Christmas day.

22

'The earth and heaven, so little known'

The earth and heaven, so little known,
Are measured outwards from my breast.
I am the midst of every zone
And justify the East and West;

The unchanging register of change
My all-accepting fixèd eye,

While all things else may stir and range
All else may whirl or dive or fly.

The swallow, favourite of the gale,
Will on the moulding strike and cling,   10
Unvalve or shut his vanèd tail
And sheathe at once his leger wing.

He drops upon the wind again;
His little pennon is unfurled.
In motion is no weight or pain,   15
Nor permanence in the solid world.

There is a vapour stands in the wind;
It shapes itself in taper skeins:
You look again and cannot find,
Save in the body of the rains.   20

And these are spent and ended quite;
The sky is blue, and the winds pull
Their clouds with breathing edges white
Beyond the world; the streams are full

And millbrook-slips with pretty pace
Gallop along the meadow grass. –
O lovely ease in change of place!
I have desired, desired to pass. . . .

23

'The stars were packed so
close that night'

The stars were packed so close that night
   They seemed to press and stare
And gather in like hurdles bright
   The liberties of air.

24

The Nightingale

'From nine o'clock till morning light
The copse was never more than grey.
The darkness did not close that night
     But day passed into day.
And soon I saw it shewing new   5
Beyond the hurst with such a hue
As silken garden-poppies do.

'A crimson East, that bids for rain.
So from the dawn was ill begun
The day that brought my lasting pain   10
     And put away my sun.
But watching while the colour grew
I only feared the wet for you
Bound for the Harbour and your crew.

'I did not mean to sleep, but found   15
I had slept a little and was chill.
And I could hear the tiniest sound,
     The morning was so still –
The bats' wings lisping as they flew
And water draining through and through   20
The wood: but not a dove would coo.

'You know you said the nightingale
In all our western shires was rare,
That more he shuns our special dale
     Or never lodges there: 25
And I had thought so hitherto –
Up till that morning's fall of dew,
And now I wish that it were true.

'For he began at once and shook
My head to hear. He might have strung   30
A row of ripples in the brook,
     So forcibly he sung,
The mist upon the leaves have strewed,
And danced the balls of dew that stood
In acres all above the wood.   35

'I thought the air must cut and strain
The windpipe when he sucked his breath
And when he turned it back again
   The music must be death.
With not a thing to make me fear,   40
A singing bird in morning clear
To me was terrible to hear.

'Yet as he changed his mighty stops
Betweens I heard the water still
All down the stair-way of the copse
   And churning in the mill.
But that sweet sound which I preferred,
Your passing steps, I never heard
For warbling of the warbling bird.'

Thus Frances sighed at home, while Luke   50
Made headway in the frothy deep.
She listened how the sea-gust shook
And then lay back to sleep.
While he was washing from on deck
She pillowing low her lily neck   55
Timed her sad visions with his wreck.

25
The Habit of Perfection

Elected Silence, sing to me
And beat upon my whorlèd ear,
Pipe me to pastures still and be
The music that I care to hear.

Shape nothing, lips; be lovely-dumb: 5
It is the shut, the curfew sent
From there where all surrenders come
Which only makes you eloquent.

Be shellèd, eyes, with double dark
And find the uncreated light: 10

This ruck and reel which you remark
Coils, keeps, and teases simple sight.

Palate, the hutch of tasty lust,
Desire not to be rinsed with wine:
The can must be so sweet, the crust   15
So fresh that come in fasts divine!

Nostrils, your careless breath that spend
Upon the stir and keep of pride,
What relish shall the censers send
Along the sanctuary side!   20

O feel-of-primrose hands, O feet
That want the yield of plushy sward,
But you shall walk the golden street
And you unhouse and house the Lord.

And, Poverty, be thou the bride   25
And now the marriage feast begun,
And lily-coloured clothes provide
Your spouse not laboured-at nor spun.

26

Nondum

'Verily Thou art a God that hidest Thyself.'
ISAIAH XLV. 15

God, though to Thee our psalm we raise
No answering voice comes from the skies;
To Thee the trembling sinner prays
But no forgiving voice replies;
Our prayer seems lost in desert ways,   5
Our hymn in the vast silence dies.

We see the glories of the earth
But not the hand that wrought them all:
Night to a myriad worlds gives birth,

Yet like a lighted empty hall
Where stands no host at door or hearth
Vacant creation's lamps appal.

We guess; we clothe Thee, unseen King,
With attributes we deem are meet;
Each in his own imagining
Sets up a shadow in Thy seat;
Yet know not how our gifts to bring,
Where seek Thee with unsandalled feet.

And still th'unbroken silence broods
While ages and while aeons run,
As erst upon chaotic floods
The Spirit hovered ere the sun
Had called the seasons' changeful moods
And life's first germs from death had won.

And still th'abysses infinite
Surround the peak from which we gaze.
Deep calls to deep, and blackest night
Giddies the soul with blinding daze
That dares to cast its searching sight
On being's dread and vacant maze.

And Thou art silent, whilst Thy world
Contends about its many creeds
And hosts confront with flags unfurled
And zeal is flushed and pity bleeds
And truth is heard, with tears impearled,
A moaning voice among the reeds.

My hand upon my lips I lay;
The breast's desponding sob I quell;
I move along life's tomb-decked way
And listen to the passing bell
Summoning men from speechless day
To death's more silent, darker spell.

Oh! till Thou givest that sense beyond,
To show Thee that Thou art, and near,
Let patience with her chastening wand
Dispel the doubt and dry the tear;

And lead me child-like by the hand
If still in darkness not in fear.

Speak! whisper to my watching heart
One word – as when a mother speaks   50
Soft, when she sees her infant start,
Till dimpled joy steals o'er its cheeks.
Then, to behold Thee as Thou art,
I'll wait till morn eternal breaks.

27

Lines for a Picture of St Dorothea

Dorothea and Theophilus

I bear a basket lined with grass.
I´ am so´ light´ and fair´
Men are amazed to watch me pass
With´; the básket I bear´,
Which in newly drawn green litter
Carries treats of sweet for bitter.

See my lilies: lilies none,
None in Caesar's garden blow.
Quínces, look´, when´ not one´
Is set in any orchard; no,   10
Not set because their buds not spring;
Spring not for world is wintering.

But´ they came´ from´ the south´,
Where winter-while is all forgot. –
The dewbell in the mallow's mouth   15
Is´ it quénchèd or not´?
In starry, starry shire it grew:
Which´ is it´, star´ or dew´?

That a quince I pore upon?
O no it is the sizing moon.   20
Now her mallow-row is gone

In tufts of evening sky. – So soon?
Sphered so fast, sweet soul? – We see
Fruit nor flower nor Dorothy.

How to name it, blessed it!   25
Suiting its grace with *him* or *her*?
Dorothea – or was your writ
Sérvèd bý méssenger´?
Your parley was not done and there!
You went into the partless air.   30

It waned into the world of light,
Yet made its market here as well:
My eyes hold yet the rinds and bright
Remainder of a miracle.
O this is bringing! Tears may swarm   35
Indeed while such a wonder's warm.

Ah dip in blood the palmtree pen
And wordy warrants are flawed through.
More will wear this wand and then
The warpèd world we shall undo.   40
Proconsul! – Is Sapricius near? –
I find another Christian here.

28

HORACE: Persicos odi, puer, apparatus

(ODES I. XXXVIII)

Ah child, no Persian-perfect art!
Crowns composite and braided bast
They tease me. Never know the part
    Where roses linger last.

Bring natural myrtle, and have done: 5
Myrtle will suit your place and mine:
And set the glasses from the sun
    Beneath the tackled vine.

29

HORACE: Odi profanum volgus et arceo

(ODES III. I)

Tread back – and back, the lewd and lay! –
Grace love your lips! – what never ear
Heard yet, the Muses' man, today
I bid the boys and maidens hear.

Kings herd it on their subject droves   5
But Jove's the herd that keeps the kings –
Jove of the Giants: simple Jove's
Mere eyebrow rocks this round of things.

Say man than man may rank his rows
Wider, more wholesale; one with claim   10
Of blood to our green hustings goes;
One with more conscience, cleaner fame;

One better backed comes crowding by: –
That level power whose word is Must
Dances the balls for low or high: 15
Her urn takes all, her deal is just.

Sinner who saw the blade that hung
Vertical home, could Sicily fare
Be managed tasty to that tongue?
Or bird with pipe, viol with air   20

Bring sleep round then? – sleep not afraid
Of country bidder's calls or low
Entries or banks all over shade
Or Tempe with the west to blow.

Who stops his asking mood at par   25
The burly sea may quite forget
Not fear the violent calender
At Haedus-rise, Arcturus-set,

For hail upon the vine nor break
His heart at farming, what between   30

The dog-star with the fields abake
And spiting snows to choke the green.

Fish feel their waters drawing to
With our abutments: there we see
The lades discharged and laded new,   35
And Italy flies from Italy.

But fears, fore-motions of the mind,
Climb quits: one boards the master there
On brazèd barge and hard behind
Sits to the beast that seats him – Care.   40

O if there's that which Phrygian stone
And crimson wear of starry shot
Not sleek away; Falernian-grown
And oils of Shushan comfort not,

Why   45
    .   .   .   .   .
Why should I change a Sabine dale
For wealth as wide as weariness?

30

The Elopement

All slumbered whom our rud red tiles
Do cover from the starry spread,
When I with never-needed wiles
    Crept trembling out of bed.
Then at the door what work there was, good lack,   5
To keep the loaded bolt from plunging back.

When this was done and I could look
I saw the stars like flash of fire.
My heart irregularly shook,
    I cried with my desire.   10
I put the door to with the bolts unpinned,
Upon my forehead hit the burly wind.

No tumbler woke and shook the cot,
The rookery never stirred a wing,
At roost and rest they shifted not,   15
   Blessed be everything.
And all within the house were sound as posts,
Or listening thought of linen-winded ghosts.

The stars are packed so thick to-night
They seem to press and droop and stare,
And gather in like hurdles bright   20
   The liberties of air.
I spy the nearest daisies through the dark,
The air smells strong of sweetbriar in the park.

I knew the brook that parts in two   25
The cart road with a shallowy bed
Of small and sugar flints, I knew
   The footway, Stephen said,
And where cold daffodils in April are
Think you want daffodils and follow as far   30

As where the little hurling sound
To the point of silence in the air
Dies off in hyacinthed ground,
   And I should find him there.
O heart, have done, you beat you beat so high,   35
You spoil the plot I find my true love by.

31

The Wreck of the Deutschland

To the
happy memory of five Franciscan nuns
exiles by the Falck Laws
drowned between midnight and morning of
Dec. 7th, 1875

PART THE FIRST

1

Thou mastering me
God! giver of breath and bread;
World's strand, sway of the sea;
Lord of living and dead;
Thou hast bound bones and veins in me, fastened me
flesh,   5
And after it almost unmade, what with dread,
Thy doing: and dost thou touch me afresh?
Over again I feel thy finger and find thee.

2

I did say yes
O at lightning and lashed rod;   10
Thou heardst me truer than tongue confess
Thy terror, O Christ, O God;
Thou knowest the walls, altar and hour and night:
The swoon of a heart that the sweep and the hurl of thee
trod
Hard down with a horror of height: 15
And the midriff astrain with leaning of, laced with fire of
stress.

3

The frown of his face
Before me, the hurtle of hell
Behind, where, where was a, where was a place?
I whirled out wings that spell   20
And fled with a fling of the heart to the heart of the
Host.

My heart, but you were dovewinged, I can tell,
    Carrier-witted, I am bold to boast,
To flash from the flame to the flame then, tower from the
    grace to the grace.

4

    I am soft sift   25
    In an hourglass – at the wall
    Fast, but mined with a motion, a drift,
    And it crowds and it combs to the fall;
I steady as a water in a well, to a poise, to a pane,
But roped with, always, all the way down from the tall   30
    Fells or flanks of the voel, a vein
Of the gospel proffer, a pressure, a principle, Christ's gift.

5

    I kiss my hand
    To the stars, lovely-asunder
    Starlight, wafting him out of it; and   35
    Glow, glory in thunder;
Kiss my hand to the dappled-with-damson west:
Since tho' he is under the world's splendour and wonder,
    His mystery must be instressed, stressed;
For I greet him the days I meet him, and bless when I
    understand.   40

6

    Not out of his bliss
    Springs the stress felt
    Not first from heaven (and few know this)
    Swings the stroke dealt –
Stroke and a stress that stars and storms deliver,   45
That guilt is hushed by, hearts are flushed by and melt –
    But it rides time like riding a river
(And here the faithful waver, the faithless fable and miss).

7

    It dates from day
    Of his going in Galilee;   50
    Warm-laid grave of a womb-life grey;
    Manger, maiden's knee;
The dense and the driven Passion, and frightful sweat:
Thence the discharge of it, there its swelling to be,

Though felt before, though in high flood yet –   55
What none would have known of it, only the heart, being
    hard at bay,

8

Is out with it! Oh,
We lash with the best or worst
Word last! How a lush-kept plush-capped sloe
    Will, mouthed to flesh-burst,   60
Gush! – flush the man, the being with it, sour or sweet,
Brim, in a flash, full! – Hither then, last or first,
    To hero of Calvary, Christ's feet –
Never ask if meaning it, wanting it, warned of it – men go.

9

Be adored among men,   65
    God, three-numberèd form;
Wring thy rebel, dogged in den,
    Man's malice, with wrecking and storm.
Beyond saying sweet, past telling of tongue,
Thou art lightning and love, I found it, a winter and
    warm;   70
    Father and fondler of heart thou hast wrung:
Hast thy dark descending and most art merciful then.

10

With an anvil-ding
    And with fire in him forge thy will
Or rather, rather then, stealing as Spring   75
    Through him, melt him but master him still:
Whether at once, as once at a crash Paul,
Or as Austin, a lingering-out swéet skíll
    Make mercy in all of us, out of us all
Mastery, but be adored, but be adored King.   80

PART THE SECOND

11

'Some find me a sword; some
    The flange and the rail; flame,
Fang, or flood' goes Death on drum,
    And storms bugle his fame.

But wé dream we are rooted in earth – Dust!   85
Flesh falls within sight of us, we, though our flower the
          same,
          Wave with the meadow, forget that there must
The sour scythe cringe, and the blear share come.

12

          On Saturday sailed from Bremen,
          American-outward-bound,   90
     Take settler and seamen, tell men with women,
          Two hundred souls in the round –
O Father, not under thy feathers nor ever as guessing
The goal was a shoal, of a fourth the doom to be
          drowned;
          Yet did the dark side of the bay of thy blessing   95
Not vault them, the million of rounds of thy mercy not reeve
          even them in?

13

          Into the snows she sweeps,
          Hurling the haven behind,
     The Deutschland, on Sunday; and so the sky keeps,
          For the infinite air is unkind,   100
And the sea flint-flake, black-backed in the regular blow,
Sitting Eastnortheast, in cursed quarter, the wind;
          Wiry and white-fiery and whirlwind-swivellèd snow
Spins to the widow-making unchilding unfathering deeps.

14

          She drove in the dark to leeward,   105
          She struck – not a reef or a rock
     But the combs of a smother of sand: night drew her
          Dead to the Kentish Knock;
And she beat the bank down with her bows and the ride
          of her keel:
The breakers rolled on her beam with ruinous shock;   110
          And canvas and compass, the whorl and the wheel
Idle for ever to waft her or wind her with, these she endured.

15

          Hope had grown grey hairs,
          Hope had mourning on,
     Trenched with tears, carved with cares,   115

Hope was twelve hours gone;
And frightful a nightfall folded rueful a day
Nor rescue, only rocket and lightship, shone,
And lives at last were washing away:
To the shrouds they took, – they shook in the hurling and
          horrible airs.   120

16

One stirred from the rigging to save
The wild woman-kind below,
With a rope's end round the man, handy and brave –
He was pitched to his death at a blow,
For all his dreadnought breast and braids of thew: 125
They could tell him for hours, dandled the to and fro
          Through the cobbled foam-fleece. What could he do
With the burl of the fountains of air, buck and the flood of
          the wave?

17

They fought with God's cold –
They could not and fell to the deck   130
(Crushed them) or water (and drowned them) or
          rolled
With the sea-romp over the wreck.
Night roared, with the heart-break hearing a heart-
          broke rabble,
The woman's wailing, the crying of child without
          check –
Till a lioness arose breasting the babble,   135
A prophetess towered in the tumult, a virginal tongue told.

18

Ah, touched in your bower of bone,
Are you! turned for an exquisite smart,
Have you! make words break from me here all alone,
Do you! – mother of being in me, heart.   140
O unteachably after evil, but uttering truth,
Why, tears! is it? tears; such a melting, a madrigal start!
Never-eldering revel and river of youth,
What can it be, this glee? the good you have there of your
          own?

19

Sister, a sister calling   145
A master her master and mine! –
And the inboard seas run swirling and hawling;
The rash smart sloggering brine
Blinds her; but she that weather sees one thing, one;
Has one fetch in her: she rears herself to divine   150
Ears, and the call of the tall nun
To the men in the tops and the tackle rode over the storm's
brawling.

20

She was first of a five and came
Of a coifèd sisterhood,
(O Deutschland, double a desperate name!   155
O world wide of its good!
But Gertrude, lily, and Luther, are two of a town,
Christ's lily and beast of the waste wood:
From life's dawn it is drawn down,
Abel is Cain's brother and breasts they had sucked the
same.)   160

21

Loathed for a love men knew in them,
Banned by the land of their birth,
Rhine refused them, Thames would ruin them;
Surf, snow, river and earth
Gnashed: but thou art above, thou Orion of light;   165
Thy unchancelling poising palms were weighing the
worth,
Thou martyr-master: in thy sight
Storm flakes were scroll-leaved flowers, lily showers – sweet
heaven was astrew in them.

22

Five! the finding and sake
And cipher of suffering Christ.   170
Mark, the mark is of man's make
And the word of it Sacrificed.
But he scores it in scarlet himself on his own bespoken,
Before-time-taken, dearest prizèd and priced –
Stigma, signal, cinquefoil token   175
For lettering of the lamb's fleece, ruddying of the rose-flake.

23

Joy fall to thee, father Francis,
Drawn to the Life that died;
With the gnarls of nails in thee, niche of the lance,
his
Lovescape crucified   180
And seal of his seraph-arrival! and these thy daughters
And five-livèd and leavèd favour and pride,
Are sisterly sealed in wild waters,
To bathe in his fall-gold mercies, to breathe in his all-fire
glances.

24

Away in the loveable west,   185
On a pastoral forehead of Wales,
I was under a roof here, I was at rest,
And they the prey of the gales;
She to the black-about air, to the breaker, the thickly
Falling flakes, to the throng that catches and quails
Was calling 'O Christ, Christ, come quickly':   200
The cross to her she calls Christ to her, christens her wild-
worst best.

25

The majesty! what did she mean?
Breathe, arch and original Breath.
Is it love in her of the being as her lover had been?
Breathe, body of lovely Death.   205
They were else-minded then, altogether, the men
Woke thee with a *We are perishing* in the weather of
Gennesareth.
Or is it that she cried for the crown then,
The keener to come at the comfort for feeling the combating
keen?

26

For how to the heart's cheering   210
The down-dugged ground-hugged grey
Hovers off, the jay-blue heavens appearing
Of pied and peeled May!
Blue-beating and hoary-glow height; or night, still
higher,

With belled fire and the moth-soft Milky Way,   215
   What by your measure is the heaven of desire,
The treasure never eyesight got nor was ever guessed what
    for the hearing?

27

   No, but it was not these.
   The jading and jar of the cart,
  Time's tasking, it is fathers that asking for ease   220
   Of the sodden-with-its-sorrowing heart,
Not danger, electrical horror; then further it finds
The appealing of the Passion is tenderer in prayer apart:
   Other, I gather, in measure her mind's
Burden, in wind's burly and beat of endragonèd seas.   225

28

  But how shall I . . . make me room there:
   Reach me a . . . Fancy, come faster –
  Strike you the sight of it? look at it loom there,
   Thing that she . . . There then! the Master,
Ipse, the only one, Christ, King, Head: 230
He was to cure the extremity where he had cast her;
   Do, deal, lord it with living and dead;
Let him ride, her pride, in his triumph, despatch and have
    done with his doom there.

29

   Ah! there was a heart right!
   There was single eye!   235
  Read the unshapeable shock night
   And knew the who and the why;
Wording it how but by him that present and past,
Heaven and earth are word of, worded by? –
   The Simon Peter of a soul! to the blast   240
Tarpeïan-fast, but a blown beacon of light.

30

   Jesu, heart's light,
   Jesu, maid's son,
  What was the feast followed the night
   Thou hadst glory of this nun? –   245
Feast of the one woman without stain.
For so conceivèd, so to conceive thee is done;

But here was heart-throe, birth of a brain,
Word, that heard and kept thee and uttered thee outright.

31

Well, she has thee for the pain, for the 250
   Patience; but pity of the rest of them!
Heart, go and bleed at a bitterer vein for the
   Comfortless unconfessed of them –
No not uncomforted: lovely-felicitous Providence
Finger of a tender of, O of a feathery delicacy, the
   breast of the 255
   Maiden could obey so, be a bell to, ring of it, and
Startle the poor sheep back! is the shipwrack then a harvest,
   does tempest carry the grain for thee?

32

I admire thee, master of the tides,
   Of the Yore-flood, of the year's fall;
The recurb and the recovery of the gulf's sides, 260
   The girth of it and the wharf of it and the
   wall;
Stanching, quenching ocean of a motionable mind;
Ground of being, and granite of it: past all
   Grasp God, throned behind
Death with a sovereignty that heeds but hides, bodes but
   abides; 265

33

With a mercy that outrides
   The all of water, an ark
For the listener; for the lingerer with a love glides
   Lower than death and the dark;
A vein for the visiting of the past-prayer, pent in prison, 270
The-last-breath penitent spirits – the uttermost mark
   Our passion-plungèd giant risen,
The Christ of the Father compassionate, fetched in the
   storm of his strides.

34

Now burn, new born to the world,
   Double-naturèd name,
The heaven-flung, heart-fleshed, maiden-furled
   Miracle-in-Mary-of-flame,

Mid-numberèd he in three of the thunder-throne!
Not a dooms-day dazzle in his coming nor dark as he
    came;
      Kind, but royally reclaiming his own;   280
A released shower, let flash to the shire, not a lightning of
    fire hard-hurled.

35

        Dame, at our door
        Drowned, and among our shoals,
    Remember us in the roads, the heaven-haven of
      the reward:
        Our King back, Oh, upon English souls!   285
Let him easter in us, be a dayspring to the dimness of
    us, be a crimson-cresseted east,
More brightening her, rare-dear Britain, as his reign
    rolls,
      Pride, rose, prince, hero of us, high-priest,
Our hearts' charity's hearth's fire, our thoughts' chivalry's
    throng's Lord.

32

Moonrise

I awoke in the Midsummer not-to-call night, | in the white and
    the walk of the morning:
The moon, dwindled and thinned to the fringe | of a fingernail
    held to the candle,
Or paring of paradisaïcal fruit, | lovely in waning but lustre-less,
Stepped from the stool, drew back from the barrow, | of dark
    Maenefa the mountain;
A cusp still clasped him, a fluke yet fanged him, | entangled
    him, not quit utterly.   5
This was the prized, the desirable sight, | unsought, presented
    so easily,
Parted me leaf and leaf, divided me, | eyelid and eyelid of
    slumber.

33
The Silver Jubilee:

To James First Bishop of Shrewsbury on the
25th Year of his Episcopate July 28, 1876.

Though no high-hung bells or din
Of braggart bugles cry it in –
   What is sound? Nature's round
Makes the Silver Jubilee.

Five and twenty years have run   5
Since sacred fountains to the sun
   Sprang, that but now were shut,
Showering Silver Jubilee.

Feasts, when we shall fall asleep,
Shrewsbury may see others keep;   10
   None but you this her true,
This her Silver Jubilee.

Not today we need lament
Your wealth of life is some way spent:
   Toil has shed round your head   15
Silver but for Jubilee.

Then for her whose velvet vales
Should have pealed with welcome, Wales,
   Let the chime of a rhyme
Utter Silver Jubilee.   20

34
The Woodlark

Teevo cheevo cheevio chee:
O where, what can thát be?

Weedio-weedio: there again!
So tiny a trickle of sóng-strain;

And all round not to be found   5
For brier, bough, furrow, or gréen ground
Before or behind or far or at hand
Either left either right
Anywhere in the súnlight.

Well, after all! Ah but hark –   10
'I am the little wóodlark.
The skylark is my cousin and he
Is known to men more than me.
Round a ring, around a ring
And while I sail (must listen) I sing.   15

To-day the sky is two and two
With white strokes and strains of the blue.
The blue wheat-acre is underneath
And the corn is corded and shoulders its sheaf,
The ear in milk, lush the sash,   20
And crush-silk poppies aflash,
The blood-gush blade-gash
Flame-rash rudred
Bud shelling or broad-shed
Tatter-tangled and dingle-a-danglèd   25
Dandy-hung dainty head.

And down . . . the furrow dry
Sunspurge oxeye
And lace-leaved lovely
Foam-tuft fumitory.   30

I ám so véry, O só very glád
That I dó thínk there is not to be had
[Anywhere any more joy to be in.
Cheevio:] when the cry within
Says Go on then I go on   35
Till the longing is less and the good gone,

But down drop, if it says Stop,
To the all-a-leaf of the tréetop.
And after that off the bough
[Hover-float to the hedge brow.]   40

Through the velvety wind V-winged
[Where shake shadow is sun's-eye-ringed]
To the nest's nook I balance and buoy
With a sweet joy of a sweet joy,
Sweet, of a sweet, of a sweet joy   45
Of a sweet – a sweet – sweet – joy.'

35

Penmaen Pool

For the Visitors' Book at the Inn

Who long for rest, who look for pleasure
Away from counter, court, or school
O where live well your lease of leisure
But here at, here at Penmaen Pool?

You'll dare the Alp? you'll dart the skiff?   5
Each sport has here its tackle and tool:
Come, plant the staff by Cadair cliff;
Come, swing the sculls on Penmaen Pool.

What's yonder? Grizzled Dyphwys dim:
The triple-hummocked Giant's Stool,   10
Hoar messmate, hobs and nobs with him
To halve the bowl of Penmaen Pool.

And all the landscape under survey,
At tranquil turns, by nature's rule,
Rides repeated topsyturvy   15
In frank, in fairy Penmaen Pool.

And Charles's Wain, the wondrous seven,
And sheep-flock clouds like worlds of wool,
For all they shine so, high in heaven,
Shew brighter shaken in Penmaen Pool.   20

The Mawddach, how she trips! though throttled
If floodtide teeming thrills her full,

And mazy sands all water-wattled
Waylay her at ebb, past Penmaen Pool.

But what's to see in stormy weather,   25
When grey showers gather and gusts are cool? –
Why, raindrop-roundels looped together
That lace the face of Penmaen Pool.

Then even in weariest wintry hour
Of New Year's month or surly Yule   30
Furred snows, charged tuft above tuft, tower
From darksome darksome Penmaen Pool.

And ever, if bound here hardest home,
You've parlour-pastime left and (who'll
Not honour it?) ale like goldy foam   35
That frocks an oar in Penmaen Pool.

Then come who pine for peace or pleasure
Away from counter, court, or school,
Spend here your measure of time and treasure
And taste the treats of Penmaen Pool.   40

36

God's Grandeur

The world is charged with the grandeur of God.
    It will flame out, like shining from shook foil;
    It gathers to a greatness, like the ooze of oil
Crushed. Why do men then now not reck his rod?
Generations have trod, have trod, have trod;   5
    And all is seared with trade; bleared, smeared with toil;
    And wears man's smudge and shares man's smell: the soil
Is bare now, nor can foot feel, being shod.

And for all this, nature is never spent;
    There lives the dearest freshness deep down things;   10
And though the last lights off the black West went
    Oh, morning, at the brown brink eastward, springs –

Because the Holy Ghost over the bent
　World broods with warm breast with ah! bright wings.

37

The Starlight Night

Look at the stars! look, look up at the skies!
　O look at all the fire-folk sitting in the air!
　The bright boroughs, the circle-citadels there!
Down in dim woods the diamond delves! the elves'-eyes!
The grey lawns cold where gold, where quickgold lies!　5
　Wind-beat whitebeam! airy abeles set on a flare!
　Flake-doves sent floating forth at a farmyard scare! –
Ah well! it is all a purchase, all is a prize.
Buy then! bid then! – What? – Prayer, patience, alms, vows.
Look, look: a May-mess, like on orchard boughs!　10
　Look! March-bloom, like on mealed-with-yellow sallows!
These are indeed the barn; withindoors house
The shocks. This piece-bright paling shuts the spouse
　Christ home, Christ and his mother and all his hallows.

38

Spring

Nothing is so beautiful as Spring –
　When weeds, in wheels, shoot long and lovely and lush;
　Thrush's eggs look little low heavens, and thrush
Through the echoing timber does so rinse and wring
The ear, it strikes like lightnings to hear him sing;　5
　The glassy peartree leaves and blooms, they brush
　The descending blue; that blue is all in a rush
With richness; the racing lambs too have fair their fling.

What is all this juice and all this joy?
   A strain of the earth's sweet being in the beginning   10
In Eden garden. – Have, get, before it cloy,

   Before it cloud, Christ, lord, and sour with sinning,
Innocent mind and Mayday in girl and boy,
   Most, O maid's child, thy choice and worthy the winning.

39
In the Valley of the Elwy

I remember a house where all were good
   To me, God knows, deserving no such thing:
   Comforting smell breathed at very entering,
Fetched fresh, as I suppose, off some sweet wood.

That cordial air made those kind people a hood   5
   All over, as a bevy of eggs the mothering wing
   Will, or mild nights the new morsels of Spring:
Why, it seemed of course; seemed of right it should.

Lovely the woods, waters, meadows, combes, vales,
All the air things wear that build this world of Wales;   10
   Only the inmate does not correspond:

God, lover of souls, swaying considerate scales,
Complete thy creature dear O where it fails,
   Being mighty a master, being a father and fond.

40
The Sea and the Skylark

On ear and ear two noises too old to end
   Trench – right, the tide that ramps against the shore;

With a flood or a fall, low lull-off or all roar,
Frequenting there while moon shall wear and wend.

Left hand, off land, I hear the lark ascend,   5
  His rash-fresh re-winded new skeinèd score
  In crisps of curl off wild winch whirl, and pour
And pelt music, till none's to spill nor spend.

How these two shame this shallow and frail town!
  How ring right out our sordid turbid time,   10
Being pure! We, life's pride and cared-for crown,

  Have lost that cheer and charm of earth's past prime:
Our make and making break, are breaking, down
  To man's last dust, drain fast towards man's first slime.

41

The Windhover:

To Christ our Lord

I caught this morning morning's minion, king-
  dom of daylight's dauphin, dapple-dawn-drawn Falcon, in
    his riding
  Of the rolling level underneath him steady air, and striding
High there, how he rung upon the rein of a wimpling wing
In his ecstasy! then off, off forth on swing,   5
  As a skate's heel sweeps smooth on a bow-bend: the hurl
    and gliding
  Rebuffed the big wind. My heart in hiding
Stirred for a bird, – the achieve of, the mastery of the thing!

Brute beauty and valour and act, oh, air, pride, plume, here
  Buckle! AND the fire that breaks from thee then, a billion   10
Times told lovelier, more dangerous, O my chevalier!

  No wonder of it: shéer plód makes plough down sillion
Shine, and blue-bleak embers, ah my dear,
  Fall, gall themselves, and gash gold-vermilion.

42

Pied Beauty

Glory be to God for dappled things –
  For skies of couple-colour as a brinded cow;
    For rose-moles all in stipple upon trout that swim;
Fresh-firecoal chestnut-falls; finches' wings;
  Landscape plotted and pieced – fold, fallow, and plough; 5
    And áll trádes, their gear and tackle and trim.
All things counter, original, spare, strange;
  Whatever is fickle, freckled (who knows how?)
    With swift, slow; sweet, sour; adazzle, dim;
He fathers-forth whose beauty is past change: 10
                Praise him.

43

Hurrahing in Harvest

Summer ends now; now, barbarous in beauty, the stooks rise
Around; up above, what wind-walks! what lovely behaviour
Of silk-sack clouds! has wilder, wilful-wavier
Meal-drift moulded ever and melted across skies?

I walk, I lift up, I lift up heart, eyes, 5
Down all that glory in the heavens to glean our Saviour;
And, éyes, heárt, what looks, what lips yet gave you a
Rapturous love's greeting of realer, of rounder replies?

And the azurous hung hills are his world-wielding shoulder
Majestic – as a stallion stalwart, very-violet-sweet! – 10
These things, these things were here and but the beholder
Wanting; which two when they once meet,
The heart rears wings bold and bolder
And hurls for him, O half hurls earth for him off under his
  feet.

44
The Caged Skylark

As a dare-gale skylark scanted in a dull cage
   Man's mounting spirit in his bone-house, mean house,
     dwells –
   That bird beyond the remembering his free fells;
This in drudgery, day-labouring-out life's age.

Though aloft on turf or perch or poor low stage,   5
   Both sing sometímes the sweetest, sweetest spells,
   Yet both droop deadly sómetimes in their cells
Or wring their barriers in bursts of fear or rage.

Not that the sweet-fowl, song-fowl, needs no rest –
Why, hear him, hear him babble and drop down to his
     nest,   10
   But his own nest, wild nest, no prison.

Man's spirit will be flesh-bound when found at best,
But uncumberèd: meadow-down is not distressed
   For a rainbow footing it nor he for his bónes rísen.

45
The Lantern out of Doors

Sometimes a lantern moves along the night,
   That interests our eyes. And who goes there?
   I think; where from and bound, I wonder, where,
With, all down darkness wide, his wading light?

Men go by me whom either beauty bright   5
   In mould or mind or what not else makes rare:
   They rain against our much-thick and marsh air
Rich beams, till death or distance buys them quite.

Death or distance soon consumes them: wind

What most I may eye after, be in at the end   10
I cannot, and out of sight is out of mind.

Christ minds: Christ's interest, what to avow or amend
    There, éyes them, heart wánts, care haúnts, foot fóllows
        kind,
Their ránsom, théir rescue, ánd first, fást, last friénd.

46
The Loss of the Eurydice

Foundered March 24, 1878

The Eurydice – it concerned thee, O Lord:
Three hundred souls, O alas! on board,
    Some asleep unawakened, all un-
warned, eleven fathoms fallen

Where she foundered! One stroke   5
Felled and furled them, the hearts of oak!
    And flockbells off the aerial
Downs' forefalls beat to the burial.

For did she pride her, freighted fully, on
Bounden bales or a hoard of bullion? –   10
    Precious passing measure,
Lads and men her lade and treasure.

She had come from a cruise, training seamen –
Men, boldboys soon to be men:
    Must it, worst weather,   15
Blast bole and bloom together?

No Atlantic squall overwrought her
Or rearing billow of the Biscay water:
    Home was hard at hand
And the blow bore from land.   20

And you were a liar, O blue March day.
Bright sun lanced fire in the heavenly bay;

But what black Boreas wrecked her? he
Came equipped, deadly-electric,

A beetling baldbright cloud thorough England   25
Riding: there did storms not mingle? and
    Hailropes hustle and grind their
Heavengravel? wolfsnow, worlds of it, wind there?

Now Carisbrook keep goes under in gloom;
Now it overvaults Appledurcombe;   30
    Now near by Ventnor town
It hurls, hurls off Boniface Down.

Too proud, too proud, what a press she bore!
Royal, and all her royals wore.
    Sharp with her, shorten sail!   35
Too late; lost; gone with the gale.

This was that fell capsize.
As half she had righted and hoped to rise
    Death teeming in by her portholes
Raced down decks, round messes of mortals.   40

Then a lurch forward, frigate and men;
'All hands for themselves' the cry ran then;
    But she who had housed them thither
Was around them, bound them or wound them with her.

Marcus Hare, high her captain,   45
Kept to her – care-drowned and wrapped in
    Cheer's death, would follow
His charge through the champ-white water-in-a-wallow,

All under Channel to bury in a beach her
Cheeks: Right, rude of feature,   50
    He thought he heard say
'Her commander! and thou too, and thou this way.'

It is even seen, time's something server,
In mankind's medley a duty-swerver,
    At downright 'No or Yes?'   55
Doffs all, drives full for righteousness.

Sydney Fletcher, Bristol-bred,
(Low lie his mates now on watery bed)

Takes to the seas and snows
As sheer down the ship goes. 60

Now her afterdraught gullies him too down;
Now he wrings for breath with the deathgush brown;
    Till a lifebelt and God's will
Lend him a lift from the sea-swill.

Now he shoots short up to the round air; 65
Now he gasps, now he gazes everywhere;
    But his eye no cliff, no coast or
Mark makes in the rivelling snowstorm.

Him, after an hour of wintry waves,
A schooner sights, with another, and saves, 70
    And he boards her in Oh! such joy
He has lost count what came next, poor boy. –

They say who saw one sea-corpse cold
He was all of lovely manly mould,
    Every inch a tar, 75
Of the best we boast our sailors are.

Look, foot to forelock, how all things suit! he
Is strung by duty, is strained to beauty,
    And brown-as-dawning-skinned
With brine and shine and whirling wind. 80

O his nimble finger, his gnarled grip!
Leagues, leagues of seamanship
    Slumber in these forsaken
Bones, this sinew, and will not waken.

He was but one like thousands more. 85
Day and night I deplore
    My people and born own nation,
Fast foundering own generation.

I might let bygones be – our curse
Of ruinous shrine no hand or, worse,
    Robbery's hand is busy to 90
Dress, hoar-hallowèd shrines unvisited;

Only the breathing temple and fleet
Life, this wildworth blown so sweet,

These daredeaths, ay this crew, in   95
Unchrist, all rolled in ruin –

Deeply surely I need to deplore it,
Wondering why my master bore it,
    The riving off that race
So at home, time was, to his truth and grace   100

That a starlight-wender of ours would say
The marvellous Milk was Walsingham Way
    And one – but let be, let be:
More, more than was will yet be. –

O well wept, mother have lost son;   105
Wept, wife; wept, sweetheart would be one:
    Though grief yield them no good
Yet shed what tears sad truelove should.

But to Christ lord of thunder
Crouch; lay knee by earth low under: 110
    'Holiest, loveliest, bravest,
Save my hero, O Hero savest.

And the prayer thou hearst me making
Have, at the awful overtaking,
    Heard; have heard and granted   115
Grace that day grace was wanted.'

Not that hell knows redeeming,
But for souls sunk in seeming
    Fresh, till doomfire burn all,
Prayer shall fetch pity eternal.   120

47
The May Magnificat

May is Mary's month, and I
Muse at that and wonder why:
    Her feasts follow reason,
    Dated due to season –

Candlemas, Lady Day;   5
But the Lady Month, May,
    Why fasten that upon her,
    With a feasting in her honour?

Is it only its being brighter
Than the most are must delight her?   10
    Is it opportunest
    And flowers finds soonest?

Ask of her, the mighty mother:
Her reply puts this other
    Question: What is Spring? –   15
    Growth in everything –

Flesh and fleece, fur and feather,
Grass and greenworld all together;
    Star-eyed strawberry-breasted
    Throstle above her nested   20

Cluster of bugle blue eggs thin
Forms and warms the life within;
    And bird and blossom swell
    In sod or sheath or shell.

All things rising, all things sizing   25
Mary sees, sympathising
    With that world of good,
    Nature's motherhood.

Their magnifying of each its kind
With delight calls to mind   30
    How she did in her stored
    Magnify the Lord.

Well but there was more than this:
Spring's universal bliss
    Much, had much to say   35
    To offering Mary May.

When drop-of-blood-and-foam-dapple
Bloom lights the orchard-apple
    And thickset and thorp are merry
    With silver-surfèd cherry   40

And azuring-over greybell makes
Wood banks and brakes wash wet like lakes
    And magic cuckoocall
    Caps, clears, and clinches all –

This ecstasy all through mothering earth   45
Tells Mary her mirth till Christ's birth
    To remember and exultation
    In God who was her salvation.

48

'Denis, whose motionable, alert,
most vaulting wit'

Denis, whose motionable, alert, most vaulting wit
Caps occasion with an intellectual fit.
Yet Arthur is a Bowman: his three-heeled timber'll hit
The bald and bóld blínking gold when áll's dóne
Right rooting in the bare butt's wincing navel in the sight   5
   of the sun.

   .   .   .   .

49

'The furl of fresh-leaved dogrose down'

The furl of fresh-leaved dogrose down
His cheeks the forth-and-flaunting sun
Had swarthed about with lion-brown
  Before the Spring was done.

His locks like all a ravel-rope's end,   5
  With hempen strands in spray –

Fallow, foam-fallow, hanks – fall'n off their ranks,
  Swung down at a disarray.

Or like a juicy and jostling shock
  Of bluebells sheaved in May   10
Or wind-long fleeces on the flock
  A day off shearing day.

Then over his turnèd temples – here –
  Was a rose, or, failing that,
Rough-Robin or five-lipped campion clear   15
  For a beauty-bow to his hat,
And the sunlight sidled, like dewdrops, like
    dandled diamonds
  Through the sieve of the straw of the plait.

50

'He mightbe slow and something feckless first'

He mightbe slow and something feckless first,
Not feck at first, and here no harm,
But earnest, always earnest, *there* the charm.

51

'What being in rank-old nature should earlier have that breath been'

What being in rank-old nature should earlier have that breath
  been
That hére pérsonal tells off these heart-song powerful peals? –
A bush-browed, beetle-brówed bíllow is it?
With a sóuth-wésterly wínd blústering, with a tide rolls reels

Of crumbling, fore-foundering, thundering all-surfy seas in;
  seen   5
Únderneath, their glassy barrel, of a fairy green.

Or a jaunting vaunting vaulting assaulting trumpet telling.

52

Binsey Poplars

felled 1879

My aspens dear, whose airy cages quelled,
  Quelled or quenched in leaves the leaping sun,
  All felled, felled, are all felled;
    Of a fresh and following folded rank
          Not spared, not one   5
        That dandled a sandalled
     Shadow that swam or sank
On meadow and river and wind-wandering
  weed-winding bank.

O if we but knew what we do
     When we delve or hew –   10
   Hack and rack the growing green!
    Since country is so tender
  To touch, her being só slender,
  That, like this sleek and seeing ball
  But a prick will make no eye at all,   15
  Where we, even where we mean
       To mend her we end her,
    When we hew or delve:
After-comers cannot guess the beauty been.
  Ten or twelve, only ten or twelve   20
    Strokes of havoc únselve
      The sweet especial scene,
   Rural scene, a rural scene,
   Sweet especial rural scene.

53
Duns Scotus's Oxford

Towery city and branchy between towers;
Cuckoo-echoing, bell-swarmèd, lark-charmèd, rook-
    racked, river-rounded;
The dapple-eared lily below thee; that country and town
    did
Once encounter in, here coped and poisèd powers;

Thou hast a base and brickish skirt there, sours   5
That neighbour-nature thy grey beauty is grounded
Best in; graceless growth, thou hast confounded
Rural rural keeping – folk, flocks, and flowers.

Yet ah! this air I gather and I release
He lived on; these weeds and waters, these walls are what 10
He haunted who of all men most sways my spirits to
    peace;

Of realty the rarest-veinèd unraveller; a not
Rivalled insight, be rival Italy or Greece;
Who fired France for Mary without spot.

54
Henry Purcell

*The poet wishes well to the divine genius of Purcell and praises him
that, whereas other musicians have given utterance to the moods of
man's mind, he has, beyond that, uttered in notes the very make and
species of man as created both in him and in all men generally.*

Have fair fallen, O fair, fair have fallen, so dear
To me, so arch-especial a spirit as heaves in Henry
    Purcell,
An age is now since passed, since parted; with the
    reversal

Of the outward sentence low lays him, listed to a heresy,
   here.

Not mood in him nor meaning, proud fire or sacred fear,   5
Or love or pity or all that sweet notes not his might
   nursle:
It is the forgèd feature finds me; it is the rehearsal
Of own, of abrúpt sélf there so thrusts on, so throngs the
   ear.

Let him oh! with his air of angels then lift me, lay me!
   only I'll
Have an eye to the sakes of him, quaint moonmarks, to
   his pelted plumage under   10
Wings: so some great stormfowl, whenever he has walked
   his while

The thunder-purple seabeach plumèd purple-of-thunder,
If a wuthering of his palmy snow-pinions scatter a
   colossal smile
Off him, but meaning motion fans fresh our wits with
   wonder.

55
'Repeat that, repeat'

Repeat that, repeat,
Cuckoo, bird, and open ear wells, heart-springs, delightfully
   sweet,
With a ballad, with a ballad, a rebound
Off trundled timber and scoops of the hillside ground,
   hollow hollow hollow ground:
The whole landscape flushes on a sudden at a sound.   5

56
The Candle Indoors

Some candle clear burns somewhere I come by.
I muse at how its being puts blissful back
With yellowy moisture mild night's blear-all black,
Or to-fro tender trambeams truckle at the eye.

By that window what task what fingers ply,   5
I plod wondering, a-wanting, just for lack
Of answer the eagerer a-wanting Jessy or Jack
There / God to aggrándise, God to glorify. –

Come you indoors, come home; your fading fire
Mend first and vital candle in close heart's vault: 10
You there are master, do your own desire;

What hinders? Are you beam-blind, yet to a fault
In a neighbour deft-handed? are you that liar
And, cast by conscience out, spendsavour salt?

57
The Handsome Heart:
at a Gracious Answer

'But tell me, child, your choice; what shall I buy
You?' – 'Father, what you buy me I like best.'
With the sweetest air that said, still plied and pressed,
He swung to his first poised purport of reply.

What the heart is! which, like carrriers let fly –   5
Doff darkness, homing nature knows the rest –
To its own fine function, wild and self-instressed,
Falls light as ten years long taught how to and why.

Mannerly-hearted! more than handsome face –

Beauty's bearing or muse of mounting vein,   10
All, in this case, bathed in high hallowing grace . . .

Of heaven what boon to buy you, boy, or gain
Not granted! – Only . . . O on that path you pace
Run all your race, O brace sterner that strain!

58

'How all's to one thing wrought!'

How all's to one thing wrought!
The members, how they sit!
O what a tune the thought
Must be that fancied it.

Nor angel insight can   5
Learn how the heart is hence:
Since all the make of man
Is law's indifference.

[Who shaped these walls has shewn
The music of his mind,   10
Made known, though thick through stone.
What beauty beat behind.]

Not free in this because
His powers seemed free to play:
He swept what scope he was   15
To sweep and must obey.

Though down his being's bent
Like air he changed in choice,
That was an instrument
Which overvaulted voice.   20

What makes the man and what
The man within that makes:
Ask whom he serves or not
Serves and what side he takes.

For good grows wild and wide,   25
Has shades, is nowhere none;
But right must seek a side
And choose for chieftain one.

Therefore this masterhood,
This piece of perfect song,   30
This fault-not-found-with good
Is neither right nor wrong.

No more than red and blue,
No more than Re and Mi,
Or sweet the golden glue   35
That's built for by the bee.

59
Cheery Beggar

Beyond Mágdalen and by the Bridge, on a place called
      there the Plain,
   In Summer, in a burst of summertime
   Following falls and falls of rain,
When the air was sweet-and-sour of the flown fineflour of
Those goldnails and their gaylinks that hang along a lime;   5

   The motion of that man's heart is fine
   Whom want could not make píne, píne
That struggling should not sear him, a gift should cheer him
Like that poor pocket of pence, poor pence of mine.

60

The Bugler's First Communion

A Bugler boy from barrack (it is over the hill
   There) – boy bugler, born, he tells me, of Irish

Mother to an English sire (he
Shares their best gifts surely, fall how things will),

This very very day came down to us after a boon he on   5
My late being there begged of me, overflowing
    Boon in my bestowing,
Came, I say, this day to it – to a First Communion.

Here he knelt then ín regimental red.
Forth Christ from cupboard fetched, how fain I of feet   10
    To his youngster take his treat!
Low-latched in leaf-light housel his too huge godhead.

There! and your sweetest sendings, ah divine,
By it, heavens, befall him! as a heart Christ's darling,
    dauntless;
    Tongue true, vaunt- and tauntless;   15
Breathing bloom of a chastity in mansex fine.

Frowning and forefending angel-warder
Squander the hell-rook ranks sally to molest him;
    March, kind comrade, abreast him;
Dress his days to a dexterous and starlight order.   20

How it dóes my heart good, visiting at that bleak hill,
When limber liquid youth, that to all I teach
    Yields tender as a pushed peach,
Hies headstrong to its wellbeing of a self-wise self-will!

Then though I should tread tufts of consolation   25
Dáys áfter, só I in a sort deserve to
    And do serve God to serve to
Just such slips of soldiery Christ's royal ration.

Nothing élse is like it, no, not all so strains
Us: fresh youth fretted in a bloomfall all portending   30
    That sweet's sweeter ending;
Realm both Christ is heir to and thére réigns.

O now well work that sealing sacred ointment!
O for now charms, arms, what bans off bad
    And locks love ever in a lad!   35
Let mé though see no more of him, and not
  disappointment

Those sweet hopes quell whose least me quickenings lift,
In scarlet or somewhere of some day seeing
    That brow and bead of being,
An our day's God's own Galahad. Though this child's
  drift   40

Seems by a divíne doom chánnelled, nor do I cry
Disaster there; but may he not rankle and roam
    In backwheels though bound home? –
That left to the Lord of the Eucharist, I here lie by;

Recorded only, I have put my lips on pleas   45
Would brandle adamantine heaven with ride and jar, did
    Prayer go disregarded:
Forward-like, but however, and like favourable heaven
  heard these.

61

Morning, Midday, and Evening Sacrifice

        The dappled die-away
        Cheek and the wimpled lip,
        The gold-wisp, the airy-grey
        Eye, all in fellowship –
        This, all this beauty blooming,   5
        This, all this freshness fuming,
        Give God while worth consuming.

        Both thought and thew now bolder
        And told by Nature: Tower;
        Head, heart, hand, heel, and shoulder   10
        That beat and breathe in power –
        This pride of prime's enjoyment
        Take as for tool, not toy meant
        And hold at Christ's employment.

        The vault and scope and schooling   15
        And mastery in the mind,

In silk-ash kept from cooling,
And ripest under rind –
What death half lifts the latch of,
What hell hopes soon the snatch of,   20
Your offering, with despatch, of!

62
Andromeda

Now Time's Andromeda on this rock rude,
With not her either beauty's equal or
Her injury's, looks off by both horns of shore,
Her flower, her piece of being, doomed dragon food.

Time past she has been attempted and pursued   5
By many blows and banes; but now hears roar
A wilder beast from West than all were, more
Rife in her wrongs, more lawless, and more lewd.

Her Perseus linger and leave her tó her extremes? –
Pillowy air he treads a time and hangs   10
His thoughts on her, forsaken that she seems,

All while her patience, morselled into pangs,
Mounts; then to alight disarming, no one dreams,
With Gorgon's gear and barebill / thongs and fangs.

63
Peace

When will you ever, Peace, wild wooddove, shy wings
   shut,
Your round me roaming end, and under be my boughs?
When, when, Peace, will you, Peace? I'll not play hypocrite

To own my heart: I yield you do come sometimes; but
That piecemeal peace is poor peace. What pure peace
   allows   5
Alarms of wars, the daunting wars, the death of it?

O surely, reaving Peace, my Lord should leave in lieu
Some good! And so he does leave Patience exquisite,
That plumes to Peace thereafter. And when Peace here
   does house
He comes with work to do, he does not come to coo,   10
               He comes to brood and sit.

64
At the Wedding March

God with honour hang your head,
Groom, and grace you, bride, your bed
With lissome scions, sweet scions,
Out of hallowed bodies bred.

Each be other's comfort kind: 5
Déep, déeper than divined,
Divine charity, dear charity,
Fast you ever, fast bind.

Then let the March tread our ears:
I to him turn with tears   10
Who to wedlock, his wonder wedlock,
Déals tríumph and immortal years.

65
Felix Randal

Felix Randal the farrier, O is he dead then? my duty all
    ended,
Who have watched his mould of man, big-boned and
    hardy-handsome
Pining, pining, till time when reason rambled in it and
    some
Fatal four disorders, fleshed there, all contended?

Sickness broke him. Impatient, he cursed at first, but
    mended 5
Being anointed and all; though a heavenlier heart began
    some
Months earlier, since I had our sweet reprieve and ransom
Tendered to him. Ah well, God rest him all road ever he
    offended!

This seeing the sick endears them to us, us too it endears.
My tongue had taught thee comfort, touch had quenched
    thy tears, 10
Thy tears that touched my heart, child, Felix, poor Felix
    Randal;

How far from then forethought of, all thy more boister-
    ous years,
When thou at the random grim forge, powerful amidst
    peers,
Didst fettle for the great grey drayhorse his bright and
    battering sandal!

66
Brothers

How lovely the elder brother's
Life all laced in the other's,

Lóve-laced! – what once I well
Witnessed; so fortune fell.
When Shrovetide, two years gone,   5
Our boys' plays brought on
Part was picked for John,
Young Jóhn; then fear, then joy
Ran revel in the elder boy.
Now the night come; all   10
Our company thronged the hall;
Henry, by the wall,
Beckoned me beside him:
I came where called, and eyed him
By meanwhiles; making mý play   15
Turn most on tender byplay.
For, wrung all on love's rack,
My lad, and lost in Jack,
Smiled, blushed, and bit his lip;
Or drove, with a diver's dip,
Clutched hands through claspèd knees;
And many a mark like these,
Told tales with what heart's stress
He hung on the imp's success.
Now the other was bráss-bóld: 25
Hé had no work to hold
His heart up at the strain;
Nay, roguish ran the vein.
Two tedious acts were past;
Jack's call and cue at last;   30
When Henry, heart-forsook,
Dropped eyes and dared not look.
Thére! the háll rúng!
Dog, he did give tongue!
But Harry – in his hands he has flung   35
His tear-tricked cheeks of flame
For fond love and for shame.
    Ah Nature, framed in fault,
There's comfort then, there's salt;
Nature, bad, base, and blind,   40
Dearly thou canst be kind;
There dearly thén, deárly,
Dearly thou canst be kind.

67

Spring and Fall:

to a young child

Márgarét, áre you gríeving
Over Goldengrove unleaving?
Leáves, líke the things of man, you
With your fresh thoughts care for, can you?
Áh! ás the heart grows older   5
It will come to such sights colder
By and by, nor spare a sigh
Though worlds of wanwood leafmeal lie;
And yet you *will* weep and know why.
Now no matter, child, the name: 10
Sórrow's spríngs áre the same.
Nor mouth had, no nor mind, expressed
What heart heard of, ghost guessed:
It ís the blight man was born for,
It is Margaret you mourn for.   15

68

Inversnaid

This darksome burn, horseback brown,
His rollrock highroad roaring down,
In coop and in comb the fleece of his foam
Flutes and low to the lake falls home.

A windpuff-bonnet of fáwn-fróth   5
Turns and twindles over the broth
Of a pool so pitchblack, féll-frówning,
It rounds and rounds Despair to drowning.

Degged with dew, dappled with dew
Are the groins of the braes that the brook treads through, 10

Wiry heathpacks, flitches of fern,
And the beadbonny ash that sits over the burn.

What would the world be, once bereft
Of wet and of wildness? Let them be left,
O let them be left, wildness and wet;   15
Long live the weeds and the wilderness yet.

69

'As kingfishers catch fire,
dragonflies draw flame'

As kingfishers catch fire, dragonflies draw flame;
  As tumbled over rim in roundy wells
  Stones ring; like each tucked string tells, each hung bell's
Bow swung finds tongue to fling out broad its name;
Each mortal thing does one thing and the same: 5
  Deals out that being indoors each one dwells;
  Selves – goes itself; *myself* it speaks and spells,
Crying *What I do is me: for that I came.*

I say more: the just man justices;
  Keeps gráce: thát keeps all his goings graces;   10
Acts in God's eye what in God's eye he is –
  Chríst. For Christ plays in ten thousand places,
Lovely in limbs, and lovely in eyes not his
  To the Father through the features of men's faces.

70

Ribblesdale

Earth, sweet Earth, sweet landscape, with leavès throng
And louchèd low grass, heaven that dost appeal

To, with no tongue to plead, no heart to feel;
That canst but only be, but dost that long –

Thou canst but be, but that thou well dost; strong 5
Thy plea with him who dealt, nay does now deal,
Thy lovely dale down thus and thus bids reel
Thy river, and o'er gives all to rack or wrong.

And what is Earth's eye, tongue, or heart else, where
Else, but in dear and dogged man? – Ah, the heir 10
To his own selfbent so bound, so tied to his turn,

To thriftless reave both our rich round world bare
And none reck of world after, this bids wear
Earth brows of such care, care and dear concern.

71

A Trio of Triolets

No. 1 – Λέγεταί τι καινόν:

'No news in the *Times* to-day,'
Each man tells his next-door neighbour.
He, to see if what they say,
'No news in the *Times* to-day,'
Is correct, must plough his way 5
Through that: after three hours' labour,
'No news in the *Times* to-day,'
Each man tells his next-door neighbour.

No. 2 – *Cockle's Antibilious Pills*

'When you ask for Cockle's Pills,
Beware of spurious imitations.'
Yes, when you ask for every ill's
Cure, when you ask for Cockle's Pills,
Some hollow counterfeit that kills 5
Would fain mock that which heals the nations.

Oh, when you ask for Cockle's Pills
Beware of heartless imitations.

No. 3 – *Wordsworth*

'The child is father to the man.'
How can he be? The words are wild.
Suck any sense from that who can:
'The child is father to the man.'
No; what the poet did write ran,   5
'The man is father to the child,'
'The child is father to the man!'
How *can* he be? The words are wild.

72

The Leaden Echo and the Golden Echo

(*Maidens' song from St Winefred's Well*)

THE LEADEN ECHO

How to kéep – is there ány any, is there none such,
    nowhere known some, bow or brooch or braid or brace,
    láce, latch or catch or key to keep
Back beauty, keep it, beauty, beauty, beauty . . . from
    vanishing away?
Ó is there no frowning of these wrinkles, rankèd wrinkles
    deep,
Dówn? no waving off of these most mournful messengers,
    still messengers, sad and stealing messengers of grey? –
No there's none, there's none, O no there's none,   5
Nor can you long be, what you now are, called fair,
Do what you may do, what, do what you may,
And wisdom is early to despair:
Be beginning; since, no, nothing can be done
To keep at bay   10
Age and age's evils, hoar hair,

Ruck and wrinkle, drooping, dying, death's worst, winding
   sheets, tombs and worms and tumbling to decay;
So be beginning, be beginning to despair.
O there's none; no no no there's none:
Be beginning to despair, to despair,   15
Despair, despair, despair, despair.

THE GOLDEN ECHO

            Spare!
There ís one, yes I have one (Hush there!),
Only not within seeing of the sun.
Not within the singeing of the strong sun,   20
Tall sun's tingeing, or treacherous the tainting of the
   earth's air,
Somewhere elsewhere there is ah well where! one,
Óne. Yes I cán tell such a key, I dó know such a place,
Where whatever's prizèd and passes of us, everything that's
   fresh and fast flying of us, seems to us sweet of us and
   swiftly away with, done away with, undone,
Undone, done with, soon done with, and yet dearly and
   dangerously sweet   25
Of us, the wimpled-water-dimpled, not-by-morning-
   matchèd face,
The flower of beauty, fleece of beauty, too apt to, ah! to
   fleet,
Never fleets móre, fastened with the tenderest truth
To its own best being and its loveliness of youth: it is an
   everlastingness of, O it is an all youth!
Come then, your ways and airs and looks, locks,
   maidengear, gallantry and gaiety and grace,   30
Winning ways, airs innocent, maiden manners, sweet
   looks, loose locks, long locks, lovelocks, gaygear, going
   gallant, girlgrace –
Resign them, sign them, seal them, send them, motion them
   with breath,
And with sighs soaring, soaring síghs, deliver
Them; beauty-in-the-ghost, deliver it, early now, long
   before death
Give beauty back, beauty, beauty, beauty, back to God,
   beauty's self and beauty's giver.   35

See; not a hair is, not an eyelash, not the least lash lost;
    every hair
Is, hair of the head, numbered.
Nay, what we had lighthanded left in surly the mere mould
Will have waked and have waxed and have walked with
    the wind what while we slept,
This side, that side hurling a heavyheaded hundredfold   40
What while we, while we slumbered.
O then, weary then whý should we tread? O why are we so
    haggard at the heart, so care-coiled, care-killed, so
    fagged, so fashed, so cogged, so cumbered,
When the thing we freely fórfeit is kept with fonder a care,
Fonder a care kept than we could have kept it, kept
Far with fonder a care (and we, we should have lost it)
    finer, fonder   45
A care kept. – Where kept? do but tell us where kept,
    where. –
Yonder. – What high as that! We follow, now we follow. –
    Yonder, yes yonder, yonder,
Yonder.

73

from St Winefred's Well

Act I. Sc. I.

Enter Teryth from riding, Winefred following.

T.   What is it, Gwen, my girl? │ why do you hover and
        haunt me?
W.   You came by Caerwys, sir? │
T.   I came by Caerwys.
W.   There
        Some messenger there might have met you from my
        uncle.
T.   Your uncle met the messenger – │ met me; and this the
        message:

Lord Beuno comes tonight. |

W.   Tonight, sir!
T.

             Soon, now: therefore   5
Have all things ready in this room. |

W.   There needs but little doing.
T. Let what there needs be done. | Stay! with him one
     companion,
     His deacon, Dirvan. Warm | twice over must the
     welcome be,
     But both will share one cell. – | This was good news,
     Gwenvrewi.

W. Ah yes!
T.   Why, get thee gone then; | tell thy mother I want
     her. *Exit Winefred.*   10
     No man has such a daughter. | The fathers of the
     world
     Call no such maiden 'mine'. | The deeper grows her
     dearness
     And more and more times laces | round and round my
     heart,
     The more some monstrous hand | gropes with clammy
     fingers there,
     Tampering with those sweet bines, | draws them out,
     strains them, strains them;   15
     Meantime some tongue cries 'What, Teryth! | what,
     thou poor fond father!
     How when this bloom, this honeysuckle, | that rides
     the air so rich about thee,
     Is all, all sheared away, | thus!' Then I sweat for fear.
     Or else a funeral, | and yet 'tis not a funeral,
     Some pageant which takes tears | and I must foot with
     feeling that   20
     Alive or dead my girl | is carried in it, endlessly
     Goes marching thro' my mind. | What sense is this? It
     has none.
     This is too much the father; | nay the mother. Fanciful!
     I here forbid my thoughts | to fool themselves with
     fears.
                     Enter Gwenlo.

.   .   .   .

Act II. – *Scene, a wood ending in a steep bank over a dry dean. Winefred having been murdered within, re-enter Caradoc with a bloody sword.*

C. My héart, where have we been? | What have we séen, my mind?

What stroke has Carádoc's right arm dealt? | what done? Head of a rebel

Struck óff it has; written | upon lovely limbs,

In bloody letters, lessons | of earnest, of revenge;

Monuments of my earnest, | records of my revenge,　　5

On one that went against me | whéreas I had warned her –

Warned her! well she knew | I warned her of this work.

What work? what harm's done? There is | no harm done, none yet;

Perhaps we struck no blow, | Gwenvrewi lives perhaps;

To make believe my mood was – | mock. O I might think so　　10

But here, here is a workman | from his day's task sweats.

Wiped I am sure this was; | it seems, not well; for still,

Still the scarlet swings | and dances on the blade.

So be it. Thou steel, thou butcher,

I cán scour thee, fresh burnish thee, | sheathe thee in thy dark lair; these drops

Never, never, never | in their blue banks again.

The woeful, Cradock, O | the woeful word! Then what,

What have we seen? Her head, | sheared from her shoulders, fall,

And lapped in shining hair, | roll to the bank's edge; then

Down the beetling banks, | like water in waterfalls,　　20

It stooped and flashed and fell | and ran like water away.

Her eyes, oh and her eyes!

In all her beauty, and sunlight | tó it is a pit, den, darkness,

Foamfalling is not fresh to it, | rainbow by it not
  beaming,
In all her body, I say, | no place was like her eyes,   25
No piece matched those eyes | kept most part much
  cast down
But, being lifted, immortal, | of immórtal brightness.
Several times I saw them, | thrice or four times turning;
Round and round they came | and flashed towards
  heaven: O there,
There they did appeal. | Therefore airy vengeances   30
Are afoot; heaven-vault fast purpling | portends, and
  what first lightning
Any instant falls means me. | And I do not repent;
I do not and I will not | repent, not repent.
The blame bear who aroused me. | What I have done
  violent
I have líke a líon dóne, | líonlíke dóne,   35
Honouring an uncontrolled royal | wrathful nature,
Mantling passion in a grandeur, | crimson grandeur.
Now be my pride then perfect, | all one piece.
  Henceforth
In a wide world of defiance | Caradoc lives alone,
Loyal to his own soul, laying his | ówn law down, no
  law nor   40
Lord now curb him for ever. | O daring! O deep
  insight!
What is virtue? Valour; | only the heart valiant.
And right? Only resolution; | will, his will unwavering
Who, like me, knowing his nature | to the heart home,
  nature's business,
Despatches with no flinching. | But wíll flesh, O can
  flésh
Second this fiery strain? | Not always; O no no!   45
We cannot live this life out; | sometimes we must
  weary
And in this darksome world | what comfort can I find?
Down this darksome world | cómfort whére can I find?
When 'ts light I quenched; its rose, | time's one rich
  rose, my hand,   50
By her bloom, fast by | her fresh, her fleecèd bloom,

Hideous dáshed dówn, leaving | earth a winter
   withering
With no now, no Gwenvrewi. | I must miss her most
That might have spared her were it | but for passion-
   sake. Yes,
To hunger and not háve, yét | hope ón for, to storm
   and strive and   55
Be at every assault fresh foiled, | worse flung, deeper
   disappointed,
The turmoil and the torment, | it has, I swear, a
   sweetness,
Keeps a kind of joy in it, | a zest, an edge, an ecstasy,
Next after sweet success. | I am not left even this;
I all my being have hacked | in half with hér neck: one
   part,   60
Reason, selfdisposal, | choice of better or worse way,
Is corpse now, cannot change; | my other self, this soul,
Life's quick, this kínd, this kéen self-feeling,
With dreadful distillation | of thoughts sour as blood,
Must all day long taste murder. | What do nów then?
   Do? Nay,
Déed-bound I am; óne deed tréads all dówn here |
   cramps all doing. What do? Not yield,
Not hope, not pray; despair; | ay, that: brazen despair
   out,
Brave all, and take what comes – | as here this rabble
   is come,
Whose bloods I reck no more of, | no more rank with
   hers
Than sewers with sacred oils. | Mankind, that mob,
   comes. Come!   70

Enter a crowd, among them Teryth, Gwenlo, Beuno.

   .   .   .   .

(C.) *After Winefred's raising from the dead and the breaking
out of the fountain.*

BEUNO. O now while skies are blue, | now while seas are
   salt,

While rushy rains shall fall | or brooks shall fleet from
    fountains,
While sick men shall cast sighs, | of sweet health all
    despairing,
While blind men's eyes shall thírst after | daylight,
    draughts of daylight,
Or deaf ears shall desire that | lípmusic that's lóst upon
    them,   5
While cripples are, while lepers, | dancers in dismal
    limbdance,
Fallers in dreadful frothpits, | waterfearers wild,
Stone, palsy, cancer, cough, | lung-wasting, womb-not-
    bearing,
Rupture, running sores, | what more? in brief, in
    burden,
As long as men are mortal | and God merciful,   10
So long to this sweet spot, | this leafy lean-over,
This Dry Dean, nów no longer dry | nor dumb, but
    moist and musical
With the uproll and the downcarol | of day and night
    delivering
Water, which keeps thy name, | (for not in róck wrítten,
But in pale water, fráil water, | wild rash and reeling
    water,   15
That will not wear a print, | that will not stain a pen,
Thy venerable record, | virgin, is recorded).
Here to this holy well | shall pilgrimages be,
And not from purple Wales only | nor from elmy
    England,
But from beyond seas, Erin, | France and Flanders,
    everywhere,   20
Pilgrims, still pilgrims, móre | pilgrims, still more poor
    pilgrims.

   ·   ·   ·   ·   ·   ·   ·   ·   ·

What sights shall be when some | that swung,
    wretches, on crutches
Their crutches shall cast from them, | on heels of air
    departing,
Or they go rich as roseleaves | hence that loathsome
    cáme hither!

t now to náme even 25
hose dearer, more divine | boons whose haven the
    heart is.

   .   .   .   .

As sure as what is most sure, | sure as that spring
    primroses
Shall new-dapple next year, | sure as to-morrow
    morning,
Amongst come-back-again things, | things with a
    revival, things with a recovery,
Thy name . . . 30

   .   .   .   .

74

The Blessed Virgin compared to the Air we Breathe

Wild air, world-mothering air,
Nestling me everywhere,
That each eyelash or hair
Girdles; goes home betwixt
The fleeciest, frailest-flixed 5
Snowflake; that's fairly mixed
With, riddles, and is rife
In every last thing's life;
This needful, never spent,
And nursing element; 10
My more than meat and drink,
My meal at every wink;
This air, which, by life's law,
My lung must draw and draw
Now but to breathe its praise 15
Minds me in many ways
Of her who not only
Gave God's infinity
Dwindled to infancy

Welcome in womb and breast,   20
Birth, milk, and all the rest
But mothers each new grace
That does now reach our race –
Mary Immaculate,
Merely a woman, yet   25
Whose presence, power is
Great as no goddess's
Was deemèd, dreamèd; who
This one work has to do –
Let all God's glory through,   30
God's glory which would go
Through her and from her flow
Off, and no way but so.
    I say that we are wound
With mercy round and round   35
As if with air: the same
Is Mary, more by name.
She, wild web, wondrous robe,
Mantles the guilty globe,
Since God has let dispense   40
Her prayers his providence:
Nay, more than almoner,
The sweet alms' self is her
And men are meant to share
Her life as life does air.   45
    If I have understood,
She holds high motherhood
Towards all our ghostly good
And plays in grace her part
About man's beating heart,   50
Laying, like air's fine flood,
The deathdance in his blood;
Yet no part but what will
Be Christ our Saviour still.
Of her flesh he took flesh: 55
He does take fresh and fresh,
Though much the mystery how,
Not flesh but spirit now
And makes, O marvellous!
New Nazareths in us.   60

Where she shall yet conceive
Him, morning, noon, and eve;
New Bethlems, and he born
There, evening, noon, and morn –
Bethlem or Nazareth,   65
Men here may draw like breath
More Christ and baffle death;
Who, born so, comes to be
New self and nobler me
In each one and each one   70
More makes, when all is done,
Both God's and Mary's Son.
   Again, look overhead
How air is azurèd;
O how! Nay do but stand   75
Where you can lift your hand
Skywards: rich, rich it laps
Round the four fingergaps.
Yet such a sapphire-shot,
Charged, steepèd sky will not   80
Stain light. Yea, mark you this:
It does no prejudice.
The glass-blue days are those
When every colour glows,
Each shape and shadow shows.   85
Blue be it: this blue heaven
The seven or seven times seven
Hued sunbeam will transmit
Perfect, not alter it.
Or if there does some soft,   90
On things aloof, aloft,
Bloom breathe, that one breath more
Earth is the fairer for.
Whereas did air not make
This bath of blue and slake   95
His fire, the sun would shake,
A blear and blinding ball
With blackness bound, and all
The thick stars round him roll
Flashing like flecks of coal,   100
Quartz-fret, or sparks of salt,

In grimy vasty vault.
    So God was god of old:
A mother came to mould
Those limbs like ours which are   105
What must make our daystar
Much dearer to mankind;
Whose glory bare would blind
Or less would win man's mind.
Through her we may see him   110
Made sweeter, not made dim,
And her hand leaves his light
Sifted to suit our sight.
    Be thou then, O thou dear
Mother, my atmosphere;   115
My happier world, wherein
To wend and meet no sin;
Above me, round me lie
Fronting my froward eye
With sweet and scarless sky;   120
Stir in my ears, speak there
Of God's love, O live air,
Of patience, penance, prayer:
World-mothering air, air wild,
Wound with thee, in thee isled,   125
Fold home, fast fold they child.

75

'The times are nightfall, look, their light grows less'

The times are nightfall, look, their light grows less;
The times are winter, watch, a world undone:
They waste, they wither worse; they as they run
Or bring more or more blazon man's distress.
And I not help. Nor word now of success: 5
All is from wreck, here, there, to rescue one –

Work which to see scarce so much as begun
Makes welcome death, does dear forgetfulness.

Or what is else? There is your world within.
There rid the dragons, root out there the sin.   10
Your will is law in that small commonweal. . . .

76

'Not of all my eyes see, wandering on the world'

Not of all my eyes see, wandering on the world,
Is anything a milk to the mind so, so sighs deep
Poetry tó it, as a tree whose boughs break in the sky.
Say it is áshboughs: whether on a December day and furled
Fast ór they in clammyish lashtender combs creep   5
Apart wide and new-nestle at heaven most high.

They touch heaven, tabour on it; how their talons sweep
The smouldering enormous winter welkin! May
Mells blue and snowwhite through them, a fringe and fray
Of greenery: it is old earth's groping towards the steep   10
    Heaven whom she childs us by.

77

'To seem the stranger lies my lot, my life'

To seem the stranger lies my lot, my life
Among strangers. Father and mother dear,
Brothers and sisters are in Christ not near
And he my peace / my parting, sword and strife.

England, whose honour O all my heart woos, wife   5
To my creating thought, would neither hear

Me, were I pleading, plead nor do I: I wear-
y of idle a being but by where wars are rife.

I am in Ireland now; now I am at a thírd
Remove. Not but in all removes I can
Kind love both give and get. Only what word

Wisest my heart breeds dark heaven's baffling ban
Bars or hell's spell thwarts. This to hoard
    unheard,
    Heard unheeded, leaves me a lonely began.

78

'I wake and feel the fell of dark, not day'

I wake and feel the fell of dark, not day.
What hours, O what black hoürs we have spent
This night! what sights you, heart, saw; ways you
    went!
And more must, in yet longer light's delay.

With witness I speak this. But where I say
Hours I mean years, mean life. And my lament
Is cries countless, cries like dead letters sent
To dearest him that lives alas! away.

I am gall, I am heartburn. God's most deep decree
Bitter would have me taste: my taste was me;
Bones built in me, flesh filled, blood brimmed the curse.

Selfyeast of spirit a dull dough sours. I see
The lost are like this, and their scourge to be
As I am mine, their sweating selves; but worse.

79
'Strike, churl; hurl, cheerless wind, then'

Strike, churl; hurl, cheerless wind, then; heltering
   hail
May's beauty massacre and wispèd wild clouds grow
Out on the giant air; tell Summer No,
Bid joy back, have at the harvest, keep Hope pale.

80
'No worst, there is none.
Pitched past pitch of grief'

No worst, there is none. Pitched past pitch of grief,
More pangs will, schooled at forepangs, wilder wring.
Comforter, where, where is your comforting?
Mary, mother of us, where is your relief?
My cries heave, herds-long; huddle in a main, a chief-   5
woe, world-sorrow; on an age-old anvil wince and sing –
Then lull, then leave off. Fury had shrieked 'No ling-
ering! Let me be fell: force I must be brief'.
O the mind, mind has mountains; cliffs of fall
Frightful, sheer, no-man-fathomed. Hold them cheap   10
May who ne'er hung there. Nor does long our small
Durance deal with that steep or deep. Here! creep,
Wretch, under a comfort serves in a whirlwind: all
Life death does end and each day dies with sleep.

81

To what serves Mortal Beauty?

To what serves mortal beauty | – dangerous; does set danc-
ing blood – the O-seal-that-so | feature, flung prouder form
Than Purcell tune lets tread to? | See: it does this: keeps warm
Men's wits to the things that are; | what good means – where
  a glance
Master more may than gaze, | gaze out of countenance.   5
Those lovely lads once, wet-fresh | windfalls of war's storm,
How then should Gregory, a father, | have gleanèd else from
  swarm-
èd Rome? But God to a nation | dealt that day's dear chance.
To man, that needs would worship | block or barren stone,
Our law says: Love what are | love's worthiest, were all
  known;   10
World's loveliest – men's selves. Self | flashes off frame and
  face.
What do then? how meet beauty? | Merely meet it; own,
Home at heart, heaven's sweet gift; | then leave, let that alone.
Yea, wish that though, wish all, | God's better beauty, grace.

82

'Not, I'll not, carrion comfort, Despair, not feast on thee'

Not, I'll not, carrion comfort, Despair, not feast on thee;
Not untwist – slack they may be – these last strands of man
In me ór, most weary, cry *I can no more*. I can;
Can something, hope, wish day come, not choose not to be.

But ah, but O thou terrible, why wouldst thou rude on me   5
Thy wring-world right foot rock? lay a lionlimb against me?
  scan
With darksome devouring eyes my bruisèd bones? and fan,

O in turns of tempest, me heaped there; me frantic to avoid
   thee and flee?
Why? That my chaff might fly; my grain lie, sheer and clear.
Nay in all that toil, that coil, since (seems) I kissed the rod,   10
Hand rather, my heart lo! lapped strength, stole joy, would
   laugh, chéer.
Cheer whom though? The hero whose heaven-handling flung
   me, fóot tród
Me? or me that fought him? O which one? is it each one?
   That night, that year
Of now done darkness I wretch lay wrestling with (my God!)
   my God.

83

'Yes. Why do we all, seeing of a soldier, bless him?'

Yes. Whý do we áll, seeing of a soldier, bless him? bless
Our redcoats, our tars? Both these being, the greater part,
But frail clay, nay but foul clay. Here it is: the heart,
Since, proud, it calls the calling manly, gives a guess
That, hopes that, makesbelieve, the men must be no less;   5
It fancies, feigns, deems, dears the artist after his art;
And fain will find as sterling all as all is smart,
And scarlet wear the spirit of wár thére express.
Mark Christ our King. He knows war, served this soldiering
   through;
He of all can reeve a rope best. There he bides in bliss   10
Now, and séeing somewhére some mán do all that man can
   do,
For love he leans forth, needs his neck must fall on, kiss,
And cry 'O Christ-done deed! So God-made-flesh does too:
Were I come o'er again' cries Christ 'it should be this'.

84
'Thee, God, I come from, to thee go'

Thee, God, I come from, to thee go,
All dáy long I like fountain flow
From thy hand out, swayed about
Mote-like in thy mighty glow.

What I know of thee I bless,   5
As acknowledging thy stress
On my being and as seeing
Something of thy holiness.

Once I turned from thee and hid,
Bound on what thou hadst forbid;   10
Sow the wind I would; I sinned:
I repent of what I did.

Bad I am, but yet thy child.
Father, be thou reconciled.
Spare thou me, since I see   15
With thy might that thou art mild.

I have life left with me still
And thy purpose to fulfil;
Yea a debt to pay thee yet:
Help me, sir, and so I will.   20

But thou bidst, and just thou art,
Me shew mercy from my heart
Towards my brother, every other
Man my mate and counterpart.

85
'Patience, hard thing! the hard thing but to pray'

Patience, hard thing! the hard thing but to pray,
But bid for, Patience is! Patience who asks

Wants war, wants wounds; weary his times, his tasks;
To do without, take tosses, and obey.

Rare patience roots in these, and, these away,   5
Nowhere. Natural heart's ivy, Patience masks
Our ruins of wrecked past purpose. There she basks
Purple eyes and seas of liquid leaves all day.

We hear our hearts grate on themselves: it kills
To bruise them dearer. Yet the rebellious wills   10
Of us we do bid God bend to him even so.

And where is he who more and more distills
Delicious kindness? – He is patient. Patience fills
His crisp combs, and that comes those ways we know.

86

'My own heart let me more have pity on'

My own heart let me more have pity on; let
Me live to my sad self hereafter kind,
Charitable; not live this tormented mind
With this tormented mind tormenting yet.

I cast for comfort I can no more get   5
By groping round my comfortless, than blind
Eyes in their dark can day or thirst can find
Thirst's all-in-all in all a world of wet.

Soul, self; come, poor Jackself, I do advise
You, jaded, let be; call off thoughts awhile   10
Elsewhere; leave comfort root-room; let joy size

At God knows when to God knows what; whose smile
's not wrung, see you; unforeseen times rather – as skies
Betweenpie mountains – lights a lovely mile.

87
To his Watch

Mortal my mate, bearing my rock-a-heart
Warm beat with cold beat company, shall I
Earlier or you fail at our force, and lie
The ruins of, rifled, once a world of art?
The telling time our task is; time's some part,   5
Not all, but we were framed to fail and die –
One spell and well that one. There, ah thereby
Is comfort's carol of all or woe's worst smart.

Field-flown, the departed day no morning brings
Saying 'This was yours' with her, but new one, worse,   10
And then that last and shortest . . .

88
Spelt from Sibyl's Leaves

Earnest, earthless, equal, attuneable, | vaulty, voluminous,
    . . . stupendous
Evening strains to be time's vást, | womb-of-all, home-of-
    all, hearse-of-all night.
Her fond yellow hornlight wound to the west, | her wild
    hollow hoarlight hung to the height
Waste; her earliest stars, earlstars, | stárs principal,
    overbend us,
Fire-féaturing heaven. For earth | her being has unbound;
    her dapple is at an end, as-   5
tray or aswarm, all throughther, in throngs; | self in self
    steepèd and páshed – qúite
Disremembering, dísmémbering | áll now. Heart, you round
    me right
With: Óur évening is over us; óur night | whélms, whélms,
    ánd will end us.

Only the beakleaved boughs dragonish | damask the tool-
   smooth bleak light; black,
Ever so black on it. Óur tale, O óur oracle! | Lét life,
   wáned, ah, lét life wind   10
Off hér once skéined stained véined varíety | upon, áll on
   twó spools; párt, pen, páck
Now her áll in twó flocks, twó folds – black, white; | right,
   wrong; reckon but, reck but, mind
But thése two; wáre of a wórld where bút these | twó tell,
   each off the óther; of a rack
Where, selfwrung, selfstrung, sheathe- and shelterless, |
   thóughts agaínst thoughts ín groans grínd.

89

On the Portrait of Two Beautiful Young People

A Brother and Sister

O I admire and sorrow! The heart's eye grieves
Discovering you, dark tramplers, tyrant years.
A juice rides rich through bluebells, in vine leaves,
And beauty's dearest veriest vein is tears.

Happy the father, mother of these! Too fast: 5
Not that, but thus far, all with frailty, blest
In one fair fall; but, for time's aftercast,
Creatures all heft, hope, hazard, interest.

And are they thus? The fine, the fingering beams
Their young delightful hour do feature down   10
That fleeted else like day-dissolvèd dreams
Or ringlet-race on burling Barrow brown.

She leans on him with such contentment fond
As well the sister sits, would well the wife;
His looks, the soul's own letters, see beyond,   15
Gaze on, and fall directly forth on life.

But ah, bright forelock, cluster that you are
Of favoured make and mind and health and youth,
Where lies your landmark, seamark, or soul's star?
There's none but truth can stead you. Christ is truth.   20

There's none but good can bé good, both for you
And what sways with you, maybe this sweet maid;
None good but God – a warning wavèd to
One once that was found wanting when Good weighed.

Man lives that list, that leaning in the will   25
No wisdom can forecast by gauge or guess,
The selfless self of self, most strange, most still,
Fast furled and all foredrawn to No or Yes.

Your feast of; that most in you earnest eye
May but call on your banes to more carouse.   30
Worst will the best. What worm was here, we cry,
To have havoc-pocked so, see, the hung-heavenward
    boughs?

Enough: corruption was the world's first woe.
What need I strain my heart beyond my ken?
O but I bear my burning witness though   35
Against the wild and wanton work of men.

.   .   .   .

90
Harry Ploughman

Hard as hurdle arms, with a broth of goldish flue
Breathed round; the rack of ribs; the scooped flank; lank
Rope-over thigh; knee-nave; and barrelled shank –
        Head and foot, shoulder and shank –
By a grey eye's heed steered well, one crew, fall to;   5
Stand at stress. Each limb's barrowy brawn, his thew
That onewhere curded, onewhere sucked or sank –
            Soared ór sánk – ,
Though as a beechbole firm, finds his, as at a rollcall, rank

And features, in flesh, what deed he each must do –   10
          His sinew-service where do.

He leans to it, Harry bends, look. Back, elbow, and liquid
   waist
In him, all quail to the wallowing o' the plough. 'S cheek
   crimsons; curls
Wag or crossbridle, in a wind lifted, windlaced –
          See his wind- lilylocks -laced;   15
Churlsgrace, too, child of Amansstrength, how it hangs or
   hurls
Them – broad in bluff hide his frowning feet lashed! raced
With, along them, cragiron under and cold furls –
          With-a-fountain's shining-shot furls.

91

Tom's Garland:

Upon the Unemployed

Tom – garlanded with squat and surly steel
Tom; then Tom's fallowbootfellow piles pick
By him and rips out rockfire homeforth – sturdy Dick;
Tom Heart-at-ease, Tom Navvy: he is all for his meal
Sure, 's bed now. Low be it: lustily he his low lot (feel   5
That ne'er need hunger, Tom; Tom seldom sick,
Seldomer heartsore; that treads through, prickproof, thick
Thousands of thorns, thoughts) swings though. Commonweal
Little Í reck ho! lacklevel in, if all had bread:
What! Country is honour enough in all us – lordly head,   10
With heaven's lights high hung round, or, mother-ground
That mammocks, mighty foot. But nó way sped,
Nor mind nor mainstrength; gold go garlanded
With, perilous, O nó; nor yet plod safe shod sound;
          Undenizened, beyond bound   15
Of earth's glory, earth's ease, all; no one, nowhere,
In wide the world's weal; rare gold, bold steel, bare

      In both; care, but share care –
This, by Despair, bred Hangdog dull; by Rage,
Manwolf, worse; and their packs infest the age.   20

92
Epithalamion

Hark, hearer, hear what I do; lend a thought now, make
   believe
We are leafwhelmed somewhere with the hood
Of some branchy bunchy bushybowered wood,
Southern dean or Lancashire clough or Devon cleave,
That leans along the loins of hills, where a candycoloured,
   where a gluegold-brown   5
Marbled river, boisterously beautiful, between
Roots and rocks is danced and dandled, all in forth and
   water-blowballs, down.
We are there, when we hear a shout
That the hanging honeysuck, the dogeared hazels in the
   cover
Makes dither, makes hover   10
And the riot of a rout
Of, it must be, boys from the town
Bathing: it is summer's sovereign good.

By there comes a listless stranger: beckoned by the noise
He drops towards the river: unseen   15
Sees the bevy of them, how the boys
With dare and with downdolphinry and bellbright bodies
   huddling out,
Are earthworld, airworld, waterworld thorough hurled, all
   by turn and turn about.

This garland of their gambol flashes in his breast
Into such a sudden zest   20
Of summertime joys
That he hies to a pool neighbouring; sees it is the best
There; sweetest, freshest, shadowiest;

Fairyland; silk-beech, scrolled ash, packed sycamore, wild
    wychelm, hornbeam fretty overstood
By. Rafts and rafts of flake leaves light, dealt so, painted
    on the air,
Hang as still as hawk or hawkmoth, as the stars or as the
    angels there,
Like the thing that never knew the earth, never off roots
Rose. Here he feasts: lovely all is! No more: off with –
    down he dings
His bleachèd both and woolwoven wear:

Careless these in coloured wisp   30
All lie tumbled-to; then with loop-locks
Forward falling, forehead frowning, lips crisp
Over finger-teasing task, his twiny boots
Fast he opens, last he off wrings
Till walk the world he can with bare his feet   35
And come where lies a coffer, burly all of blocks
Built of chancequarrièd, selfquainèd, hoar-huskèd rocks
And the water warbles over into, filleted | with glassy
    grassy quicksilvery shivès and shoots
And with heavenfallen freshness down from moorland still
    brims,
Dark or daylight on and on. Here he will then, here he will
    the fleet   40
Flinty kindcold element let break across his limbs
Long. Where we leave him, froliclavish, while he looks
    about him, laughs, swims.

Enough now; since the sacred matter that I mean
I should be wronging longer leaving it to float
Upon this only gambolling and echoing-of-earth note –   45

What is . . . . the delightful dean?
Wedlock. What the water? Spousal love.

   ·   ·   ·   ·   ·   ·
    ·   ·   ·   ·   ·   ·

                                    turns
Father, mother, brothers, sisters, friends
Into fairy trees, wildflowers, woodferns   50
Rankèd round the bower

   ·   ·   ·   ·   ·   ·

93

'The sea took pity: it interposed with doom'

The sea took pity: it interposed with doom:
'I have tall daughters dear that heed my hand:
Let Winter wed one, sow them in her womb,
And she shall child them on the New-world strand.'

94

That Nature is a Heraclitean Fire and of the comfort of the Resurrection

Cloud-puffball, torn tufts, tossed pillows ⎮ flaunt forth, then
   chevy on an air-
built thoroughfare: heaven-roysterers, in gay-gangs ⎮ they
   throng; they glitter in marches.
Down roughcast, down dazzling whitewash, ⎮ wherever an
   elm arches,
Shivelights and shadowtackle in long ⎮ lashes lace, lance,
   and pair.
Delightfully the bright wind boisterous ⎮ ropes, wrestles,
   beats earth bare   5
Of yestertempest's creases ⎮ in pool and rutpeel parches
Squandering ooze to squeezed ⎮ dough, crust, dust; stanches,
   starches
Squadroned masks and manmarks ⎮ treadmire toil there
Footfretted in it. Million-fuelèd, ⎮ nature's bonfire burns on.
But quench her bonniest, dearest ⎮ to her, her clearest-selvèd
   spark   10
Man, how fast his firedint, ⎮ his mark on mind, is gone!
Both are in an unfathomable, all is in an enormous dark
Drowned. O pity and indig ⎮ nation! Manshape, that shone
Sheer off, disseveral, a star, ⎮ death blots black out; nor mark
         Is any of him at all so stark   15

But vastness blurs and time ˡ beats level. Enough! the
  Resurrection,
A heart's-clarion! Away grief's gasping, ˡ joyless days,
  dejection.
                Across my foundering deck shone
A beacon, an eternal beam. ˡ Flesh fade, and mortal trash
Fall to the residuary worm; ˡ world's wildfire, leave but ash: 20
                In a flash, at a trumpet crash,
I am all at once what Christ is, ˡ since he was what I am,
  and
This Jack, joke, poor potsherd, ˡ patch, matchwood, immortal
  diamond,
                Is immortal diamond.

95

In honour of

St Alphonsus Rodriguez

Laybrother of the Society of Jesus

Honour is flashed off exploit, so we say;
And those strokes once that gashed flesh or galled shield
Should tongue that time now, trumpet now that field,
And, on the fighter, forge his glorious day.
On Christ they do and on the martyr may;   5
But be the war within, the brand we wield
Unseen, the heroic breast not outward-steeled,
Earth hears no hurtle then from fiercest fray.
Yet God (that hews mountain and continent,
Earth, all, out; who, with trickling increment,   10
Veins violets and tall trees makes more and more)
Could crowd career with conquest while there went
Those years and years by of world without event
That in Majorca Alfonso watched the door.

96

'Thou art indeed just, Lord, if I contend'

*Justus quidem tu es, Domine, si disputem tecum; verumtamen
justa loquar ad te: Quare via impiorum prosperatur? &c.*

Thou art indeed just, Lord, if I contend
With thee; but, sir, so what I plead is just.
Why do sinners' ways prosper? and why must
Disappointment all I endeavour end?

Wert thou my enemy, O thou my friend,   5
How wouldst thou worse, I wonder, than thou dost
Defeat, thwart me? Oh, the sots and thralls of lust
Do in spare hours more thrive than I that spend,

Sir, life upon thy cause. See, banks and brakes
Now, leavèd how thick! lacèd they are again   10
With fretty chervil, look, and fresh wind shakes

Them; birds build – but not I build; no, but strain,
Time's eunuch, and not breed one work that wakes.
Mine, O thou lord of life, send my roots rain.

97

'The shepherd's brow, fronting forked lightning'

The shepherd's brow, fronting forked lightning, owns
The horror and the havoc and the glory
Of it. Angels fall, they are towers, from heaven – a story
Of just, majestical, and giant groans.
But man – we, scaffold of score brittle bones;   5
Who breathe, from groundlong babyhood to hoary
Age gasp; whose breath is our *memento mori* –
What bass is *our* viol for tragic tones?
He! Hand to mouth he lives, and voids with shame;
And, blazoned in however bold the name   10

Man Jack the man is, just; his mate a hussy.
And I that die these deaths, that feed this flame,
That . . . in smooth spoons spy life's masque mirrored: tame
My tempests there, my fire and fever fussy.

98

To R. B.

The fine delight that fathers thought; the strong
Spur, live and lancing like the blowpipe flame,
Breathes once and, quenchèd faster than it came,
Leaves yet the mind a mother of immortal song.

Nine months she then, nay years, nine years she long   5
Within her wears, bears, cares and combs the same:
The widow of an insight lost she lives, with aim
Now known and hand at work now never wrong.

Sweet fire the sire of muse, my soul needs this;
I want the one rapture of an inspiration.   10
O then if in my lagging lines you miss

The roll, the rise, the carol, the creation,
My winter world, that scarcely breathes that bliss
Now, yields you, with some sighs, our explanation.

Early Diaries and Journals

Early Diaries

1863

Note on water coming through a lock.

There are openings near the bottom of the gates (which allow the water to pass through at all times, I suppose.) Suppose three, as there often are. The water strikes through these with great force and extends itself into three fans. The direction of the water is a little oblique from the horizontal, but the great force with which it runs keeps it almost uncurved except at the edges. The end of these fans is not seen for they strike them under a mass of yellowish boiling foam which runs down between the fans, and meeting covers the whole space of the lock-entrance. Being heaped up in globes and bosses and round masses the fans disappear under it. This turpid mass smooths itself as the distance increases from the lock. But the current is strong and if the basin into which it runs has curving banks it strikes them and the confusion of the already folded and doubled lines of foam is worse confounded.

Flick, fillip, flip, fleck, flake.

Flick means to touch or strike lightly as with the end of a whip, a finger etc. To *fleck* is the next tone above flick, still meaning to touch or strike lightly (and leave a mark of the touch or stroke) but in a broader less slight manner. Hence substantively a *fleck* is a piece of light, colour, substance etc. looking as though shaped or produced by such touches. *Flake* is a broad and decided *fleck*, a thin plate of something, the tone above it. Their connection is more clearly seen in the applications of the words to natural objects than in explanations. It would seem that *fillip* generally pronounced *flip* is a variation of *flick*, which however seems connected with *fly, flee, flit,* meaning to make fly off. Key to meaning of *flick, fleck* and *flake* is that of striking or cutting off the surface of a thing; in *flick* (as to flick off a fly) something little or light from the surface, while *flake* is a thin scale of surface. *Flay* is therefore connected, perhaps *flitch*.

Whitby Abbey. I have not seen any parallel to this kind of tracery in French or Italian Gothic. The style did not last long I think and seems to me to have been more capable of grand development than any other. The bars split at the ends, which connect the bights or recesses of the four-sided openings with other parts of the tracery are at a distance and in effect straight and yet harmonise completely. This is the only successful manner of introducing them in Decorated windows that I know, for those in early geometrical are poor and the instance in Merton choir erected in finest style and in company with other windows of exquisite tracery is quite unworthy of the others and a failure. The above window I have restored as far as possible from a photograph by Uncle George. There was probably no circle or other opening within the four-sided ones. The mouldings I have not given. The whole rough.

1864

April 14. Walked with Gurney to Elsfield. Sketched E. window of Church, which is in transition from decorated to perpendicular, or rather decorated with traces of perpendicularity. It had strange all its windows except the E. and two or perhaps three others. The E. had original tracery (see sketch book). These others were 3-lighted square-headed; as far as I remember the lights were lancet-shaped and cinquefoiled. The mullions were carried up to the head. The parson's son kindly let us in to see the Easter decorations. The widest and most charming views from Elsfield. A plain lies on the opposite side to Oxford with villages crowned with square church-towers shining white here and there. The lines of the fields, level over level, are striking, like threads in a loom. Splendid trees – elms, and farther on great elliptic-curve oaks. Bloomy green of larches. Standing on a high field on all sides over the hedge the horizon balanced its blue brim. The cowslips' heads, I see, tremble in wind. Noticed also frequent partings of ash-boughs.

Moonlight hanging or dropping on treetops like blue cobweb.

May 3. Walked with Addis to Staunton Harcourt. The Church is cruciform and rather large, with a Norman door and several windows etc., Early English East end and other windows, windows in tower (probably) Decorated, a Decorated or more probably Perpendicular parapet, and Perpendicular windows. The Early English is certainly unattractive, however the Church is evidently in Egypt and Churchwardenship. We did not go into it, nor into the tower (close to the church, in Perpendicular, rather shorter than that of the church,) in the top storey of which Pope finished his 5th volume of Homer, or of the Iliad, nor into the Octagon-roofed kitchen, which except one at Glastonbury is unparalleled in England, nor into the chapel, which with the tower and kitchen belonged to Staunton Harcourt Manorhouse, I believe. Pope lived here two years, Gay some time. We saw to our great surprise the tablet (on Church walls) raised to William (or John) Hewett and Sarah Drew, affianced lovers, killed by lightning; one of Pope's epitaphs is on the tablet. *Vide* the account, and writings which rose on subject. Charming place, rather of my ideal Stratford-on-Avon kind; willows, lovely elms. Pool of inky black water with leaves in it. Vertical shortish grass. Orchards with trunks of trees smeared over with the common white mixture, whatever it is, rather pretty than otherwise. Primroses, large, in wet, cool, shady place. – On way fields yellow with cowslip and dandelion. Found purple orchis, which opens flowers from ground, then rises the stem pushing upward. Crossed Isis at Skinner's Weir, or as people about call it, *Wire*. Beautiful effect of cloud. Wild apple(?) beautiful in blossom. Caddis-flies on stones in clear stream, water-snails and leeches. Round-looking glossy black fieldmouse of some kind or water-rat in ditch on Witney Road. Cuckoo. Peewits wheeling and tumbling, just as they are said to do, as if with a broken wing. They pronounce *peewit* pretty distinctly, sometimes querulously, with a slight metallic tone like a bat's cry. Their wings are not pointed, to the eye, when flying, but broad, white and of a black or reddish purple apparently.

Saw one day dead (water-?) rat floating down Isis. The head was downward, hind legs on surface . . .

Snakes'-heads.

Like drops of blood. Buds pointed and like snakes' heads, but the reason of name from mottling and scaly look.

Saw a curious thing on, I think, Oct 1 – A cloud hid the sun and its edges were so brilliant that the lustre prevented one seeing outlines which swam in the light. Happening to look in a pond, I saw the cloud reflected and therefore with much diminution of light, of course, and the outlines of the lighted part of the cloud were distinct and touched here and there with spots of colours.

1865

Sunrise at Chagford. There was a remarkable fan of clouds traced in fine horizontals, which afterwards lost their levels, some becoming oblique. Below appearing bright streaks which crowded up one after another. A white mist in the churchyard, trees ghostly in it.

Sunset here also. Over the nearest ridge of Dartmoor. Sky orange, trail of Bronze-lit clouds, stars and streak of brilliant electrum underneath, but not for this, but effect of dark intensified foreground. Long rounded ridge of Dartmoor deep purple, then trees on the descending hill, and a field with an angle so that the upper level was lighter green the lower darker, then a purplish great brown field, then the manufactory with grey white timbers (it is built of wood) and grey shingle(?) roofs.

Grey sky at Hampstead lately. Clouds showing beautiful and rare curves like curds, comparable to barrows, arranged of course in parallels.

Rain railing off something.

The butterfly perching in a cindery dusty road and pinching his scarlet valves. Or wagging, one might say. And also valvèd eyes.

Mallowy red of sunset and sunrise clouds.

Journals

1866

May 2. We came into these lodgings, Addis and I, at beginning of this term – 18, New Inn Hall Street.

Weather cold and raw, chestnut leaves touched with frost and limp. Sun today. Swallows playing over Ch. Ch. meadows with a wavy and hanging flight and shewing their white bellies. Snakes'-heads. Yellow wagtails. Almost think you can hear the lisp of the swallow's wings.

· Coaching with W. H. Pater this term. Walked with him on Monday evening last, April 30. Fine evening bitterly cold. 'Bleak-faced Neology in cap and gown': no cap and gown but very bleak. Same evening Hexameron met here: Addis read on the Franciscans: laughter. Thought all the next day of the terrible history of Fra Dolcino. Same day, I believe, Case at one of the cricket grounds saw three Ch. Ch. men laughing loudly at a rat with back broken, a most ghastly sight, flying at the dog. He kicked away the dog, put his heel on the rat's head and killed it, and drove away the crowd of cads. Wonder what would be the just statement of the effects of cruelty to animals, cruel sports, etc.

Little girls singing about May Day under the windows yesterday.

Never heard this before the other day –

> Violante
> In the pantry
> Gnawing at a mutton bone
> How she gnawed it,
> How she clawed it,
> When she felt herself alone.

Reading Maurice de Guérin's Remains, enjoying but without sufficient knowledge of French.

This day week brought forward motion in defence of the Fenians at the Balliol Debating Society. Wandered about S. Hinksey that day with most sad distracting scruple, as bad as any single one almost ever was.

May 3. Cold. Morning raw and wet, afternoon fine. Walked then with Addis, crossing Bablock Hythe, round by Skinner's Weir through many fields into the Witney road. Sky sleepy blue without liquidity. From Cumnor Hill saw St Philip's and the other spires through blue haze rising pale in a pink light. On further side of the Witney road hills, just fleeced with grain or other green growth, by their dips and waves foreshortened here and there and so differenced in brightness and opacity the green on them, with delicate effect. On left, brow of the near hill glistening with very bright newly turned sods and a scarf of vivid green slanting away beyond the skyline, against which the clouds shewed the slightest tinge of rose or purple. Copses in grey-red or grey-yellow – the tinges immediately forerunning the opening of full leaf. Meadows skirting Seven-bridge road voluptuous green. Some oaks are out in small leaf. Ashes not out, only tufted with their fringy blooms. Hedges springing richly. Elms in small leaf, with more or less opacity. White poplars most beautiful in small grey crisp spray-like leaf. Cowslips capriciously colouring meadows in creamy drifts. Bluebells, purple orchis. Over the green water of the river passing the slums of the town and under its bridges swallows shooting, blue and purple above and shewing their amber-tinged breasts reflected in the water, their flight unsteady with wagging wings and leaning first to one side then the other. Peewits flying. Towards sunset the sky partly swept, as often, with moist white cloud, tailing off across which are morsels of grey-black woolly clouds. Sun seemed to make a bright liquid hole in this, its texture had an upward northerly sweep or drift from the W, marked softly in grey. Dog violets. Eastward after sunset range of clouds rising in bulky heads moulded softly in tufts or bunches of snow – so it looks – and membered somewhat elaborately, rose-coloured. Notice often imperfect fairy rings. Apple and other fruit trees blossomed beautifully . . .

Yellow and green in the fields charming. Ferryman said 'I can't justly tell you', and they call *weir* as if *wire*,

I think that thread in smooth rivers is made by water being drawn or retained at right angles to the current.

May 4. Fine. Alone in Powder Hill wood. Elms far off have that flaky look now but nearer the web of springing green with long curls moulds off the skeleton of the branches. Fields pinned with daisies. Buds of apple blossoms look like nails of blood. Some ashes are out. I reckon the spring is at least a fortnight later than last year for on Shakspere's birthday, April 21, it being the tercentenary, Ilbert crowned a bust of Shakspere with bluebells and put it in his window, and they are not plentiful yet. Beauty of hills in blue shadow seen through lacy leaf of willows.

May 10. Ascension Day. Fair, with more clouds than sun. Walked alone to Fyfield or rather to a step beyond the great elm (perhaps the greatest I have ever seen) and made a sketch at the turning point. The road went under elms their light green darker printed by shadows, chestnut, sweet-smelling firs etc. Rooks cawing. Beddingfield church with good and curious E. and W. windows, but sadly neglected. Fine elms there with ground-running boughs. In timbered pasture etc beside road bluebells thick, and tufts of primrose, and campion, the two latter or two former matching gracefully but not so well the three. One effect of sky was a straight line as by a ruler parting white and soft blue, and rolling reefs shaded with pearl grey hanging from this to the earthline.

May 14. Chestnuts in bloom. The blooms are, as one feels, not straight but the tips bent inwards: then being thrown in some cases forwards, a good deal out of the upright, the curved type is easily seen in multiplicity which in one might be unnoticed. A brown tulip is a noble flower, the curves and close folding of the petals delightful. Anthers thick furry black. Young copper beech leaves seen against the sky pale brown with rosy blush along the ribs of each leaf. Solomon's seal.

May 15. Fair or fine and cold, evening remarkably so and very clear. Walking in Magdalen walks. Green-white of lower leafage especially in elms and beeches: of course in the beeches it is almost the natural hue. Elm trunks are blue or purple rich moist black at this time, as thrown out by the thick heaps and armfuls of the wet pellets of young green of which their leafing now 'stands'. To see the long forward-creeping curls of the newly-leaved trees, in sweeps and rows all lodged one with another down the meadow edge, beautiful, but distraction and the want of the canon only makes these graceful shapes in the keen unseasonable evening air to 'carve out' one's thought with painful definiteness. Hemlock in clouds of bloom. The shallow shelves of beech branches hang with light and certain poise, dividing the air, say just over one's head, with level-grown pieces of pale window-like green spotted with soft darks by the now and then overlapping of the leaves. May in bloom. Irises blooming.

May 18. Charming to see in the Garden Quadrangle the strong relief of the dark green and the balls of light in the close grass and the mixture of sunlit leaf and dewy-looking shadow in the chestnuts high up and moving in the wind. Squares of green out-of-doors, as a window or garden-door, are delightful and the green then suggests rose in an unusually recondite way, as if it were a translation of rose or rose in another key. Plane in full leaf but not sycamore. Mulberry budding. Lilac in full blow. – Things look sad and difficult.

May 19. Summer. Draughts of warm wind through doors or windows are pleasanter than out of doors.

May 24. Grey in morning, then fine. Cold, with E. wind, skin being parched and lips cut. Buttercups in Magdalen meadow put out the green in their yellow and from their just visible distinction and countlessness throw the trees of the Walks 'to finer distance'. Some of the chestnuts have blooms touched with bright rose, not faint and at a distance confused and put out by the yellow as in the common ones, but shining with red and white purely and beautifully.

June 3. Showers, but mostly bright and hot. Clouds growing in beauty at end of the day. In the afternoon a white rack of two parallel spines, vertebrated as so often. At sunset, when the sky had charm and beauty, very level clouds, long pelletted sticks of shade-softened grey in the West, with gold-colour splashed sunset-spot, then more to the S. grey rows rather thicker and their oblique flake or thread better marked, above them on a ground of indistincter grey a drift of spotty tufts or drops, a 'dirty' looking kind of clouds, scud-like, rising. With Garrett in Binsey Lane. The green was softening with grey. The meadows yellow with buttercups and under-reddened with sorrel and containing white of oxeyes and puff-balls. The cuckoo singing one side, on the other from the ground and unseen the wood-lark, as I suppose, most sweetly with a song of which the structure is more definite than the skylark's and gives the link with that of the rest of birds. – Yellow meadows shining through the willow-rods pretty . . . At sunset too there was much of that delicate lock-of-hair horizontal streaking. The map of the sky was a rhomboid of grey round-moulded cloud in one great cloth stretching over the sky with one part resting somewhere on the skyline in the S. or S. W., and the other rows were meteorologically parallel but perspectively converging and diverging with respect to this, clear sky being between. Wafts of very warm wind came now and then all day.

June 6. Aspens thick in leaf but not so the sycamores even yet, or possibly they are this summer or at this time of the summer very thin. A mass of buttercup floating down under one of the Godstow bridges. A barge, I find, not only wrinkles smooth water by a wedge outlined in parallel straight lap-waves but also, before and without these, shallower ones running, say midway, between those of the wedge and a perpendicular to the current.

June 13. Grace of willow bushes with their sprays shooting over and reversed in water. – Was happily able to see composition of the crowd in the area of the theatre, all the heads looking one way thrown up by their black coats relieved only by white shirt-fronts etc.: the short strokes of eyes, nose, mouth, repeated hundred of times I believe it is which gives the visible law: looked at in any one instance it flies. I could find a sort of beauty in this, certainly character – but in fact that is almost synonymous with finding order, anywhere. The short parallel strokes spoken of are like those something in effect on the cusp-ends of six-foils in the iron tracery of the choir gates in our chapel.

June 19. Smart showers in morning with bright between; this cleared till it was very fine, with flying clouds casting shadows on the Wye hills. Fine sunset. – Tintern to Ross by Monmouth – The afternoon way we much enjoyed, in especial we turned down a grass lane to reach the river at the ferry. It was steep down at first and I remember blue sprays of wych-elm or hazel against the sunlight green further on. Then the fields rose high on each side, one crowned with beautiful trees (there was particularly an ash with you could not tell how many contradictory supple curvings in the boughs), and then orchards, of which this country is full; on the other, with a narrow plot of orchard in which sheep grazed between the rise and the lane, was Goderich castle of red sandstone on the height. Close by the river was a fine oak with long lunging boughs. The country is full of fine trees, especially oaks, and is, like Devonshire, on red soil. We crossed the river whirling down with a swollen stream, and then by lanes to Ross. From the hotel there you see the river enclosing the Oak Meadow and others in its bends. We walked by twilight and moonlight up it, flush, swift, and oily, the moon streaking it with hairs, Addis said, of light. Aspens blackened against the last light seem to throw their scarcer leaves into barbs or arrowheads of mackerel patterns. – Addis' idea of fondness or friendship he says is of feeling and not of acts of kindness. – He thinks passing through a country associated with someone who has been before you, as Hereford-shire partly with Prichard, is deeply sad, but it is not with associations of the dead.

June 21. Saw Gloucester cathedral, where everything is very sadly done. Addis was very melancholy. Home in storms of rain. – Morning bright, then dull, with sky in long strips from which dirty scud clouds were swept upwards like flying skirts. Saw Cumnor Hurst far off and could partly feel Addis' feeling. Sunset fine, soft round curdled clouds bathed with fleshy rose-colour in wedges, for a dark spoke struck up in the midst. Then thunder and lightning and then hard rain.

July 6. Hard thunder-showers, fine between, passing clouds. Sun coming out after one of these showers in morning hotly made ground smoke, gravel as well as lawn, some time. Lawn shews half-circle curves of the scythe in parallel ranks. Beeches seen from behind the house scatter their tops in charming tufted sheep-hooks drooping towards each other and every way. Lay-ers or shelves of the middle cedar not level but in waved lips like silver plate. Soft vermilion leather just budded leaves on the purple beech, and the upper sprays ruddy in the sunlight: whole effect rich, the leaves too being crisply pinched like little fingered papers. Carnations if you look close have their tongue-shaped petals powdered with spankled red glister, which no doubt gives them their brilliancy: sharp chip shadows of one petal on another: the notched edge curls up and so is darked, which gives them graceful precision. Green windows of cabbages in sun-shine. The roses: their richness, variety, etc. will no doubt always make them necessary to the poets. Take colour: there are some pink-grey or lilac a little way off upon their dead-green bushes, there are the yellow ones with packed pieces blushing yellower at the foot, the *coupe d'Hebe* pink outside and dry bright-grained rose-pink where the leaves turn out, etc. Then for shape, some flat and straggling have fissures twisting inwards upon the centre, some are globed and with the inner petals drawn geometrically across each other like laces of boddices at the opera with chipped-back little tight rolls at the edge. – Grandmamma looking thin but pretty, this bringing out the delicacy of her features.

July 11. Dull and shallow sunlight. Saw an olive-coloured snake on hedge of Finchley wood and just before its slough in the road – or at all events a slough. Oats: hoary blue-green sheaths and stalks, prettily shadow-stroked spikes of pale green grain. Oaks: the organisation of this tree is difficult. Speaking generally no doubt the determining planes are concentric, a system of brief contiguous and continuous tangents, whereas those of the cedar would roughly be called horizontals and those of the beech radiating but modified by droop and by a screw-set towards jutting points. But beyond this since the normal growth of the boughs is radiating and the leaves grow some way in there is of course a system of spoke-wise clubs of green – sleeve-pieces. And since the end shoots curl and carry young and scanty leaf-stars these clubs are tapered, and I have seen also the pieces in profile with chiselled outlines, the blocks thus made detached and lessening towards the end. However the star knot is the chief thing: it is whorled, worked round, a little and this is what keeps up the illusion of the tree: the leaves are rounded inwards and figure out ball-knots. Oaks differ much, and much turns on the broadness of the leaf, the narrower giving the crisped and starry and Catherine-wheel forms, the broader the flat-pieced mailed or shard-covered ones, in which it is possible to see composition in dips etc. on wider bases than the single knot or cluster. But I shall study them further.

July 13. Fine. All day faint long tails, getting thicker as the day went on, and at one time there were some like long ringlets, namely curls shaping out a hollow screw. Rows of cloud lay across sky at sun-set, their lit parts yellow, below which was the curious opaque blue one sometimes sees with that colour. – To Midhurst, then walked to West Lavington and back, seeing the church, built 15 years ago. I should like to see it again for it looked immature and strange. The bowered lanes to Lavington skirting Cowdery Park were charming and the gloom in the

thicket of the park, where yews shewed and chestnut leaves –
hoary opaque green. Walked again later towards the downs,
heard more woodlarks, and found a glowworm. Just beyond
the town (of Midhurst) runs the canal water looking like a river
and on the steeper-rising further side the park trees make a
towering and noble wall which runs along to the left and turns
and embays a quarter of a mile away, the whole having the
blocky short cresting which freely grown park trees show. There
were oaks and other trees, one beech I noticed especially scatter-
ing forwards from the press brown point-sprays, but the great
feature is the Spanish chestnut, their round knots tufted with
white heaps of flour-and-honey blossom: this gives splendour
and difference to such a growth of trees. I know now too what
a tinkling brook is.

July 19. Fine, but the sunlight becoming faint. – Macfarlane
arrived. – Alone in the woods and in Mr Nelthorpe's park,
whence one gets such a beautiful view southwards over the
county. I have now found the law of the oak leaves. It is of
platter-shaped stars altogether; the leaves lie close like pages,
packed, and as if drawn tightly to. But these old packs, which
lie at the end of their twigs, throw out now long shoots
alternately and slimly leaved, looking like bright keys. All the
sprays but markedly these ones shape out and as it were
embrace greater circles and the dip and toss of these make the
wider and less organic articulations of the tree.

July 21. There is a large-leaved kind of ash which grows in tall
close bushes: when the wind blows it the backs of the sprays,
which are silvery, look like combs of fish-bones, the leaves
where they border their rib-stem appearing, when in repetition
all jointed on one rib, to be angularly cut at the inner end. The
two bindweeds are in blossom.

July 24. The wild parsley (if it is that) growing in clumps by the
road side a beautiful sight, the leaf being delicately cut like rue.
There is a tree that has a leaf like traveller's-joy, curled, and
with brick-like veinings. It has clusters of berries which are
flattened like some tight-mouthed jars, yellow when unripe, then
cherry-coloured, then quickly turning glossy black if gathered.
The traveller's joy winds over it and they then are hard to tell
apart, unless that it has rougher duller leaves. There was a

graceful bit, a stile, with this tree hanging over on the left side, hazel and large-leaved ash on the right, and a spray of the ash stood forward like a bright blind of leaves drawing and condensing the light. Under the bushes on each side was suggestive woolly darkness (and giving on one hand onto the dry stoned bed of a streamlet, where on looking under one saw more light filtering in) and soft round-bladed tufts of grass grew in half-darkness under the stone at the foot of the stile. – No, the berries belong, I now remember, to a rough round-leaved tree (the underside being white). Merely the white-beam, I believe.

1867

July 10. Flames of mist rose from the French brooks and meadows, and sheets of mist at a distance led me to think I saw the sea: at sunrise it was fog. Morning star and peach-coloured dawn. The scales of colour in the landscape were more appreciable before than after sunrise: all was 'frank'. The trees were irregular, scarcely expressing form, and the aspens blotty, with several concentric outlines, and as in French pictures. In the facing sunlight there was very little colour but bright grey shine and glister, with trees interposing in their stems and leafage poles and strokes of bluish shadow. The day was fine, everything bright: even the iron rings in the walls of the Seine wharfs dropped long slant pointed shadows like birds do.

July 18. Showers and fine; rainbow. – The reason Shakspere calls it 'the blue bow' – to put it down now precisely – is because the blue band edged by and ending in violet, though not the broadest, is the deepest expression of colour in the bow and so becomes the most decisive and emphatic feature there. – At sunset the air rinsed after the rain.

July 28. I am three and twenty. – Bright extremely, though a shower or more fell; distances all fine blues; the sky working blue-silver; the clouds, which far off were in chains, were there covered in a blue light and shaded with blue shadow, and in the afternoon indeed shewed silver lips only and then were indistinguishable from blue sky below that; sunset bright – an edge of gold shewing amidst wet sandy gold; afterwards glowing ranks. – The timbered side of Frognal – Mr Claypen's that was, Oak Hill, etc. – from the fields towards Mr Joseph Hoare's looked finer than I had ever seen it before: the foliage was so vivid with the breaks and the packing; the poplars there are there looked like velvet, shewing all dark except an edge of bright sprays along the top.

Aug. 14. Hot; fine, with haze; at six in the evening a wonderful rack of what I hear they call 'flock-of-sheep' clouds, a dapple of plump rounds half parted, half branching from one another like madrepores: the edge was pulled straight, and where in the west the rack sunk to the earth they were somewhat bright and gaily waved in diminishing pieces: as time went on through all the rack the parts seemed to close up more and form yokes – whether this was really so or only that the shadows, which continued to grow and run up, bound them together in mack-erelling to the eye.

Aug 22. Bright. Walked to Finchley and turned down a lane to a field where I sketched an appletree. Their sprays against the sky are gracefully curved and the leaves looping over edge them, as it looks, with rows of scales. In something the same way I saw some tall young slender wych-elms of thin growth the leaves of which enclosed the light in successive eyebrows. From the spot where I sketched – under an oak, beyond a brook, and reached by the above green lane between a park-ground and a pretty field – there was a charming view, the field, lying then on the right of the lane, being a close-shaven smoothly-rounded shield of bright green ended near the high road by a row of viol-headed or flask-shaped elms – not rounded merely but squared – of much beauty – dense leafing, rich dark colour, ribs and spandrils of timber garlanded with leaf between tree and tree. But what most struck me was a pair of ashes in going up the lane again. The further one was the finer – a globeish just-sided head with one launching-out member on the right; the nearer one was more naked and horny. By taking a few steps one could pass the further behind the nearer or make the stems close, either coincidingly, so far as disagreeing outlines will coincide, or allowing a slit on either side, or again on either side making a broader stem than either would make alone. It was this which was so beautiful – making a noble shaft and base to the double tree, which was crested by the horns of the nearer ash and shaped on the right by the bosom of the hinder one with its springing bough. The outline of the double stem was beautiful to whichever of the two sides you slid the hinder tree – in one (not, I think, in both) shaft-like and narrowing at the ground. Besides I saw how great the richness and subtlety is of the curves in the clusters, both in the forward bow mentioned before and in some most graceful hangers on the other side: it combines somewhat-slanted outward strokes with rounding, but I cannot very well characterise it now. – Elm-leaves: – they shine much in the sun – bright green when near from underneath but higher up they look olive: their shapelessness in the flat is from their being made διὰ τὸ πεφυκέναι, to be dimpled and dog's-eared: their leaf-growth is in this point more rudimentary than that of oak, ash, beech, etc that the leaves lie in long rows and do not subdivide or have central knots but tooth or cog their woody twigs.

For July 6, 1866 I have a note on elm-leaves, that they sit crisp, dark, glossy, and saddle-shaped along their twigs, on which at that time an inner frill of soft juicy young leaves had just been run; they chip the sky, and where their waved edge turns downwards they gleam and blaze like an underlip sometimes will when seen against the light.

Aug 24. Bright. In the middle of, I think, this day Lionel had a piece of sky-blue gauze for butterfly-nets lying on the grass in the garden. It was a graceful mixture of square folds and winding tube-folds. But the point was the colour as seen by sunlight in a transparent material. The folds, which of course doubled the stuff, were on the sun's side bright light blue and on the other deep blue – *not shadow-modified*, but real blue, as in tapestries and some paintings. Then the shadowed sides had cobweb-streaks of paler colour across, and in other parts became transparent and shewed the grass below, which was lit by the sun through the gauze.

Aug 29. Miss Warren told me that she had heard the following vision of an old woman from Mr Baring-Gould. She saw, she said, white doves flying about her room and drops of blood falling from their 'nibs' – that is their beaks.

The story comes in Henderson's book of Folklore. The woman was a good old woman, Widow Freeman by name, of Horbury. The room was full of bright light, the 'nibs' bathed in blood, and the drops fell on her. Then the light became dazzling and painful, the doves were gone, and our Lord appeared displaying His five wounds.

Aug 30. Fair; in afternoon fine; the clouds had a good deal of crisping and mottling. – A round by Plumley. – Stands of ash in a copse: they consisted of two or three rods most gracefully leaved, for each wing or comb finally curled inwards, that is upwards. – Putting my hand up against the sky whilst we lay on the grass I saw more richness and beauty in the blue than I had known of before, not brilliance but glow and colour. It was not transparent and sapphire-like but turquoise-like, swarming and blushing round the edge of the hand and in the pieces clipped in by the fingers, the flesh being sometimes sunlit, sometimes glassy with reflected light, sometimes lightly shadowed in that violet one makes with cobalt and Indian red.

Sept 2. The furze on the moor is thick in bloom. The composition of the bloom is this – the head of a spike has, let us say, eight flowers, the nibs of which – I do not know the botanical name – point outwards, arranged as below, thus suggesting a square by way of Union Jack; the wings or crests rising behind make a little square with four walls, as in the drawing, these crests being those of the bigger flowers and those of the smaller, I fancy, being suppressed; these little walls are like the partitions in honeycombs; the nibs when looked down upon are as in the diagram, something like a Jew's-harp, enclosing a split tongue; the whole makes a pretty diaper. Some again might have six flowers, as in the third drawing. The regularity however of the drawings is of course – though the flowers are regular – that of the type.

1868

June 20. To Madame Leupold's concert, where Madle. Mela sang in a tenor and a girl played the violin and another, Madle. Vogt, the finger-glasses (Mattauphône), and certainly that instrument is chromatically more perfect than the violin even and of course the tone what one knows and magical. But 'it is the sport' to watch her fingers flying, and at the distance the articulations vanishing, they wave like flakes or fins or leaves of white. Madam Leupold played four short pieces of Schumann.

[On a walking tour of Switzerland with Edward Bond, an Oxford friend, July 1868]

July 6. By railway to Basel. Beautiful view from the train of the hills near Mülheim etc. They were clothed with wood and at the openings in this and indeed all upward too they were charactered by vertical stemming, dim in the distance. Villages a little bare like Brill rise in blocks of white and deep russet tiling. The nearer hills terraced with vine-yards deep and vertical, the pale grey shaven poles close on the railway leaning capriciously towards one another. – Here we met the young Englishman who had been to see Charlotte Brontë's school in Brussels. – The whole country full of walnut and cherry trees; oleanders in bloom; creeper is trained on houses and even the stations and waves in the wind.

But Basel at night! with a full moon waking the river and sending up straight beams from the heavy clouds that overhung it. We saw this from the bridge. The river runs so strong that it keeps the bridge shaking. Then we walked about the place and first of all had the adventure of the little Englishwoman with her hat off. We went through great spacious streets and places dead still and came to fountains of the clearest black water through which pieces of things at the bottom gleamed white. We got up to a height where a bastion-shaped vertical prominence shaded with chestnut trees looked down on the near roofs, which then in the moonlight were purple and velvety and edged along with ridges and chimneys of chalk white. A woman came to a window with a candle and some mess she was

making, and then that was gone and there was no light anywhere but the moon. We heard music indoors about. We saw
the courtyard of a charming house with some tree pushing to
the windows and a fountain. A church too of immensely high
front all dead and flush to the top and next to it three most
graceful flamboyant windows.

July 9. Before sunrise looking out of window saw a noble scape
of stars – the Plough all golden falling, Cassiopeïa on end with
her bright quains pointing to the right, the graceful bends of
Perneus underneath her, and some great star whether Capella
or not I am not sure risen over the brow of the mountain.
Sunrise we saw well: the north landscape was blighty but the
south, the important one, with the Alps, clear; lower down all
was mist and flue of white cloud, which grew thicker as day
went on and like a junket lay scattered on the lakes. The sun lit
up the bright acres of the snows at first with pink but afterwards
clear white: the snow of the Bernese Highland remained from
its distance pinkish all day. – The mountain ranges, as any series
or body of inanimate like things not often seen, have the air of
persons and of interrupted activity; they are multitudinous too,
and also they express a second level with an upper world or
shires of snow. – In going down between Pilatus and a long
streak of cloud the blue sky was greenish. Since I have found
this colour is seen in looking from the snow to the sky but why
I do not understand: can there possibly be a rose hue suppressed
in the white (– *purpurea candidior nive*)?

July 11. Fine.
We took a guide up the Wylerhorn but the top being clouded
dismissed him and stayed up the mountain, lunching by a
waterfall. Presently after long climbing – for there was a good
chance of a clearance – we nearly reached the top, when a cloud
coming on thick frightened me back: had we gone on we should
have had the view, for it cleared quite. Still we saw the neighbouring mountains well. The snow is often cross-harrowed and
lies too in the straightest paths as though artificial, which again
comes from the planing. In the sheet it glistens yellow to the
sun. How fond of and warped to the mountains it would be
easy to become! For every cliff and limb and edge and jutty has
its own nobility. – Two boys came down the mountain yodel-
ling. – We saw the snow in the hollows for the first time. In one

the surface was crisped across the direction of the cleft and the other way, that is across the broader crisping and down the stream, combed: the stream ran below and smoke came from the hollow: the edge of the snow hewn in curves as if by moulding-planes. – Crowd of mountain flowers – gentians; gentianellas; blood-red lucerne; a deep blue glossy spiked flower like plantain, flowering gradually up the spike, so that at the top it looks like clover or honeysuckle; rich big harebells glistening black like the cases of our veins when dry and heated from without; and others. All the herbage enthronged with every fingered or fretted leaf. – Firs very tall, with the swell of the branching on the outer side of the slope so that the peaks seem to point inwards to the mountain peak, like the lines of the Parthenon, and the outline melodious and moving on many focuses. – I wore my pagharee and turned it with harebells below and gentians in two rows above like double pan-pipes. – In coming down we lost our way and each had a dangerous slide down the long wet grass of a steep slope.

July 12. To mass at the church. It was an odd sight: all the women sat on one side and you saw hundreds of headdresses all alike. The hair is taken back and (apparently) made into one continuous plait with narrow white linen, which crosses the lock of hair not always the same way but zigzag (or that perhaps there must be more than one linen strip), and the alteration of lock and linen gives the look of rows of regular teeth. The fastening is by a buckle (Bädeker calls it) or plate of silver generally broadened at the ends or sometimes by a silver or gold pin, wavy and headed by a blunted diamond-shaped piece gracefully enamelled. Over the middle of the pin or buckle or just above it the linen is broadened out and covers the inside of the two concentric circles which the plaits of hair make and, below, one of the plaits is looped up in the middle.

July 15. The mountains and in particular the Silberhorn are shaped and nippled like the sand in an hourglass and the Silberhorn has a subsidiary pyramidal peak naped sharply down the sides. Then one of their beauties is in nearly vertical places the fine pleatings of the snow running to or from one another, like the newness of lawn in an alb and sometimes cut off short as crisp as celery.

There are round one of the heights of the Jungfrau two ends

or falls of a glacier. If you took the skin of a white tiger or the deep fell of some other animal and swung it tossing high in the air and then cast it out before you it would fall and so clasp and lap round anything in its way just as this glacier does and the fleece would part in the same rifts: you must suppose a lazuli under-flix to appear. The spraying out of one end I tried to catch but it would have taken hours: it was this which first made me think of a tiger-skin, and it ends in tongues and points like the tail and claws: indeed the ends of the glaciers are knotted or knuckled like talons. Above, in a plane nearly parallel to the eye, becoming thus foreshortened, it forms saddle-curves with dips and swells.

July 17. Rain, but the heights westwards and southwards sharp, the sun hidden by a straight-edged canvas of rain-cloud. It began to come out and a rainbow appeared shewing nearly two thirds of its whole wheel. In the midst of its arc rose milk-white cloud shewing the angled shadow of a height sharply upon it and on the edges of this shadow were amber and pale green colours. – Richness of the greens – nearest the hollow of the Bättenalp below us, then the blue-green of the lake, then again the grass-green of the heights beyond, and to add a fourth note the sun coming out accented the forward brows and edges of the Bättenalp with a butter-bright lustre. – The sunset itself was in a bank with sharp level strands above it, and on the mountains to the S. rested long straight pellets of muddy cloud hiding their tops. – The after-glow gave a reddish look to the snow.

July 18. Then we saw the three falls of the Reichenbach. The upper one is the biggest. At the take-off it falls in discharges of rice or meal but each cluster as it descends sharpens and tapers, and from halfway down the whole cascade is inscaped in fretted falling vandykes in each of which the frets or points, just like the startings of a just-lit lucifer match, keep shooting in races, one beyond the other, to the bottom. The vapour which beats up from the impact of the falling water makes little feeder rills down the rocks and these catching and running in drops along the sharp ledges in the rock are shaken and delayed and chased along them and even cut off and blown upwards by the blast of the vapour as it rises: saw the same thing at Handeck too. – In the second fall when facing the great limbs in which the water is packed saw well how they are tretted like open sponge or light breadcrumb where the yeast has supped in the texture in big and little holes.

July 20. Fine.

Walked down to the Rhone glacier. It has three stages – first a smoothly-moulded bed in a pan or theatre of thorny peaks, swells of ice rising through the snow-sheet and the snow itself tossing and fretting into the sides of the rock walls in spray-like points: this is the first stage of the glaciers generally; it is like bright-plucked water swaying in a pail – ; second, after a slope nearly covered with landslips of moraine, was a ruck of horned waves steep and narrow in the gut: now in the upper Grindel-wald glacier between the bed or highest stage was a descending limb which was like the rude and knotty bossings of a strombus shell – ; third the foot, a broad limb opening out and reaching the plain, shaped like the fan-fin of a dolphin or a great bivalve shell turned on its face, the flutings in either case being suggested by the crevasses and the ribs by the risings between them, these being swerved and inscaped strictly to the motion of the mass. Or you may compare the three stages to the heel, instep, and ball or toes of a foot. – The second stage looked at from nearer appeared like a box of plaster of Paris or starch or toothpowder, a little moist, tilted up and then struck and jarred so that the powder broke and tumbled in shapes and rifts.

Aug 30. Grey till past four; then fine.

I saw the phenomenon of the sheepflock on the downs again from Croham Hurst. It ran like the water-packets on a leaf – that collectively, but number of globules so filmed over that they would not flush together is the exacter comparison: at a gap in the hedge they were huddled and shaking open as they passed outwards they behaved as the drops would do (or a handful of shot) in reaching the brow of a rising and running over.

1869

Sept. About the same time a fine sunset, which, looked at also from the upstairs windows, cut out the yews all down the approach to the house in bright flat pieces like wings in a theatre (as once before I noticed at sunrise from Magdalen tower), each shaped by its own sharp-cut shadow falling on the yew-tree behind it, since they run E. and W. Westward under the sun the heights and groves in Richmond Park looked like dusty velvet being all flushed into a piece by the thick-hoary golden light which slanted towards me over them.

Also that autumn my eye was suddenly caught by the scaping of the leaves that grow in allies and avenues: I noticed it first in an elm and then in limes. They fall from the two sides of the branch or spray in two marked planes which meet at a right angle or more. This comes from the endeavour to catch the light on either side, which falls left and right but not all round. Thus each branch is thatched with a double blade or eave of leaves which run up to a coping like the roof-crest all along its stem, and seen from some places these lie across one another all in chequers and x's.

Dec. Another day in the evening after Litanies as Father Rector was giving the points for meditation I shut my eyes, being very tired, and without ceasing to hear him began to dream. The dream-images seemed to rise and overlie those which belonged to what he was saying and I saw one of the Apostles – he was talking about the Apostles – as if pressed against by a piece of wood about half a yard long and a few inches across, like a long box with two of the long sides cut off. Even then I could not understand what the piece of wood did encumbering the apostle. Now this piece of wood I had often seen in an outhouse and being that week 'A Secretis' I had seen it longer together and had been that day wondering what it was: in reality it is used to hold a little heap of cinders against the wall which keep from the frost a piece of earthenware pipe which there comes out and goes in again making a projection in the wall. It is just the things which produced dead impressions, which the mind, either because you cannot make them out or because they were perceived across other more engrossing thoughts, has made nothing of and brought into no scaping, that force themselves up in this way afterwards. – It seems true what Ed. Bond said, that you can trace your dreams to something or other in your waking life, especially of things that have been lately – I would not say this universally however. But the connection may be capricious almost punning: I remember in one case to have detected a real pun but what it was I forget.

The dream-images also appear to have little or no projection, to be flat like pictures, and often one seems to be holding one's eyes close to them – I mean even while dreaming. This probably due to a difference still felt between images brought by ordinary use of function of sight and those seen as these are 'between our eyelids and our eyes' – though this is not all, for we also see the colours, brothy motes and figures, and at all events the positive darkness, made by the shut eyelids by the ordinary use of the function of sight, but these images are brought upon that dark field, as I imagine, by a reverse action of the visual nerves (the same will hold of the sounds, sensations of touch, etc of dreams) – or by other nerves, but it seems reasonable to suppose impressions of sight belong to the organ of sight – and once lodged there are stalled by the mind like other images: only you cannot make them at will when awake, for the very effort and advertence would be destructive to them, since the eye in its sane waking office kens only impressions brought from without, that is to say either from beyond the body or from the body itself produced upon the dark field of the eyelids. Nevertheless I have seen in favourable moments the images brought from within lying there like others: if I am not mistaken they are coarser and simpler and something like the spectra made by bright things looked hard at. I can therefore believe what Chandler told E. B., that at waking he could see – which is a step beyond seeing them on the fields of the eyelids – the images of his dream upon the wall of his room.

1870

One day in the Long Retreat (which ended on Xmas Day) [1869] they were reading in the refectory Sister Emmerich's account of the Agony in the Garden and I suddenly began to cry and sob and could not stop. I put it down for this reason, that if I had been asked a minute beforehand I should have said that nothing of the sort was going to happen and even when it did I stood in a manner wondering at myself not seeing in my reason the traces of an adequate cause for such strong emotion – the traces of it I say because of course the cause in itself is adequate for the sorrow of a lifetime. I remember much the same thing on Maundy Thursday when the presanctified Host was carried to the sacristy. But neither the weight nor the stress of sorrow, that is to say of the thing which should cause sorrow, by themselves move us or bring the tears as a sharp knife does not cut for being pressed as long as it is pressed without shaking of the hand but there is always one touch, something striking sideways and unlooked for, which in both cases undoes resistance and pierces, and this may be so delicate that the pathos seems to have gone directly to the body and cleared the understanding in its passage. On the other hand the pathetic touch by itself, as in dramatic pathos, will only draw slight tears if its matter is not important or not of import to us, the strong emotion coming from a force which was gathered before it was discharged: in this way a knife may pierce the flesh which it had happened only to graze and only grazing will go no deeper.

The winter was called severe. There were three spells of frost with skating, the third beginning on Feb. 9. No snow to speak of till that day. Some days before Feb. 7 I saw catkins hanging. On the 9th there was snow but not lying on the roads. On the grass it became a crust lifted on the heads of the blades. As we went down a field near Caesar's Camp I noticed it before me *squalentem*, coat below coat, sketched in intersecting edges bearing 'idiom', all down the slope: – I have no other word yet for that which takes the eye or mind in a bold hand or effective sketching or in marked features or again in graphic writing, which not being beauty nor true inscape yet gives interest and makes ugliness even better than meaninglessness. – On the Common the snow was channelled all in parallels by the sharp driving wind and upon the tufts of grass (where by the dark colour shewing through it looked greyish) it came to turret-like clusters or like broken shafts of basalt. – In the Park in the afternoon the wind was driving little clouds of snow-dust which caught the sun as they rose and delightfully took the eyes flying up the slopes they looked like breaks of sunlight fallen through ravelled cloud upon the hills and again like deep flossy velvet blown to the root by breath which passed all along. Nearer at hand along the road it was gliding over the ground in white wisps that between trailing and flying shifted and wimpled like so many silvery worms to and from one another.

Feb 12. The slate slabs of the urinals even are frosted in graceful sprays. [Dec 31, 1870. I have noticed it here also at the seminary: it comes when they have been washed.]

March 12. A fine sunset: the higher sky dead clear blue bridged by a broad slant causeway rising from right to left of wisped or grass cloud, the wisps lying across; the sundown yellow, moist with light but ending at the top in a foam of delicate white pearling and spotted with big tufts of cloud in colour russet between brown and purple but edged with brassy light. But what I note it all for is this: before I had always taken the sunset and the sun as quite out of gauge with each other, as indeed physically they are, for the eye after looking at the sun is blunted to everything else and if you look at the rest of the sunset you must cover the sun, but today I inscaped them together and made the sun the true eye and ace of the whole, as it is. It was all active and tossing out light and started as strongly forward from the field as a long stone or a boss in the knop of the chalice-stem: it is indeed by stalling it so that it falls into scape with the sky.

May. I do not think I have ever seen anything more beautiful than the bluebell I have been looking at. I know the beauty of our Lord by it. Its inscape is mixed of strength and grace, like an ash tree. The head is strongly drawn over backwards and arched down like a cutwater drawing itself back from the line of the keel. The lines of the bells strike and overlie this, rayed but not symmetrically, some lie parallel. They look steely against the paper, the shades lying between the bells and behind the cockled petal-ends and nursing up the precision of their distinctness, the petal-ends themselves being delicately lit. Then there is the straightness of the trumpets in the bells softened by the slight entasis and by the square splay of the mouth. One bell, the lowest, some way detached and carried on a longer foot-stalk, touched out with the tips of the petals an oval not like the rest in a plane perpendicular of the axis of the bell but a little atilt, and so with the square-in-rounding turns of the petals . . . There is a little drawing of this detached bell. It looks square-cut in the original.

December. Hailstones are shaped like the cut of diamonds called brilliants. – I found one morning the ground in one corner of the garden full of small pieces of potsherd from which there rose up (and not dropped off) long icicles carried on in some way each like a forepitch of the shape of the piece of potsherd it grew on, like a tooth to its root for instance, and most of them bended over and curled like so many tusks or horns or / best of all and what they looked likest when they first caught my eye / the first soft root-spurs thrown out from a sprouting chestnut. This bending of the icicle seemed so far as I could see not merely a resultant, where the smaller spars of which it was made were still straight, but to have flushed them too. – The same day and others the garden mould very crisp and meshed over with a lace-work of needles leaving (they seemed) three-cornered openings: it looked greyish and like a coat of gum on wood. Also the smaller crumbs and clods were lifted fairly up from the ground on upright ice-pillars, whether they had dropped these from themselves or drawn them from the soil: it was like a little Stonehenge – Looking down into the thick ice of our pond I found the imprisoned air-bubbles nothing at random but starting from centres and in particular one most beautifully regular white brush of them, each spur of it a curving string of beaded and diminishing bubbles – The pond, I suppose from over pressure when it was less firm, was mapped with a puzzle of very slight clefts branched with little springs: the pieces were odd-shaped and sized – though a square angular scaping could be just made out in the outline but the cracks ran deep through the ice markedly in planes and always the planes of the cleft on the surface. They remained and in the end the ice broke up in just these pieces.

1871

March. What you look hard at seems to look hard at you, hence the true and the false instress of nature. One day early in March when long streamers were rising from over Kemble End one large flake loop-shaped, not a streamer but belonging to the string, moving too slowly to be seen, seemed to cap and fill the zenith with a white shire of cloud. I looked long up at it till the tall height and the beauty of the scaping – regularly curled knots springing if I remember from fine stems, like foliation in wood or stone – had strongly grown on me. It changed beautiful changes, growing more into ribs and one stretch of running into branching like coral. Unless you refresh the mind from time to time you cannot always remember or believe how deep the inscape in things is.

1874

Nov 8. Walking with Wm. Splaine we saw a vast multitude of starlings making an unspeakable jangle. They would settle in a row of trees; then, one tree after another, rising at a signal they looked like a cloud of specks of black snuff or powder struck up from a brush or broom or shaken from a wig; then they would sweep round in whirlwinds – you could see the nearer and farther bow of the rings by the size and blackness; many would be in one phase at once, all narrow black flakes hurling round, then in another; then they would fall upon a field and so on. Splaine wanted a gun: then 'there it would rain meat', he said. I thought they must be full of enthusiasm and delight hearing their cries and stirring and cheering one another.

1875

Feb. Denbigh is a taking picturesque town. Seen from here, as Henry Kerr says, it is always beautiful. The limekiln under a quarried cliff on this side of the town is always sending out a white smoke and this, and the greyer smoke of Denbigh, creeping upon the hill, what with sun and wind give fairy effects which are always changing.

The day was bright, the sun sparkling through a frostfog which made the distance dim and the stack of Denbigh hill, as we came near, dead mealy grey against the light: the castle ruins, which crown the hill, were punched out in arches and half arches by bright breaks and eyelets of daylight. We went up to the castle but not in: standing before the gateway I had an instress which only the true old work gives from the strong and noble inscape of the pointedarch. We went to eat our lunch to a corner opening by a stone stile upon a wilderness by which you get down to the town, under the outer wall, overgrown with ivy, bramble, and some graceful herb with glossy lush green sprays, something like celery.

Feb 7. I asked Miss Jones in my Welsh lesson the Welsh for *fairy* for we were translating Cinderella. She told me *cĭpenăper* (or perhaps *cĭpernăper, Anglice kippernapper*): the word is nothing but *kidnapper*, moulded, according to their fashion, to give it a Welsh etymology, as she said, from *cĭpio* to snatch, to whisk away. However in coming to an understanding between ourselves what fairies (she says *fairess* by the way for a she-fairy) and kippernappers were, on my describing them as little people 'that high', she told me quite simply that she had seen them. It was on or near the Holywell road (she indicated the spot). She was going to her grandfather's farm on the hill, not far from where Justice Williams lived, on the slope of the Rhuallt. It was a busy time, haymaking I think. She was going up at 5 o'clock in the morning, when she saw three little boys of about four years old wearing little frock coats and odd little caps running and dancing before her, taking hands and going round, then going further, still dancing and always coming together, she said. She would take no notice of them but went on to the house and there told them what she had seen and wondered that children could be out so early. 'Why she has seen the kipper-nappers' her grandmother said to her son, Susannah Jones' father. They were

[The journal breaks off at this point]

Letters

To his Father

            23 New Inn Hall Street, Oxford. 16/17 Oct 1866
My Dear Father, – I must begin with a practical immediate
point. The Church strictly forbids all communion in sacred
things with non-Catholics. I have only just learnt this, but it
prevents me going to chapel, and so yesterday I had to inform
the Dean of the Chapel. Today the Master sent for me and said
he cd. not grant me leave of absence without an application
from you. As the College last term passed a resolution admitting
Catholics and took a Catholic into residence it has no right to
alter its principle in my case. I wish you therefore not to give
yourself the pain of making this application, even if you were
willing: I am of age moreover and am alone concerned. If you
refuse to make the application, the Master explains that he shall
lay my case before the common-room. In this case there is very
little doubt indeed that the Fellows wd. take the reasonable
course and give me leave of absence fr. chapel, and if not, I am
quite contented: but in fact I am satisfied as to the course our
Fellows will take and the Master will at the last hesitate to lay
the matter before them perhaps even. I want you therefore to
write at once, if you will, – not to the Master who has no right
to ask what he does, but to me, with a refusal: no harm will
follow.
    The following is the position of things with me. You ask me
to suspend my judgment for a long time, or at the very least
more than half a year, in other words to stand still for a time.
Now to stand still is not possible, thus: I must either obey the
Church or disobey. If I disobey, I am not suspending judgment
but deciding, namely to take backward steps fr. the grounds I
have already come to. To stand still if it were possible might be
justifiable, but to go back nothing can justify. I must therefore
obey the Church by ceasing to attend any service of the Church
of England. If I am to wait then I must either be altogether
without services and sacraments, which you will of course know
is impossible, or else I must attend the services of the Church –

still being unreceived. But what can be more contradictory than, in order to avoid joining the Church, attending the services of that very Church? Three of my friends, whose conversions were later than mine, Garrett, Addis, and Wood, have already been received, but this is by the way. Only one thing remains to be done: I cannot fight against God who calls me to His Church: if I were to delay and die in the meantime I shd. have no plea why my soul was not forfeit. I have no power in fact to stir a finger: it is God Who makes the decision and not I.

But you do not understand what is involved in asking me to delay and how little good you wd. get from it. I shall hold as a Catholic what I have long held as an Anglican, that literal truth of our Lord's words by which I learn that the least fragment of the consecrated elements in the Blessed Sacrament of the Altar is the whole Body of Christ born of the Blessed Virgin, before which the whole host of saints and angels as it lies on the altar trembles with adoration. This belief once got is the life of the soul and when I doubted it I shd. become an atheist the next day. But, as Monsignor Eyre says, it is a gross superstition unless guaranteed by infallibility. I cannot hold this doctrine confessedly except as a Tractarian or a Catholic: the Tractarian ground I have seen broken to pieces under my feet. What end then can be served by a delay in wh. I shd. go on believing this doctrine as long as I believed in God and shd. be by the fact of my belief drawn by a lasting strain towards the Catholic Church?

About my hastiness I wish to say this. If the question which is the Church of Christ? cd. only be settled by laborious search, a year and ten years and a lifetime are too little, when the vastness of the subject of theology is taken into account. But God must have made his Church such as to attract and convince the poor and unlearned as well as the learned. And surely it is true, though it will sound pride to say it, that the judgment of one who has seen both sides for a week is better than his who has seen only one for a lifetime. I am surprised you shd. say fancy and aesthetic tastes have led me to my present state of mind: these wd. be better satisfied in the Church of England, for bad taste is always meeting one in the accessories of Catholicism. My conversion is due to the following reasons mainly (I have put them down without order) – (i) simple and strictly drawn arguments partly my own, partly others', (ii) common sense, (iii) reading the Bible, especially the Holy Gospels, where texts like 'Thou art Peter' (the evasions proposed for this alone are enough to make one a Catholic) and the manifest position of St Peter among the Apostles so pursued me that at one time I thought it best to stop thinking of them, (iv) an increasing knowledge of the Catholic system (at first under the form of Tractarianism, later in its genuine place), which only wants to be known in order to be loved – its consolations, its marvellous ideal of holiness, the faith and devotion of its children, its multiplicity, its array of saints and martyrs, its consistency and unity, its glowing prayers, the daring majesty of its claims, etc. etc. You speak of the claims of the Church of England, but it is to me the strange thing that the Church of England makes no claims: it is true that Tractarians make them for her and find them faintly or only in a few instances borne out for them by her liturgy, and are strongly assailed for their extravagances while they do it. Then about applying to Mr Liddon and the Bp. of Oxford. Mr Liddon writes begging me to pause: it wd. take too long to explain how I did not apply to him at first and why it wd. have been useless. If Dr Pusey is in Oxford tomorrow I will see him, if it is any satisfaction to you. The Bishop is too much engaged to listen to individual difficulties and those who do apply to him may get such answers as young Mr Lane Fox did, who gave up £30,000 a year just lately to become a Catholic. He wrote back about a cob which he wanted to sell to the Dean of some place and wh. Lane Fox was to put his own price on and ride over for the Bishop to the place of sale. In fact Dr Pusey and Mr Liddon were the only two men in the world who cd. avail to detail me: the fact that they were Anglicans kept me one, for arguments for the Church of England I had long ago felt there were none that wd. hold water, and when that influence gave way everything was gone.

You are so kind as not to forbid me your house, to which I have no claim, on condition, if I understand, that I promise not to try to convert my brothers and sisters. Before I can promise this I must get permission, wh. I have no doubt will be given. Of course this promise will not apply after they come of age. Whether after my reception you will still speak as you do now I cannot tell.

You ask me if I have had no thought of the estrangement. I have had months to think of everything. Our Lord's last care on the cross was to commend His mother to his Church and His Church to His mother in the person of St John. If even now you wd. put yourselves into that position wh. Christ so unmistakably gives us and ask the Mother of sorrows to remember her three hours' compassion at the cross, the piercing of the sword prophesied by Simeon, and her seven dolours, and her spouse Joseph, the lily of chastity, to remember the flight into Egypt, the searching for his Foster-Son at twelve years old, and his last ecstasy with Christ at his death-bed, the prayers of this Holy Family wd. in a few days put an end to estrangements for ever. If you shrink fr. doing this, though the Gospels cry aloud to you to do it, at least for once – if you like, only once – approach Christ in a new way in which you will at all events feel that you are exactly in unison with me, that is, not vaguely, but casting yourselves into His sacred broken Heart and His five adorable Wounds. Those who do not pray to Him in His Passion pray to God but scarcely to Christ. I have the right to propose this, for I have tried both ways, and if you will not give one trial to this way you will see you are prolonging the estrangement and not I.

After saying this I feel lighter-hearted, though I still can by no means make my pen write what I shd. wish. I am your loving son,

GERARD M. HOPKINS

P.S. I am most anxious that you shd. not think of my future. It is likely that the positions you wd. like to see me in wd. have no attraction for me, and surely the happiness of my prospects depends on the happiness to me and not on intrinsic advantages. It is possible even to be very sad and very happy at once and the time that I was with Bridges, when my anxiety came to its height, was I believe the happiest fortnight of my life. My only strong wish is to be independent.

If you are really willing to make the application to the Master, well and good; but I do not want you to put yourself to pain. I have written a remonstrance to him.

To his Mother

Oxford Union Society. 20 Oct 1866

... I am to be received into the church tomorrow at Birming-
ham by Dr Newman. It is quite the best that any hopes should
be ended quickly, since otherwise they wd. only have made the
pain longer. Until then the comforts you take are delusive, after
it they will be real. And even for me it is almost a matter of
necessity, for every new letter I get breaks me down afresh, and
this cd. not go on. Your letters, wh. shew the utmost fondness,
suppose none on my part and the more you think me hard and
cold and that I repel and throw you off the more I am helpless
not to write as if [it] were true. In this way I have no relief. You
might believe that I suffer too. I am your very loving son

To Kate Hopkins (sister)

Stonyhurst, 25 April, 1871

My Dear Kate, – Many thanks for your letter, which I was
delighted to get. When it first came to hand I stood balancing in
my mind who it could be from, there was such a youngladyship
and grownupdom about the address, until I remembered that
you were older than you used to be. As for me, I will say no
more than this, that I have prescribed myself twenty four
hourglasses a day (which I take even during sleep, such is the
force of habit) and that even this does not stop the ravages of
time.

What month in the year it may be at Hampstead I will not be
sure; with us it is a whity-greeny January. What with east winds,
cloud, and rain I think it will never be spring. If we have a
bright afternoon the next morning it is winter again.

We were all vaccinated the other day. The next day a young
Portuguese came up to me and said 'Oh misther 'Opkins, do
you feel the cows in *yewer* arm?' I told him I felt the horns
coming through. I do I am sure. I cannot remember now
whether one ought to say the calf of the arm or the calf of the
leg. My shoulder is like a shoulder of beef. I dare not speak
above a whisper for fear of bellowing – there now, I was going

to say I am obliged to speak low for fear of lowing. I dream at night that I have only two of my legs in bed. I think there is a split coming in both my slippers. Yesterday I could not think why it was that I would wander about on a wet grass-plot: I see now. I chew my pen a great deal. The long and short of it is that my left forequarter is swollen and painful (I meant to have written arm but I cowld not). Besides the doctor has given us medicine, so that I am in a miserable way just now.

From cows I will turn to lambs. Our fields are full of them. When they were a little younger and nicer and sillier they wd. come gambolling up to one as if one were their mother. One of them sucked my finger and my companion took another up in his arms. The ewes then came up and walked round us making suspicious sheep's eyes at us, as people say. Now, when they are not sucking the breast (to do which they make such terrific butts and digs at the old dam that two of them together will sometimes lift her off her hind legs) they spend their time in bounding and spinning round as if they were tumblers. The same thing is I daresay to be seen (and earlier than this) about Hampstead: still as many of these lambs are ours I cannot pass it by and must tell you of it in black and white.

One thing made me very sad the day we were vaccinated. I was coming away: I left a number of my companions in a room in the infirmary – some had come from the doctor and others were waiting for their turn – all laughing and chatting. As I came down one of the galleries from the room I saw one of our young men standing there looking at a picture. I wondered why he stayed by himself and did not join the rest and then afterwards I remembered that he had had the smallpox and was deeply marked with it and all his good looks gone which he would have had and he did not want to face the others at that time when they were having their fun taking safe precautions against catching what it was too late for him to take any precautions against.

I want to know two things by the next person who writes – first some particulars from Arthur about the American yacht Sappho which seems to have had such great successes last year and next whether it is true that the cuckoo has come unusually early this year, as I heard said. It has not come here yet and I do not know if it will.

To Robert Bridges

Stonyhurst, Whalley, Lancashire. Aug 2, 1871
My dear Bridges, – Our holidays have begun, so I will write
again. I feel inclined to begin by asking whether you are
secretary to the International as you seem to mean me to think
nothing too bad for you but then I remember that you never
relished 'the intelligent artisan'. I must tell you I am always
thinking of the Communist future. The too intelligent artisan is
master of the situation I believe. Perhaps it is what everyone
believes, I do not see the papers or hear strangers often enough
to know. It is what Carlyle has long threatened and foretold.
But his writings are, as he might himself say, 'most inefficacious-
strenuous heaven-protestations, caterwaul, and Cassandra-wail-
ings'. He preaches obedience but I do not think he has done
much except to ridicule instead of strengthening the hands of
the powers that be. Some years ago when he published his
Shooting Niagara he did make some practical suggestions but
so vague that they should rather be called '*too* dubious moon-
stone-grindings and on the whole impracticable-practical unver-
acities'. However I am afraid some great revolution is not far
off. Horrible to say, in a manner I am a Communist. Their ideal
bating some things is nobler than that professed by any secular
statesman I know of (I must own I live in bat-light and shoot at
a venture). Besides it is just. – I do not mean the means of
getting to it are. But it is a dreadful thing for the greatest and
most necessary part of a very rich nation to live a hard life
without dignity, knowledge, comforts, delight, or hopes in the
midst of plenty – which they make. They profess that they do
not care what they wreck and burn, the old civilisation and
order must be destroyed. This is a dreadful look out but what
has the old civilisation done for them? As it at present stands in
England it is itself in great measure founded on wrecking. But
they got none of the spoils, they came in for nothing but harm
from it then and thereafter. England has grown hugely wealthy
but this wealth has not reached the working classes; I expect it
had made their condition worse. Besides this iniquitous order
the old civilisation embodies another order mostly old and what
is new in direct entail from the old, the old religion, learning,
law, art, etc and all the history that is preserved in standing
monuments. But as the working classes have not been educated

they know next to nothing of all this and cannot be expected to care if they destroy it. The more I look the more black and deservedly black the future looks, so I will write no more.

St Beuno's, St Asaph. Aug 21 1877

Dearest Bridges, – Your letter cannot amuse Father Provincial, for he is on the unfathering deeps outward bound to Jamaica: I shd. not think of telling you anything about his reverence's goings and comings if it were it not that I know that fact has been chronicled in the Catholic papers.

Enough that it amuses me, especially the story about Wooldridge and the Wagnerite, wh. is very good.

Your parody reassures me about your understanding the metre. Only remark, as you say that there is no conceivable licence I shd. not be able to justify, that with all my licences or rather laws, I am stricter than you and I might say anybody I know. With the exception of the *Bremen* stanza, which was, I think, the first written after 10 years' interval of silence, and before I had fixed my principles, my rhymes are rigidly good – to the ear – and such rhymes as *love* and *prove* I scout utterly. And my quantity is not like 'Fiftytwō Bĕdfŏrd Squāre', where *fifty* might pass but *Bĕdfŏrd* I should never admit. Not only so but Swinburne's dactyls and anapaests are halting to my ear: I never allow e.g. *I* or *my* (that is diphthongs, for *I = a + i* and *my = ma + i*) in the short or weak syllables of those feet, excepting before vowels, semi-vowels, or *r*, and rarely then, or when the measure becomes (what is the word?) molossic – thus: ᵕ–ᵕ|ᵕ–ᵕ|ᵕ–ᵕ, for then the first short is almost long. If you look again you will see. So that I may say my apparent licences are counterbalanced, and more, by my strictness. In fact all English verse, except Milton's, almost, offends me as 'licentious'. Remember this.

I do not of course claim to have invented *sprung rhythms* but only sprung rhythm; I mean that single lines and single instances of it are not uncommon in English and I have pointed them out in lecturing – e.g. 'why should this : desert be?' – which the editors have variously amended; 'There to meet : with Macbeth' or 'There to meet with Mac : beth'; Campbell has some throughout the '*Battle of the Baltic*' – 'and their fleet along the deep : proudly shone' – and '*Ye Mariners*' – 'as ye sweep : through the deep' etc; Moore has some which I cannot recall; there is one in

'*Grongar Hill*' and, not to speak of *Pom pom*, in Nursery Rhymes, Weather Saws, and Refrains they are very common – but what I do in the '*Deutschland*' etc is to enfranchise them as a regular and permanent principle of scansion.

There are no outriding feet in the '*Deutschland*'. An outriding foot is, by a sort of contradiction, a recognised extra-metrical effect; it is and it is not part of the metre; not part of it, not being counted, but part of it by producing a calculated effect which tells in the general success. But the long, e.g. seven-syllabled, feet of the 'Deutschland' are strictly metrical. Outriding feet belong to counterpointed verse, which supposes a well-known and unmistakable or unforgettable standard rhythm: the '*Deutschland*' is not counterpointed; counterpoint is excluded by sprung rhythm. But in some of my sonnets I have mingled the two systems: this is the most delicate and difficult business of all.

The choruses in '*Samson Agonistes*' are intermediate between counterpointed and sprung rhythm. In reality they are sprung, but Milton keeps up a fiction of counterpointing the heard rhythm (which is the same as the mounted rhythm) upon a standard rhythm which is never heard but only counted and therefore really does not exist. The want of a metrical notation and the fear of being thought to write mere rhythmic or (who knows what the critics might not have said?) even unrhythmic prose drove him to this. Such rhythm as French and Welsh poetry has is sprung, counterpointed upon a counted rhythm, but it differs from Milton's in being little calculated, not more perhaps than prose consciously written rhythmically, like orations for instance; it is in fact the *native rhythm* of the words used bodily imported into verse; whereas Milton's mounted rhythm is a real poetical rhythm, having its own laws and recurrence, but further embarrassed by having to count.

Why do I employ sprung rhythm at all? Because it is the nearest to the rhythm of prose, that is the native and natural rhythm of speech, the least forced, the most rhetorical and emphatic of all possible rhythms, combining, as it seems to me, opposite and, one wd. have thought, incompatible excellences, markedness of rhythm – that is rhythm's self – and naturalness of expression – for why, if it is forcible in prose to say 'lashed : rod', am I obliged to weaken this in verse, which ought to be stronger, not weaker, into 'láshed birch-ród' or something?

My verse is less to be read than heard, as I have told you before; it is oratorical, that is the rhythm is so. I think if you will study what I have here said you will be much more pleased with it and may I say? converted to it.

You ask may you call it 'presumptious jugglery'. No, but only for this reason, that *presumptious* is not English.

I cannot think of altering anything. Why shd. I? I do not write for the public. You are my public and I hope to convert you.

You say you wd. not for any money read my poem again. Nevertheless I beg you will. Besides money, you know, there is love. If it is obscure do not bother yourself with the meaning but pay attention to the best and most intelligible stanzas, as the two last of each part and the narrative of the wreck. If you had done this you wd. have liked it better and sent me some serviceable criticisms, but now your criticism is of no use, being only a protest memorialising me against my whole policy and proceedings.

I may add for your greater interest and edification that what refers to myself in the poem is all strictly and literally true and did all occur; nothing is added for poetical padding.

Stonyhurst College, Blackburn (or Whalley). May 13 1878
I enclose you my Eurydice, which the *Month* refused. It is my only copy. Write no bilgewater about it: I will presently tell you what that is and till then excuse the term. I must tell you I am sorry you never read the Deutschland again.

Granted that it needs study and is obscure, for indeed I was not over-desirous that the meaning of all should be quite clear, at least unmistakeable, you might, without the effort that to make it all out would seem to have required, have nevertheless read it so that lines and stanzas should be left in the memory and superficial impressions deepened, and have liked some without exhausting all. I am sure I have read and enjoyed pages of poetry that way. Why, sometimes one enjoys and admires the very lines one cannot understand, as for instance 'If it were done when 'tis done' sqq., which is all obscure and disputed, though how fine it is everybody sees and nobody disputes. And so of many more passages in Shakspere and others. Besides you would have got more weathered to the style and its features – not really odd. Now they say that vessels sailing from the port of

London will take (perhaps it should be / used once to take) Thames water for the voyage: it was foul and stunk at first as the ship worked but by degrees casting its filth was in a few days very pure and sweet and wholesomer and better than any water in the world. However that may be, it is true to my purpose. When a new thing, such as my ventures in the Deutschland are, is presented us our first criticisms are not our truest, best, most homefelt, or most lasting but what come easiest on the instant. They are barbarous and like what the ignorant and the ruck say. This was so with you. The Deutschland on her first run worked very much and unsettled you, thickening and clouding your mind with vulgar mudbottom and common sewage (I see that I am going it with the image) and just then unhappily you *drew off* your criticisms all stinking (a necessity now of the image) and bilgy, whereas if you had let your thoughts cast themselves they would have been clearer in themselves and more to my taste too. I did not heed them therefore, perceiving they were a first drawing-off. Same of the Eurydice – which being short and easy please read more than once.

Catholic Church, St Giles's, Oxford. Jan 19 1879.
When we met in London we never but once, and then only for a few minutes before parting, spoke on any important subject, but always on literature. This I regret very much. If it had ended in nothing or consisted in nothing but your letting me know your thoughts, that is some of them, it would have been a great advantage to me. And if now by pen and ink you choose to communicate anything I shall be very glad. I should also like to say one thing. You understand of course that I desire to see you a Catholic or, if not that, a Christian or, if not that, at least a believer in the true God (for you told me something of your views about the deity, which were not as they should be). Now you no doubt take for granted that your already being or your ever coming to be any of these things turns on the working of your own mind, influenced or uninfluenced by the minds and reasonings of others as the case may be, and on that only. You might on reflection expect me to suggest that it also might and ought to turn on something further, in fact on prayer, and that suggestion I believe I did once make. Still under the circumstances it is one which it is not altogether consistent to make or adopt. But I have another counsel open to no objection and yet

I think it will be unexpected. I lay great stress on it. It is to give alms. It may be either in money or in other shapes, the objects for which, with your knowledge of several hospitals, can never be wanting. I daresay indeed you do give alms, still I should say give more: I should be bold to say / give, up to the point of sensible inconvenience. *Fieri non potest ut idem sentiant qui aquam et qui vinum bibant*: the difference of mind and being between the man who finds comfort all round him unbroken unless by constraints which are none of his own seeking and the man who is pinched by his own charity is too great for forecasting, it must be felt: I do not say the difference between being pinched and being at one's ease, that one may easily conceive and most people know, willynilly, by experience, but the difference between paying heavily for a virtue and not paying at all. It changes the whole man, if anything can; not his mind only but the will and everything. For here something applies like the French bishop's question to his clergy whenever one of them came to tell him that he had intellectual difficulties and must withdraw from the exercise of his priestly functions – *What is her name?* in some such way a man may be far from belief in Christ or God or all he should believe, really and truly so; still the question to be asked would be (not *who is she?*, for that to him is neither here nor there) but *what good have you done?* I am not talking pure christianity, as you may remember, but also I am talking pure sense, as you must see. Now you may have done much good, but yet it may not be enough: I will say, it is not enough. I say this, you understand, on general grounds; I am not judging from particular knowledge, which I have no means to do and it would be very wrong and indiscreet.

Jan 23 – I feel it is very bold, as it is uncalled for, of me to have written the above. Still, if we care for fine verses how much more for a noble life!

St Giles's, Oxford. Jan 29 1879.

Dearest Bridges, – Morals and scansion not being in one keeping, we will treat them in separate letters and this one shall be given to the first named subject: the Preface will wait.

You so misunderstand my words (it seems they ought never to have been written: if they meant what you take them to mean I should never have written them) that I am surprised, and not only surprised but put out. For amongst other things I am made to appear a downright fool.

Can you suppose I should send Pater a discipline wrapped up in a sonnet 'with my best love'? Would it not be mad? And it is much the same to burst upon you with an exhortation to mortification (under the name of 'sensible inconvenience') – which mortification too would be in your case aimless. So that I should have the two marks of the foolish counsellor – to advise what is bad to follow and what will not be followed.

But I said that my recommendation was not open to objection. I did not mean as the doctrine of the Real Presence, which is true and yet may be objected against; I meant what could not be and was not objected against. Unless you object to doing good and call it 'miserable' to be generous. All the world, so to speak, approves of charity and of the corporal works of mercy, though all the world does not practise what it approves of. Even Walt Whitman nurses the sick.

I spoke, then, of alms – alms whether in money or in medical or other aid, such as you from the cases you come across at the hospital might know to be called for. And I said 'sensible inconvenience'; that is, for instance, you might know of someone needing and deserving an alms to give which would require you in prudence to buy no books till next quarter day or to make some equivalent sacrifice of time. These are sensible inconveniences. And to submit to them you cannot, nevertheless, call the reverse of sensible. But to 'derweesh' yourself (please see the Cairo letter in the last *Athenaeum* – or possibly *Academy*), that would *not* be sensible and that is what you took me to mean and that is what it would have been supremely senseless of me to mean.

I added something about it needing the experience to know what it feels like to have put oneself out for charity's sake (or one might say for truth's sake, for honour's sake, for chastity's sake, for any virtue's sake). I meant: everybody knows, or if not can guess, how it feels to be short of money, but everybody may not know, and if not cannot well guess, how it feels to be short of money for charity's sake, etc as above.

All the above appears to me to be put plainly. It reads to me in the blustering bread-and-cheese style. You will ask why I was not as plain at first. Because the blustering bread-and-cheese style is not suited for giving advice, though it may be for defending it. Besides I did not foresee the misunderstanding.

What I did fear, and it made me keep the letter back, was that you would be offended at my freedom, indeed that you would not answer at all. Whereas, for which I heartily thank you, you have answered three times.

It is true I also asked you to give me, if you liked, an account of your mind – which wd. call for, you say, self examination, and at all events one cannot say what one thinks without thinking. But this and the almsgiving are two independent things mentioned in one letter. No doubt I see a connection, but I do not need you to.

However if I must not only explain what I said but discover what I thought, my thoughts were these – Bridges is all wrong, and it will do no good to reason with him nor even to ask him to pray. Yet there is one thing remains – if he can be got to give alms, of which the Scripture says (I was talking to myself, not you) that they resist sins and that they redeem sins and that they will not let the soul go out into darkness, to give which Daniel advised Nabuchodonosor and Christ the Pharisees, the one a heathen, the other antrichristians, and the whole scripture in short so much recommends; of which moreover I have heard so-and-so, whose judgment I would take against any man's on such a point, say that the promise is absolute and that there is for every one a fixed sum at which he will ensure his salvation, though for those who have sinned greatly it may be a very high sum and very distressing to them to give – or keep giving: and not to have the faith is worse than to have sinned deeply, for it is like not being even in the running. Yet I will advise something and it must improve matters and will lead to good. So with hesitation and fear I wrote. And now I hope you see clearly, and when you reply will make your objections, if any, to the practice of almsgiving, not to the use of hairshirts. And I take leave to repeat and you cannot but see, that it is a noble thing and not a miserable something or other to give alms and help the needy and stint ourselves for the sake of the unhappy and deserving. Which I hope will take the bad taste away. And at any rate it is good of you only to misunderstand and be vexed and not to bridle and drop correspondence.

St Giles's, Oxford. Aug 14 1879.
By the by, inversions – As you say, I do avoid them, because they weaken and because they destroy the earnestness or in-

earnestness of the utterance. Nevertheless in prose I use them more than other people, because there they have great advantages of another sort. Now these advantages they should have in verse too, but they must not seem to be due to the verse: that is what is so enfeebling (for instance the finest of your sonnets to my mind has a line enfeebled by inversion plainly due to the verse, as I said once before. ''Tis joy the falling of her fold to view' – but how it should be mended I do not see). As it is, I feel my way to their use. However in a nearly finished piece I have a very bold one indeed. So also I cut myself off from the use of *ere, o'er, wellnigh, what time, say not* (for *do not say*), because, though dignified, they neither belong to nor ever cd. arise from, or be the elevation of, ordinary modern speech. For it seems to me that the poetical language of an age shd. be the current language heightened, to any degree heightened and unlike itself, but not (I mean normally: passing freaks and graces are another thing) an obsolete one. This is Shakespeare's and Milton's practice and the want of it will be fatal to Tennyson's Idylls and plays, to Swinburne, and perhaps to Morris.

St Joseph's, Bedford Leigh, near Manchester. Oct 22 1879
But now in general. And first to visit the workhouse. Oct. 25 – You seem to want to be told over again that you have genius and are a poet and your verses beautiful. You have been told so, not only by me but very spontaneously by Gosse, Marzials, and others; I was going to say Canon Dixon, only, as he was acknowledging your book, it was not so spontaneous as Gosse's case. You want perhaps to be told more in particular. I am not the best to tell you, being biassed by love, and yet I am too. I think then no one can admire beauty of the body more than I do, and it is of course a comfort to find beauty in a friend or a friend in beauty. But this kind of beauty is dangerous. Then comes the beauty of the mind, such as genius, and this is greater than the beauty of the body and not to call dangerous. And more beautiful than the beauty of the mind is beauty of character, the 'handsome heart'. Now every beauty is not a wit or genius nor has every wit or genius character. For though even bodily beauty, even the beauty of blooming health, is from the soul, in the sense, as we Aristotelian Catholics say, that the soul is the form of the body, yet the soul may have no other beauty, so to speak, than that which it expresses in the symmetry of the

body – barring those blurs in the case which wd. not be found in the die or the mould. This needs no illustration, as all know it. But what is more to be remarked is that in like manner the soul may have no further beauty than that which is seen in the mind, that there may be genius uninformed by character. I sometimes wonder at this in a man like Tennyson: his gift of utterance is truly golden, but go further home and you come to thoughts commonplace and wanting in nobility (it seems hard to say it but I think you know what I mean). In Burns there is generally recognised on the other hand a richness and beauty of manly character which lends worth to some of his smallest fragments, but there is a great want in his utterance; it is never really beautiful, he had no eye for pure beauty, he gets no nearer than the fresh picturesque expressed in fervent and flowing language (the most strictly beautiful lines of his that I remember are those in Tam o' Shanter: 'But pleasures are like poppies spread' sqq. and those are not). Between a fineness of nature which wd. put him in the first rank of writers and a poverty of language which puts him in the lowest rank of poets, he takes to my mind, when all is balanced and cast up, about a middle place. Now after all this introduction I come to what I want to say. If I were not your friend I shd. wish to be the friend of the man that wrote your poems. They shew the eye for pure beauty and they shew, my dearest, besides, the character which is much more rare and precious. Did time allow I shd. find a pleasure in dwelling on the instances, but I cannot now. Since I must not flatter or exaggerate I do not claim that you have such a volume of imagery as Tennyson, Swinburne, or Morris, though the feeling for beauty you have seems to me pure and exquisite; but in point of character, of sincerity or earnestness, of manliness, of tenderness, of humour, melancholy, human feeling, you have what they have not and seem scarcely to think worth having (about Morris I am not sure: his early poems had a deep feeling). I may then well say, like St Paul, *aemulor te Dei aemulatione*. To have a turn for sincerity has not made you sincere nor a turn for earnest / in earnest; Sterne had a turn for compassion, but he was not compassionate; a man may have natural courage, a turn for courage, and yet play the coward . . .

I hardly know what you allude to at Oxford, it is better that I should not. I used indeed to fear when I went up about this time last year that people wd. repeat against me what they remembered to my disadvantage. But if they did I never heard of it. I saw little of University men: when you were up it was an exceptional occasion, which brought me into contact with them. My work lay in St Clement's, at the Barracks, and so on. However it is perhaps well I am gone; I did not quite hit it off with Fr. Parkinson and was not happy. I was fond of my people, but they had not as a body the charming and cheering heartiness of these Lancashire Catholics, which is so deeply comforting; they were far from having it. And I believe they criticised what went on in our church a great deal too freely, which is d—d impertinence of the sheep towards the shepherd, and if it had come markedly before me I shd. have given them my mind.

      Rose Hall, Lydiate, Lancashire. Oct 26 1880.
Dearest Bridges, – I daresay you have long expected as you have long deserved an answer to your last kind and cheering – let us say, number or issue. But I never could write; time and spirits were wanting; one is so fagged, so harried and gallied up and down. And the drunkards go on drinking, the filthy, as the scripture says, are filthy still: human nature is so inveterate. Would that I had seen the last of it.

I must first speak of your book, the last one. I have not got it here, but can make some remarks without reference. What is the place described in *Indolence*? Is it Abingdon? There are two lines I am not satisfied with in it. One is 'And charmèd Indolence in languor lay'. This is open, I think, to the objection made to 'Let observation with extensive view Survey mankind from China to Peru', which meant: Let observation with extensive observation observe all that is observable. For one might as well have said 'And charmèd Languor indolently lay'; the two abstractions are not distinct enough, it seems they ought not to come together and one be personified and the other not, when you are on personifying you might turn out a lot, as Milton does in *L'Allegro* and *Il Penseroso*. And 'pleasurable' is a prosaic word, I think: can you not find something better? It is not a bad word, but it falls flatly. (This reminds me that 'test' is to my ear prosaic in 'Thou didst delight', but could scarcely be changed.) Otherwise the poem is very beautiful, very fine in execution and style. Style seems your great excellence, it is really classical. What fun if you were a classic! So few people have style, except individual style or manner – not Tennyson nor Swinburne nor Morris, not to name the scarecrow misbegotton Browning crew. Just think the blank verse these people have exuded, such as *Paracelsus, Aurora Leigh*, Baillie's or Bayley's *Festus* and so on. The Brownings are very fine too in their ghastly way.

That reminds me. First you misquote, then you insult me. I wrote 'Dog, he did give tongue!' not, what you call like Browning, 'Dog, did he give tongue?' It means, so to say, 'And by George, sir, when the young dog opened his mouth at last he did make a noise and no mistake'.

London Snow is a most beautiful and successful piece. It is charmingly fresh, I do not know what is like it. The rhythm, as I told you, is not quite perfect. That of the child-piece is worse and that piece is worse, indeed *it is* Browningese, if you like; as for instance 'To a world, do we think, that heals the disaster of this?' or something like that. You are certainly less at your ease in sprung rhythm. In the snow-piece this has not been a hindrance however, but perhaps has helped it, by making it more original in diction. Truth compels, and modesty does not forbid, me here to say that this volume has at least three real echoes (or echoes) of me: I do not wish them away, but they are there. The 'snow-mossed wonder' line recalls 'For though he is under' in the Deutschland, 'O look at the trees' the first line of the Starlight sonnet, and 'throned behind' again comes from the Deutschland. I fancy there is another I cannot now recall. O yes, it is in the Voice of Nature – 'Precipitate all o'er-rides and swerves nor abides' (is it?): this is in the Deutschland too, I cannot quote it but it ends with 'abides'. It is easy to see why this is: that is the longest piece of extant in sprung rhythm and could not help haunting your memory. I do not want them altered, and 'throned behind' having found its way into the midst of a lovely image would not like to be parted from its company.

Jan 26 1881. 8 Salisbury Street, Liverpool.
Dearest Bridges, – This is that promised letter, begun on St Agnes' Eve, an Eve as bitter as in Keats, but found fault with and begun again. The weather we are undergoing in Liverpool is not remarkable except for its severity, or so at least I wrote at first, but since then I have been into the country a little way and

seen deep frozen snowdrifts – yet these parts have felt the storm as little, I think, as any – and I am shortly going down to see the ice in the Mersey and the infinite flocks of seagulls of which I hear. But however I want you, as you are χιονουργός or χιονότεχνος, a snowwright or snowsmith or whatever one should say, to write me a graphic account of what London and its neighbourhood have been and looked like at this time.

Jan. 27 – Well, I went. The river was coated with dirty yellow ice from shore to shore; where the edges could be seen it seemed very thick; it was not smooth but many broken pieces framed or pasted together again; it was floating down stream with the ebb tide; it everywhere covered the water, but was not of a piece, being continually broken, ploughed up, by the plying of the steam ferryboats, which I believe sometimes can scarcely make their way across. The gulls were pampered; throngs of people were chucking them bread; they were not at all quick to sight it and when they did they dipped towards it with infinite lightness, touched the ice, and rose again, *but generally missed the bread*: they seem to fancy they cannot or ought not to rest on the ground. – However I hear the Thames is frozen and an ox roasted whole. Today there is a thaw, and the frostings, which have been a lovely fairyland on the publicans' windows, are vanished from the panes.

Manresa House, Roehampton, S.W. June 10 1882
Dearest Bridges, – It was a needless and tedious frenzy (no, the phrase is *not* like Flatman's 'serene and rapturous joys' to which poor Purcell had to drudge the music): another train came up on that train's tail, and indeed it was a dull duncery that overhung us both not to see that its being Ascot day ensured countless more trains and not fewer. There was a lovely and passionate scene (for about the space of the last trump) between me and a tallish gentleman (I daresay he was a cardsharper) in your carriage who was by way of being you; I smiled, I murmured with my lips at him, I waved farewells, but he would not give in, till with burning shame (though the whole thing was, as I say, like the duels of archangels) I saw suddenly what I was doing.

I wish our procession, since you were to see it, had been better: I find it is agreed it was heavy and dead. Now a Corpus Christi procession shd. be stately indeed, but it shd. be brisk and joyous. But I grieve more, I am vexed, that you had not a book to follow the words sung: the office is by St Thomas and contains all his hymns, I think. These hymns, though they have the imperfect rhetoric and weakness in idiom of all medieval Latin verse (except, say, the Dies Irae: I do not mean weakness in classical idiom – that does not matter – but want of feeling for or command of *any* idiom), are nevertheless remarkable works of genius and would have given meaning to the whole, even to the music, much more to the rite.

It is long since such things had any significance for you. But what is strange and unpleasant is that you sometimes speak as if they had in reality none for me and you were only waiting with a certain disgust till I too should be disgusted with myself enough to throw off the mask. You said something of the sort walking on the Cowley Road when we were last at Oxford together – in '79 it must have been. Yet I can hardly think you do not think I am in earnest. And let me say, to take no higher ground, that without earnestness there is nothing sound or beautiful in character and that a cynical vein much indulged coarsens everything in us. Not that you do overindulge this vein in other matters: why then does it bulk out in that diseased and varicose way in this?

Stonyhurst College, Blackburn. Sept 26 1882.
I wish I could show you this place. It is upon my word worth seeing. The new college, though there is no real beauty in the design, is nevertheless imposing and the furniture and fittings are a joy to see. There is always a stirring scene, contractors, buildings, masons, bricklayers, carpenters, stonecutters and carvers, all on the spot; a traction engine twice a day fetches stone from a quarry on the fells; engines of all sorts send their gross and foulsmelling smoke all over us; cranes keep swinging; and so on. There are acres of flat roof which, when the air is not thick, as unhappily it mostly is, commands a noble view of this Lancashire landscape, Pendle Hill, Ribblesdale, the fells, and all round, bleakish but solemn and beautiful. There is a garden with a bowling green, walled in by massive yew hedges, a bowered yew-walk, two real Queen Ann summerhouses, observatories under government, orchards, vineries, green-houses, workshops, a plungebath, fivescourts, a mill, a farm, a fine cricketfield besides a huge playground; then the old man-

sion, ponds, towers, quadrangles, fine cielings, chapels, a church, a fine library, museums, MSS illuminated and otherwise, coins, works of art; then two other dependent establishment[s], one a furlong, the other ¾ a mile off; the river Hodder with lovely fairyland views, especially at the bathingplace, the Ribble too, the Calder, Whalley with an abbey, Clitheroe with a castle, Ribchester with a strange old chapel and Roman remains; schoolboys and animation, philosophers and foppery (not to be taken too seriously) a jackdaw, a rookery, goldfish, a clough with waterfalls, fishing, grouse, an anemometer, a sunshine gauge, a sundial, an icosihedron, statuary, magnetic instruments, a laboratory, gymnasium, ambulacrum, studio, fine engravings, Arundel chromos, Lancashire talked with *naïveté* on the premises (Hoo said this and hoo did that) – and, what caps all, if I were shewing it you, as I hope to do (I have to shew it too often: it takes from an hour and a half to three hours: I do it with more pride than pleasure) you could not make me wretched now by either stealing or buying fruit.

Stonyhurst College, Blackburn. Oct 18 1882.
Dearest Bridges, – I have read of Whitman's (1) 'Pete' in the library at Bedford Square (and perhaps something else; if so I forget), which you pointed out; (2) two pieces in the *Athenaeum* or *Academy*, one on the Man-of-War Bird, the other beginning 'Spirit that formed this scene'; (3) short extracts in a review by Saintsbury in the *Academy*: this is all I remember. I cannot have read more than half a dozen pieces at most.

This, though very little, is quite enough to give a strong impression of his marked and original manner and way of thought and in particular of his rhythm. It might be even enough, I shall not deny, to originate or, much more, influence another's style: they say the French trace their whole modern school of landscape to a single piece of Constable's exhibited at the Salon early this century.

The question then is only about the fact. But first I may as well say what I should not otherwise have said, that I always knew in my heart Walt Whitman's mind to be more like my own than any other man's living. As he is a very great scoundrel this is not a pleasant confession. And this also makes me the more desirous to read him and the more determined that I will not.

Nevertheless I believe that you are quite mistaken about this piece [poem 72] and that on second thoughts you will find the fancied resemblance diminish and the imitation disappear.

And first of the rhythm. Of course I saw that there was to the eye something in my long lines like his, that the one would remind people of the other. And both are in irregular rhythms. There the likeness ends. The pieces of his I read were mostly in an irregular rhythmic prose: that is what they are thought to be meant for and what they seemed to me to be. Here is a fragment of a line I remember: 'or a handkerchief designedly dropped'. This is in a dactylic rhythm – or let us say anapaestic; for it is great convenience in English to assume that the stress is always at the end of the foot; the consequence of which assumption is that in ordinary verse there are only two English feet possible, the iamb and the anapaest, and even in my regular sprung rhythm only one additional, the fourth paeon: for convenience' sake assuming this, then the above fragment is

$$\overset{1\ \ 2\ \ \ 3}{}\quad\overset{1\ \ \ 2\ \ \ \ 3}{}\quad\overset{1\ \ 2\ 3}{}\quad\overset{1\ \ 2\ \ \ \ 3}{}$$

anapaestic – 'or a hánd | kerchief . . . | . desígn | edly drópped' – and there is a break down, a designed break of rhythm, after 'handkerchief', done no doubt that the line may not become downright verse, as it would be if he had said 'or a handkerchief purposely dropped'. Now you can of course say that he meant

$$\overset{1\ \ 2\ \ \ 3}{}\quad\overset{1\ \ 2}{}$$

pure verse and that the foot is a paeon – 'or a hánd | kerchief

$$\overset{3\quad\ 4}{}\quad\overset{1\ 2}{}\quad\overset{3}{}$$

desígn | edly drópped'; or that he means, without fuss, what I should achieve by looping the syllable *de* and calling that foot an outriding foot – for the result might be attained either way. Here then I must make the answer which will apply here and to all like cases and to the examples which may be found up and down the poets of the use of sprung rhythm – *if they could have done it they would*: sprung rhythm, once you hear it, is so eminently natural a thing and so effective a thing that if they had known of it they would have used it. Many people, as we say, have been 'burning', but they all missed it; they took it up and mislaid it again. So far as I know – I am enquiring and presently I shall be able to speak more decidedly – it existed in full force in Anglo saxon verse and in great beauty; in a degraded and doggrel shape in *Piers Ploughman* (I am reading that famous poem and am coming to the conclusion that it is not worth reading); Green was the last who employed it at all consciously and he never continuously; then it disappeared – for one cadence in it here and there is not sprung rhythm and one swallow does not make a spring. (I put aside Milton's case, for it is altogether singular.) In a matter like this a thing does not exist, is not *done* unless it is wittingly and willingly done; to recognise the form you are employing and to mean it is everything. To apply this: there is (I suppose, but you will know) no sign that Whitman means to use paeons or outriding feet where these breaks in rhythm occur; it seems to me a mere extravagance to think he means people to understand of themselves what they are slow to understand even when marked or pointed out. If he does not mean it then he does not do it; or in short what he means to write – and writes – is rhythmic prose and that only. And after all, you probably grant this.

Good. Now prose rhythm in English is always one of two things (allowing my convention about scanning upwards or from slack to stress and not from stress to slack) – either iambic or anapaestic. You may make a third measure (let us call it) by intermixing them. One of these three simple measures then, all iambic or all anapaestic or mingled iambic and anapaestic, is what he in every case means to write. He dreams of no other and he *means* a rugged or, as he calls it in that very piece 'Spirit that formed this scene' (which is very instructive and should be read on this very subject), a 'savage' art and rhythm.

Extremes meet, and (I must for truth's sake say what sounds pride) this savagery of his art, this rhythm in its last ruggedness and decomposition into common prose, comes near the last elaboration of mine. For that piece of mine is very highly wrought. The long lines are not rhythm run to seed: everything is weighed and timed in them. Wait till they have taken hold of your ear and you will find it so. No, but what it *is* like is the rhythm of Greek tragic choruses or of Pindar: which is pure sprung rhythm. And that has the same changes of cadence from point to point as this piece. If you want to try it, read one till you have settled the true places of the stress, mark these, then read it aloud, and you will see. Without this these choruses are prose bewitched; with it they are sprung rhythm like that piece of mine.

Besides, why did you not say *Binsey Poplars* was like Whitman? The present piece is in the same kind and vein, but developed, an advance. The lines and the stanzas (of which there are two in each poem and having much the same relation to one another) are both longer, but the two pieces are greatly alike: just look. If so how is this a being untrue to myself? I am sure it is no such thing.

The above remarks are not meant to run down Whitman. His 'savage' style has advantages, and he has chosen it; he says so. But you cannot eat your cake, and keep it: he eats his off-hand, I keep mine. It makes a very great difference. Neither do I deny all resemblance. In particular I noticed in 'Spirit that formed this scene' a preference for the alexandrine. I have the same preference: I came to it by degrees, I did not take it from him.

About diction the matter does not allow me so clearly to point out my independence as about rhythm. I cannot think that the present piece owes anything to him. I hope not, here especially, for it is not even spoken in my own person but in that of St Winefred's maidens. It ought to sound like the thoughts of a good but lively girl and not at all like – not at all like Walt Whitman. But perhaps your mind may have changed by this.

Stonyhurst, Blackburn. Dec 1 1882.

I agree with you that English compounds do not seem real single words or properly unified till by some change in form or spelling or slur in pronunciation their construction is disguised. This seems in English a point craved for and insisted on, that words shall be single and specific marks for things, whether self-significant or not; and it is noticeable how unmeaning our topographical names are or soon become, while those in Celtic languages are so transparent – not that their unmeaningness is any virtue, rather a vice; still it shews the tendency. But your instances are not fair: if icebergs had been common in British seas a name would have been found for them either not compounded at all or if compound as good as *iceberg* is or better and certainly a great deal better than *icelump*, which is caricature. *Thimble* is singler than *thumbstall* (I do not believe it comes from that but from *thumb-le*), but it is a meaner word. The absurdity of 'finger hut' is not in its being a compound but in its impropriety, in the particular trope employed. *Fingerhood* or indeed *fingerstall* seem to me to be well enough. *Potato* is certainly one of the ugliest and most laughable words in the language and cannot well be used in verse, whereas *earthapple* is stately: *potato* has one virtue only, the being specific.

Stonyhurst College, Blackburn. Feb 3 1883.

I quite understand what you mean about gentlemen and 'damfools'; it is a very striking thing and I could say much on the subject. I shall not say that much, but I say this: if a gentleman feels that to be what we call a gentleman is a thing essentially higher than without being a gentleman to be ever so great an artist or thinker or if, to put it another way, an artist or thinker feels that were he to become in those ways ever so great he wd. still essentially be lower than a gentleman that was no artist and no thinker – and yet to be a gentleman is but on the brim of morals and rather a thing of manners than of morals properly – then how much more must art and philosophy and manners and breeding and everything else in the world be below the least degree of true virtue. This is that chastity of mind which seems to lie at the very heart and be the parent of all other good, the seeing at once what is best, the holding to that, and the not allowing anything else whatever to be even heard pleading to the contrary. Christ's life and character are such as appeal to all the world's admiration, but there is one insight St Paul gives us of it which is very secret and seems to me more touching and constraining than everything else is: This mind he says, was in Christ Jesus – he means as man: being in the form of God – that is, finding, as in the first instant of his incarnation he did, his human nature informed by the godhead – he thought it nevertheless no snatching-matter for him to be equal with God, but annihilated himself, taking the form of servant; that is, he could not but see what he was, God, but he would see it as if he did not see it, and be it as if he were not and instead of snatching at once at what all the time was his, or was himself, he emptied or exhausted himself so far that was possible, of godhead and behaved only as God's slave, as his creature, as man, which also he was, and then being in the guise of man humbled himself to death, the death of the cross. It is this holding of himself back, and not snatching at the truest and highest good, the good that was his right, nay his possession from a past eternity in his other nature, his own being and self, which seems to me the root of all his holiness and the imitation of this the root of all moral good in other men. I agree then, and vehemently, that a gentleman, if there is such a thing on earth, is in the position to despise the poet, were he Dante or Shakespere, and the painter, were he Angelo or Apelles, for anything in him that shewed him *not* to be a gentleman. He is in the position to do it, I say, but if he is a gentleman perhaps this is what he will not do. Which leads me to another remark.

The quality of a gentleman is so very fine a thing that it seems to me one should not be at all hasty in concluding that one possesses it. People assume that they have it, take it quite for granted, and claim the acknowledgement from others: now I should say that this also is 'no snatching-matter'. And the more a man feels what it means and is – and to feel this is certainly some part of it – the more backward he will be to think he can have realised in himself anything so perfect. It is true, there is nothing like the truth and 'the good that does itself not know scarce is'; so the perfect gentleman will know that he is the perfect gentleman. But few can be in the position to know this and, being imperfect gentlemen, it will perhaps be a point of their gentlemanliness, for a gentleman is modest, to feel that they are not perfect gentlemen.

By the by if the English race had done nothing else, yet if they left the world the notion of a gentleman, they would have done a great service to mankind.

As a fact poets and men of art are, I am sorry to say, by no means necessarily or commonly gentlemen. For gentlemen do not pander to lust or other basenesses nor, as you say, give themselves airs and affectations nor do other things to be found in modern works. And this adds a charm to everything Canon Dixon writes, that you feel he is a gentleman and thinks like one. But now I have prosed my prose and long enough.

University College, St Stephen's Green, Dublin. Sept 1 1885.
I shall shortly have some sonnets to send you, five or more. Four of these came like inspirations unbidden and against my will. And in the life I lead now, which is one of a continually jaded and harassed mind, if in any leisure I try to do anything I make no way – nor with my work, alas! but so it must be.

Mr Patmore lent me Barnes' poems – 3 volumes, not all, for indeed he is prolific. I hold your contemptuous opinion an unhappy mistake: he is a perfect artist and of a most spontaneous inspiration; it is as if Dorset life and Dorset landscape had taken flesh and tongue in the man. I feel the defect or limitation or whatever we are to call it that offended you: he lacks fire; but who is perfect all round? If one defect is fatal what writer could we read?

An old question of yours I have hitherto neglected to answer, am I thinking of writing on metre? I suppose thinking too much and doing too little. I do greatly desire to treat that subject; might perhaps get something together this year; but I can scarcely believe that on that or on anything else anything of mine will ever see the light – of publicity nor even of day. For it is widely true, the fine pleasure is not to do a thing but to feel that you could and the mortification that goes to the heart is to feel it is the power that fails you: *qui occidere nolunt Posse volunt*; it is the refusal of a thing that we like to have. So with me, if I could but get on, if I could but produce work I should not mind its being buried, silenced, and going no further; but it kills me to be time's eunuch and never to beget. After all I do not despair, things might change, anything may be; only there is no great appearance of it. Now because I have had a holiday though not strong I have some buoyancy; soon I am afraid I shall be ground down to a state like this last spring's and summer's, when my spirits were so crushed that madness seemed to be making approaches – and nobody was to blame, except myself partly for not managing myself better and contriving a change.

University College, St Stephen's Green, Dublin. June 1 '86
This leads me to say that a kind of touchstone of the highest or most living art is seriousness; not gravity but the being in earnest with your subject – reality. It seems to me that some of the greatest and most famous works are not taken in earnest enough, are farce (where you ask the spectator to grant you something not only conventional but monstrous). I have this feeling about *Faust* and even about the Divine Comedy, whereas *Paradise Lost* is most seriously taken. It is the weakness of the whole Roman literature.

University College, Stephen's Green, Dublin. Oct 13 1886
By the bye, I say it deliberately and before God, I would have you and Canon Dixon and all true poets remember that fame, the being known, though in itself one of the most dangerous things to a man, is nevertheless the true and appointed air,

element, and setting of genius and its works. What are works of art for? to educate, to be standards. Education is meant for the many, standards are for public use. To produce then is of little use unless what we produce is known, if known widely known, the wider known the better, for it is by being known it works, it influences, it does its duty, it does good. We must then try to be known, aim at it, take means to it. And this without puffing in the process or pride in the success. But still. Besides, we are Englishmen. A great work by an Englishman is like a great battle won by England. It is an unfading bay tree. It will even be admired by and praised by and do good to those who hate England (as England is most perilously hated), who do not wish even to be benefited by her. It is then even a patriotic duty τῇ ποιήσει ἐνεργεῖν and to secure the fame and permanence of the work. Art and its fame do not really matter, spiritually they are nothing, virtue is the only good; but it is only by bringing in the infinite that to a just judgment they can be made to look infinitesimal or small or less than vastly great; and in this ordinary view of them I apply to them, and it is the true rule for dealing with them, what Christ our Lord said of virtue, Let your light shine before men that they may see your good works (say, of art) and glorify yr. Father in heaven (that is, acknowledge that they have an absolute excellence in them and are steps in a scale of infinite and inexhaustible excellence).

University College, St Stephen's Green, Dublin. July 30 1887
On Irish politics I had something to say, but there is little time. 'It only needs the will,' you say: it is an unwise word. It is true, it (that is, to govern Ireland) does 'only need the will'; but Douglas Jerrold's joke is in place, about Wordsworth (or whoever it was) that could write plays as good as Shakespeare's 'if he had the mind', and 'only needed the mind'. It is a just reproach to any man not to do what lies in his own power and he could do if he would: to such a man you may well say that the task in question only needs the will. But where a decision does *not* depend on us and we cannot even influence it, then it is only wisdom to recognise the facts – the will or want of will in those, not us, who have control of the question; and that is the case now. The will of the nation is divided and distracted. Its judgment is uninformed and misinformed, divided and distracted, and its action must be corresponding to its knowledge.

It has always been the fault of the mass of Englishman to know and care nothing about Ireland, to let be what would there (which, as it happened, was persecution, avarice, and oppression): and now, as fast as these people wake up and hear what wrong England has done (and has long ceased doing) to Ireland, they, like that woman in Mark Twain, 'burst into tears and rushing upstairs send a pink silk parasol and a box of hairpins to the seat of war'. If you in your limited but appreciable sphere of influence can bring people to a just mind and a proper resolution about Ireland (as you did, you told me, take part in your local elections) do so: you will then be contributing to that will which 'only is wanting'; but do not reproach me, who on this matter have perhaps both more knowledge and more will than most men. If however you think you could do but little and are unwilling even to do that (for I suppose while you are writing plays you cannot be canvassing electors), then recognise with me that with an unwavering will, or at least a flood of passion, on one, the Irish, side and a wavering one or indifference on the other, the English, and the Grand Old Mischiefmaker loose, like the Devil, for a little while and meddling and marring all the fiercer for his hurry, Home Rule is in fact likely to come and even, in spite of the crime, slander, and folly with which its advance is attended, may perhaps in itself be a measure of a sort of equity and, considering that worse might be, of a kind of prudence.

To Coventry Patmore

Milltown Park, Milltown, Dublin May 6 1888
Since I last wrote I have reread Keats a little and the force of your criticism on him has struck me more than it did. It is impossible not to feel with weariness how his verse is at every turn abandoning itself to an unmanly and enervating luxury. It appears too that he said something like 'O for a life of impressions instead of thoughts!' It was, I suppose, the life he tried to lead. The impressions are not likely to have been all innocent and they soon ceased in death. His contemporaries, as Wordsworth, Byron, Shelley, and even Leigh Hunt, right or

wrong, still concerned themselves with great causes, as liberty and religion; but he lived in mythology and fairyland the life of a dreamer. Nevertheless I feel and see in him the beginnings of something opposite to this, of an interest in higher things and of powerful and active thought. On this point you shd. if possible read what Matthew Arnold wrote. His mind had, as it seems to me, the distinctively masculine powers in abundance, his character the manly virtues, but while he gave himself up to dreaming and self indulgence of course they were in abeyance. Nor do I mean that he wd. have turned to a life of virtue – only God can know that – , but that this genius wd. have taken to an austerer utterance in art. Reason, thought, what he did not want to live by, would have asserted itself presently and perhaps have been as much more powerful than that of his contemporaries as his sensibility or impressionableness, by which he did want to live, was keener and richer than theirs. His defects were due to youth – the self indulgence of his youth; its ill-education; and also, as it seems to me, to its breadth and pregnancy, which, by virtue of a fine judgment already able to restrain but unable to direct, kept him from flinging himself blindly on the specious Liberal stuff that crazed Shelley and indeed, in their youth, Wordsworth and Coleridge. His mind played over life as a whole, so far as he a boy, without (seemingly) a dramatic but still with a deeply observant turn and also without any noble motive, felt at first hand, impelling him to look below its surface, cd. at that time see it. He was, in my opinion, made to be a thinker, a critic, as much as a singer or artist of words. This can be seen in certain reflective passages, as the opening to *Endymion* and others in his poems. These passages are the thoughts of a mind very ill instructed and in opposition; keenly sensible of wrongness in things established but unprovided with the principles to correct that by. Both his principles of art and his practice were in many things vicious, but he was correcting them, even eagerly; for *Lamia* one of his last works shews a deliberate change in manner from the style of *Endymion* and in fact goes too far in change and sacrifices things that had better have been kept. Of construction he knew nothing to the last: in this same *Lamia* he has a long introduction about Mercury, who is only brought in to disenchant Lamia and ought not to have been employed or else ought to be employed again. The story has a moral element or interest; Keats was aware of this and touches on it at times, but could make nothing of it; in fact the situation at the end is that the sage Apollonius does more harm than the witch herself had done – kills the hero; and Keats does not see that this implies one of two things, either some lesson of the terrible malice of evil which when it is checked drags down innocence in its own ruin or else the exposure of Pharisaic pretence in the wouldbe moralist. But then if I could have said this to Keats I feel sure he wd. have seen it. In due time he wd. have seen these things himself. Even when he is misconstructing one can remark certain instinctive turns of construction in his style, shewing his latent power – for instance the way the vision is introduced in *Isabella*. Far too much now of Keats.

Devotional Writings

from a sermon at Bedford Leigh, 23 November 1879
[on Luke 2:33]

Our Lord Jesus Christ, my brethren, is our hero, a hero all the world wants. You know how books of tales are written, that put one man before the reader and shew him off handsome for the most part and brave and call him My Hero or Our Hero. Often mothers make a hero of a son; girls of a sweetheart and good wives of a husband. Soldiers make a hero of a great general, a party of its leader, a nation of any great man that brings it glory, whether king, warrior, statesman, thinker, poet, or whatever it shall be. But Christ, he is the hero. He too is the hero of a book or books, of the divine Gospels. He is a warrior and a conqueror; of whom it is written he went forth conquering and to conquer. He is a king, Jesus of Nazareth king of the Jews, though when he came to his own kingdom his own did not receive him, and now, his people having cast him off, we Gentiles are his inheritance. He is a statesman, that drew up the New Testament in his blood and founded the Roman Catholic Church that cannot fail. He is a thinker, that taught us divine mysteries. He is an orator and poet, as in his eloquent words and parables appears. He is all the world's hero, the desire of nations. But besides he is the hero of single souls; his mother's hero, not out of motherly foolish fondness but because he was, as the angel told her, great and the son of the Most High and all that he did and said and was done and said about him she laid up in her heart. He is the true-love and the bridegroom of men's souls: the virgins follow him whithersoever he goes; the martyrs follow him through a sea of blood, through great tribulation; all his servants take up their cross and follow him. And those even that do not follow him, yet they look wistfully after him, own him a hero, and wish they dared answer to his call. Children as soon as they can understand ought to be told about him, that they may make him the hero of their young hearts. But there are Catholic parents that shamefully neglect their duty: the grown children of Catholics are found that scarcely know or do not know his name. Will such parents say they left instruction to the priest or the schoolmaster? Why, if they sent them very early to the school they might make that excuse, but when they do not what will they say then? It is at the father's or the mother's mouth first the little one should learn. But the parents may be gossiping or drinking and the children have not heard of their lord and saviour. Those of you, my brethren, who are young and yet unmarried resolve that when you marry, if God should bless you with children, this shall not be but that you will have more pity, will have pity upon your own.

There met in Jesus Christ all things that can make man lovely and loveable. In his body he was most beautiful. This is known first by the tradition in the Church that it was so and by holy writers agreeing to suit those words to him / Thou art beautiful in mould above the sons of men: we have even accounts of him written in early times. They tell us that he was moderately tall, well built and tender in frame, his features straight and beautiful, his hair inclining to auburn, parted in the midst, curling and clustering about the ears and neck as the leaves of a filbert, so they speak, upon the nut. He wore also a forked beard and this as well as the locks upon his head were never touched by razor or shears; neither, his health being perfect, could a hair ever fall to the ground. The account I have been quoting (it is from memory, for I cannot now lay my hand upon it) we do not indeed for certain know to be correct, but it has been current in the Church and many generations have drawn our Lord accordingly either in their own minds or in his images. Another proof of his beauty may be drawn from the words *proficiebat sapientia et aetate et gratia apud Deum et homines* (Luc. ii 52) / he went forward in wisdom and bodily frame and favour with God and men; that is / he pleased both God and men daily more and more by his growth of mind and body. But he could not have pleased by growth of body unless the body was strong, healthy, and beautiful that grew. But the best proof of all is this, that his body was the special work of the Holy Ghost. He was not born in nature's course, no man was his father; had he been born as others are he must have inherited some defect of figure or of constitution, from which no man born as fallen men are born is wholly free unless God interfere to keep him so. But his body was framed directly from heaven by the power of the Holy Ghost, of whom it would be unworthy to leave any the least botch or failing in his work. So the first Adam was moulded by God himself and Eve built up by God too out of Adam's rib and they could not but be pieces of both, of faultless workmanship: the same then and much more must Christ have been. His constitution too was tempered perfectly, he had neither disease nor the seeds of any: weariness he felt when he was wearied, hunger when he fasted, thirst when he had long gone without drink, but to the touch of sickness he was a stranger. I leave it to you, brethren, then to picture him, in whom the fulness of the godhead dwelt bodily, in his bearing how majestic, how strong and yet how lovely and lissome in his limbs, in his look how earnest, grave but kind. In his Passion all this strength was spent, this lissomness crippled, this beauty wrecked, this majesty beaten down. But now it is more than all restored, and for myself I make no secret I look forward with eager desire to seeing the matchless beauty of Christ's body in the heavenly light.

from a sermon at St Joseph's, Bedford, 30 November 1879
[on Romans 13: 11–14]

Now, brethren, as the time of Christ's second coming is uncertain so is the time of our death. Both are certain to come, both are uncertain when. But one thing may be said of both and the apostle says it: The night has got on, the day is nearer. This is, my brethren, always true and always getting truer. Mark these two things: every minute true, for it is at any minute true to say our life has got some way on, our death made some approach, or again that the world has gone on some time since Christ's first coming and made some approach to his second; and also every minute truer for every minute we and the world are older, every minute our death and the world's end are nearer than before. For life and time are always losing, always spending, always running down and running out, therefore every hour that strikes is a warning of our end and the world's end, for both these things are an hour nearer than before. But there is a difference between our death and the world's end: the world's end though every generation, one after another, is warned of it, yet one only will be overtaken by it, the rest will have passed away before; but death comes to every one and none escapes.

Therefore God has given us more warnings of death: age is a warning, sickness is a warning, and the deaths of others that go before us are a great warning. For the last day none have seen, but almost all men have seen death.

However, whether for the world's end or death, the apostle's warning is the same, to walk honestly, that is honourably, becomingly, wellbehavedly, as in the day, not etc. And Christ's warning is like it (Luke xxi 34): But take heed to yourselves that your hearts be not loaded with overeating and drunkenness and cares of this life, and that day come upon you unawares. And these things that they warn us of, they abound; who needs the warning more than we? for the evils abound. Now more than ever is there riotous company, drunkenness, lewdness, strife, brawling, even bloodshed. To speak against all these things is too much. But look, brethren, at the order of them. First comes rioting or revelry, unruly company: here is the beginning of evil, bad company. Bad company seem hearty friends, goodnatured companions and such as a man should have: must not a man have his friend, his companion, unbend from his work at times, see company and life? Must he sit mum? must he mope at home? But, brethren, look at these things nearer. A friend is a friend, he loves you, he thinks of you and not only of his own pleasure. A rout of drinking companions do not love one another, they are selfish, they do not love their own, how can you think they care for strangers? Their own children may be hungry, their mothers or their wives in tears, their homes desolate and they are so good as to spend their time, their money, and their health with you. One of two things: you treat them or they you. If you treat them you like a fool spend your money on the worthless; if they treat you often you are eating their children's bread, you are draining the blood of their little ones. There is no friendship here, no love; there is no love, I say, where nothing comes in but selfishness.

An unruly company leads to drunkenness. Though many and many a tongue is now telling of it what tongue *can* tell the evils of drunkenness? – Drunkenness is shameful, it makes the man a beast; it drowns noble reason, their eyes swim, they hiccup in their talk, they gabble and blur their words, they stagger and fall and deal themselves dishonourable wounds, their faces grow blotched and bloated, scorpions are in their mind, they see devils and frightful sights. A little drunkenness is sad, a thing pitiful to see, and drunkenness confirmed and incurable is a world of woe. It defiles and dishonours the fresh blooming roses of youth, the strength of manhood, the grey hairs of age. It corrupts the children yet unborn, it gives convulsions to the poor sucking child. It is ugly in man, but in woman it is hideous beyond what words can say. And the world is laid waste with it.

It lays waste a home. There is no peace, there is no reverence or honour. The children are scandalised and taught to sin. Nay, it breaks home quite up, breaks the bond that God fastens, what he has joined it puts asunder, wife runs from drunken husband or husband from dunken wife.

It wastes, it spends, it brings on poverty. Times may be good, wages may abound, and yet in the house is seen want and slovenly disorder, for gold and silver and clothes and furniture and all are gone one way, down the belly. Or times may be had and then surely there is nothing to spend on drink. But there is: feet may go bare and hearth be cold but the fire in the throat must be quenched with liquor or rather with liquor fanned to flame. And not only must the body want but the soul too is to fast and lose its food: the family cannot go to mass, obey the Church's commandment, worship God on his holy day in his holy place and be present at the great sacrifice; though it should cost not a penny they cannot do it, because the clothes are pawned.

from a sermon at St Francis Xavier's, Liverpool, 11 January 1880
[on God's Kingdom: 'Thy Kingdom come']

God is our king. *The lord is a great king*, says the Scripture, and it tells us of what, of sea and land, the heights of the mountains and all the bounds of the earth; it calls them his and says / *But we are his people and the sheep of his pasture: come let us adore him.* So then God is a king and men are his people, his subjects, the nation he rules over. But how does God come to be our king? is it because he created us? – The same Psalm seems to say so, for it says: The sea is his *and he made it* and *his hands founded the dry land* / and again: Let us bewail before *the Lord who made us*, for he is the Lord our God (Ps. xciv.), as if to have created anything were to be king over it.

But no. God is our king, but creating us did not make him so. God is our owner and master, but creating us did not make him so. God is our father, but creating us did not make him so. This may sound surprising, yet I must repeat it. We are God's subjects; and again we are God's things, his goods and chattels, his property, his slaves; and lastly we are God's children; but yet his creating us did not of itself make us any of these three things. Most certainly it gave him a title to them all: there was a crown for him if he chose to wear it; there was an estate for him if he chose to own it; there were children for him if he chose to adopt them. But it did not follow that he would. The crowns of the earth sometimes go begging among men and do not always find a wearer; there are pieces of property which are no man's and may be owned, *or disowned*, by the first finder; and as for children, who would dream that men are either bound to adopt or always do adopt children they have never begotten: now God created us by nature, he did not beget us; by nature then we are his creatures, not his sons, nor yet his property nor yet his subjects. Nay God has not only created us but every moment preserves us, giving us ever fresh and fresh being, whereas an earthly father begets but once upon a time: yet this does not make God a father; again God holds us and all things with a faster hold not only than man can hold his goods, for how can the wealthy landowner grasp his acres in the palm of his hand? even than the miser grips his gold: yet this does not make God an owner; once more, whereas it is sometimes said of constitutional sovereigns, that the king or queen reigns but does not govern, meaning that he of his dignity gives a name and marks a period but does not manage the state by his own mastery, God on the contrary must govern, must direct and master the world, or it would fly to pieces: yet this governing is not reigning, as reigning it not governing, and does not make God a king. A fresh act of his will is needed: to make us sons he must adopt us; to make us of his property he must own us; to make us his subjects he must ascend our throne. He has the right and title but he must employ it, he must make the claim; if he should not then *we* cannot claim *him: we* cannot father ourselves on God to be his children; *we* cannot bestow ourselves on God to be his property; *we* cannot force a crown on God to be his subjects. For certainly we have not the power, and we have not the right either.

Nevertheless *now* we *are* God's subjects and he our king; we are his property and he our master and owner; we are his sons and he our father. Was this always so? – No. Was it so in the beginning? – Yes. It was so at the beginning, then it must have ceased to be, and now it is again: here there is a world of things to be known; but this evening I wish to speak of what was in the beginning and after what manner it was that God was then man's king and master and father. Now, my brethren, what I am going to say may be dark, it may be dry; yet I shall make it as clear as I can, and men's thoughts may well be spent in taking pains to master the things of God.

Wherever there is a sovereign power, a king, an emperor, any kind of prince, ruler, governor, one such or more of them, or even a whole people selfgoverning and selfgoverned, there must always some understanding have gone before about the governing and the being governed – I mean those who are governed must have agreed to be governed and those who govern, they too must have accepted the task of government. Whether this understanding is well-known and a matter of history, as suppose the people have chosen a king and offered him the crown, or whether it is lost in the darkness of the past how it came about, nevertheless at any particular time when orderly government is going on there *is* such an agreement, there exists such an understanding: the subjects obey, at least they are not in rebellion; the rulers govern, at least they have not thrown up the reigns of power. For if the governed had never, neither at first nor after, submitted to be ruled / all would be riot, order could never have come about; if the ruling power had never, neither at first nor after, accepted the task of government how could he or his house or heirs or representatives be now upon the throne? The agreement, the understanding, the contract, must have somehow *come about*, and it will always have been brought about for the good of both parties, governor and governed, for their common good, their *common weal*; and this is what we call a commonwealth. For men are met in towns and assembled into states for their common wellbeing, to buy and sell, to marry and be given in marriage, for mutual defence, for learning's sake and company's sake, for a thousand reasons all gathered up in the words common weal or commonwealth. A leader and lawgiver for them there must be and they may choose one, but for the most part there is no need to enquire who was chosen or when, for people are born to things and rest content with them much as they are: look at ourselves, we have no two thoughts about the matter; we find the queen on her throne, houses of parliament, judges sitting or going, the army, the police, the postoffice at work; the common good is being provided for, we share it more or less, we share the common weal, we are part of the commonwealth; we may dislike this or that ministry or measure, move and agitate to get it changed, but as for refusing to be ruled at all and putting ourselves out of the commonwealth, to most people the very thought would never occur; they are born to share its advantage and therefore they suppose themselves born to share in its duties and be in its allegiance. I do not wish to speak of an oppressed country, where the burdens and not the blessings of government are felt, that sighs under a heavy yoke, but of a fairly well-governed one, and in such I say that those who find themselves born to the blessings and avail themselves of those blessings know they must be born to bear the burdens and that it is their duty to bear them.

Remark these two words, wellbeing or advantage and duty, for on them the commonwealth turns. The aim of every commonwealth is the wellbeing, the welfare of all and this welfare of all is secured by a duty binding all. For, as we have said, there is an understanding, there is a contract, which once made, once allowed, is in justice binding: he that undertook to govern bound himself to look to the common good and for that he makes his laws; they that undertook to be governed bound themselves to obey his laws and perform what should be by them commanded. Hold fast this thought, I say it once more: a commonwealth is the meeting of many for their common good, for which good all are solemnly agreed to strive and being so agreed are then in duty bound to strive, the ruler by planning, the ruled by performing, the sovereign by the weight of his authority, the subject by the stress of his obedience.

from a semon at St Francis Xavier's, Liverpool, 25 January 1880
[on Matthew 12: 25]

Eve was alone. It was no sin to be alone, she was in her duty, God had given her freedom and she was wandering free, God had made her independent of her husband and she need not be at his side. Only God had made her for Adam's companion; it was her office, her work, the reason for her being to companion him and she was not doing it. There is no sin, but there is no delicacy of duty, no zeal for the sovereign's honour, no generosity, no supererogation. And Adam, he too was alone. He had been commanded to dress and keep Paradise. What flower, what fruitful tree, what living thing was there in Paradise so lovely as Eve, so fruitful as the mother of all flesh, that needed or could repay his tendance and his keeping as she? There was no sin; yet at the one fatal moment when of all the world care was wanted care was not forthcoming, the thing best worth keeping was unkept. And Eve stood by the forbidden tree, which God had bidden them not to eat of, which *she* said God had bidden them not even touch; she neither sinned nor was tempted to sin by standing near it, yet she would go to the very bounds and utmost border of her duty. To do so was not dangerous of itself, as it would be to us. When some child, one of Eve's poor daughters, stands by a peachtree, eyeing the blush of colour on the fruit, fingering the velvet bloom upon it, breathing the rich smell, and in imagination tasting the sweet juice, the nearness, the mere neighbourhood is enough to undo her, she looks and is tempted, she touches and is tempted more, she takes and tastes. But in Eve there was nothing of this; she was not mastered by concupiscence, *she* mastered *it*. There she stood, beautiful, innocent, with her original justice *and with nothing else*, nothing to stain it, but nothing to heighten and brighten it: she felt no cravings, for she was mistress of herself and would not let them rise; she felt no generous promptings, no liftings of the heart to give God glory, for she was mistress of herself and gave them no encouragement. Such was Eve before her fall.

Now, brethren, fancy, as you may, that rich tree all laden with its shining fragrant fruit and swaying down from one of its boughs, as the pythons and great snakes of the East do now, waiting for their prey to pass and then to crush it, swaying like a long spray of vine or the bine of a great creeper, not terrible but beauteous, lissome, marked with quaint streaks and eyes or flushed with rainbow colours, the Old Serpent. We must suppose he offered her the fruit, as though it were the homage and the tribute of the brute to man, of the subject to his queen, presented it with his mouth or swept it from the boughs down before her feet; and she declined it. Then came those studied words of double meaning the Scripture tells us of: *What! and has God forbidden you to eat of the fruit of Paradise?* – Now mark her answer: you would expect her to reply: No, but of this one fruit only: he has given us free leave for all the trees in Paradise excepting one – but hear her: *Of the fruit of the trees in Paradise we do eat* – no mention of God's bounty here, it is all their freedom, what they do: 'we do eat' – *but the fruit of the tree in the midst of Paradise* – as though she would say / of the best fruit of all – *God has commanded us not to eat of, nor so much as touch it, or we shall die; then* she remembers God when it is question of a stern and threatening law. She gave her tempter the clew to his temptation – that God her sovereign was a tyrant, a sullen lawgiver; that God her lord and landlord was envious and grudging, a rackrent; that God her father, the author of her being, was a shadow of death. The serpent took the hint and bettered it. Well was he called subtle: he does not put her suggestion into words and make it blacker; she would have been shocked, she would have recoiled; he gives the thing another turn, as much as to say: Why yes, God would be all this if you took his law according to the letter. No no; what does 'death' mean? you will not *die*: you will die to ignorance, if you will, and wake to wisdom: *God knows, on the day you eat of it your eyes will be opened and you will be as gods, knowing good and evil.* And with these words he dealt three blows at once against God's kingdom – at God as a lawgiver and judge, at God as an owner or proprietor, at God as a father; at God as a lawgiver and judge, for the Serpent said / God has made this the tree of the knowledge of good and evil, that is / which shall decide for him whether to call you good or evil, good if you keep from it, evil if you touch it: be your own lawgivers and judges of good and evil; be as God yourselves, be divinely independent, why not? make it *good* to try the tree, *evil* to leave it untasted; at God as a proprietor, for as owner of man and the earth and all therein and sovereign of the commonwealth God had given the other trees of Paradise to his subjects but reserved this one to the crown: the Serpent advised them to trepass boldly on these rights and seize crown-property; and at God as a father, for God like a fatherly providence found them food and forbad them poison: the Serpent told them the deadly poison was life-giving food. It was enough: Eve would judge for herself. She *saw that the tree was good to eat*, that it was *not* poison, it was the food of life – and here was the pride of life; *that it was beautiful to the eyes*, a becoming object to covet and possess – and here was the desire of the eyes; *and that it was delightful to behold*, that is / sweet and enjoyable in imagination even and forecast, how much more in the eating and the reality! – and here was the desire of the flesh; she freely yielded herself to the three concupiscences; *she took and eat* of this devil's-sacrament; she rebelled, she sinned, she fell.

from a sermon at St Francis Xavier's, Liverpool, 30 May 1880
[on Luke 14: 16–24]

The parable itself is not a hard one, it needs no very long explanation. However I shall speak of one or two points or difficulties in it; next I shall give its meaning and application to the world and history; lastly I shall speak of how it applies to ourselves.

The first of the difficulties or strange points to be found in the parable is that many were asked to the supper, we are told, and *all* of these refused to come – which seems a thing incredible; for one man might make one excuse, another another, out of many, and not come, that might happen, but that all should refuse, that out of those many not one should do his duty; shew common civility; nay if it were no more than care for a handsome entertainment, not even care for that, how do we account for this? – how, brethren, but by remarking those words *with one accord*? 'With one accord', we read more clearly in the Greek, 'they began to excuse themselves' – at one signal, as it were. For so it was, it was a conspiracy, a thing got up among them to pass a joint and public slight on the most eminent of their fellow citizens, a slight much more grievous than individual neglect and more shamefully thankless, graceless, heartless, and malignant. How else could they have refused with one accord? This then is how that came to pass. They meant him with his empty hall and untasted banquet to be the laughingstock of the whole town: it turned out otherwise. He laughs best that laughs last, he laughs best that has the most to laugh with him; and so it happened with their host and them.

So then instead of the well-to-do guests who were above coming were called the poor that had never thought to be asked and for those the men of business, the men of action, the men of pleasure that went off after their own enterprises, their newbought farms and oxen, or stayed at home with their brides, were brought in the feeble and the blind and the lame, those that could scarcely come if they wished, that must be carried, led, or helped to the banquet hall, and after these again for townsfolk and neighbours the farm hands and outlying country people, that had not so much as seen from out of doors the splendour of a city feast, all these were led, carried, drawn, or driven in till the house was filled.

This must have taken time. For suppose the supper or dinner, as we should rather call it, had first been fixed for, say, two in the afternoon, then when each of the invited guests had made his excuse and the servant had returned with these to his master and gone forth again with orders to bring the poor, feeble, blind, and lame and had brought them or got them brought, which could scarcely be over before evening, after this, I say, when he was gone the third time forth and further, into the open country, had scoured the country, the lanes and hedges, and with his fellowservants and men under him brought the throng of country people in, it must have been nightfall and dark before the house was full and the supper served to all of them. The hall would be lit up, the town alive with the guests flocking thither, no supper would be so famous as that one.

The parable ends with the words 'But I say unto you that none of those men that were invited shall taste of my supper' and in these there is something that may seem surprising. For why, one might ask, what need of saying that? Of course they will not taste of it; it is what they do not care to do, do not want to do, have expressly refused to do, have gone out of town not to do: why then does the host lay such a stress on his not giving the thing they will not take? Is it that the first bidden guests repented and would gladly have come when it was too late and every place was filled? And why should they repent? – Because the tables were turned; because – no other word puts it so clearly – the tables had been turned on them. They had meant to leave their host's house empty and it was filled, his supper untasted and all the world, so to say, tasted it but themselves; they had meant him to be left by himself a laughing-stock to the town, and town and country had gathered to him; they only were left out; they were the laughingstock; they had meant to give the chief citizen a slight which should lower him below the least of themselves and they found themselves replaced by strangers, put below beggars and cripples. This then is what those words mean, 'But I say unto you that none of

those men that were invited shall taste of my supper', that is /
They say they will not taste of it, they shall not; they shall find
the tables turned on them; it shall not be they that refuse me, I
tell you I refuse them; my feast shall go forward with lights and
wine and music into the night, I have my guests in plenty, but
they – no, not one of *them* shall taste my supper.

from a sermon at St Francis Xavier's, Liverpool, 25 October 1880
                [on Divine Providence and the Guardian Angels]
Notes – God knows infinite things, all things, and heeds them
all in particular. We cannot 'do two things at once', that is
cannot give one full heed and attention to two things at once.
God heeds all things at once. He takes more interest in a
merchant's business than the merchant, in a vessel's steering
than the pilot, in a lover's sweetheart than the

> [In consequence of this word *sweetheart* I was in a manner
> suspended and at all events was forbidden (it was some time
> after) to preach without having my sermon revised. However
> when I was going to take the next sermon I had to give after
> this regulation came into force to Fr. Clare for revision he
> poohpoohed the matter and would not look at it]

lover, in a sick man's pain than the sufferer, in our salvation
than we ourselves. The hairs of our heads are numbered before
him. He heeds all things and cares about all things, but not
· alike; he does not care for nor love nor provide for all alike, not
for little things so much as great, brutes as men, the bad as the
good, the reprobate who will not come to him as the elect who
will. It was his law that the ox should not be muzzled that trod
out the corn, but this provision was made for an example to
men, not for the sake of the beast; for: Does God care for oxen?
asks St Paul; that is to say, compared with his care for men he
does not care for them. Yet he does care for them and for every
bird and beast and finds them their food. Not a sparrow, our
Lord says, falls to the ground without your Father, that is /
without his noticing and allowing and meaning it. But we men,
he added, are worth many, that is / any number of, sparrows.
So then God heeds all things and cares and provides for all
things but for us men he cares most and provides best.

Therefore all the things we see are made and provided for us,
the sun, moon, and other heavenly bodies to light us, warm us,
and be measures to us of time; coal and rockoil for artificial

light and heat; animals and vegetables for our food and clothing; rain, wind, and snow again to make these bear and yield their tribute to us; water and the juices of plants for our drink; air for our breathing; stone and timber for our lodging; metals for our tools and traffic; the songs of birds, flowers and their smells and colours, fruits and their taste for our enjoyment. And so on: search the whole world and you will find it a million-million fold contrivance of providence planned for our use and patterned for our admiration.

But yet this providence is imperfect, plainly imperfect. The sun shines too long and withers the harvest, the rain is too heavy and rots it or in floods spreading washes it away; the air and water carry in their currents the poison of disease; there are poison plants, venomous snakes and scorpions; the beasts our subjects rebel, not only the bloodthirsty tiger that slaughters yearly its thousands, but even the bull will gore and the stallion bite or strike; at night the moon sometimes has no light to give, at others the clouds darken her; she measures time most strangely and gives us reckonings most difficult to make and never exact enough; the coalpits and oilwells are full of explosion, fires and outbreaks of sudden death, the sea of storms and wrecks, the snow has avalanches, the earth landslips; we contend with cold, want, weakness, hunger, disease, death, and often we fight a losing battle, never a triumphant one; everything is full of fault, flaw, imperfection, shortcoming; as many marks as there are of God's wisdom in providing for us so many marks there may be set against them of more being needed still, of something having made of this very providence a shattered frame and a broken web.

Let us not now enquire, brethren, why this should be; we most sadly feel and know that so it is. But there is good in it; for if we were not forced from time to time to feel our need of God and our dependance on him, we should most of us cease to pray to him and to thank him. If he did everything we should treat him as though he did nothing, whereas now that he does not do all we are brought to remember how much he does and to ask for more. And God desires nothing so much as that his creatures should have recourse to him.

But there is one great means he has provided for every one of us to make up for the shortcomings of his general and common providence. This great and special providence is the giving each of us his guardian angel. *He has given*, the Scripture says *his angels commands about thee, to keep thee in all thy ways.* And we learn from what our Lord said to his disciples that every child, that every human being, however low and of little account, is given in charge to a blessed and heavenly spirit, a guardian angel: *Beware*, said he, *of despising one of these little ones* (which means not only children but all who are in any other way little or of little account): *I tell you their angels always see the face of my Father in heaven* (Matt. xviii 10).

Consider, brethren, what a wonderful honour this is. We men are cared for by angels, fallen men by blissful spirits; we who are so full of the miseries of the flesh that we cannot bear at times to be in each other's presence are watched without ceasing by these glorious beings, and while they have us poor wretches in their sight they are at the same time gazing on the face of God. How much does God make of us when he will have his very courtiers, those who are about his throne, to look after us men, even the lowest amongst us! It may fill us with shame to be so honoured; it may also fill us with shame to think how we are watched and seen, for there is nothing we do but comes under the eye not of God only but of another witness besides, our guardian angel. He counts all our steps, he knows every hair of our heads, he is witness of all our good deeds and all our evil; he sees all and remembers all. Even our hearts he searches, for he sees them in the light of God's knowledge and God reveals to him all that can be of service to him in his charge and duty of leading the human being entrusted to him to the kingdom of heaven. But though he knows and remembers all the harm we have done he will not be our accuser; where he cannot help us he will be silent; he will speak but of our right deeds and plead in our defence all the good he has observed in us. His whole duty is to help us to be saved, to help us both in body and soul. We shall do well therefore to be ashamed of ourselves before our guardian angel, but not to have no other feelings than shame and dread towards him; for he is our good faithful and charitable friend, who never did and never could sleep one moment at his post, neglect the least thing that could be of service to us, or leave a stone unturned to help us all the days that we have been in his keeping. We should deeply trust him, we should reverence and love him, and often ask his aid.

Here, brethren, I must meet an objection which may be

working on your minds. If everyone has so watchful and so strong a keeper at his side why is there such a thing as sudden death, as catching fever, as taking poison by mistake, as being shot or any way injured, even as a stumble or a fall, a scald or a sprain? What are the guardian angels doing that they let such things be? – To begin with, many mischiefs that might befall us our guardian angels do ward off from us: that is the first answer to be made. Next their power over us depends in part on the power we give them and by willingly putting ourselves into their hands, by expressly asking them to help us, we enable them to do so; for always God's special providences are for his special servants. They are not to save us from all the consequences of our own wickedness or folly or even from the wickedness and folly of other men; for we are our own masters, are free to act and then must take the consequences; moreover man is his brother's keeper and may be well or ill kept, as Abel was by wicked Cain not kept but killed. But the fullest answer is this – that in appointing us guardian angels God never meant they should make us proof against all the ills that flesh is heir to, that would have been to put us in some sort back into the state of Paradise which we have lost; but he meant them, accompanying us through this world of evil and mischance, sometimes warding off its blows and buffets, sometimes leaving them to fall, always to be leading us to a better; which better world, my brethren, when you have reached and with your own eyes opened look back on this you will see a work of wonderful wisdom in the guidance of your guardian angel. In the meantime God's providence is dark and we cannot hope to know the why and wherefore of all that is allowed to befall us.

From Notes on The Spiritual Exercises of St Ignatius Loyola

On the First Principle and Foundation

Man was created to praise, reverence and serve God Our Lord, and by so doing to save his soul. And the other things on the face of the earth were created for man's sake and to help him in the carrying out of the end for which he was created. Hence it follows that man should make use of creatures so far as they help him to attain his end and withdraw from them so far as they hinder him from so doing. For that, it is necessary to make ourselves indifferent in regard to all created things in so far as it is left to the choice of our free will and there is no prohibition; in such sort that we do not on our part seek for health rather than sickness, for riches rather than poverty, for honour rather than dishonour, for a long life rather than a short one; and so in all other things, desiring and choosing only those which may better lead us to the end for which we were created.

on *Principium sive Fundamentum*

'Homo creatus est' – Aug 20 1880: during this retreat, which I am making at Liverpool, I have been thinking about creation and this thought has led the way naturally through the exercises hitherto. I put down some thoughts. – We may learn that all things are created by consideration of the world without or of ourselves the world within. The former is the consideration commonly dwelt on, but the latter takes on the mind more hold. I find myself both as man and as myself something most determined and distinctive, at pitch, more distinctive and higher pitched than anything else I see; I find myself with my pleasures and pains, my powers and my experiences, my deserts and guilt, my shame and sense of beauty, my dangers, hopes, fears, and all my fate, more important to myself than anything I see. And when I ask where does all this throng and stack of being, so rich, so distinctive, so important, come from / nothing I see can answer me. And this whether I speak of human nature or of my individuality, my selfbeing. For human nature, being more highly pitched, selved, and distinctive than anything in the world, can have been developed, evolved, condensed, from the vastness of the world not anyhow or by the working of common powers but only by one of finer or higher pitch and determination than itself and certainly than any that elsewhere we see, for this power had to force forward the starting or stubborn elements to the one pitch required. And this is much more true when we consider the mind; when I consider my selfbeing, my consciousness and feeling of myself, that taste of myself, of *I* and *me* above and in all things, which is more distinctive than the taste of ale or alum, more distinctive than the smell of walnutleaf or camphor, and is incommunicable by any means to another man (as when I was a child I used to ask myself: What must it be to be someone else?). Nothing else in nature comes near this unspeakable stress of pitch, distinctiveness, and selving, this selfbeing of my own. Nothing explains it or resembles it, except so far as this, that other men to themselves have the same feeling. But this only multiplies the phenomena to be explained so far as the cases are like and do resemble. But to me there is no resemblance: searching nature I taste *self* but at one tankard, that of my own being. The development, refinement, condensation of nothing shews any sign of being able to match this to me or give me another taste of it, a taste even resembling it.

One may dwell on this further. We say that any two things however unlike are in something like. This is the one exception: when I compare my self, my being-myself, with anything else whatever, all things alike, all in the same degree, rebuff me with blank unlikeness; so that my knowledge of it, which is so intense, is from itself alone, they in no way help me to understand it. And even those things with which I in some sort identify myself, as my country or family, and those things which I own and call mine, as my clothes and so on, all presuppose the stricter sense of *self* and *me* and *mine* and are from that derivative.

Meditation on Death

Preparatory prayer.
Introductory remark – Death is certain and uncertain, certain to come, uncertain when and where. Did any man yet escape death? – Adam lived long, Methusalem longer, near 1000 years, but died. It is *appointed* to men once to die, once at least: Enoch and Elias the prophets are living yet, God preserves their life, but their death is appointed, it is foretold in Scripture; they too will die. Once to die: some have died twice, been raised to life after death, as Lazarus and many others, but then they died again; twice they had the pangs of death; they did not escape. It is appointed to man once to die and after this the judgment: these men were not judged, God foresaw and put off judgment

at their first death, but they died again and are judged now. We do not hope to be raised again, if we did what real difference would it make? The truth remains then, it is appointed to men to die, and we shall die.

And it is uncertain when or where – not so *un*certain as it is certain that we shall die; a man sick to death has a strong likelihood that he will die, say, within a week and in that house or even in that bed; still there hangs over death a great, a harassing uncertainty. *When* shall each of us die? – I cannot tell, but *all within a century* (I say what no one doubts), some long hence, some soon, one perhaps this year. Express it no further: it is a great uncertainty. *And where?* – Some here no doubt and some elsewhere; some in their beds, others suddenly in some unlikely place, where now they little think: this too is a great uncertainty. But one thing is certain and let that be the *1st prelude* to the meditation – *We shall die in these bodies*. I see you living before me, with the mind's eye, brethren, I see your corpses: those same bodies that sit there before me are rows of corpses that will be. And I that speak to you, you hear and see me, you see me breathe and move: this breathing body is my corpse and I am living in my tomb. This is one thing certain of your place of death; you are there now, you sit within your corpses; look no farther: there where you are you will die.

2nd prel. – What we want is so deep a sense of the certainty and uncertainty of death, to have death so before us, that we may dread to sin now and when we die die well.

1st point – *The terrors of death* – (1) It is the greatest of earthly evils. It robs us of our all. Do you love sunshine, starlight, fresh air, flowers, fieldsports? – Despair then: you will see them no more; they will be above ground, you below; you will lose them all. Do you love townlife, homelife, the cheerful hearth, the sparkling fire, company, the social glass, laughter, frolic among friends? – Despair then: you will have no more of them for ever, the churchyards are full of such men as you are now, that feasted once and now worms feast on; the dark day is coming; slow or sudden, death is coming; then rottenness and dust and utterly to be forgotten. Do you dearly love wife or husband, child or friend? – Despair then: death shall part you, from your dearest, though they may hang round your bed yet you shall go into the dark unbefriended, alone. Do you love money? – Despair then: death shall make you drop it, death shall wring it from you; though your funeral were costly, yet poor shall you lie. Do you love fame in your day and to make yourself felt, to play your part somewhere in the world? do you take an interest in politics and watch how the world goes? – Despair then: the world will do without you and you must do without the world, for you shall be where you cannot stir hand or foot to make it worse or better. Do you love what is better than all these, to do God's work, to do good to others, to give alms, to pray, to make God's kingdom come? Make haste then, work while it is day, and despair of any other chance than this: *the night is coming*, says your master, *when no man can work* and again *There is neither work nor reason nor wisdom nor knowledge in the grave where thou art hastening fast.* And again Ecclus. xiv 17. *Before thy death do justice, for there is no finding food in the grave* / 'Ante obitum tuum operare justitiam, quoniam non est apud inferos invenire cibum.' On one ground or another, do you love life, dear life? – Despair, all of you: death is coming that shall rob you even of dear life. Is there no help? – No, none. If it were poverty we might escape it or not escaping it we could bear it; we should still have life. If it were pain and sickness we might escape them or not escaping them get over them or not getting over them we might still live. If it were shame, if it were the death of others – but no, we may lose health, wealth, fame, friends, peace of mind, and all that makes life dear and still keep, and glad to keep, dear life; and then besides, we need not lose them – death might be our first sickness, we might live all our lives well to do, honoured, with our best friends round us; but *life we must lose* and with life all the goods of life; other evils need not come, but death, *the worst of evils, must* come, and rob us of our only chance, rob us of our all. This is the first terror of death: it is the worst of earthly evils and robs us of our all, and it is the only evil certain to come.

(2) The next terror of death are *the pains of death*. Death mostly is the end of fatal sickness and when is sickness, fatal sickness, without pain? And its pain is not as other pains, which either we surmount and get the better of or at least we can keep up with; but fatal sickness and its pains are for the dying man a losing battle, he bears them and is worse, he may have patience and they do not spare, bad they may be but they will be worse, things will come to the worse and then not mend, making the

proverb a lie; the pains of fatal sickness are the pains of death; a woman is in pangs and she brings forth a child, she is at peace and from her pangs has come new life, but we shall be in pangs and bring forth death. I do not mean that the pain of dying is always great; I know well and have seen that often it is not so, so far as from outside we can judge; but often it is; and great pain or little or none, it is terror enough that life is ebbing away. And even for those who seem to die peacefully, if they have their senses to the last, one cannot without shrinking think of that very last moment when flesh and spirit are rent asunder and the soul goes out into the cold, leaving the body its companion dear a corpse behind. This will be to every one of you; I see your corpses here before me.

But there are worse pangs of death than those of the body. There is the sweat of fear, *there is the dread of what is to come after*. Saints have feared: St Hilarion, St Jerome, that all their lives did penance, trembled when they came to pass away. The Devil rages then, for he knows that his time is short: one thought of mortal sin at the last gasp is enough, it will do his work for ever, and he watches well, he knows when death is near. And what, my brethren, if you should find yourselves dying and in mortal sin? hurriedly you will send for the priest, counting the minutes till he comes; and what if he should be away, some miscarriage happen, as there always may, even where all seems best provided for? I could tell you even from my own experiences tales to make you tremble and more from that of others. The last sacraments are a tower of strength if you can get them, but who can tell you that you will? God does not promise that. Will you trust a priest? May not even a wise and zealous man for once be careless or misjudge and think there is no danger when there is? Few are the parish priests that never, as the saying is, let one slip through their hands. (Here one may tell the story of the woman that died calling on St Winefred to curse Fr – for not coming; also of the woman in Page Street, Liverpool, when the bell was not answered, no one knows why; and of my man in Wm. Henry Street.) If things like this should happen to any of you make an act of sorrow for your sins, earnestly asking God to give you the grace, which he will: do this and you will be saved; but yet I say it is a wretched wretched thing to die in fear, without the sacraments.

(3) The third terror of death is its uncertainty, that *it may be*

sudden and find us unprepared. This is worse than the rest. Few people die sudden deaths, but a few do and what of those few? Here you are many, most of you then will not die suddenly, but some few of you will; some few, some one or two that hear me, will die suddenly. There are dangers by land and sea, wrecks, railway accidents, lightning, mischances with machinery, fires, falls; there are murders – I have talked with the widows and the orphaned children of suddenly murdered men; there are heart complaints and other sudden strokes of death. Now a sudden death *need* not be a bad death; holy men have sometimes prayed to die suddenly and their prayer been heard; it has its advantages, for if we then are in the grace of God we have no time to fall away; but yet consider, brethren, how many men live in unbroken mortal sin, who if they died suddenly must therefore die in mortal sin; consider how many more go indeed to confession and are forgiven, but sin again shortly and so spend most of their days in mortal sin and if they were cut off suddenly would (not certainly indeed, but) *most likely*, O dreadful likelihood! be then in mortal sin. Others would be as likely as not, others not so likely, but even one chance, how terrible it is! And then follows the judgment of damnation. This is a terror then that far exceeds the rest.

From Retreat Notes in Ireland 1888

Jan 1 1888. St Stanislaus' College, Tullabeg
Principium seu Fundamentum: 'Homo creatus est ut laudet' etc. – All moral good, all man's being good, lies in two things – in being right, being in the right, and in doing right; in being on the right side, on the side of good, and on that side of doing good. Neither of these will do by itself. Doing good but on the wrong side, promoting a bad cause, is rather doing wrong. Doing good but in no good cause is no merit: of whom or what does the doer deserve well? Not at any rate of God. Nor plainly is it enough to be on the right side and not promote it.

But men are variously constituted to make much of one of these things and neglect the other. The Irish think it enough to be Catholics or on the right side and that it is no matter what they say and do to advance it; practically so, but what they think is that all they and their leaders do to advance the right side is and must be right. The English think, as Pope says for them, he can't be wrong whose life is in the right. Marcus Aurelius seems in his Meditations to be leading the purest and most unselfish life of virtue; he thinks, though with hesitation, that Reason governs the Universe and that by this life he ranks himself on the side of that Reason; and indeed, if this was all he had the means of doing, it was enough; but he does not know of any particular standard the rallying to which is the appointed signal of, taking God the sovereign Reason's, God the Word's, side; and yet that standard was then raised in the world and the Word and sovereign Reason was then made flesh and he persecuted it. And in any case his principles are principles of despair and, again, philosophy is not religion.

But how is it with me? I was a Christian from birth or baptism, later I was converted to the Catholic faith, and am enlisted 20 years in the Society of Jesus. I am now 44. I do not waver in my allegiance, I never have since my conversion to the Church. The question is how I advance the side I serve on. This may be inwardly or outwardly. Outwardly I often think I am employed to do what is of little or no use. Something else which I can conceive myself doing might indeed be more useful, but still it is an advantage for there to be a course of higher studies for Catholics in Ireland and that that should be partly in Jesuit hands; and my work and my salary keep that up. Meantime the Catholic Church in Ireland and the Irish Province in it and our College in that are greatly given over to a partly unlawful cause, promoted by partly unlawful means, and against my will my pains, laborious and distasteful, like prisoners made to serve the enemies' gunners, go to help on this cause. I do not feel then that outwardly I do much good, much that I care to do or can much wish to prosper; and this is a mournful life to lead. In thought I can of course divide the good from the evil and live for the one, not the other: this justifies me but it does not alter the facts. Yet it seems to me that I could lead this life well enough if I had bodily energy and cheerful spirits. However these God will not give me. The other part, the more important, remains, my inward service.

I was continuing this train of thought this evening when I began to enter on that course of loathing and hopelessness

which I have so often felt before, which made me fear madness
and led me to give up the practice of meditation except, as now,
in retreat and here it is again. I could therefore do no more than
repeat *Justus es, Domine, et rectum judicium tuum* and the like,
and then being tired I nodded and woke with a start. What is
my wretched life? Five wasted years almost have passed in
Ireland. I am ashamed of the little I have done, of my waste of
time, although my helplessness and weakness is such that I
could scarcely do otherwise. And yet the Wise Man warns us
against excusing ourselves in that fashion. I cannot then be
excused; but what is life without aim, without spur, without
help? All my undertakings miscarry: I am like a straining
eunuch. I wish then for death: yet if I died now I should die
imperfect, no master of myself, and that is the worst failure of
all. O my God, look down on me.

Jan. 2 – This morning I made the meditation on the Three Sins,
with nothing to enter but loathing of my life and a barren
submission to God's will. The body cannot rest when it is in
pain nor the mind be at peace as long as something bitter distills
in it and it aches. This may be at any time and is at many: how
then can it be pretended there is for those who feel this anything
worth calling happiness in this world? There is a happiness,
hope, the anticipation of happiness hereafter: it is better than
happiness, but it is not happiness now. It is as if one were
dazzled by a spark or star in the dark, seeing it but not seeing
by it: we want a light shed on our way and a happiness spread
over our life.

Afternoon: on the same – more loathing and only this
thought, that I can do my spiritual and other duties better with
God's help. In particular I think it may be well to resolve to
make the examen every day at 1.15 and then say vespers and
compline if not said before. I will consider what next

Jan. 3 – Repetition of 1st and 2nd exercise – Helpless loathing.
Then I went out and I said the Te Deum and yet I thought what
was needed was not praise of God but amendment of life

Jan. 5th – Repetition of meditations on Incarnation and Nativity
– All that happens in Christendom and so in the whole world
affected, marked, as a great seal, and like any other historical
event, and in fact more than any other event, by the Incarnation;

at any rate by Christ's life and death, whom we by faith hold to
be God made man. Our lives are affected by the events of
Roman history, by Caesar's victory and murder for instance.
Yet one might perhaps maintain that at this distance of time
individuals could not find a difference in their lives, except in
what was set down in books of history and works of art, if
Pompey instead of Caesar had founded the Empire or Caesar
had lived 20 years longer.

But our lives and in particular those of religious, as mine, are
in their whole direction, not only inwardly but most visibly and
outwardly, shaped by Christ's. Without that even outwardly the
world could be so different that we cannot even guess it. And
my life is determined by the Incarnation down to most of the
details of the day. Now this being so that I cannot even stop it,
why should I not make the cause that determines my life, both
as a whole and in much detail, determine it in greater detail still
and to the greater efficiency of what I in any case should do,
and to my greater happiness in doing it?

It is for this that St Ignatius speaks of the angel *discharging
his mission*, it being question of action leading up to, as now
my action leads from, the Incarnation. The Incarnation was for
my salvation and that of the world: the work goes on in a great
system and machinery which even drags me on with the collar
round my neck though I could and do neglect my duty in it. But
I say to myself that I am only too willing to do God's work and
help on the knowledge of the Incarnation. But this is not really
true: I am not willing enough for the piece of work assigned me,
the only work I am given to do, though I could do others if they
were given. This is my work at Stephen's Green. And I thought
that the Royal University was to me what Augustus's enrolment
was to St Joseph: *exiit sermo a Caesare Augusto etc.*; so
resolution of the senate of the R. U. came to me, inconvenient
and painful, but the journey to Bethlehem was inconvenient and
painful; and then I am bound in justice, and paid. I hope to
bear this in mind.

John Middleton Murry (1919)

We happen to have been born into an age without perspective; hence our idolatry for the one living poet and prose writer who has it and comes, or appears to come, from another age. But another rhythm is possible. No doubt it would be mistaken to consider this rhythm as in fact wholly divorced from the rhythm of personality; it probably demands at least a minimum of personal coherence in its possessor. For critical purposes, however, they are distinct. This second and subsidiary rhythm is that of technical progression. The single pursuit of even the most subordinate artistic intention gives unity, significance, mass to a poet's work. When Verlaine declares 'de la musique avant toute chose', we know where we are. And we know this not in the obvious sense of expecting his verse to be predominantly musical; but in the more important sense of desiring to take a man seriously who declares for anything 'avant toute chose'.

It is the 'avant toute chose' that matters, not as a profession of faith – we do not greatly like professions of faith – but as the guarantee of the universal in the particular, of the *dianoia* in the episode. It is the 'avant toute chose' that we chiefly miss in modern poetry and modern society and in their quaint concatenations. It is the 'avant toute chose' that leads us to respect both Mr Hardy and Mr Bridges, though we give all our affection to one of them. It is the 'avant toute chose' that compels us to admire the poems of Gerard Manley Hopkins; it is the 'avant toute chose' in his work, which, as we believe, would have condemned him to obscurity today, if he had not (after many years) had Mr Bridges, who was his friend, to stand sponsor and the Oxford University Press to stand the racket. Apparently Mr Bridges himself is something of our opinion, for his introductory sonnet ends on a disdainful note:

> Go forth: amidst our chaffinch flock display
> Thy plumage of far wonder and heavenward flight!

It is from a sonnet written by Hopkins to Mr Bridges that we take the most concise expression of his artistic intention, for the poet's explanatory preface is not merely technical, but is written in a technical language peculiar to himself. Moreover, its scope is small; the sonnet tells us more in two lines than the preface in four pages.

> O then if in my lagging lines you miss
> The roll, the rise, the carol, the creation ...

There is his 'avant toute chose'. Perhaps it seems very like 'de la musique'. But it tells us more about Hopkins's music than Verlaine's line told us about his. This music is of a particular kind, not the 'sanglots du violon', but pre-eminently the music of song, the music most proper to lyrical verse. If one were to seek in English the lyrical poem to which Hopkins's definition could be most fittingly applied, one would find Shelley's 'Skylark'. A technical progression onwards from the 'Skylark' is accordingly the main line of Hopkins's poetical evolution. There are other, stranger threads interwoven; but this is the chief. Swinburne, rightly enough if the intention of true song is considered, appears hardly to have existed for Hopkins, though he was his contemporary. There is an element of Keats in his epithets, a half-echo in 'whorlèd ear' and 'lark-charmèd'; there is an aspiration after Milton's architectonic in the construction of the later sonnets and the most lucid of the fragments, 'Epithalamion'. But the central point of departure is the 'Skylark'. The 'May Magnificat' is evidence of Hopkins's achievement in the direct line:

> Ask of her, the mighty mother:
> Her reply puts this other
> > Question: What is Spring? –
> > Growth in everything –
>
> Flesh and fleece, fur and feather,
> Grass and greenworld all together;
> > Star-eyed strawberry-breasted
> > Throstle above her nested
>
> Cluster of bugle blue eggs thin
> Forms and warms the life within; ...

When drop-of-blood-and-foam-dapple
Bloom lights the orchard-apple
    And thicket and thorp are merry
    With silver-surfèd cherry

And azuring-over greybell makes
Wood banks and brakes wash wet like lakes
    And magic cuckoocall
    Caps, clears, and clinches all –

That is the primary element manifested in one of its simplest, most recognisable, and some may feel most beautiful forms. But a melody so simple, though it is perhaps the swiftest of which the English language is capable without the obscurity which comes of the drowning of sense in sound, did not satisfy Hopkins. He aimed at complex internal harmonies, at a counterpoint of rhythm; for this more complex element he coined an expressive word of his own:

> But as air, melody, is what strikes me most of all in music and design in painting, so design, pattern, or what I am in the habit of calling *inscape* is what I above all aim at in poetry.

Here, then, in so many words, is Hopkins's 'avant toute chose' at a higher level of elaboration. 'Inscape' is still, in spite of the apparent differentiation, musical; but a quality of formalism seems to have entered with the specific designation. With formalism comes rigidity; and in this case the rigidity is bound to overwhelm the sense. For the relative constant in the composition of poetry is the law of language which admits only a certain amount of adaptation. Musical design must be subordinate to it, and the poet should be aware that even in speaking of musical design he is indulging a metaphor. Hopkins admitted this, if we may judge by his practice, only towards the end of his life. There is no escape by sound from the meaning of the posthumous sonnets, though we may hesitate to pronounce whether this directness was due to a modification of his poetical principles or to the urgency of the content of the sonnets, which, concerned with a matter of life and death, would permit no obscuring of their sense for musical reasons.

·   I wake and feel the fell of dark, not day.

What hours, O what black hoürs we have spent
This night! what sights you, heart, saw; ways you went!
And more must, in yet longer light's delay.

With witness I speak this. But where I say
Hours I mean years, mean life. And my lament
Is cries countless, cries like dead letters sent
To dearest him that lives alas! away.

There is compression, but not beyond immediate comprehension; music, but a music of overtones; rhythm, but a rhythm which explicates meaning and makes it more intense.

Review in *The Athenaeum*, June 1919

Frederick Page S. J. (1920)

Mr Bridges is a poet of exquisite and usually right sensibility, unjust almost only to Catholics. He laughs at us – some of us – for preferring the least original of Father Gerard Hopkins' poems, which he excludes from his collection. The present writer is in a position to recognise the justice of Mr Bridges' criticism, while still resenting the haughty urbanity with which he assures Catholics that we should not feel at home at this new feast he has spread. But when he deprecates the 'exaggerated Marianism' of some of the poems he now prints (and by implication, the 'exaggerated Marianism' of Catholic dogma) it is not our self-love which is hurt. We can but wonder how so fine a mind can see in the Mother of Our Lord the patroness of a fad, she the Destroyer of Heresies ...

This might be a false start in writing of the poetry of Gerard Hopkins, were it not that it easily leads to yet another Catholic divergence from this Protestant editor. Necessarily he is alive to the human import of these poems (if you tickle them, they laugh; if you prick them, they bleed), but except in his own beautiful prefatory sonnet, he prefers to speak of their author almost solely as a prosodist, we (the murder is out!) as a priest. Nor yet so much a priest, as a pastor, *Pastor in parochia*, who lays down his life for the sheep.

The prosody is as difficult as Mr Bridges' own in his later and least welcome development. The difficulty of Browning's or Meredith's syntax is as nothing to the difficulty here from impermissible omissions and the clumsiest of inversions. The diction is as rough-hewn as Mr Hardy's: the *Oxford Dictionary* would not have been large enough for Hopkins, but he must call in the *English Dialect Dictionary* to his aid. It is with malicious enjoyment that we note a Browningism in a *protégé* of Mr Bridges, whose appreciation of Browning (we think Miss Mary Coleridge has told us) is confined to two lines. Gerard Hopkins, hesitating for, making shots at, the right word, the fitting phrase, as every poet must, does not wait for them, but sets down his hesitations, his pot-shots, as Browning may do legitimately enough for his *dramatis personae*. But when Hopkins, in a great religious lyric, writes as follows, we may enjoy it, yet find it hard to justify:

> But how shall I . . . make me room there:
> Reach me a . . . Fancy, come faster –
> Strike you the sight of it? look at it loom there,
> Thing that she . . . There then! the Master, . . .

It is only fair to say that, if another stanza from this same poem reminds us also of Browning, it is chiefly of the ardour of 'Prospice', and of the divine close of 'Abt Vogler', not of the queerness of 'Mater Hugues':

> The frown of his face
> Before me, the hurtle of hell
> Behind, where, where was a, where was a place?
> I whirled out wings that spell
> And fled with a fling of the heart to the heart of the Host.
> My heart, but you were dovewinged, I can tell,
> Carrier-witted, I am bold to boast,
> To flash from the flame to the flame then, tower from the grace
> to the grace.

For the extenuation of Gerard Hopkins' too-learned perversities and self-indulged whims, I refer my reader to Mr Bridges' editorial notes, and now proceed to speak of that 'fatherliness', that humanity, in Father Hopkins which we are sure Mr Bridges must see as some set-off to his friend's Romanism, and which is for us the very essence of his sacerdotal character: we have not here a priest who cannot be touched by a feeling of our infirmities. He seems to have had a special feeling for children; there are more than two or three poems evincing the same tenderness, which yearns for the consecration of their innocence. One little boy is exquisitely docile: and Father Hopkins is anxious that his docility should be perfected. Another boy is pathetically proud of his younger brother, and Father Hopkins is touched by this 'radiance of Eden unquenched by the Fall' (to use Patmore's words). He gives Holy Communion to a bugler boy, he administers Extreme Unction to a farrier, and it means as much to him as to them, their emotion is his, and is recollected in verse. His 'passion for souls' is the motive of many another poem. He notes a candle burning behind some window he passes, he watches a lantern moving through the dark, he remembers the hospitable cottages of Wales, in each case to yearn that the human actor may be worthy of the homely or mysterious or lovely scene. In 'The Candle Indoors' (and in another, unfinished, sonnet) he presses the point of his meditations home to his own bosom as who should say: 'A passion for souls? What then of your own?' It is with something of this same pastoral character that he envisages 'The Loss of the Eurydice' (a poem that offers a curious parallel to Cowper's 'The Loss of the *Royal George*' in that both seem intent to reproduce all the newspaper facts). There is pastoral responsibility here, but transferred to God:

> The Eurydice – it concerned thee, O Lord:
> Three hundred souls, O alas! on board,
>   Some asleep unawakened, all un-
> warned, eleven fathoms fallen,
>
> Where she foundered!

His own priesthood makes prayer for them. And so similarly with his longest and most ambitious poem, 'The Wreck of the Deutschland', 1975; for though the compelling occasion of this poem might seem to be the presence in the wreck of five German nuns expelled from Germany, yet the first part of the poem is (without any explicit reference to the shipwreck) a long, impassioned, and beautiful (though difficult) apostrophe to God, as the constrainer of men's wills, who has contrived this wreck for His own purpose as surely as Prospero contrived *his*. In the second part, where the wreck is narrated, one of the nuns (the Miranda of this tempest, and of the poet's love and wonder) becomes the interpreter and the mediatress of this purpose to the shipwrecked crew and passengers. The subject is still the salvation of souls.

'He calleth his own sheep by name': in 'The Loss of the Eurydice' it is 'Marcus Hare, high her captain', 'Sydney Fletcher, Bristol-bred'; in other poems, Felix Randal, the farrier; the 'boy-bugler, born, he tells me, of Irish mother to an English sire' (how obviously a jotting from the notebook of a parish-priest!); the brothers Henry and John; the young child, Margaret ('grieving over Goldengrove unleaving'); Tom and Dick, the navvies; Harry, the ploughman. Even if these last are but the generic 'Tom, Dick and Harry', they yet bear witness to Father Hopkins' need to individualise his flock. Of great significance is the following confession. Passing 'the candle indoors':

> By that window what task what fingers ply,
> I plod wondering, a-wanting, just for lack
> Of answer the eagerer a-wanting Jessy or Jack
> There / God to aggrándise, God to glorify. –

You have there, and throughout these poems, a double passion, the human affection for each Jessy and Jack, and the 'passion for souls': that they should glorify God. The theme is varied and developed in poems which express his love of, yet unsatisfaction with, beauty, and his imperious necessity of connecting it with God; and the beauty of the strength of manhood – a frequent theme, coinciding with Whitman. Of one such poem, ' a direct picture of a ploughman, without afterthought' – almost uniquely so in him – he writes: 'Let me know if there is anything like it in Walt Whitman, as perhaps there may be, and I should be sorry for that.' There *is*, and he should not have been sorry that at least sometimes this self-chartered libertine might coincide in feeling with a Jesuit father!

Review in *The Dublin Review*, vol. 167 (September 1920)

F. R. Leavis (1932)

Hopkins's originality was radical and uncompromising: there was, as he owns, some excuse for the dismay of his first readers. He could not himself, as the *Author's Preface* shows, be reconciled to his originality without subterfuge. His prosodic account in terms of Logaoedic Rhythm, Counterpoint Rhythm, Sprung Rhythm, Rocking Feet and Outriders will help no one to read his verse – unless by giving the sense of being helped: it merely shows how subtle and hard to escape is the power of habits and preconceptions. The prescription he gives when warm from reading his verse – 'take breath and read it with the ears, as I always wish to be read, and my verse becomes all right' – is a great deal more to the point, and if we add 'and with the brains and the body' it suffices.

This is a measure of the genuineness of his originality.[1] For the peculiarities of his technique appeal for sanction to the spirit of the language: his innovations accentuate and develop bents it exhibits in living use and, above all, in the writings of the greatest master who ever used it. Hopkins might have said about each one of his technical idiosyncrasies what he says about the rhythm of 'The Wreck of the Deutschland'; the idea was not altogether new, but no one had professedly used it and made it a principle throughout as he had. Paradoxical as it may sound to say so, his strength was that he brought poetry much closer to living speech. How badly some such regeneration was needed may be judged from the inability of critics avowedly interested in him, as Bridges and Dixon were, to appreciate his significance: the habits and conventions he defeated were so strong. They are strong still. Mr Charles Williams, the editor of the second edition of the *Poems* concludes in his *Critical Introduction* that the 'poet to whom we should most relate Gerard Hopkins' is Milton. Now if one were seeking to define the significance of Hopkins by contraries, Milton is the poet to whom one would have recourse: the relation is an antithesis. But, alas! Mr Williams leaves no room to suppose that he means that.

The way in which Hopkins uses the English language (that is the primary order of consideration; 'consciousness of the universe'[2] is an unprofitable abstraction apart from it) contrasts him with Milton and associates him with Shakespeare. There is no essential characteristic of his technique of which it might not be said that it is a matter of 'using professedly' and 'making a principle' of something that may be found in Shakespeare:

> . . . the world-without-end hour[3]

> . . . bloody, bawdy villain!
> Remorseless, treacherous, lecherous kindless villain![4]

> . . . cabin'd, cribb'd, confined[5]

> what thou wouldst highly,
> That wouldst thou holily.[6]

> If it were done when 'tis done, then 'twere well
> It were done quickly: if the assassination
> Could trammel up the consequence, and catch
> With his surcease success; that but this blow
> Might be the be-all and the end-all here,
> But here, upon this bank and shoal of time,
> We'd jump the life to come . . .[7]

This last passage takes us beyond technical devices, found in embryo in Shakespeare. Indeed, it would be a mistake to insist too much on these (they could be exemplified indefinitely); it might distract attention from the more essential likeness illustrated by the passage as a whole. Hopkins' imagery, and his way of using the body and movement of the language, are like Shakespeare's.

> O the mind, mind has mountains; cliffs of fall
> Frightful, sheer, no-man-fathomed. Hold them cheap
> May who ne'er hung there. Nor does long our small
> Durance deal with that steep or deep. Here! creep, . . .

That is Shakespearian, but quite un-Miltonic. And this ('what's not meet' being made to suggest at the same time 'not what's meet') handles grammar and syntax in the spirit of Hopkins:

> In a rebellion,
> When what's not meet, but what must be, was law,
> Then were they chosen: in a better hour,

> Let what is meet be said it must be meet,
> And throw their power in the dust.[8]

If we look for a parallel to a characteristic Shakespearian rendering of the very movement of consciousness:

> My thought, whose murder yet is but fantastical,
> Shakes so my single state of man, that function
> Is smother'd in surmise, and nothing is,
> But what is not[9]

> > Only what word
> Wisest my heart breeds dark heaven's baffling ban
> Bars or hell's spell thwarts. This to hoard unheard,
> Heard unheeded, leaves me a lonely began.[10]

It is not that he derives from Shakespeare (Shakespeare, we have often been told, is a dangerous model). We cannot doubt that he knew his Shakespeare well, but if he profited he was able to do so because of his own direct interest in the English language as a living thing. The bent of his genius was so strong that we are forced to believe that his experimenting would have taken much the same lines even if there had been no Shakespeare. The similarities arise out of a similar exploitation of the resources and potentialities of the language. Hopkins belongs with Shakespeare, Donne, Eliot and later Yeats as opposed to Spenser, Milton and Tennyson. He departs very widely from current idiom (as Shakespeare did), but nevertheless current idiom is, as it were, the presiding spirit in his dialect, and he uses his medium not as a literary but as a spoken one. That is the significance of his repeated demand to be tested by reading aloud: 'read it with the ears, as I always wish to be read, and my verse becomes all right'. It is not merely the rhythm that he has in mind.

> I laughed outright and often, but very sardonically, to think you and the Canon could not construe my last sonnet; that he had to write to you for a crib. It is plain I must go no further on this road: if you and he cannot understand me who will? Yet, declaimed, the strange constructions would be dramatic and effective.

It is not only the constructions that gain, and 'dramatic' has a further sense here than perhaps Hopkins intended. His words and phrases are actions as well as sounds, ideas and images, and

must, as I have said, be read with the body as well as with the
eye: that is the force of his concern to be read aloud.

New Bearings in English Poetry, 1932

T. S. Eliot (1934)

At this point, having called attention to the difficulties experienced by Mr Pound and Mr Yeats through no fault of their own,
you may be expecting that I shall produce Gerard Hopkins, with
an air of triumph, as the orthodox and traditional poet. I wish
indeed that I could; but I cannot altogether share the enthusiasm
which many critics feel for this poet, or put him on a level with
those whom I have just mentioned. In the first place, the fact that
he was a Jesuit priest, and the author of some very beautiful
devotional verse, is only partially relevant. To be converted, in
any case, while it is sufficient for entertaining the hope of
individual salvation, is not going to do for a man, as a writer,
what his ancestry and his country for some generations have
failed to do. Hopkins is a fine poet, to be sure; but he is not
nearly so much a poet of our time as the accidents of his
publication and the inventions of his metric have led us to
suppose. His innovations certainly were good, but like the mind
of their author, they operate only within a narrow range, and are
easily imitated though not adaptable for many purposes; furthermore, they sometimes strike me as lacking inevitability – that is
to say, they sometimes come near to being purely *verbal*, in that
a whole poem will give us *more* of the same thing, an accumulation, rather than a real development of thought or feeling.

I may be wrong about Hopkins's metric and vocabulary. But
I am sure that in the matter of devotional poetry a good deal
more is at issue than just the purity and strength of the author's
devotional passion. To be a 'devotional poet' is a limitation: a
saint limits himself by writing poetry, and a poet who confines
himself to even this subject matter is limiting himself too.
Hopkins is not a religious poet in the more important sense in
which I have elsewhere maintained Baudelaire to be a religious
poet; or in the sense in which I find Villon to be a religious poet;

or in the sense in which I consider Mr Joyce's work to be penetrated with Christian feeling. I do not wish to depreciate him, but to affirm limitations and distinctions. He should be compared, not with our contemporaries whose situation is different from his, but with the minor poet nearest contemporary to him, and most like him: George Meredith. The comparison is altogether to Hopkins's advantage. They are both English nature poets, they have similar technical tricks, and Hopkins is much the more agile. And where Meredith, beyond a few acute and pertly expressed observations of human nature, has only a rather cheap and shallow 'philosophy of life' to offer, Hopkins has the dignity of the Church behind him, and is consequently in closer contact with reality. But from the struggle of our time to concentrate, not to dissipate; to renew our association with traditional wisdom; to re-establish a vital connexion between the individual and the race; the struggle, in a word, against Liberalism: from all this Hopkins is a little apart, and in this Hopkins has very little aid to offer us.

After Strange Gods, 1934

Christopher Devlin S. J. (1935)

Hopkins and Duns Scotus

Gerard Hopkins at one period of his life, 1875–9, drew his poetry almost entirely from Nature. In this he appears to have been aided by Scotus, for in 1875 he wrote, 'I was flush with a new enthusiasm. Whenever I took in an inscape of the sea or sky, I thought of Scotus . . .' to anyone who has taken in an inscape and then opened a page of Scotus this remark should come as a shock. For Scotus presents at first nothing but a mass of bristling syllogisms. Nevertheless behind this barrier savagely guarded is the sleeping beauty. That is why Scotus is not served in the ordinary course of scholastic philosophy. Scholastic philosophy must not go beyond what the average man with the unaided use of reason can attain; for a scholastic to appeal to private inspiration would be ludicrous. Actually Scotus knew this and never does appeal beyond reason. But he achieves his effect by hiatuses – as one might draw from all angles any number of lines correct but meaningless till you step back and see a radiant figure shaped not by the lines but by the points where they stop. Knowledge ceases on the threshold that Desire may enter in: he warns you about that at the beginning of his book. Hence as an intelligent everyman's guide to a harmonious solution of all intellectual problems, he is greatly inferior to St Thomas Aquinas. Yet to a poet so interwoven with the beauty of earth that heaven would seem agony without it, he might well be what he was to Hopkins, in 1879 'he who of all men most sways my spirits to peace', even if it was not peace with victory in theological examinations.

One ought really to approach this dramatically, showing by effect how to Hopkins through the murky air of the mediaeval lecture-room there dawned the revelation. But in the space available all one can do is to indicate some of the points where the minds of Scotus and Hopkins found themselves in unison. A convenient standpoint is the Scotist formal distinction between the Nature in a thing and its Individuality. Each man's nature is the Nature of all the world, elemental, vegetative, sensitive, human. But one man differs utterly from another because by his Individuality he possesses the common nature in an especial degree. The individual degree is the degree in which he lacks the Infinite; it knits together in the one man all his natural activities, animal, rational etc, and gives them direction God-wards. The effect of this metaphysical lack of the Infinite when felt physically by sympathy, seems to be the 'stress' of the opening verses of the 'Wreck of the Deutschland' – the 'touch' of God upon the very centre of the being: 'over again I feel Thy finger and find thee': cf also 'Thee God, I come from, to thee go'. Hence also the idea in 'In the Valley of the Elwy' and 'Ribblesdale', that only through man can earth go back to its Creator. It is important to note that according to Scotus, Christ as Man possesses His created Nature in the highest possible degree summing up all other degrees. Fittingly therefore the sonnet on individualities, 'As kingfishers catch fire, dragonflies draw flame', ends up with

> Chríst – for Christ plays in ten thousand places,
> Lovely in limbs, and lovely in eyes not his,
> To the Father through the features of men's faces.

This must lead on to a description however inadequate of the
Scotist theory of knowledge. The source and the object of all
knowledge in man is the common nature which he possesses: it
is that which gives colour, warmth, meaning etc, in response to
external excitations of the nervous system. Every distinct act of
knowing which takes in the adapted world of habit and practical necessity, has been preceded by a first act wherein sense and
intellect are one, a confused intuition of Nature as a living
whole, though the effect of the senses is to contract this intuition
to a particular 'glimpse', which is called the 'species specialis-
sima'. Ordinarily, no sooner has the glimpse occurred than
conation enters in and by abstraction adapts knowledge to suit
needs. But if the first act is dwelt on (by 'instress'?) to the
exclusion of succeeding abstractions, then you can feel, see, hear
or somehow experience the Nature which is yours and all
creation's as 'pattern, air melody, – what I call *inscape*'. And if
you can hold that, then you have a poem 'in petto' to which
with the abstractive intelligence you must return in order to
express it. That seems to be why Hopkins's images so tumble
over each other intertwining so as to keep pace with and capture
a single 'species' which has broken from his consciousness –
'How a lush-kept plush-capped sloe Will, mouthed to flesh-
burst, Gush! . . . Brim, in a flash, full!' The vividness of the
'glimpse' depends upon its nearness to the individual degree;
and its fertility depends upon the kindred 'species' which it
arouses to be re-experienced in the memory. The more perfect
the harmony between sensation and memory the more fully will
one glimpse Nature. Hopkins could justify himself when he
'knew the beauty of our Lord by a bluebell,' and in the flight of
a windhover, because in Christ is the fulness of Nature.

Scotus's theory of knowledge has been adapted for mystical
and for ascetic purposes. The mystical adaptation must be
passed over in silence except to opine that it does not support
the late Abbé Bremond's thesis in *Prayer and Poetry* though he
quotes it as doing so. But the ascetic adaptation is one which
seems to have had a very marked influence on Hopkins's poetry.
Holding, as 'To R. B.' shows him to have done, an inspirational
view of poetry, he seems to have connected Scotus's 'first act'
with that artistic inspiration which under differing names will
be familiar to all who know the aesthetic theories of various
nineteenth- and early twentieth-century psychologists. A useful

résumé of them is given by Professor Stewart in the second part of his book on Plato's Ideas where he is trying to explain the ἐξαίφνης κατόψεταί τι τὸ καλόν in current terminology. Now according to Scotus, this act being a spontaneous expression of Nature, is good but neither right nor wrong. To make it 'right' the individual will must step in and direct it to God by an act of love. Only thus can natural beauty be transformed into super-natural – 'God's better beauty, Grace.' This is the whole point of the poem 'How all's to one thing wrought': he praises the inspiration as a masterpiece of Nature, but mourns that it may have no more immortal value than 'sweet the golden glue that's builded by the bee.' And frequently one notes the same distrust of natural inspiration – perhaps because it really is as Bergson says akin to the hypnotic trance. In his unfinished poems, e.g. 'Moonrise', 'Ashboughs', 'The Woodlark', he abandons himself to it swaying in unison with nature. But in finished poems such as 'The Golden Echo', 'Sybil's Leaves', 'The Windhover' there is a deliberate intervention of the will-guided intelligence to give 'beauty back to God – beauty's self and beauty's giver'. And a terror lest natural beauty fade unharvested is the dominant note of all his poems on people. With such startling clearness did he realise that only through man's mind is Nature made transitorily beautiful – 'quench this clearest-selved spark' and '*both* are in an unfathomable dark drowned' – yet only in Christ by man's free will can both be made beautiful for ever.

How God the Son 'personifies' nature, is in the world yet not of it, Scotus strives to explain. Passages about Matter and the source of Light suggest that in such lines as 'lovely-asunder starlight wafting Him out of it' Hopkins was aiming at truth rather than fancy; and passages in the book on the Blessed Sacrament make the 'Hurrahing in Harvest' sonnet much less and much more than 'affectation in metaphor'.

But they meet, philosopher and poet, rather as fellow-pilgrims than as master and disciple. Both were trying in their different languages to express the vision of St Francis of Assisi. Perhaps they failed. It is difficult to say because at the end of both their lives failure in expression fulfilling the philosopher's tenet, became achievement in the will.

New Verse, No. 14 (April 1935)

Charles Madge (1935)

What is all this juice?

From Wordsworth to Hopkins the expanding universe has
not ceased to expand at an accelerating rate. Wordsworth
embraced nature in its calm and desolate aspects; he liked the
monumental quality of stones, the passionate quality of waterfalls, the eloquent isolation of a single acorn dropping in
the middle of a forest. By Hopkins's time however the cry had
gone out for life, life and more life. Instincts of hunting and
tearing to pieces, traces of Bacchantic or Corybantic psychology,
had been transferred into a furious and devouring love of
nature:

> The glassy peartree leaves and blooms, they brush
> The descending blue; that blue is all in a rush
> With richness; the racing lambs too have fair their fling.
> What is all this juice and all this joy?

Nature is felt to be naturally juicy and ripe. One can compare
the American Walt Whitman:

> Hefts of the moving world at innocent gambols silently rising,
>   freshly exuding,
> Scooting obliquely high and low.
> Something I cannot see puts upward libidinous prongs,
> Seas of bright *juice* suffuse heaven.

These images make their appeal straight to the salivary glands,
those telltale sources of moisture which have been so fruitful
a subject for Pavlov and physiological psychology. Note that
there is no attempt to inhibit their unrestrained, all-deluging
flow in such a key image as this in 'The Wreck of the
Deutschland':

> Is out with it! Oh,
> We lash with the best or worst
> Word last! How a lush-kept plush-capped sloe
> Will, mouthed to flesh-burst,
> Gush! – flush the man, the being with it, sour or sweet,
> Brim, in a flash, full! – Hither then, last or first, . . .

Walt Whitman was a peasant who wrote as he did out of sheer simplicity, but Hopkins was a Jesuit, and so these physiological excesses are with him complicated by religious sublimation. He was half ashamed of a kinship with Whitman which he could not disown.

Leaves of Grass appeared in 1855. Hopkins's poems were written between 1862 and 1889. Lear's Book of Nonsense was first published in 1846. Lewis Carroll produced his works between 1870 and 1880, period also of Maldoror and La Saison en Enfer – ceci pour les amateurs de chronologie synoptique.

In prospecting Victorian literature, one finds that the main streams are subterranean. Under cover of Tennyson and Long-fellow, a silent revolution took place[11]: the annihilation of the self. This annihilation was undertaken in two historic directions, Inwards, by the solipsist technique of Lear:

> We think so then and we thought so still[12]

and Outwards by the Whitmanesque identification of the self with Nature:

> I depart as air, I shake my white locks at the runaway sun
> I effuse my flesh in eddies, and drift it in lacy jags
> I bequeath myself to the dirt to grow from the grass I love,
> If you want me again look for me under your bootsoles[13]

In Hopkins the direction remains, to the end, undecided; one may find in him the solipsist rhetoric of dislocated syntax, discordia concors etc., but none the less it is as an exponent of lacy jags – the violent self-identification with kinaesthetic Nature, and the exalted physical states of empathic hyperaesthesia – that he is interesting in 1935.

The following phrases from 'A Vision of the Mermaids' shows the vocabulary of hyperaesthesia already prominent in his earliest writing, where indeed his luxurious sensuality is that of Keats:

> ... fretted falls ...
> lace of rosy weed ...
> flesh-flowers ...
> dainty-delicate fretted fringe of fingers ...

In his last poems he contrasts the laciness of nature with his own sterility:

> . . . See, banks and brakes
> Now, leavèd how thick! lacèd they are again
> With fretty chervil, look, and fresh wind shakes
> Them; birds build – but not I build; no, but strain,
> Time's eunuch, and not breed one work that wakes.

In the intermediate period one can collect phrases such as 'the midriff astrain with leaning of, laced with fire of stress,' 'fresh youth fretted in a bloomfall', 'How lovely the elder brother's/ Life all laced in the other's/Love-laced!', 'lace', . . . 'footfretted', 'hornbeam fretty'.

Lacy and *fretty* should not be described as typical of Hopkins's imagery, because they are *not* images, but modes of sensation, and Hopkins poured all his consciousness into these sensations. Nature takes laced and fretted forms to express its violent intricacy, its identity with the exploring fingers which are the amoeboid pseudopodia of consciousness itself, pushing out into every cranny of shape, figure and sensation. In Hopkins, as in Whitman, locks blown in the wind have the significance of flames rising from the physical being and searching the air of nature with fingers and tongues: 'Finger of a tender of, O of a feathery delicacy,' '. . . curls/Wag or crossbridle, in a wind lifted, windlaced – /See his wind-lilylocks-laced', 'clammyish lashtender combs', 'monstrous hand gropes with clammy fingers' . . .

The Whitman of *Leaves of Grass* and *Scented Herbage of my Breast* adopted the character of a poetic herbivore, and Hopkins is fond of an edible and potable nature: 'ale like goldy foam/ That frocks an oar'. . . . 'broth of goldish flue', 'golden glue'.

There is no space to describe the opposite tendency in Hopkins towards metallic, glacial, fibrous forms, his *winter world*. The Bergsonian fountain falls back into abstraction. The price of hyperaesthetic ecstasy is the rigidity of death.

> O slender leaves [writes Whitman],
> O blossoms of my blood! I permit you to tell me in your own way
>   of the heart that is under you
> O I do not know what you mean there underneath yourselves,
>   you are not happiness.
> You are often more bitter than I can bear, you burn and sting me
> Yet you are beautiful to me you faint-tinged roots, you make me
>   think of death.

And Hopkins writes

> A juice rides rich through bluebells, in vine leaves,
> And beauty's dearest, veriest vein is tears.

There is always a leaden echo; and Hopkins dreading the sound attempts to hear a golden echo, the false gold of religion, where Whitman professes himself indifferent.

New Verse, no. 14 (April 1935)

Geoffrey Grigson (1935)

Blood or Bran

Only for the most select and most balanced minds does it seem possible to guard the perceived picture of external reality against the distortion to which it is otherwise subjected in its transit through the psychic individuality of the one perceiving it.

Freud, *Psychopathology of Everyday Life*

As much as to any poet this statement by Freud applies to Gerard Manley Hopkins, though if it is to be applied at all to artists, one must emphasise and extend the word 'distortion,' and distinguish, as instruments, the 'psychic individuality' from 'imagination,' which is its highest conscious function. Mr Madge shows in his article [see above], or partly shows, how the psychic and physiological individuality of Hopkins unconsciously twisted the reality which he perceived. One can say more after examining Hopkins's language, his images, and his letters. It will not injure Hopkins – I disagree with Mr Madge's conclusion – but it will show in him the attempt to control (not suppress) certain phenomena of his mental life in favour of the imagination, i.e. in favour of being an artist.

In one of the letters a play by Bridges is attacked for the unreality of its characters: 'The characters from men become puppets, *their bloodshed becomes a leakage of bran.*' That is typical: for Hopkins blood had to be blood, not bran. Actively as well as passively he was interested in pain. He was interested in the gash, the bloody flow, the bloody hour of the martyrs. Self-humiliation, and pain in others, did not obsess him, but they were always important to him. They entered into a great many of his poems. 'Gash', with the implications of opened flesh and squirting blood was a word frequently used and blood was part of descriptions in which it might least be expected. The sky was gashed and bloody (1862), cinders gash themselves (1877), poppies are 'blood-gush blade-gash' and apple blossom 'drop-of-blood-and-foam-dapple'. This interest is obvious in the extraordinary letter to Bridges (1888) in which he talks of reading Dana's *Two Years Before the Mast*, which describes the flogging of two spread-eagled sailors, 'a flogging, which is terrible and instructive *and it happened* – ah, that is the charm and the main point', and in the letter following, giving details of how a young man, a medical student who 'possibly knew how to proceed,' put his eyes out with a stick and some wire. 'The eyes were found among nettles in a field.' Most thoroughly and consistently this algolagnia appears in Hopkins's writings about martyrdom. These begin with his first extant poem *The Escorial* (1860):

> For that staunch saint still prais'd his Master's name
> While his cracked flesh lay hissing in the grate.

This poem and 'In honour of St Alphonsus Rodriguez' ('and those strokes that once gashed flesh') are the only ones dealing with martyrdom which were completed, but martyrdom is incidental in each. 'Margaret Clitheroe', in honour of the Catholic martyr who was pressed to death ('within her womb the child was quick'), a poem on the martyrdom of Campion, Sherwin and Bryant (of which nothing survives) and his tragedy of passion on St Winefred ('I all my being hacked in half with her neck'), were never finished and I incline to believe that this was not due to Hopkins's habitual failure to complete various things begun, but to half (and only half) realised suspicion that he was not interested in martyrdom purely, or with a full religious intention.

What is corybantic, sadistic (the images of anvils, forging, etc., are near the images of blood), connected with masculine beauty, with storm and big seas and death by drowning, etc., in Hopkins's poetry fixes him sharply in his time between Keats and T. S. Eliot, Beddoes and Aubrey Beardsley: what takes him out of his time is this honest half-knowledge of his own situation. He wished to achieve 'the pure art, morally neutral', in which such interests without being suppressed can be controlled and philosophically employed; and Hopkins knew himself, vaguely or at least without enough definition, to be a bit 'blackguardly': 'I always knew in my heart Walt Whitman's mind to be more like my own than any other man's living. As he is a very great scoundrel that is not a pleasant confession.' He makes another such confession when he writes to Bridges about R. L. Stevenson: 'You are certainly wrong about Hyde being overdrawn: my Hyde is worse,' and it is in contrast with himself that he praises Dixon for 'pure imagination, either arising from images in nature (as in the Rainbow poem) or expressing itself in them', for being a gentleman and thinking like one. In the sense of his letter on the gentleman, Hopkins felt himself to be inferior. Though he had more of it than most poets he knew that he had not enough of the 'true virtue' which he describes as 'that chastity of mind which seems to lie at the very heart and be the parent of all other good, the seeing at once what is best, the holding to that, and the not allowing anything else whatever to be even pleading to the contrary'.[14]

The more balanced and Miltonic style which Hopkins wished to evolve would have been the style of a poetry less dominated by his psychic individuality. That is certain; and his poems, many of those which have been most praised, are damaged by morbid exuberance, and damaged (or made, I would also agree) by the sense of guilt from unforgiven 'blackguardliness,' which the 'blackguard' half understood. The wrong way to consider Hopkins in these facts is the way which upset Robert Bridges or the ignorant way in which Charles Kingsley (whom Hopkins detested) wrote of Webster (Whom Hopkins probably admired[15]); 'the stength of Webster's confest mastership lies simply in his acquaintance with vicious nature in general. We will say no more on this matter, save to ask "cui bono?" Was the art of which this was the highest manifestation likely to be of much use to mankind?' This simply is suppression of the greasy truth by hiding it under the antimacassar. It was not Hopkins's way. He was prepared to admit the evil in himself, the significance of which he did not fully understand. He could not, as an artist, separate himself from that evil, which is the evil of humanity; and use it, as Webster did, to the fuller imaginative ends of a tragic art.

Hopkins would have been a more excellent poet, had he known himself better; and those who read his poems will not be good readers unless they also examine themselves. The danger is to find Hopkins either repellent or attractive because of half knowledge or ignorance of one's own psychogenic or physiological nature.

New Verse, no. 14 (April 1935)

Donald Davie (1952)

In 1878 appeared another guiding principle in Hopkins's criticism, his devotion to Milton:

> The same M. Arnold says Milton and Campbell are our two greatest masters of *style*. Milton's art is incomparable, not only in English literature, but, I should think, almost in any; equal, if not more than equal, to the finest of Greek or Roman. And considering that this is shown especially in his verse, his rhythm and metrical system, it is amazing that so great a writer as Newman should have fallen into the blunder of comparing the first chorus of the *Agonistes* with the opening of *Thalaba* as instancing the gain in smoothness and correctness of versification made since Milton's time ...

Milton is, for Hopkins, always the final court of appeal. And it is worth remarking that those modern readers who have most readily embraced Hopkins's poetry and his criticism are very often those who have called in question Milton's prestige, or at any rate the fruitfulness of his influence. Hopkins is quite unambiguous. He puts forward Milton, time and again, as a model; and in so doing he flies in the face not only of modern poets, Ezra Pound and T. S. Eliot, but also of Keats and Cowper. In effect, he challenges one of the best authenticated working principles in the English poetic tradition – the principle that Milton, however great in himself, is a bad example for other poets. Was Hopkins alive to certain Miltonic aspects of his own poetry which his modern critics conspire to ignore, or merely cannot see? Of course he was indebted to Milton for the first hints of his novel prosody, and this is certainly one aspect of his art which has not engaged his later readers so much as he expected. But this does not entirely explain the matter; for Milton repeatedly appears in connection with 'Style' and, while this term is never fully explained by Hopkins, it plainly involves for him much more than prosody. It is quite possible of course that the critics may have seen the nature of Hopkins's achievement more clearly than he saw it himself; and that where he thought himself indebted to Milton, he was mistaken. But for students of his criticism the problem remains. Milton's practice is central to that criticism; and this must make it very different from the criticism of Keats, of Cowper or of Mr Eliot. It is worth asking where and how Hopkins differs from these authorities, and whether he differs for the better or for the worse.

'Miltonic style' soon appears in connection with another important principle, as novel as that of 'Parnassian', the idea of 'inscape':

> No doubt my poetry errs on the side of oddness. I hope in time to have a more balanced and Miltonic style. But as air, melody, is what strikes me most of all in music and design in painting, so design, pattern or what I am in the habit of calling 'inscape' is what I above all aim at in poetry. Now it is the virtue of design, pattern, or inscape to be distinctive and it is the vice of distinctiveness to become queer. This vice I cannot have escaped.

It has been found by critics of Hopkins's poetry that to explain 'inscape' it is necessary to explore the poet's theology and philosophy, especially his admiring study of Duns Scotus. The same, of course, is true of his criticism. Every system of criticism rests, explicitly or not, upon a moral philosophy, and to do justice to the criticism one should ideally set it in that context. On the other hand I am concerned with how far Hopkins's standards of criticism are viable, how far they can be adopted with profit by readers professing quite different philosophies. And for this purpose it is enough to point out that, for Hopkins, since 'it is the virtue of design, pattern, or inscape to be distinctive', this principle is closely related to 'the Parnassian'. Hopkins shows himself here aware of some of the dangers inherent in giving to 'distinctiveness' such value as he does. It is interesting to know how he intended to guard against those dangers, or whether he thought them only a risk that must be run.

To 1870 belong most of the snap-judgments that show Hopkins at his best. There is the comment on Swinburne, for instance:

> I do not think that kind goes far: it expresses passion but not feeling, much less character. This I say in general or of Swinburne in particular. Swinburne's genius is astonishing, but it will, I think, only do one thing.

Or this on Tennyson:

> . . .there may be genius uninformed by character. I sometimes wonder at this in a man like Tennyson: his gift of utterance is truly golden, but go further home and you come to thoughts common-place and wanting in nobility (it seems hard to say it but I think you know what I mean). In Burns there is generally recognised a richness and beauty of manly character which lends worth to some of his smallest fragments, but there is a great want in his utterance; it is never really beautiful, he had no eye for pure beauty, he gets no nearer than the fresh picturesque expressed in fervent and flowing language . . .

Or the comment on the age:

> For it seems to me that the poetical language of an age should be the current language heightened, to any degree heightened and unlike itself, but not (I mean normally: passing freaks and graces are another thing) an obsolete one. That is Shakespeare's and Milton's practice and the want of it will be fatal to Tennyson's Idylls and plays, to Swinburne, and perhaps to Morris.

Or, more generally, on obscurity:

> One of two kinds of clearness one should have – either the meaning to be felt without effort as fast as one reads or else, if dark at first reading, when once made out *to explode*.

This certainly does not exhaust the question of how a poet transmits his meanings, but it could hardly be bettered as a handy rule-of-thumb. In the same way, many readers will admire the way the critic goes at once to the heart of the matter, in the judgments on his contemporaries. But even here there are puzzling elements. However warmly we may agree that 'the poetical language of an age should be the current language heightened', we are not used to seeing Milton cited as an authority for it. Keats, we remember, discarded the Miltonic 'Hyperion' just because 'English must be kept up'. And in the same way, we may be sure that Hopkins is right about Tennyson and yet wonder if he is right about Burns. 'He had no eye for pure beauty . . .' – we suspect that 'pure beauty' never meant anything exact, and we should blush to see it in critical parlance today. Whatever the force of 'pure' we may find it a narrow notion of beauty that cannot find room for 'the fresh picturesque'. And does not such a narrowness reflect upon the critic?

Purity of Diction in English Verse, 1952

Geoffrey Grigson (1955)

The poetry of Gerard Manley Hopkins might be called a 'passionate science'. Like other poets and like painters of his era, this poet and priest delighted in the observation and grasping of nature. With the greatest delicacy, strength, and intelligence he possessed his environment, making it the inseparable, intimate vehicle for the passionate praises of his belief.

Hopkins is 'strange'; and for a long while his poems, which were first published in 1918, twenty-nine years after his death, had to be excused or grudged or argued about on that score. Yet the strangeness of Hopkins is only concentrated in the excess and force of his qualities; there was nothing strange about his turn to a strong naturalism, to a passionate science, at his particular time, in the nineteenth century; he was born five years after Cézanne, four years after Thomas Hardy, a year after Henry James. The scientific mind had slowly formed, slowly extroverted itself on to nature, and at an even slower rate the concerns of the artist had been extroverted in the same direction, at least outwardly. The process had already known its phases and varieties. A being and a personality had been ascribed to nature; some artists had been pantheists, some nature-drunkards. Passionate emotions declined to an easy, popular, sentiment: poets and painters then corrected themselves by looking carefully at the select details of nature.

In the eighteen-sixties, at home and at school in London, at the university in Oxford, Hopkins was familiar with the poems of Tennyson, Browning, Coventry Patmore, with the prose of Ruskin, and with the careful painting of the Pre-Raphaelites. Nature, he could well detect, had become something to employ: the selected details were presented almost for themselves, or else as ornaments of a moral tale. Tennyson in the 'sixties was talking upon one occasion about Irish landscape: 'I saw wonderful things there: twenty different showers at once in a great expanse – a vast yellow cloud with a little bit of rainbow stuck on one corner.' William Allingham, who put this on record, says that Tennyson swept his arm round for the cloud and gave a nick in the air with his thumb for the bit of rainbow; and then added 'I wish I could bring these things in'. Or again, Allingham and Tennyson talked of the kinship between white lilies and white peacocks; Allingham quoted Browning on a passage in Tennyson's *Princess*: 'Tennyson,' said Browning, 'has taken to white peacocks. I always intended to use them. The Pope has a number of white peacocks.'

Browning intended to *use* white peacocks; Tennyson has *taken to* them, Tennyson always wanted to *bring in* those things which he so delicately noticed. Hopkins, coming after them, more intelligent, more passionate, did not select details and add them up. He did not make rhetorical gestures towards nature; no wave of an arm for the yellow cloud, no nick of a thumb for the rainbow. A first and central fact of his poems is their birth in a science of passionate empathy, carried so far that it distinguishes Hopkins entirely from every other English poet. So, to begin with, what was the manner and what was the method of this earnest empathic possession of his environment?

As well as the poems, we have luckily these journals which Hopkins kept from 1868 to 1875. They are not very long, and they are nature journals or journals of observation. But they are difficult to read because of the extremely solid and packed quality of that observation. In the journals one notices, although Hopkins is personal and selective, not so much of his immediate passion as a certain more or less scientific neutrality; this selective observer is free from most of our common associative poetic preferences. In 1871 Hopkins put down an observation upon the leaves of Wood Sorrel, a common enough European and English plant. 'The half-opened wood-sorrel leaves,' he wrote, 'the centre or spring of the leaflets rising foremost and the leaflets dropping back like ears, leaving straight-chipped clefts between them, look like some green lettering.' That is easy for the reader to take. Though wood sorrel is not a species like rose or columbine or iris or lily in the tradition of aesthetic preference, a poet of the mid- or later nineteenth century may be expected to like an organism so crisp and delicate; and the accuracy of description is quite obvious, the analogue is not immediately too peculiar. This comparison of the tiny, crisp leaves to green lettering by itself de-limits the leaves and gives to their colour its correct sharpness.

In 1872, on a Holy Saturday warm with thunder, Hopkins observed 'odd tufts of thin-textured very plump round clouds something like' – and the convincing analogue is less expected – 'something like the eggs in an opened ant-hill'. Clouds, as well, are poetic properties of the century: they would do for other English poets, Patmore or Tennyson or Barnes or Bridges; yet now the explicative object is more peculiar, the clouds are like ants' eggs in the opened nest, they are different altogether from Tennyson's clouds in water-colour; and the nature of the Hopkins science is more revealed. The more excessive peculiarity begins to demand more knowledge and attention; although in his poems Hopkins does check too much eccentricity of observation, too much intrusion of peculiar things which are outside the likely experience of readers. The journal was for himself alone.

In 1870, concerned with the beauties and severities of the winter and neutrally alive to things as much in one place as another, Hopkins observed that 'the slate slabs of the urinals even are frosted with graceful sprays'. Or in Lancashire in 1873 he watched a dying sheep under a stone hedge, making of it an entirely matter-of-fact record without sentiment: 'There ran slowly from his nostril a thick flesh-coloured ooze, scarlet in places, coiling and roping its way down, so thick that it looked like fat.'

Here, with letter-leaves, ant's egg clouds, roping ooze and frost-sprayed urinals, we are divorced from the averagely fine poetic detection of the nineteenth century. Here – and almost everywhere in Hopkins – we knock our sensibilities against exactitudes and starknesses which may still repel or dismay either those who live aesthetically in older, gentler modes or those who do not require to live outwardly at all. The peculiarity goes further, in one respect. In these notes out of the journal Hopkins uses 'like' – *like* fat, *like* ants' eggs in the opened nest, *like* green lettering. In his greater intensities 'like' disappears: adjectives, compound adjectives, compound nouns, active and embracing and characterising verbs, take its place; words have been as starkly and freshly scrutinised and possessed as any other relevant part or property of the poet's environment, until the selected words are as close an equivalent as they can be to the things and the actions and the states which they convey. Thus pigeons go 'strutting and *jod-jodding* with their heads'. 'Jod' is a rare verb, yet its revival and adaptation are not frigid or eccentric. One acknowledges at once that pigeons behave exactly so.

In the acceptance of his poems, in the critical unravelling of their verbal knots, in the general consideration of Hopkins as a poet of his time who was as yet absolutely distinct, this peculiar science of his does not receive enough attention. To know this poet one does not need dictionaries alone, or a fine recognition of ambiguities alone, or only a knowledge of the Ignatian Exercises or of Duns Scotus, 'Of realty the rarest-veined unraveller': one must also have or must also cultivate some equivalence of pure sensation, some of Hopkins's own accurate empathic cognition of the plants, trees, fruit, metals, skies, clouds, sunsets, birds, waters, surfaces, grains, activities, perfumes, of all the phenomena at which he stared or to which he opened his senses.

Gerard Manley Hopkins, 'Writers and their Work'
no. 59 booklet, British Council, 1955

David Jones (1962)

For the 'poet' or the 'artist' the 'past' is much what 'nature' is to him – it is the raw stuff which he uses. But when that 'past' is virtually forgotten and available perhaps (as in the Welsh case), in another linguistic tradition and moreover a tradition separated from us by centuries of a contrary tradition, that *poeta* is in a real jam. I don't pretend to know what the answer is. But I do believe that this is [a] *main and a mental* difficulty (there are others) for the Welshman – or the half-Welshman, writing in English. The name 'Rhiannon' is a very good symbol of what I am trying to say. The name means a very great deal to me – it means as much as some Classical name or some biblical name, but when one writes it down one *knows* that not only will the reader be unable to pronounce it but that its connotations, the Celtic Mother Goddess, 'Ragantona', the 'Great Queen', the woman who did penance at the horse-block, etc. etc. etc., will be *wholly* lost on the 'English' reader and, alas, on many 'Welsh' readers also. It is this 'break' with a whole extremely complex, cultural, religious and linguistic tradition that is the real buggeration for those of us who, while able only to use English, have our deepest roots (in some way or other) in the Welsh past.

I expect this is the reason why part-Welshmen (such as myself) have drawn so much on Malory and the English-French Arthurian sources. For there alone there is a connecting link between the tradition of Wales and that of England. But this is far from satisfactory. For one thing the 'Arthurian' material has been vitiated by a kind of Tennysonian romanticism, which is so very other from Malory, *let alone* from the Welsh deposits. As I say, I don't know *what* the answer is. Perhaps there isn't one!

But at all events those of us who chance to be in some way 'Welsh' cannot (except by total silence) do other than continue to draw upon such fragmentary bits and pieces of our national heritage as may be available to us in an alien tongue (*I speak only for myself*) and try to embody it as best we may (a poor best) in our English writings.

That (in my view) very great poet, Gerard Manley Hopkins, did, (in quite another way – technically that is) envigorate the English language[16] by his study of Welsh metrical forms. It was an outstanding achievement, the implications of which are still barely understood – perhaps less understood now than twenty years ago. But that is rather another matter. I am here thinking more of 'content' than of 'form'. And as far as 'content' is concerned Hopkins seems to me very 'Victorian' English[17], though, of course, with the great difference of being profoundly of a Catholic mind. One thing that I find interesting but hardly ever referred to is that the 'English Metaphysicals' of the seventeenth century were so very largely of the Welsh border-lands. This is interesting because, as far as I can gather, the Welsh poets writing in Welsh in the medieval period and before did not, except for some exceptions, show this metaphysical tendency at all. Yet, what must be called the first generation of anglicised Welshmen or part-Welshmen of more or less aristo-cratic status such as Vaughan and Herbert and for that matter Donne etc., comprise the core of the 'English Metaphysical' poetry. I wonder why this was? Then it ended as abruptly as it started.

Letter to Vernon Watkins, 11 April 1962

John Wain (1966)

Those commentators who have portrayed him against a back-ground, showing us a Hopkins not isolated but nourished by a corporate life and a corporate vision, have always had to make that background one of piety and duty. Never of art, never of imagination. As a priest among priests, as a scholar among scholars, Hopkins knew fulfilment and the commentators have been able to show us that fulfilment. But as a poet among poets he was lonely. 'I have made writing so difficult,' he complained in a moment of weariness; weariness with the long critical struggle to rethink the problem of poetics from an isolated position; weariness with the incomprehension of those who should have been his allies. 'A perfect organisation for crippling me exists and the one for "encouragemental purposes" (modern English) is not laid down yet,' he wrote, wryly, to Bridges. And to Dixon, a poet far from widely recognised, 'It is sad to think what disappointment must many times over have filled your heart for the darling children of your mind . . . For disappoint-ment and humiliations embitter the heart and make an aching in the very bones.'

It will be my purpose in this essay to sketch a Hopkins both isolated and involved, both idiosyncratic and completely central. With regard to the immediate circumstances of his life – his life, that is, as a poet – he was eccentric, running counter to the whole accepted system. But in a wider perspective he appears as the one traveller who has found the path. What I take to be a wider perspective will begin from the fact that Hopkins was born in 1844. Already by that date the new kind of society had developed in every western European country; the civilised world had finally made the crossing from an agricultural to an industrial economy. And by the time Hopkins grew up to maturity the changed demands which confronted everyone – the artist, the priest, the ruler, the citizen, even the criminal and the madman – had become pressing and inescapable. In the world created by industrialism, nothing would work in quite the same way as it had worked before. Tradition and habit were still valuable, but to remain effective they had to be re-examined. From this point of view it is Bridges, Patmore, and Dixon who are peripheral and Hopkins who is central. His re-examination is so much more fundamental than theirs; it is on a level with the re-examination that was currently being undertaken on the other side of the Channel. Hopkins seems lonely and idiosyncratic compared with Bridges, Poet Laureate and resident of Boar's Hill. But compare him with Baudelaire, Rimbaud, Verlaine, Laforgue, and one sees a major artist moving naturally among his peers. Like them, he was writing the new poetry. He had faced the problems, carried out the initial reassessment of the means that were to hand, and had already started on the task.

From this point of view, it is arguable that Hopkins was strengthened, rather than crippled, by the fact of his being a Jesuit and therefore isolated in the most literal, physical sense from the ordinary life of his time. A detachment such as his was hard to achieve in the densely-organised intellectual and artistic world of nineteenth-century England. The other writers, even when they are protesting against their age, seem so very much *of* it. Not that it is a handicap, generally speaking, for an artist to be strongly characteristic of his time. But there are certain moments in the history of the arts when the need is for boldness, for a new and independent programme. It was not lack of talent that kept English writers from coming up with this new programme, but lack of freedom. They reacted against their age so much in its own terms. They denounced it in its own vocabulary. In all that burst of intellectual energy, only one English writer found it possible to transform his imaginative procedures with a completeness that matched the transformation in industrial, scientific, and social procedures. Only one, and he the most isolated.

If my argument appears to contain contradictions, I must ask for your patience. For the situation I am describing does in fact include contradictory elements. Hopkins *was* isolated. He felt keenly that he was considered eccentric and that he could count on no support. 'A perfect organisation for crippling me exists.' Yet it is also true that he *was* central, and that the amiable but rather ineffectual club of lettered gentlemen who made up the official literary scene were by comparison peripheral. The club functioned too smoothly; it was too comfortable; to belong to it was to make a bargain with industrial society. The French poets knew better than to make any such bargain. In the latter half of the nineteenth century French poetry is far more interesting than English, and the reason seems to be not only that it is technically bolder but that it is also more honest and serious. The French poets are not concerned with keeping up a position in society, making poetry a respectable profession, standing well with the Royal Family, or making provision for their descendants. They are concerned with only one thing – to tell the truth. Modern industrial civilisation has become intolerable and they have no objection to saying so openly. Modern rationalistic thinking has impoverished the human spirit by banishing dreams to the pillow and nonsense to the nursery; they will restore them to dignity. Modern linguistic usage, developed to meet the needs of a scientific and commercial world, is incapable of ranging over a wide enough field of significance; they will give back to it the richness of a primitive vocabulary. English poets were restrained from doing these things, not by lack of talent but by an over-developed social instinct. When Verlaine tried to explain to Yeats why he had turned aside from the task of translating *In Memoriam*, he put his finger on just this quality. 'Tennyson is too noble, too *anglais*; when he should have been broken-hearted, he had many reminiscences.'

Above all, the French poets were the enemies of what is nowadays called 'culture'. In a consumer-orientated world the artist and the thinker are encouraged to see themselves as producing a commodity, which, by means of government departments, Foundations, Ministries, and the like, can be exported, imported, weighed and measured by officials, and generally treated as one undifferentiated substance. It is this substance to which the modern bureaucrat gives the name 'culture'. In Hopkins's day the production and marketing of culture had not yet become highly organised; still, I think I make myself clear when I say that Hopkins was like Baudelaire or Rimbaud, but unlike Tennyson or Bridges, in being outside the world of 'culture' and indifferent to it.[18] The French poets achieved their immunity from culture partly by being disreputable, poor, and diseased; Rimbaud in particular, whose ambition was to murder culture, attacked it so hard that he went straight through and came out on the other side, reducing himself to silence after the age of eighteen. Yet in those few years he had already shown himself a great poet. Hopkins does not, in any detail of his life, resemble these poets; yet the overall pattern of his life resembles theirs ...

If we cast about for anything in Victorian verse that resembles the work of Hopkins in boldness and originality, we shall find that the most serious candidates are the nonsense poets. For it was in the work of Dodgson and Lear that the English imagination, dammed up by institutional respectability and rationalistic good manners, burst out into the open. The extent to which the 'official' literature of the twentieth century has derived from, and paid tribute to, the unofficial literature of the nineteenth is a striking testimony to this. When he goes into the nursery, the Victorian poet is free to forget his social responsibilities and say what is in his mind ...

Alone among the English poets, he is willing to try anything, to desert logic, to wrench language, to treat the individual word as a mystery and a challenge. To him, the iron curtain between 'sense' and 'nonsense' does not exist.

> The blue wheat-acre is underneath
> And the braided ear breaks out of the sheath,
> And ear in milk, lush the sash,
> And crush-silk poppies aflash,
> The blood-gush blade-gash
> Flame-rash rudred

Bud shelling or broad-shed
Tatter-tassel-tangled and dingle-a-danglèd
Dandy-hung dainty head.

Essays on Literature and Ideas, 1966

John Berryman (1968)

Father Hopkins, teaching elementary Greek
whilst his mind climbed the clouds, also died here.
O faith in all he lost.
Swift wandered mad through his rooms & could not speak.
A milkman sane died, the one one, I fear.
His name was gone almost.

Hopkins's credits, while the Holy Ghost
rooted for Hopkins, hit the Milky Way.
This is a ghost town.
It's Xmas. Henry, can you reach the post?
Yeats did not die here – died in France, they say,
brought back by a warship & put down.

Joyce died overseas also but Hopkins died here:
where did they plant him, after the last exam?
To his own lovely land
did they rush him back, out of his hole unclear,
barbaric & green, or did they growl 'God's damn'
the lousy Jesuit, canned.

No. 377 in *His Toy, His Dream, His Rest*, 1968

'How Meet Beauty':
A Broadcast Symposium (1977)

CHRISTOPHER RICKS: If one wonders how the original readers of Hopkins – whether they were his friends, like Bridges, or

whether they were his first readers in 1918, thirty years after his death – how they could have missed what Hopkins himself calls 'the roll, the rise, the carol, the creation', one answer must surely be that the verse seemed to them to move so strangely. They perhaps could see that it bristled with life, but it seemed to bristle with difficulties, too. Roy Fuller started us off on a discussion of the prosody and on whether or not we need to know, as readers, some of the things which Hopkins needed to know as the writer.

ROY FULLER: I think the question of looking at these poems without all that hoo-ha about the prosody is extremely difficult. I'll take just one example. Hopkins is quite likely, when he's writing strong rhythm to have a foot of one syllable. Now this is very upsetting, I think, if you're looking at it from a theoretical point of view. If you're looking at it from a practical point of view there's no difficulty. If it's one of Hopkins's very strong words – it might be 'thong' or something – you're quite prepared to linger on that and treat it as a foot. But if you're trying to count the number of feet in the line; if it's a sonnet and you know, you've been told, that it's a sonnet of Alexandrines or a sonnet of five stress lines, that you have a couple of one syllable feet, then you're up a gum tree, aren't you? So far as your counting is concerned, your reading of the poem is made so much more difficult; so that I think, really, having done your homework, as it were, on the metrics, the best thing is to forget them.

GRAHAM STOREY: It was stress that he aimed at, the maximum stress or emphasis – for him the essence of poetry, above all, and he kept on insisting on this in letter after letter, on poetry heard as against read, performed. Sprung rhythm makes verse stressy: it gave him infinitely greater flexibility than the conventional standard or running rhythm. He could put his stresses where he wanted. Abruptly juxtaposed, bumping up against each other, hence the spring, or with any number of weak, unaccented syllables in-between. So that sprung rhythm – surely his main poetic innovation – constantly, as he put it, 'fetched his meaning out'.

D. W. HARDING: When you examine the scheme of prosody that he put forward – his sprung rhythm – it's so filled with provisos and reservations and exceptions that it becomes an extremely flexible scheme that could really accommodate all the rhythms that he wanted to use, and I don't think that you could ever derive the proper reading of a line of his verse from applying his metrical scheme, and you get a kind of balance in the line that is not symmetrical. It's rather like an asymmetrical balance in a painting. A couple of lines from the poem for St Alphonsus where he says that God could 'Crowd career with conquest while there went/Those years and years by of world without event'. You could of course get two flowing lines. Just say 'Could crowd career with conquest while there went/Those years and years of world without event'. But he breaks it. The effect of the break is to drag out the first rhythmical unit: 'those years and years by'.

MARTIN JARRETT-KERR: The point I think that is worth making is that it's an oddity not only of his poetry but also of his prose, and not only of his studies in prose but even of his quite occasional prose, even in his own letters when he's writing off the cuff. I mean . . . a couple of quotations from letters: 'dine out, we seldom do', and even more striking 'meant to write I have every day for long'. Well, when you're writing somebody saying, 'I'm terribly sorry, I meant to answer your letter a long time ago and I've been meaning to answer it for a long time,' you don't normally turn your words around like that, and I suppose this must have been a quirk of the man. I think he had a tortuous mind, and he was always twisting himself spiritually, as well as intellectually, into knots: and I suppose this affected his style. I think it was a search for honesty.

ALFRED THOMAS: He gives one of the finest instructions he ever gave about his poetry when he says, 'I wish to be read with the ears'.

GEOFFREY HILL: The interest for me is mainly in the fact that Hopkins – if you recall in the definition that he himself gives of sprung rhythm where he says that one stress makes one foot, no matter how many or few the syllables – then adds, 'I should add that the word "sprung" means something like "abrupt"'. Now this word 'abrupt' I find extremely interesting because it's the same word that occurs, with rather different connotation, in the sonnet on Henry Purcell. I'm thinking of the lines 'It is the forgèd feature finds me; it is the rehearsal/Of own, of abrùpt sèlf there so thrusts on, so throngs the ear'. Now, it's clear that Hopkins was a very careful, very precise, user of words and even if his conscious mind were not brooding upon this word 'abrupt' I think that possibly unconsciously the metrical and the psychological were coming together in a fascinating way there. It's as though the abruptness that he speaks about in connection with rhythm relates to his delight in the revelation of the distinctive self and this unity of spiritual or psychological concern with intimate metrical and rhythmical concerns is, I think, the crux of Hopkins' achievement as a poet ...

GRAHAM STOREY: I think that stress, the maximum aimed-at expressiveness which underlies the sprung rhythm also explains most of the apparent syntactical distortions or idiosyncrasies as well: the inversions, the telescopings, the omitted relative pronouns: almost all the things he had to explain in letter after letter to Bridges. All are ways of concentrating, energising the meaning, lessening or omitting what didn't matter to him, just as the strong stresses of his sprung rhythm lessened in their way the slack, unaccented syllables in-between. Both the syntactical concentration and the stresses are what, in one letter, he called 'bidding', discarding everything that does not 'bid', does not *tell*. It's in one of my favourite poems, 'Henry Purcell', the musician whom Hopkins himself most loved. And it's the beginning and, again, it's a fairly famous syntactical crux. 'Have fair fallen, O fair, fair have fallen, so dear/To me, so arch-especial a spirit as heaves in Henry Purcell'. On the 'Have fair fallen', I will simply read out his own explanation to Bridges: ' "Have" is the singular imperative or optative, if you like, of the past, a thing possible and actual both in logic and grammar, but naturally a rare one. As in the second person we say, "have done", or making appointments, "have had your dinner beforehand": so one can say in the third person not only "fair fall", what is present or future, but also "have fair fallen" of what is past.'

ROY FULLER: There are a number of absolutely stunning images which in a way I suppose have not been equalled, have they, in English poetry. I mean, I would give an example of the image 'like shining from shook foil' which is rather extraordinary because it's only in our day, when we put things in – you know – roasting bags, where I think this comes home to everybody.

ELIZABETH JENNINGS: Everything in Hopkins is dynamic. That is the thing. He's a very, very dynamic writer. Full of energy. He can halt. He can use words and phrases and images, use them in a very sort of athletic kind of way. And whatever the subject, when it is most dark ... the energy pulses through and then ends in a wonderful simplicity of a line like 'all/Life death does end and each day dies with sleep'. You know it's really Shakespearian, that.

D. W. HARDING: He's working at the far remove from cliché. He's gone to the opposite extreme. He accepts a minimum of ready-made moulds for putting his thought into and consequently he's looking just for the terms that convey most of the force of his feeling, and he uses those compressed as closely as possible and in whatever order fits the rhythm but also expresses the emotion that he's conveying in the words.

GEORGE BARKER: I think he's one of the few English poets that can invest intellectual operations with a tremendous sensuality so that the words, which are so often Anglo-Saxon words, in fact have the most tremendous intellectual responsibility. I think it's De Quincey who says Latin is the language of the intellect, Saxon the language of the emotions. I personally think that the extraordinary thing about Hopkins is he reversed just precisely that proposition!

GEOFFREY HILL: From Coleridge on, it has been observed, quite rightly, that literature demands attention. That reading is not skimming, but an act of attention, and this sense that I think we have so strongly now that when we speak of *reading* we speak of reading a newspaper, we speak of reading a poem. I think we feel – I think we are *right* to feel – that really you want two words to describe two quite different functions. If what you do with a newspaper is called reading then what you do with a poem should be described in a different way. It is an act of passionate attention. I think Coleridge created the strategy, the 'drama of reason', which I think is one of his own phrases, for trying to comprehend what happens to a culture, what happens to a society when the physical, when the scientific advancement of the age enables a certain kind of superficial fluency at the loss of what art, I think, requires more than anything: this brooding meditation. Now, what I'm trying to say about Hopkins is that either consciously or with the deep intuition of the creative mind, he sensed this divergence. He sensed this flowing away of time into a world of machinery and specious communication. And that against this specious flowing away, against this terrible divergence, he poised a faith and a technique and both the faith and the technique turn on the realisation of abrupt selfhood and the realisation that in order to passionately meditate upon the truth of being, upon the reality of nature, you must slow down the medium of communication . . .

HALLAM TENNYSON: Actually, a fascinating comparison springs to my mind and that is between Hopkins and the great German poet, Rainer Maria Rilke, who, without ever having read a word of Hopkins of course, achieved an extraordinary similarity of view in his poetry. He had a concept of *innigkeit*, the inwardness of things with which he could associate his own personality and experience actually the life of nature and the life of the trees, the life of flowers, the life of roses; and he wrote in the most extraordinarily beautiful way about this innerness of things and in his great outburst of sonnets, the sonnets to Orpheus, he says at one point that Orpheus, the first poet, has taught us to be 'hearers with tongues for creation's praise', that man in fact is on earth only in order to be able to name the world in which he lives. And this similarity of thought between Rilke and Hopkins goes also to a similarity of style to some extent. I mean, I think the Duino Elegies are written in an extraordinarily complex stressed and dislocated style which is very similar to the style that Hopkins developed. And this leads one, I think, to think of Hopkins as an influence. What has been the result of Hopkins's publication on other poets?

CHRISTOPHER RICKS: Well I think it has been much exaggerated. I think perhaps the fashion for exaggerating it has passed somewhat. I mean, when W. H. Gardner was doing some of his pioneering literary historical and critical work he made much of the fact that many of the poets of the thirties learned from Hopkins particularly. And it's true, clearly, that Dylan Thomas again and again sounds very like Hopkins and is likely to have been influenced by Hopkins, but there may be behind that some common Welsh influence working upon them both. I think that influence is perhaps the simplest way of seeing somebody's achievement. The crucial comparison for me would be with Eliot, neither of them of course mystics, both of them profoundly argumentative or arguing poets, in a way I think the great mystics are not; but Eliot's own testimony about Hopkins, I think, is of great interest. He tries to say why Hopkins's achievements with words, though easily imitable, are not very adaptable for many purposes and he also tries to give reasons for setting quite strict limits to his admiration for Hopkins so that – I am persuaded by Eliot – there is for me a severe limit to the achievement. It comes out perhaps in the excessive weight which Hopkins gives to the idea of mastery. There's a mastery over language, as God masters us, and I think the notion of mastery is itself too narrow in the end for the relationship of the greatest poets to the English language, and to experience. They do more I think than 'master' it. But the opposite point of view was put, very passionately, and I think very stirringly, by John Wain.

JOHN WAIN: Part of the reason why one thinks of him as the greatest poet of the Victorian era and I mean of all the years that Victoria was on the throne, is partly of course his way with language. To write poetry I think essentially is to liberate the power that is in language. Most of us use language in a way that's just like pushing counters around but the greatest poet is the poet like Shakespeare who over the whole range of what is possible liberates the power of language. Hopkins isn't a Shakespeare, he's the other thing. He's a poet who suddenly appears on a different part of the stage: suddenly liberates power that nobody else has liberated for a long time. There were certain strengths in the English language which, on the whole, the English poetic tradition throughout the nineteenth century had neglected. The music that English poets have got out of the English language was, on the whole, a rather mellifluous music and when it was rugged like Browning it tended to be amusingly idiosyncratic. Well, Hopkins isn't amusingly idiosyncratic. He is somebody who gets the power of – the rhythmic power, the emotional power – of a strong, hard, rugged language that breaks apart into chunks of granite which quite possibly had never really been heard since before the Norman Conquest, before Norman French came in. Hopkins was the chap who works on his own and has very little truck with the mainstream that's going through. And in his case, of course, he was a first-rate scholar, a very original thinker, an extremely intelligent man as well as being a very sensitive artist; and the reason he was isolated was because he belonged to a religious minority and spent his life in such close discipline that he very often had no opportunity to read the work of contemporary English poets. But in his case it was not a misfortune because he had to forge his art out of the silence of his own mind. He had to respond directly to the situation without any clamour of what was going on around him. And I think that Hopkins's isolation in fact made him a great artist and it was just as natural as when you breathe out you then breathe in that, having got a new vision, he got a new language. I can never get the two apart and I wouldn't *like* to try to get the two apart. He deals with extremes of feeling. He deals with life at its flashpoints and very often the imagery is bizarre and strong in a way that one can find at certain points in seventeenth-century poetry, one can find in a Baroque tradition, one can find here and there, and one can find in modern poetry of the twentieth century, but not very often in his time. For example, the extraordinary daring of the sexual imagery in that poem in which he apologises to Bridges for not writing better and more: 'The fine delight that fathers thought; the strong/Spur, live and lancing like the blowpipe flame,/Breathes once and, quenchèd faster than it came,/Leaves yet the mind a mother of immortal song./Nine months she then, nay years, nine years she long/Within her wears, bears, cares and combs the same'. Now the sexual imagery there – that the mind is impregnated by this spasm of delight which is live and lancing like the blowpipe flame – this is the kind of thing you're always finding in Hopkins. It's bedrock, it's pared away to basic and rather extreme situations which is why the poems of suffering, the poems of despair, are so shattering even in our age where everybody goes in for extreme statements and you can't get a hearing for any statement *unless* it's extreme. They remain the most powerful expressions of suffering that one can think of, except possibly Shakespeare's sonnets.

'How Meet Beauty': An Enquiry into the Current Reputation of Gerard Manley Hopkins, arranged by Christopher Ricks and Hallam Tennyson, transmitted by the BBC, 23 June 1977. Other contributors, not included in this excerpt, were Bernard Bergonzi, Mary Douglas, Paddy Kitchen, Gerald Roberts, and Wallace Robson.

Seamus Heaney (1980)

> O rose, thou art sick!
> The invisible worm
> That flies in the night,
> In the howling storm,
>
> Has found out thy bed
> Of crimson joy:
> And his dark secret love
> Does thy life destroy.

These eight lines of Blake's are like four loaves and four fishes that shoal and crumble as we try to consume their meaning. A rose is a rose is a rose but not when it's sick. Then it becomes a canker, a corruption, a tainted cosmos. The poem drops petal after petal of suggestion without ever revealing its stripped core: it is an open invitation into its meaning rather than an assertion of it.

Now I wonder if we can say the same of this poem, also short, also living off the life of its images:

> Heaven-Haven
> *A nun takes the veil*
> I have desired to go
>   Where springs not fail
> To fields where flies no sharp and sided hail
>   And a few lilies blow.
>
> And I have asked to be
>   Where no storms come,
> Where the green swell is in the havens dumb
>   And out of the swing of the sea.

In each case the verse lives by its music and suggestiveness, but with one important difference: the suggestiveness here condenses on a stated theme, 'a nun takes the veil', and the heaven–purity–cold idea equates with the haven–nunnery–quiet images in a relationship that is essentially allegorical rather than symbolic. The Hopkins poem is fretted rather than fecund. In the Blake poem the rose might be a girl but it remains a rose. Yet it is also a rose window, bloodshot with the light of other possible meanings. The rose and the sickness are not illustrative in the way the lilies and the haven are. In 'Heaven-Haven' it is the way things are exquisitely wrought, the way a crystal is sharp and sided and knowable rather than the way a rose is deep and unknowable that counts. Hopkins's art here is the discovery of verbal equivalents, in mingling the purity of images with the idea of a vow of chastity. The words are crafted together more than they are coaxed out of one another, and they are crafted in the service of an idea that precedes the poem, is independent of it and to which the poem is perhaps ultimately subservient. So much for the dark embryo. We are now in the realm of flint-spark rather than marshlight. 'Heaven-Haven' is consonantal fire struck by idea off language. The current of its idea does not fly the bound it chafes but confines itself within delightful ornamental channels.

To take another comparison with a poet whose nervous apprehension of phenomena and ability to translate this nervous energy into phrases reminds us also of Hopkins: take this line by Keats, describing autumn as the season of fulfilment:

> Close bosom-friend of the maturing sun

and compare it with a Hopkins line that also realises a sense of burgeoning and parturition, imagining Jesus in Mary's womb:

> Warm-laid grave of a womb-life grey.

Both lines rely on the amplitude of vowels for their dream of benign, blood-warm growth, but where Keats's vowels seem like nubs, buds off a single *uh* or *oo*, yeasty growths that are ready at any moment to relapse back into the original mother sound, Hopkins's are defined, held apart, and in relation to one another rather than in relation to the original nub: if they are full they are also faceted. Hopkins's consonants alliterate to maintain a design whereas Keats's release a flow. I am reminded of something T. S. Eliot wrote comparing Shakespeare and Ben Jonson. In Jonson, Eliot remarked in *The Sacred Wood*:

> unconscious does not respond to unconscious; no swarms of inarticulate feelings are aroused. The immediate appeal of Jonson is to the mind; his emotional tone is not in the single verse but in the design of the whole.

We must say much the same of the Keats and Hopkins lines. Keats has the life of a swarm, fluent and merged; Hopkins has the design of the honeycomb, definite and loaded. In Keats, the rhythm is narcotic, in Hopkins it is a stimulant to the mind. Keats woos us to receive, Hopkins alerts us to perceive.

Preoccupations, 1980

Anthony Burgess (1989)

He had already written the most original poetry of the nineteenth century (if we except the work of Emily Dickinson and Walt Whitman), but none of this had been published. His friend Robert Bridges, whose elegant mediocrity as a poet was to earn him the laureateship, had kept all Hopkins's work carefully filed but delayed publication until 1918.

This belated issue by the Oxford University Press of what amounted to a literary hand grenade had the effect of placing Hopkins dead in the middle of the Modernist movement. The book sold little but, with its second edition in 1930, it began to influence poets like Auden and Day Lewis, who imitated Hopkins's startling technique to an end very different from his own.

Hopkins, a devout priest whose conversion to Catholicism followed in Newman's wake, either wrestled with or praised God. Auden and Day Lewis wrestled with the social system of the 1930s and praised Stalin. The effect of reading their early works is that of watching a *défroqué* waxing drunk and spouting blasphemies.

Like all artistic innovators, Hopkins did something very simple. He saw there was no essential difference between the rhythm of music and that of poetry. Traditional verse had followed the French and Italian example of counting the number of syllables in a line, so that prosodists could speak of Milton's and Wordsworth's iambic pentameters. But, said Hopkins, English did not behave like Latin or Greek. It was a Germanic tongue and went in for heavy stresses. A poetic line was not a syllabic matter; you named it according to the number of stresses it had. In a line like 'To be or not to be, that is the question' you counted five stresses and argued that Shakespeare could, if he wished, have used as many unstressed syllables as was feasible. 'To be or conceivably not to be, that is indubitably the question' remains, if you stutter over those added syllables, still a five-beat line.

The parallel with music is pretty exact. Music stutters, slows down, interposes moments of silence, but always watches the conductor's beat-counting baton. Hopkins called his musicalised poetic line by a new name. It contained, he said, sprung rhythm. The rhythm sprang out of the stresses.

Sprung rhythm, he said, was present in nursery rhymes. 'One, two/Buckle my shoe' is a perfect example. There are two stresses to a line, but the first line has only two syllables while the second line has four. The number of syllables doesn't matter; it's the steady beat that counts. The line, 'Morn, eve, noon, night' has four stresses but only four syllables. Change it to 'Morning, evening, noontime, night' and you have increased the syllables without changing the stresses. Go further and write 'In the morning, in the evening, at noontime, also at night' and you have loaded it to the near-limit with syllables but not at all modified the conductor's steady beat.

The problem with writing verse in sprung rhythm was that you couldn't clarify the beats to the eye of the reader without using stress-marks. Ideally, sprung rhythm required a method of notation analogous to that of music. But readers of poetry, and poets themselves for that matter, are rarely musicians as well. There are still readers of Hopkins around who claim that his verses don't scan. But Hopkins was himself an amateur composer and, in the 1860s, was anticipating ultra-modern practice by using microtones. We need his recorded voice to show us how his sprung rhythm works. If we have had musical training we have little difficulty with lines like

> Glory be to God for dappled things –
> For skies of couple-colour as a brinded cow . . .

The first line is traditional enough – no syllabic overloading – but the second demands that you hurry over the 'couple-colour'. If you chant it with a steadily maintained (and highly soporific) equal syllabic weight, you'll want to put six stresses there. But there are only five.

This eschewal of the chanting *da-di-da-di-da* of traditional

verse brings sprung rhythm, as Hopkins recognised, rather close
to the irregular melody of prose. But prose is a medium for the
unexcited, and Hopkins was always excited. He was excited by
the variegated patterns of nature, seeing that God's creation was
characterised by a kind of harmonised conflict – 'dapple', in
fact, the 'pied beauty' which is the title of the sonnet I've just
quoted. Nature is full of individuality; things 'selve', announce
what they are, sustain a personal 'inscape'.

It was necessary for Hopkins to invent words, resurrect dead
ones, draw on dialect, indulge in verbal and rhythmical surprises
which would match the always astonishing impact on himself
of external nature. In a late sonnet he prophesies that the dapple
of life will break down because of man's unwillingness to accept
harmonious conflict. At the end of the 1880s, he fears the
reduction of life to political or metaphysical abstrations:
'thoughts against thoughts in groans grind'.

When I was about fourteen I knew most of Hopkins's poetry
by heart. It was poetry that demanded the acceptance of the ear,
not the eye, and cried out to be recited. The effect of hearing
'The Wreck of the Deutschland' performed by a virtuoso (John
Gielgud has done it well) is not unlike that of assisting at some
symphonic poem by Richard Strauss, with a vast amount of
tone-colour, an emotional urgency occasionally expressed in
what sounds like grotesquerie.

Hopkins does not sound like Tennyson, and he is never prosy
like Browning. He comes close to James Joyce in his exploitation
of new sounds. Indeed, the two writers seem to be contemporary, but Joyce was only seven when Hopkins died, and, when
Joyce became a student at University College Dublin, Hopkins
was not even a remembered name. Joyce read Hopkins when he
had already formed his mature style and said that he was an
English Mallarmé – a not very prespicacious judgment. Hopkins
was an English Joyce who wrote verse not prose, and retained
his Jesuit rigour to the end. Joyce did too, but he jettisoned the
theology.

Hopkins is a poet's poet and probably has little relevance to
the pragmatic world, despite the fact that his renewal of
language – always the poet's aim – reminds even the unpoetic
that language allowed to grow banal, weary and cliché-ridden
is one of the devices of political oppression. It is sadly ironic
that Hopkins's second-hand influence used to be found in food

advertisements. 'Brown-as-dawning-skinned', which describes a drowned sailor in 'The Loss of the Eurydice', was, I remember, once applied to a junk-food roast chicken. The compression of a multiple epithet, the clang of alliteration are in the armoury of the publicists who, being no fools, read poetry. There is a glossy attractiveness about some of Hopkins's lines which would fit well on a page of *Vogue*

> . . . blue-bleak embers, ah my dear,
> Fall, gall themselves, and gash gold-vermilion.

There are good words there for describing new synthetic fabrics.

All this is blasphemy. Hopkins was a great religious poet whose linguistic innovation and deliberately twisted syntax were in the service of registering the shock of the divine creation (whose pollution the poet foresaw: 'bears man's smell and wears man's smudge'). In this bicentenary of the French Revolution it is seemly to remember other revolutions, however small. A suffering English Jesuit remains one of the revolutionaries.

Irish Times, 14 October, 1989

John Wain (1989)

I have never been troubled by any poet's being Christian. My personal attitude towards Christianity, that is to its formal dogmas and beliefs, has varied a good deal during my life and never stood still for long. There were times in my youth, particularly when I was much under the influence of people of strong character like C. S. Lewis and Charles Williams, who were Anglicans, when I used to think what a great blessing it must be to have a religious faith and I made consistent efforts to hypnotise myself into accepting Christian doctrine as amenable to reason. I gave that up at about the age of thirty and I believe I have been happier since. The arguments, considered simply as arguments, seem to me to sway back and forth and end up as six of one and half-a-dozen of the other; given the sheer size and range of the unknowables, the reasons for accepting or rejecting any metaphysic are just about equal in force, so it comes down to individual mood and temperament. I have times when faith seems to me very natural, and other times when it seems so far away as to be unthinkable. It is like a wind that blows through me (to use, in a different way, that metaphor of Lawrence's), sometimes veering a few degrees to one side or another, sometimes turning completely round, now and then ceasing to blow altogether and leaving me inwardly becalmed, in that state that mystics describe as 'the dark night of the soul' but which to me seems more like a Bank Holiday. I never strain after religious faith; sometimes it comes to me, stays as long as it seems to want to, and goes again. I never cease to enjoy and admire Hopkins's poems, and I do not have to wait for my moods of religious faith to enjoy them more.

Everything I have said up to now applies not only to Hopkins but to Donne, Milton, George Herbert, Eliot, and for that matter to Dante, though I read him only in translation. I was brought up in a civilisation whose values were founded on Christianity, and I can't imagine myself not responding to the beautiful piety that underlies so much Christian art, that one feels in Chartres and Durham Cathedral and in the Miracle Plays and carols and medieval illuminated manuscripts and the Christian poetry of Anglo-Saxon England. But your question narrows down from that. Why do I not (if I don't) feel any alienation from Hopkins's Catholicism – his 'almost sixteenth-century Catholicism', come to that?

This question is of great interest to me personally because I have always considered Hopkins a great poet and yet my view of him has changed over the decades. When I first fell in love with his poetry (I was nineteen) I had a very low awareness of its specifically Catholic content. I knew of course that he had been converted, largely by the personal example of Newman, and was a Jesuit; I knew he put his life unquestionably at the service of his Order; I knew he was a Scotist. But it was not in the forefront of my attention. What caught my eye, and my ear, immediately, was his one-man struggle with the language, the need he felt to rethink and renew English as the linguistic vehicle for major statements in poetry. I could see that this struggle, and the 'counter, original, spare, strange' language that resulted from it, had isolated him from the literary community of his time, but I took that isolation to be no more than the normal and predictable isolation of the artist who forges ahead of his time, who works today in tomorrow's idiom, and therefore does not gain widespread acceptance. I came to Hopkins fresh from an immersion in Ezra Pound with his breezy assumption that 'artists are the antennae of the race' and hence will never speak the language of 'the bullet-headed many'.

In short I failed, in those days, to see the depth, the range, the inclusiveness of Hopkins's separation from the culture of his time. It was no mere matter of the language of verse, the idiom of this art and that, though these, both in what they are and in what they indicate, are far from trivial matters. Hopkins was much more than a literary rebel, intent on finding new ways of writing. It was, quite simply, *impossible* for him to share the language and style of Victorian poets generally because he shared none of their assumptions. He felt profoundly at odds with the society he lived among. Deeply as he loved England, truly and discerningly as he loved the beauty of her landscape and birds and flowers and waters and stones, deeply as he loved the English language and the finer things in the English tradition, he thought that England had wandered outside the pale of true religion and therefore, as he saw it, of true civilisation.

Hopkins was not alone in this attitude. One meets it in a propagandist like Hilaire Belloc half a century later; it is the stock in trade of Chesterton, of Arnold Lunn, of Ronald Knox. But in Hopkins it is not a succession of debating points as it tends to be with them. It is a deep, elegiac sorrow. He grieves for an England that he sees as lost and wandering. He prays and watches for her return to the fold. He did genuinely have hopes that, some three centuries after what he would certainly not have thought of as 'the Reformation', that might actually become a possibility and then an achieved reality.

It was from this that Hopkins's isolation proceeded. He found himself really at home with nothing that expressed English civilisation since the end of the seventeenth century saw the final triumph of Protestant values. The England of the eighteenth century, mercantile, legalistic and adventurist, had developed into the England of the nineteenth, industrial, capitalistic, imperialist, and jingoistic. Hopkins could recognise no good quality in all this. He found its art as false as its values generally. Where he praises a poet it is usually someone like William Barnes, who looks towards some neglected corner of sensibility soon to be jettisoned in the march towards centralisation and empire preference. (How could Barnes's Dorset poems be set for study in Indian schools to give the sub-continental children that healing dip in English culture that would make a reliable middle class of them?) He likes Dryden; and what qualities in Victorian verse are Drydenian? He was interested in Welsh poetry and the Welsh language, and at the time he was studying them most intently they were generally regarded in England as a quaint survival that was ineluctably doomed to die out as a rural population was recruited into urban occupations, and as 'Progress' marched up the mountainsides.

Most of the sensitive people of the nineteenth century felt themselves to be isolated from the culture within which they lived. As industrialism spread ugliness, and not only spread it but standardized it, sensitive natures of one kind retreated into aestheticism. (Walter Pater burning with a hard gem-like flame in the Banbury Road); as scientific materialism seeped down through the mass of the populace and inevitably took the form, which it never takes with actual scientists, of mere crude disbelief in the invisible and intangible in any guise, sensitive natures of another stripe were driven towards the more arcane and ritualistic forms of Christianity and even into the sub-world of the cults, as Yeats was. None of these could be majority movements, enjoying any sense of solidarity with the large numbers and vast resources of Victorian England. The embattled Catholic minority had similar feelings and, to add to them, a history of dispossession, persecution and disbarment. When Hopkins briefly returned to Oxford in 1878, not as a student now but as a priest, his second period there coincided with the first wave of purpose-built Catholic churches allowed to go up in England since the mid-sixteenth century. A church like St Aloysius', at the beginning of the Woodstock Road close to Somerville College, is a handsome enough place, but every sensitive person who worshipped there, and in similar Victorian Catholic churches all over the country, must have thought, every time they walked past a venerable medieval church or a soaring cathedral, 'That, too, was once ours'.

'Walford Davies interviews John Wain',
The New Welsh Review (Winter 1989–90)

Ernest Ferlita S. J. (1990)

Towards the end of Hopkins's life, a new invention was made available to the public – the phonograph. Now, Hopkins thought, a record could be kept of 'fine spoken utterance' and it would be, he was persuaded, 'a lovely art'.[19] But the tape recorder was still several decades away. If such an instrument had been available to him, we can be sure he would have put it to good use. '[. . .] such verse as I do compose is oral', he once said, 'made away from paper, and I put it down with repugnance'. Well, we, of course, are grateful that he did put it down, but it *is* important to remember that, for Hopkins, his verse is first and foremost something heard. The 'sprung' rhythm that he employed in his verse originated, after all, in the ear – 'I had long had haunting my ear the echo of a new rhythm which I now realised on paper' – and again he insisted that his 'verse is less to be read than heard [. . .]; it is oratorical, that is the rhythm is so'.

He was convinced that the difficulties in his verse would disappear if only it were recited well, and he was 'sweetly soothed' by his brother Everard saying so: 'that is what I always hoped, thought, and said; it is my precise aim'. Poetry, he says, *his* poetry, 'must be spoken; *till it is spoken it is not performed*, it does not perform, it is not itself.'[20] He underlines: *till it is spoken it is not performed*, and then to stress the point yet further, changes from a transitive to an intransitive use of the verb *perform*: it *does* not perform. We speak of a machine performing badly or well, but it would never occur to me to say that a poem performs, with or without a modifier. It strikes me that Hopkins is trying to say something self-evident, and self-evident things are not easily put into words. What the anthropologist Victor Turner says about performance in relation to experience may shed some light on the matter.

> Through the performance process itself, what is normally sealed up, inaccessible to everyday observation and reasoning, in the depth of socio-cultural life, is drawn forth [. . .] 'Meaning' is squeezed out of an event which has either been directly experienced by the dramatist or poet, or cries out for penetrative, imaginative understanding [. . .] An experience is itself a process

which 'presses out' to an 'expression' which completes it. Here the etymology of 'performance' may give us a helpful clue, for it has nothing to do with 'form', but derives from Old French *parfournir*, 'to complete' or 'carry out thoroughly'. A performance, then, is the proper finale of an experience.[21]

When Hopkins says 'till [his verse] is spoken it does not perform' he is saying, quite simply: till it is spoken it falls short of the 'expression' which completes it, it has not yet achieved its proper finale; or, as he himself puts it, 'it is not [yet] itself'.

In the very next sentence Hopkins links the self of a poem to sprung rhythm. 'Sprung rhythm,' he says, 'gives back to poetry its true soul and self.' Since poetry 'is emphatically speech, speech purged of dross like gold in the furnace', it must have all the essential elements of speech.

> Now emphasis itself, stress, is one of these: rhythm makes verse stressy; it purges it to an emphasis as much brighter, livelier, more lustrous than the regular but commonplace emphasis of common rhythm as poetry in general is brighter than common speech.[22]

The common rhythm of common speech – *that* rhythm gives rise to sprung rhythm. That's why Hopkins employs it: 'Because it is the nearest to the rhythm of prose, that is the native and natural rhythm of speech, the least forced, the most rehtorical and emphatic of all possible rhythms'. He is speaking, of course, of English speech, whose accent is not primarily *tonic* but *emphatic*: though it commonly includes *tone*, or *pitch* of note, it is essentially *stress*. And stress, as we know, is at the heart of sprung rhythm: '*one stress makes one foot*, no matter how many or few the syllables'. It is a rhythm 'which is altogether for recital, not for perusal'.

If sprung rhythm is so natural to English speech, why did Hopkins feel it necessary to put stress marks over certain accents? Because, with performance very much in mind, Hopkins wanted to make sure that *we* heard what *he* heard. Some lines could be scanned in more than one way, and the way Hopkins scanned them was by no means the most natural. Admittedly, the rhythm he marks out can seem at times to be forced, as in his revision of the early poem 'For a Picture of St Dorothea', when he first began to experiment with 'sprung rhythm'. But in most instances his markings serve to 'press out' to its most cogent 'expression' the meaning of a line. Consider that mighty, weighty poem 'Spelt from Sibyl's Leaves', a poem replete with Hopkins's own stress marks. In one line all six stresses are marked. I will read it first with the six stresses we would most likely give it *without* his markings:

Our évening is óver us: our níght whélms, whélms and will énd us.

Here is how Hopkins marks it:

Óur évening is over us; óur night whélms, whélms ánd will end us.

Note especially that unnatural stress on the conjunction 'and'. A small word but because it contains a nasal, it lends itself to sustained vocalisation, and the effect is actually to enable the voice to fall with even greater weight upon the syllables that follow it: 'ánd will end us'. Now the mere perusal of the poem could never bring this out. Nor is it enough merely to read it aloud. That is still not to perform it as he intended it should be performed. In connection with another poem, 'The Loss of the Eurydice', Hopkins says:

> to perform it quite satisfactorily is not at all easy, I do not say I could do it; but this is nothing against the truth of the principle maintained. A composer need not be able to play his violin music or sing his song. Indeed the higher wrought the art, clearly the wider severance between the parts of the author and the performer.

He compares the doubters to those who have never heard plain chant '(or worse, have heard it murdered) and cannot conceive the performance; for to read and even play it, without the secret, is no good'.[23]

Let's be clear about what Hopkins is saying here. You can't just read one of my poems to yourself and think you've got it. That's out. You can't just read it aloud. That's still not enough. You have to be as skilled in performing it as a violinist in playing a piece of music or a singer in singing a song. The two comparisons he makes are well chosen. Is there anything more painful to the ear than violin-playing that doesn't quite make it or singing that is even just slightly off? I think it's safe to say that Hopkins in his lifetime never heard his verse performed in the way that he required except, like a deaf Beethoven, in his own inner ear. What a dilemma! He would send his poems to

Bridges and Bridges would read them and shudder. Did Bridges ever even read them aloud? I suppose he did, since Hopkins insisted on it so. But Bridges could never quite catch the music.

Yes, Hopkins often thought of the performance of his works in musical terms. Regarding 'Spelt from Sibyl's Leaves', he writes to Bridges:

> Of this long sonnet above all, remember what applies to all my verse, that it is, as living art should be, made for performance and that its performance is not reading with the eye but loud, leisurely, poetical (nor rhetorical) recitation, with long rests, long dwells on the rhyme and other marked syllables, and so on. This sonnet shd. be almost sung: it is most carefully timed in *tempo rubato*.

The term *rubato*, meaning 'robbed' or 'stolen', is used of a tempo in which the strict value of certain notes is disregarded *in favour of greater expressiveness in performance*, some notes lengthened by stealing time from others. It may also entail the accenting of certain notes that are not normally accented. Some critics will fault Hopkins for this, often citing the last line as an instance of his perverseness or subjectivity or what have you, but it happens to be the very line in which the *rubato* is felt with special force: the last half of the line, read with normal stress, would be:

> thoúghts against thoúghts in groáns grínd.

But Hopkins has it:

> thóughts agaínst thoughts ín groans grínd.

I would like to call attention to another term he uses in that note on the performance of 'Spelt from Sibyl's Leaves': it is not, he says, 'reading with the eye but loud, leisurely, poetical (not rhetorical) recitation'. That 'not rhetorical' puzzled me. After all, we heard him say that the reason he employed 'sprung rhythm' at all was because 'it is [. . .] the most rhetorical and emphatic of all possible rhythms'. But we also heard him say: my verse 'is oratorical, that is the rhythm is so'. There is a difference, after all, between the rhythm of a piece and its recitation. The rhythm is 'oratorical', which in the context is another word for 'rhetorical', because, as he says, it is 'nearest to the rhythm of prose, that is the native and natural rhythm of speech', but a poem must not be recited rhetorically, that is, in the manner of a persuasive speech, which is after all prose. 'Poetical recitation' demands something more, which he seems to describe by what follows: 'with long rests, long dwells on the rhyme and other marked syllables, and so on'.

There is another poem whose performance he explicitly conceives of in musical terms. It is identified by its first line, an exact rendering of a text from Jeremiah: 'Thou art indeed just, Lord'. 'This sonnet,' he tells Bridges, 'must be read *adagio molto* and with great stress.' It's too bad that performance directions are not published with poems as they are with music. In this case, at least, I think they are essential. Without them the first four lines, for instance, would, I imagine, be rendered as follows:

> Thóu art indéed júst, Lord, if I conténd
> With thée; but, sír, só what I pléad is júst.
> Whý do sínners' ways prósper? and whý múst
> Dísappóintment áll I endéavour énd?

But hear the difference, when read *adagio molto* and with great stress: [the four lines are here re-read]. One might object that I put more feeling in it the second time, but feeling comes precisely through the *adagio molto* and the great stress. In this connection I should mention something else essential to its performance – and to the performance of other poems of the same genre. This sonnet is a dramatic lyric. It is written in the first person, there is a speaker in the poem, the poet's second self, his persona, his mask; and the performer must put on this mask if he is truly to perform the poem; he must become the 'I' that speaks it.

Most of the poems that Hopkins wrote in his last years, there in Ireland, all of them of intense feeling, are dramatic lyrics. It was also at this time that he was working on an actual drama, *St Winefred's Well*. It's no wonder that he was moving in this direction: of dramatic poetry especially, one must say: *till it is spoken it is not performed*.

I should tell you that I have on several occasions performed *St Winefred's Well* as a one-man show. All we have from Hopkins's hand are an opening dialogue, three monologues, and the choral song 'The Leaden Echo and the Golden Echo'. These I have placed within a dramatic narration to provide continuity and to give the story a beginning, middle, and end. As a performer, I discovered and was very grateful for three things in Hopkins's dramatic language: first, its power to express passion. 'Sprung rhythm', Hopkins says, 'lends itself to expressing passion.' He doesn't say why but he certainly demonstrates it, especially in Caradoc's soliloquy after he has murdered Winefred. No doubt it is partly due to the fact that it is, again, 'the most [. . .] emphatic of all possible rhythms' and partly to that *abruptness* which is what he understands by *sprung*, strictly speaking, 'where one stress follows another running, without syllable between', as in this line and a half in which there are two such instances and three others where the syllable between is very slight.

> What I have done violent
> I have líke a líon dóne, líonlíke dóne,
> (All stresses are marked by Hopkins himself).

A second quality to be found in this soliloquy is that 'nameless quality which is of the first importance both in oratory and drama'.

He sometimes calls it *bidding* and first mentions it in reference to Bridges's first play, *Prometheus the Firegiver*, which he found somewhat lacking in this quality, and for this reason has his doubts about the acting of it. By *bidding*, you will recall, he means

> the art or virtue of saying everything right *to* or *at* the hearer, interesting him, holding him in the attitude of correspondent or addressed or at least concerned, making it everywhere an act of intercourse – and of discarding everything that does not bid, does not tell.

He grants that it is most difficult to combine this bidding, 'such a fugitive thing', with a monumental style and Bridges's style, he says, is monumental. 'But it can be done.' It can be done, and in this soliloquy Hopkins certainly does it.

A third quality discovered in performance, one that is of the utmost importance for the performance of a dramatic work, is what I call the gestural dimension of his language. By that I simply mean that the language itself often suggests gesture. No need for stage directions: the very language brings hands, face, body into play. There is one especially good example of this. It happens also to be an arresting use of dramatic foreshadowing, making it visual as well as aural. Teryth, the father of Winefred, or Gwenvrewi, as she is called in the play, looks lovingly on her as she goes from him and he is suddenly seized with the fearful thought of losing her.

> What, Teryth! What, thou
>   poor fond father!
> How when this bloom, this honeysuckle, that rides the
>   air so rich about thee,
> Is all, all sheared away, thus!

Then, after the murder has taken place, it is re-enacted, as it were, by a repetition of this same gesture demanded by very similar words, this time uttered by the murderer himself. Caro- doc wonders where 'in the darksome world' he can ever again find comfort now that he has quenched its light.

>   its rose, time's one rich rose, my hand,
> By her bloom, fast by her fresh, her fleeced bloom,
> Hideous dáshed dówn, leaving earth a winter withering
> With no now, no Gwenvrewi.

Performance, I have been saying, is for Hopkins a *sine qua non*. In so doing I have simply taken Hopkins at his word: his verse 'is not itself' until performed. Furthermore, it's not just anybody who can perform his verse, no more than just anybody can perform a Beethoven sonata. 'I do not say I could do it', wrote Hopkins. In one of his sermons, Hopkins says: 'Correspondence with grace and seconding of God's designs is like a taking part in [our] own creation, the creation of [our] best selves.' Simi- larly, I would say, in conclusion, that the performer seconds the poet's designs and cooperates in the creation of the poem's very self.

> P. Bottalla, G. Marra and F. Marucci (eds.), *Gerard Manley Hopkins: Tradition and Innovation*, Ravenna, 1991

Christopher Ricks (1996)

Against the claims of theory, I set the counterclaims of principle. These may sometimes be counterclaims in the sense that they are at odds with theory's claims, and sometimes in the sense that they put in a competing bid for what will always, in teaching and out of it, be limited resources, notably those severely limited resources time and energy and attention. Very often my beliefs have been best expressed by others; this is for me not an admission but an acknowledgement, since it makes thought about literature continuous with literature, where too I repeatedly find my beliefs best expressed by others.

When Hopkins wrote of the 'teachable element' in literature, it was not of theory that he was thinking, and his words may remind us of one continuing alternative claim upon the attentions of teachers and taught, whether in school, college, or graduate school. Hopkins speaks of how poets should learn, and what he says is consonant with how we might learn about as well as from poets.

> The strictly poetical insight and inspiration of our poetry seems to me to be of the very finest, finer perhaps than the Greek; but its rhetoric is inadequate – seldom firstrate, mostly only just sufficient, sometimes even below par. By rhetoric I mean all the common and teachable element in literature, what grammar is to speech, what thoroughbass is to music, what theatrical experience gives to playwrights.

Hopkins enunciates a principle; because it is a principle and not a theory he is moved naturally to speak of experience, to which principle, as by definition less comprehensively ideate than theory gives a correspondingly greater weight. Rhetoric, this teachable element in literature, is not theory, and it still has its legitimate claims and must not be ousted. Rhetoric, granted, is not literature, but that is not because this teachable element departs, rather because something else arrives, a ministering to wisdom, or to justice or to vitality or to magnanimity, such as does not rest content with persuasion. Literature is, among other things, principled rhetoric, and Hopkins's words need to be complemented by T. S. Eliot's, when, having embarked upon editorship of *The Criterion*, he spoke of principles:

> A literary review should maintain the application, in literature, of principles which have their consequences also in politics and in private conduct ... To maintain the autonomy, and the disinterestedness, of every human activity, and to perceive it in relation

to every other, require a considerable discipline. It is the function of a literary review to maintain the autonomy and disinterestedness of literature, and at the same time to exhibit the relations of literature – not to 'life', as something contrasted to literature, but to all the other activities, which, together with literature, are the components of life.

Such a sense of literature's relations is itself a statement of principle, and is incompatible with subservience. Literary study, like literature itself, has always needed to resist not only the imperialism of science, which is often frankly adversarial, but also those humanities which are literature's allies but do have their neo-imperialistic ambitions ...

Hopkins, who was a great critic, pre-eminently in his letters, set down an unforgettable and endlessly applicable principle in his unfolding of Tennyson and 'Parnassian'. Hopkins's letter to A. W. M. Baillie moves with beautiful pertinence:

> Sept. 10, 1864.
>
> Dear Baillie,
>
> Your letter has been sent to me from Hampstead. It has just come, and I do a rare thing with me, begin at once on an answer. I have just finished *The Philippics* of Cicero and an hour remains before bedtime; no one except Wharton would begin a new book at that time of night, so I was reading *Henry IV*, when your letter was brought in – a great enjoyment.
>
> The letter-writer on principle does not make his letter only an *answer*, it is a work embodying perhaps answers to questions put by his correspondent but that is not its main motive. Therefore it is as a rule not well to write with a received letter fresh on you. I suppose the right way is to let it sink into you, and reply after a day or two. I do not know why I have said all this.
>
> Do you know, a horrible thing has happened to me. I have begun to *doubt* Tennyson. (Baillejus ap. Hopk.) It is a great *argumentum*, a great clue, that our minds jump together even if it be a leap into the dark. I cannot tell you how amused and I must say pleased and comforted by this coincidence I am.

From reading Cicero and *Henry IV*, to reading a letter, to thinking about the principles of writing a letter ('The letter-writer on principle does not make his letter only an *answer*'), to thinking about those principles of poetry and of 'poetical criti-

cism' which are to be the letter's enterprise: the modulation and
momentum are superb, and so is Hopkins's finding appropriate
amusement, pleasure, and comfort in his being so in sympathy
with Baillie about this new qualifying of his sympathy with
Tennyson.

Hopkins's letter, famous and inexhaustible, sets out the principles which distinguish 'the language of inspiration' from 'Parnassian', which 'can only be spoken by poets, but is not in the
highest sense poetry'. The movement of Hopkins's mind is as
naturally a move from a principle to an instance as then from
instance back to principle – but never into theory.

> Great men, poets I mean, have each their own dialect as it were
> of Parnassian, formed generally as they go on writing, and at last,
> – this is the point to be marked, – they can see things in this
> Parnassian way and describe them in this Parnassian tongue,
> without further effort of inspiration. In a poet's particular kind of
> Parnassian lies most of his style, of his manner, of his mannerism
> if you like. But I must not go farther without giving you instances
> of Parnassian. I shall take one from Tennyson, and from *Enoch
> Arden*, from a passage much quoted already and which will be no
> doubt often quoted, the description of Enoch's tropical island.

> > The mountain wooded to the peak, the lawns
> > And winding glades high up like ways to Heaven,
> > The slender coco's drooping crown of plumes,
> > The lightning flash of insect and of bird,
> > The lustre of the long convolvuluses
> > That coil'd around the stately stems, and ran
> > Ev'n to the limit of the land, the glows
> > And glories of the broad belt of the world,
> > All these he saw.

> Now it is a mark of Parnassian that one could conceive oneself
> writing it if one were the poet. Do not say that *if* you were
> Shakesepare you can imagine yourself writing Hamlet, because
> that is just what I think you can*not* conceive.

What makes this statement of principle, with its persuasive
instance, so thrilling is its own inspiration, especially in that last
leap.

Now it is a mark of Parnassian that one could conceive oneself
writing it if one were the poet. Do not say that *if* you were
Shakespeare you can imagine yourself writing Hamlet, because
that is just what I think you can*not* conceive.

For it is a mark of Hopkins's genius that though I could, I
suppose, conceive of myself coming up with some distinction
between the inspired and the not inspired, I cannot conceive of
myself creating the penetrating terms of this principle itself:
'Now it is a mark of Parnassian that one could conceive oneself
writing it if one were the poet.' More, Hopkins's critical feat
at once goes beyond critical Parnassianism; do not say that *if*
you were Hopkins you can imagine yourself writing these sentences, because that is just what I think you can*not* conceive.
Inspiration there is perfectly at one with courtesy, as it was in
the opening of this immediately-answering letter, when Hopkins, 'on principle', goes into a letter's needing to be more
than an answer; the courtesy within the astonishing, and
immediately convincing, appeal to Shakespeare and *Hamlet* is
manifest in the sequence, 'because that is just what I think
you can*not* conceive.' Not 'just what you can*not* conceive',
but 'just what I think you can*not* conceive'. This is the perfection of two kinds of consideration, the co-operation of a considered principle with a considerate tact. Principle and tact are
as intimately co-operative in criticism as are comparison and
analysis; and it can be a grounded objection to theory that its
being reasoned is on occasion no compensation for its being
tactless.

Essays in Appreciation, 1996

References (Original footnotes to the above essays)

(F. R. LEAVIS)

1 'The poem which is absolutely original is absolutely bad; it
   is, in the bad sense "subjective" with no relation to the
   world to which it appeals. Originality, in other words, is by
   no means a simple idea in the criticism of poetry. True
   originality is merely development.' – T. S. Eliot, Introduction
   to *Selected Poems: Ezra Pound*

2 'The simultaneous consciousness of a controlled universe,
   and yet of division, conflict, and crises within that universe,

is hardly so poignantly expressed in any other English poets
than those two.' – *Poems* (Second Edition), Introduction.

3 *Sonnet 57.*
4 *Hamlet, II. ii.*
5 *Macbeth, III. iv.*
6 *Macbeth, I. v.*
7 *Macbeth, I. vii.*
8 *Coriolanus, III. i.*
9 *Macbeth, I. iii.*
10 'To seem the stranger lies my lot, my life'.

(CHARLES MADGE)

11 A visitor asked Tennyson what he thought of Whitman.
   'Whitman? Whitman? you want to know what I think about
   Whitman? I don't know that I think about him. I wonder if
   I ever really think about him? But I am aware of his
   existence: he is a vast monster of some sort – a monster, sir:
   I can't make him out: but I hear the noise he makes and see
   the commotion of the waters as he dashes along: I suppose I
   do not think of him – think of him: but I acknowledge and
   respect him: he is a force that without explaining itself to
   me I still acquiesce in.'

> (For though no one speaks of it, everyone knows
> He has got no webs between his toes!)

12 Pelican Chorus.
13 Song of Myself, 52.

(GEOFFREY GRIGSON)

14 It is instructive to compare Hopkins's satisfaction over 'The
   Windhover' with his uneasiness over 'The May Magnificat'.
15 Hopkins never mentions Webster, but though he was strong
   against literary echoes 'The Caged Skylark' begins with an
   obvious echo of Bosola's speech in the torture scene of *The
   Duchess of Malfi*: 'Didst thou ever see a Larke in a cage?
   such is the soule in the body: this world is like her little turfe
   of grasse,' etc.

(DAVID JONES)

16 I may be wrong but my impression is that Dylan Thomas
   learned a lot from Hopkins.

17 Even that great, very great, poem 'The Wreck of the
Deutschland' is characteristically Victorian in its choice of
subject – they were very sentimentally inclined toward ship-
wrecks etc. weren't they – Grace Darling etc. And again
'The Bugler's First Communion' and lots of others – the
nature thing (rocks, Ruskin) show Hopkins to have been
very much of his epoch. But his Catholicism gave it a
different twist and his study of Welsh metric metamor-
phosed the stuff entirely – at least that's how I see it.

(JOHN WAIN)
18 Cf. The youthful Aragon: 'L'habitude artistique est une
mascarade qui compromet toute dignité humaine.'

(ERNEST FERLITA S. J.)
19 *Hopkins Research Bulletin*, 4 (1973), p. 12.
20 Ibid., p. 6.
21 *From Ritual to Theatre*, New York, Performing Arts Journal
Publication, 1982, p. 13.
22 *Hopkins Research Bulletin*, 4 (1973), p. 10.
23 *Hopkins Research Bulletin*, 4 (1973), p. 12.

EXPLANATORY NOTES TO THE POEMS

'. . . we should explain things, plainly state them, clear them up,
explain them'

(Hopkins, letter to Bridges, 25 May 1888)

*Apart from the titles and the key-words to be explained
(which are in bold), all words and phrases quoted exactly
from the poems are in italics, and explanatory paraphrases
within inverted commas*

1. **The Escorial** (1860) Highgate (*p. 3*):
The poem won for Hopkins the School Poetry Prize at Highgate
School, Easter 1860, at the age of sixteen. The title was the one
set for Oxford University's Newdigate Prize the same year. The
absence of stanza 9 and the fact that stanza 3 is one line short
were the result of Hopkins having to meet the set limit of 125
lines. Despite its Romantic derivativeness, it shows a precocious
deployment of the traditional Spenserian stanza form and an
understanding of the differences between Greek and Gothic art,
a subject of contemporary debate.

(Title) **The Escorial:** El Escorial or El Escurial, a village in
central Spain, northwest of Madrid, the site of a complex
comprising a palace, a college and a monastery, built by
Philip II between 1563 and 1584.
(Epigraph): the Greek translates as 'I compete as a frog does
against the cicadas' (Theocritus Idyll VII, l.41).

The following are Hopkins's own notes to the poem:
Stanza 2: at the battle of St Quentin, between the French and
the Spaniards, Philip II vowed the Escorial to St Laurence, the
patron Saint of the day, if he gained victory.
Stanza 3: St Laurence is said to have been roasted to death on
a gridiron.
Stanza 4: the escorial was built in the form of a gridiron, the

rectangular convent was the grate, the cloisters the bars, the towers the legs inverted, the palace the handle.

The building contained the royal Mausoleum; and a gate which was opened only to the newborn heir apparent, and to the funeral of a monarch.

41. the stubborn Fleming: Philip endeavoured to establish the Inquisition in the Netherlands.

Stanza 6: Philip did not choose the splendid luxuriance of the Spanish Gothic as the style of architecture fitted for the Escorial,

Stanza 7: nor the Classic.

58. brilliant-hued: The Parthenon etc. were magnificently coloured and gilded.

60. horsemen: the horsemen in the Panathenaic processions.

63. Fair relics: the Alhambra etc.

Stanza 8: the Architect was Velasquez; the style Italian Classic, partly Ionic partly Doric. The whole is sombre in appearance, but grand and imposing.

Stanza 10: the interior was decorated with all the richest productions of art and nature. Pictures, statues, marble, fountains, tapestry, etc. (*He* refers to Philip.)

75. the virgin mother etc: in one of Raphael's pictures the Madonna and St Joseph play with their Child in a wide meadow; behind is a palm-tree.

78. where the crownals droop'd: alluding to Raphael's 'Lo Spasimo', which is, I believe, in the Escorial.

81. darkened landscape: alluding to the dark colouring of landscapes to be seen in Rubens, Titian etc.

85. Antinous: a beautiful youth drowned in the Nile; the statue has the position described.

88. Chang'd to a flower: Hyacinthus.

89. Apollo: the Belvidere Apollo.

Stanza 12: the Escorial was adorned by succe[e]ding kings, until the Peninsular war, when the French as a piece of revenge for their defeats, sent a body of dragoons under La Houssaye, who entered the Escorial, ravaged and despoiled it of some of its greatest treasures. The monks then left the convent. Since that time it has been left desolate and uninhabited. The twelfth stanza describes this.

97. Blades ... in circles: alluding to the practise [sic] of arranging swords in circles, radiating from their hilts.

Stanza 13: the Escorial is often exposed to the attacks of the storms which sweep down from the mountains of Guadarrama.

114. **fearing ravage:** some years ago, fearing that the Carlists would plunder the Escorial, they removed the choicest remaining treasures to Madrid.

117. **royal discord:** the civil wars of late years in Spain.

121. **Eighth wonder:** the Spaniards call it eighth wonder of the world.

2. Winter with the Gulf Stream (1863) Highgate (*p. 7*):

A precocious poem in 'terza rima', the subject prompted by the unseasonally warm winter of 1862–3. Published (probably through the influence of the schoolboy's father) in the magazine *Once a Week* in February 1863, and therefore one of the few poems published during Hopkins's lifetime.

27. **Pactolus:** the golden river that cured Midas of the affliction whereby everything he touched turned to gold.

3. Spring and Death (1863) Highgate (*p. 8*):

A poem probably under the influence of his father's poetry, but also anticipating 'Spring and Fall' seventeen years later.

4. New Readings (1864) (*p. 9*):

The influence is clear of George Herbert, one of Hopkins's favourite English poets, and a remaining connection with the Anglican church.

5. Heaven-Haven (1864) (*p. 9*):

The theme of retreat or rest in holy or idyllic places was a common secular as well as religious one in Victorian poetry. Cf., in particular, Tennyson's description of Avilion in his 'Morte d'Arthur' (ll. 260–61): 'Where falls not hail, or rain or any snow,/Nor ever wind blows loudly . . .'

(Title) **Heaven-Haven:** cf. the last line of George Herbert's 'The Size': 'These seas are tears, and heav'n the haven'.

6. 'I must hunt down the prize' (1864) Oxford (*p. 10*):

A sequel to the previous poem, 'Heaven-Haven'. An alternative to the second stanza reads:

> Must see the green seas roll
> > Where waters set

Towards those wastes where the ice-blocks tilt and fret,
     Not so far from the pole.

7. 'Why should their foolish bands' (1864) (p. 10):
The next three poems (the third only partly) were written while
Hopkins was on a reading holiday in Wales with two Oxford
friends in August 1864.

8. 'It was a hard thing' (1864) Maentwrog (p. 10).

9. 'Miss Story's character' (1864) Maentwrog (p. 11):
'We have four Miss Storys staying in the house, girls from
Reading. This is a great advantage – but not to reading'.

10. Io (1864) (p. 12):
In Greek mythology, Io was the first priestess of Hera, the wife
of Zeus. Zeus fell in love with her and, to save her from Hera's
jealousy, turned her into a white heifer.

   16. vigil-organ: Zeus arranged that Argos, who had eyes all
   over his body, should guard Io.

11. To Oxford (April 1865) Oxford (p. 13):
Hopkins was in his second year at Oxford, as a Classics
exhibitioner at Balliol College.

(First sonnet)
   1. the terms that reappear: the three annual academic terms
   of the University.
   6. pleasaunce: both 'pleasance' (a secluded part of a garden,
   set out with walks etc) and the archaic abstract word 'pleasaunce' from Old French = pleasure.
   10. towers musical: cf. the reference to Oxford as 'bell-
   swarmèd' in the later sonnet, 'Duns Scotus's Oxford'.
   11. Window-circles: the rose-windows of some of the Oxford
   college chapels.

(Second sonnet)
This is highly characteristic of the poet's vision in more mature
poems in that it delights in viewing the world from odd angles.
Looking up steeply at the façade of an Oxford college chapel,
Hopkins makes the straight lines of the architectural *levels*,
courses and *horizontals* appear curved (*in bows*). And in the
sestet he questions whether his own unique vision is that of
mankind in general.

5. visual compulsion: optical illusion.

9. bye-ways: combining the fact that it is often along narrow lanes that one comes *underneath* a *chapel-side* in Oxford and the fact that the sonnet's odd perspective produces an out-of-the-ordinary effect, a *bye-ways beauty.*

12. The Alchemist in the City (May 1865) Oxford (*p. 14*):
An 'alchemist' – a person seeking to turn base metals into gold and to discover an elixir for eternal life – is a potent metaphor for Hopkins, at a low ebb as a second-year undergraduate at Oxford, wondering whether it is too late to join instead the busy world of men outside his window. Helping the metaphor is the fact that a medieval townscape seen through a window would be similar to the views still possible from Hopkins's rooms in Balliol in mid-Victorian Oxford.

25. belvedere: a summer house or roofed gallery, sited so as to command a pleasant view.

13. To Oxford (June 1865) (*p. 15*):
Written as a sonnet, it lacks its last two lines which, on entering the poem in his journal, Hopkins said he had 'forgotten and must get'.

6. Belleisle: a code name for Oxford that Hopkins was fond of using because of its closeness in sound to the name of his own college, Balliol. Cf. the fragment 'Bellisle', entered in his journal a few weeks previously:

> Bellisle! that is a fabling name, but we
> Have here a true one, echoing the sound;
> And one to each of us is holy ground;
> But let me sing that which is known to me.

14. 'Myself unholy' (June 1865) Hampstead (*p. 16*):
As also in the next sonnet, in this summer of 1865 Hopkins is clearly working through from a sense of doubt and self-disgust to a deeper religious commitment.

3. the rook: a frequent self-mocking term. Eleven years later he was to sign a Welsh poem written at St Bueno's College as having been written by 'Brân Maenefa', the Crow of Maenefa.

15. 'See how Spring opens' (June 1865) Hampstead (*p. 16*):
A sonnet caught emotionally between early disappointments,

including sexual frustration, and the beginning of the feelings that brought about his conversion to Rome in the following year.

7. the good sower: Matthew 13.
10. the waste done in unreticent youth: both sexual *waste* (a Victorian term for masturbation) and the *waste* of his previous years as a Protestant.

16. 'My prayers must meet a brazen heaven' (September 1865) Hampstead (*p. 17*):
Another poem of self-doubt from the summer months at home before returning to Oxford for his third year.

1. brazen heaven: 'χάλκεου ουρανόν', brazen heaven, in Homer, *Iliad* xvii, ll. 424–5. Hopkins later quoted Homer's phrase in a journal entry for 8 July 1871, describing thunder 'echoing round like brass'. In the present poem, the fuller context of Homer's line is relevant: 'The iron clang arose to the brazen heaven through the air where no harvest is reaped'.

17. Shakspere (September 1865) (*p. 17*):
The previous year (1864) had been the tercentary of Shakespeare's birth, the occasion of much celebration. Cf. Matthew Arnold's sonnet 'Shakespeare', published 1849.

18. 'Let me be to Thee' (October 1865) Oxford (*p. 18*):
In Hopkins's early diaries in October 1865, this and the next poem, 'The Half-way House', follow directly on an entry in which the poet raises the specific question of leaving the Church of England for Roman Catholicism. The poems are in turn followed by an entry (for 6 November) deciding to forgo aesthetic pleasures – including, for a while, poetry: 'On this day by God's grace I resolved to give up all beauty until I had His leave for it'.

19. The Half-way House (October 1865) (*p. 18*):
A poem very much in the manner of George Herbert, one of Hopkins's favourite poets. See also the note to the previous poem.

(Title) The Half-way House: John Henry Newman's *Apologia Pro Vita Sua* (1864) had claimed that the Church of

England was an institution half-way between Roman Catholicism and atheism.

7. **Egyptian reed:** 2 Kings 18:21 and Isaiah 36:6. A reference
here to the Church of England, now giving way, in Hopkins's
allegiance, to Roman Catholicism.
8. **vine:** John 15:1–10.
8. **cross-barred rod or rood:** the Roman Catholic church.

20. **A Complaint** (late autumn 1865) (*p. 19*):
Lightheartedly written, as if spoken by his sister Milicent.
Hopkins's letters show that he had also forgotten her birthday
in 1863, but there is bibliographical evidence for the later dating
of the poem, suggesting another occasion for making amends in
this engaging poem.

8. **seventeenth of next October:** Milicent Hopkins was born
17 October 1849.

21. **'Moonless darkness stands between'** (Christmas Day 1865)
Hampstead (*p. 20*).

22. **'The earth and heaven, so little known'** (January 1866)
Hampstead (*p. 20*).

23. **'The stars were packed so close that night'** (January 1866)
(*p. 21*).

24. **The Nightingale** (January 1866) (*p. 22*).

25. **The Habit of Perfection** (January 1866) (*p. 23*):
An expression of the paradoxical exquisiteness of the experience
of withdrawing into ascetic religious self-dedication, away from
the world and from the normal enjoyment of the five senses.
Religious retreat was a subject pictorially externalised by a good
number of recent Pre-Raphaelite paintings. Cf. 'Heaven-Haven'
above.

10. **uncreated light:** the 'lux increata', epitomising the pure
mind of God.
12. **Coils, keeps:** in the sense of 'embroils' and 'confines'.
13. **hutch:** a place for storing.
18. **keep:** 'upkeep'.
24. **unhouse and house:** a reference to the Host in the
Eucharist being 'taken from' and 'returned to' the tabernacle

of the altar where it is kept; but also *housed* in the sense of being taken into the communicant's own body.
27–8. See Matthew 6:28–9.

26. Nondum (Lent 1866) (*p. 24*):

A poem concerned with the idea of God as a 'Deus Absconditus', an absent God, a theme memorably expressed in Tennyson's *In Memoriam* (eg. sections LVI and CXXIV).

(Title) **Nondum:** the Latin means 'Not yet'.
19–24. Genesis 1:1–13.
27. **Deep calls to deep:** Psalms 42:7.

27. Lines for a Picture of St Dorothea (1866) (*p. 26*):

A revised version of an 1864 poem, 'For a Picture of Saint Dorothea', which was the first that Hopkins ever showed to Robert Bridges. A little after the present poem, Hopkins also wrote a version in 'dramatic' form with three voices. The poem is of particular interest because it represents Hopkins's first experiments in 'Sprung Rhythm' (see Introduction, pp. xli–xliv)

(Subtitle) **Dorothea and Theophilus:** Dorothea was reputedly killed at Caesarea in Cappadocia under Diocletian for refusing to marry and worship idols. A young lawyer, Theophilus, taunted her on her way to execution by challenging her to send him fruit and flowers from paradise. On receiving these, Theophilus was converted to Christianity and subsequently himself martyred. The legend was embodied in *The Virgin-Martyr* by Massinger (1622) and also in a poem by Swinburne.

Stanza 2: cf. *The Virgin-Martyr*, v.i.
10. **set:** in the gardening sense of being planted to produce fruit or seed.
23. **Sphered:** placed, like the moon and stars, beyond reach.
28. **Served by messenger:** Theophilus is in doubt as to whether the revisitation is by Dorothea herself or by an angel.
31. **into the world of light:** an echo of Henry Vaughan's poem 'They are all gone into the world of light'.
39. **wand:** that of the palm, symbol of martyrdom.
42. **another Christian:** i.e., the converted Theophilus.

28. Horace: Persicos odi, puer, apparatus (late 1867–early 1868) The Oratory, Edgbaston (*p. 27*):

Horace's original is from the end of Book 1 of the Odes. In their characteristic praise for the simple life, this translation and the next one remind us that there are classical, secular equivalents to Hopkins's religious interest in retreat – and from a very different culture.

1. **child**: the young slave serving the wine.

1. **Persian-perfect**: because Persia had connotations of sumptuousness.

2. **bast**: fibrous material obtained from jute, hemp, lime etc., used for making rope and string, and thus for binding garlands.

5. **natural myrtle**: myrtle leaves provided the base for weaving garlands.

8. **tackled vine**: i.e., the vine is 'tied' to a trellis.

29. **Horace**: *Odi profanum volgus et arceo* (late 1867–early 1868) The Oratory, Edgbaston (*p. 28*):
Horace's original is from Book 3 of the Odes.

2. **Grace love your lips!**: in effect, 'say nothing' (a textual variant was 'Grace guard your tongues!'). At certain rituals, some newcomers were told they were not welcome (*Tread back*) and others told simply to be quiet (*Grace love your lips!*).

17. **the blade**: the sword hanging by a hair above the sycophant Damocles, to force him to reconsider his claim that being a king was a happy state.

18. **Sicily fare**: Sicily was famous for its feasting.

24. **Tempe**: a wooded valley in Thessaly, between the mountains of Olympus and Ossa, famously referred to in Keats's 'Ode on a Grecian Urn'.

28. **Haedus ... Arcturus**: the stars that mark the parameters of winter.

31. **dog-star**: Sirius, the star associated with extremely hot weather.

34. **abutments**: 'encroachments' – as if human domestic life were expanding even into the sea, the domain of fishes.

41. **Phrygian stone**: marble was a renowned product of Phrygia, in west central Asia Minor.

42. **starry shot**: the changeable colour-effect of certain textiles.

43. **Falernian grown**: i.e., Falernian wine.

44. oils of Shushan: *Shushan* was the Biblical name for Susa, capital of the Persian empire.

30. The Elopement (early 1868) The Oratory, Edgbaston (*p. 29*):

A piece influenced by Keats's 'The Eve of St Agnes'. It was contributed to a short-lived, handwritten weekly journal (three copies only) produced at the Oratory School, where Hopkins was a junior master. It only survived through being quoted in The Oratory School Magazine in November 1895.

1. rud red: the red of red ochre (ruddle).
21. hurdles: fences. Cf. 'The Starlight Night': 'This piece-bright paling shuts the spouse/Christ home, Christ and his mother and all his hallows' (*p. 45*).
22. liberties: the right or privilege of access to particular places.

31. The Wreck of the Deutschland (1875) St Beuno's (*p. 31*):

'What refers to myself in the poem is all strictly and literally true and did all occur.' The real structure of the poem is the bringing into relationship of the poet's profound inner experience and a parallel to it in an event in the outer historical world. The unevadable reality of that outer event was horrifyingly brought home in the reports in *The Times* and the *Illustrated London News*, sent to the poet at St Beuno's by his mother:

> One brave sailor, who was safe in the rigging, went down to try and save a child or woman who was drowning on deck. He was secured by a rope to the rigging, but a wave dashed him against the bulwarks, and when daylight dawned his headless body, detained by the rope, was swaying to and fro with the waves.
>
> *The Times*, 11 December 1875 (cf. stanza 16)

It was in fact with the narrative of the wreck itself that Hopkins started writing the poem (at stanza 12). But he insisted that 'The principal business is lyrical': the work is ultimately an ode rather than a narrative poem. In celebrating and exploring the tragedy, rather than simply recording it, the problem was to find significance in that which appeared merely 'unshapeable' (stanza 29) and cruel, while rejecting any simple notion that the wreck was directly caused by God (stanza 6). The significance for Hopkins lay in the fact that terror and beauty are inevitable parts of any religious experience of the world. It is a duality made inevitable by the Fall, and made meaningful by the Incarnation which signalled God's own participation in a world of pain. That central fact is what is recorded in 'Part the First'; and the literalness of what is described there (see stanza 2) is attested by a private Journal entry of 18 September 1873 describing

> a nervous collapse of the same sort as when one is very tired and holding oneself at stress not to sleep yet/suddenly goes slack and seems to fall and wakes, only on a greater scale and with a loss of muscular control reaching more or less deep; this one to the chest and not further, so that I could speak, whispering at first, then louder ... I had lost all muscular stress elsewhere but not sensitive, feeling where each limb lay and thinking that I could recover myself if I could move my finger, I said, and then the arm and so the whole body. The feeling is terrible: the body no longer swayed as a piece by the nervous and muscular instress seems to fall in and hang like a dead weight on the chest.

Hopkins sees the wreck as presenting a renewed challenge to his intellectual ability to accept that kind of experience: 'And after it almost unmade, what with dread,/Thy doing: and dost thou touch me afresh?/Over again I feel thy finger and find thee'. It is this fact of a public event testing personal experience that causes the whole poem to pivot on the interpretation (in stanzas 19–30) of the nun's invocation of Christ at the height of the suffering aboard the *Deutschland*. As Hopkins sees it, the nun's sense of Christ's presence *in* the suffering is equivalent to His rebirth in time (stanza 30). It is in this way that the wreck is ultimately seen (stanzas 34–35) as an important sign for Britain: 'Dame, at our door/Drowned . . . Remember us in the roads'.

PART THE FIRST

Stanza 1

1. **mastering me**: a composite adjective, describing *God*.

6. **almost unmade**: bouts of spiritual crisis always involved for Hopkins a sense of physical disintegration.

6. **what with dread**: 'with what dread'.

8. **Over again**: once again (in the event of the shipwreck). Hopkins recognises God's terrible working, and remembers,

in the next two stanzas, its earlier manifestation in his own personal life.

Stanza 2

9. I did say yes: the paradox of responding positively to, and accepting, the terror of the experience.

13. Thou knowest etc.: i.e. the details of that actual former experience.

16. the midriff astrain etc.: straining with the pressure (*leaning*) of the *stress*, and pierced (*laced*) with its fire.

Stanza 3

19. where was a place?: i.e. of peace and refuge.

20. wings that spell: i.e. words of prayer as a means of escape.

21. heart of the Host: the *host* is the consecrated bread of the Eucharist (Latin 'hostia' = victim).

23. Carrier-witted: the poet's heart has the right homing instinct – that of a carrier-pigeon.

24. from the flame to the flame etc.: God is in what is fled from, as much as in what is fled to; his *grace* is implicit even in the terror.

Stanza 4

25. I am soft sift etc.: the image is of sand (*soft sift*) in the top part of the hourglass – appearing unmoved at the sides (*at the wall/Fast*), but under-*mined* and sifting downwards in the middle.

30. But roped with etc.: the hourglass image for inner disintegration is replaced by an image of poise and balance. The steady surface of the well is supported by (*roped with*) the hillside rivulets which feed it. This symbolises the effect of grace – an aspect (*vein*) and revelation (*pressure*) of the promise (*proffer*) of the gospel.

Stanza 5

35. wafting him out of it: *him* = Christ.

36. glory in thunder: emphasising Hopkins's acceptance of the dark as well as the more obviously beautiful side of God's presence in the world.

38. since, tho' etc.: though God is always present in the world, that presence must be activated by man's disciplined response (*instressed*), and kept at stress and proclaimed (*stressed*). Cf. l. 35 '*wafting him out of it*, and the end of 'Hurrahing in Harvest' (p. 48).

Stanza 6

41. Not out of his bliss etc.: this disciplined perception of God's presence in the world does not have its source in either the beauty (*bliss*) or the disasters (*storms*) of nature. (The latter are in any case not directly caused by God.) It is, rather, something more deeply involved in history (*it rides time*).

Stanza 7

49. It dates from day etc.: it dates from Christ's actual presence in the world (*his going in Galilee*): his conception, with the *womb* forecasting the *grave*; his birth (*Manger*); and his subsequent *Passion* at Gethsemane and Calvary.

54. Thence the discharge of it etc.: 'there is its source', as though of an electrical charge, and its growth-point (*swelling*) – though these were forecast in Classical and Old Testament times (*felt before*) and are still in force (*in high flood yet*).

56 (and into Stanza 8). only the heart, being hard at bay etc.: it is the individual in extremity who releases this recognition (*Is out with it!*) of God's most essential revelation in Christ's suffering.

Stanza 8

58–9. the best or worst/Word last!: a response to the fact that it takes personal extremity to recognise Christ's suffering. This is half celebrated and half lamented by Hopkins: it is our *best word* in being a real recognition, and our *worst word* in being delayed and painful.

59. lush-kept plush-capped sloe etc.: the sloe is the bitter plum-like fruit of the blackthorn. The image of it being bitten and burst evokes the sense of something suddenly revealing its exact nature. Here, it suggests (a) Christ's dramatic revelation of his full nature in his cruel death; (b) man's sudden realisation of the significance of that death in time; and (c) man's sudden sense of the bitter-sweet fullness of his own response.

62. Hither then, last or first etc.: 'late or soon, then', men come to recognise Christ's sacrifice – whether voluntarily and knowingly or not.

Stanza 9

67. Wring thy rebel: continues the sense of *flush the man* from the previous stanza – this time flushing out man from the kennel (*den*) of his own malice.

70. lightning and love etc.: the paradox is now firmly established in the poem – the co-identity of the dark and the merciful side of God's dealings with the world.

Stanza 10

73. With an anvil-ding etc.: God is enjoined to *master* man either suddenly or gradually.

77–8. Paul,/Or . . . Austin: contrasting the sudden conversion of St Paul on the road to Damascus with the gentler and gradual conversation of St Augustine of Hippo (A.D. 354–430).

PART THE SECOND

Stanza 11

83. goes Death on drum: Death proclaims, as if beating a drum, the various forms it takes – the *sword*, *flame*, *flood* etc. of the previous two lines.

85. but wé dream etc.: man imagines that he is permanent (*rooted in earth*); but man, like earth, is only *Dust*!

88. the sour scythe cringe: *cringe* in the archaic sense of 'cause to cringe'.

Stanza 12

91. Take settler and seamen, tell men with women etc.: i.e. 'taking' account of the passengers and crew, and 'counting' all the men and women, the number was 200.

93. not under thy feathers: not being conscious Christians (cf. Matthew 23:37).

94. a shoal: the Kentish Knock, the sandbank on which the ship was wrecked in the Thames estuary.

94. of a fourth etc.: the syntax runs 'not guessing that it was the fate (*doom*) of a quarter of them to be drowned'.

95. the bay of thy blessing etc.: the nautical meaning of *bay* leads to the later word *reeve* ('to rope together, and rope in'); but the architectural meaning of *bay* is also present, in the word *vault*.

Stanza 13

99. so the sky keeps: i.e. 'so the sky remains' (filled with the snow-storm), because *the infinite air is unkind*.

101. And the sea flint-flake etc.: 'and so also the sea remains' – sliced and raised from great depths (hence *black-backed*) by the *regular blow* of the storm.

103. Wiry: because the snow spirals in the wind.

Stanza 14

107. combs: ridges.

108. Kentish Knock: the most dangerous sandbank in the Thames Estuary.

111. whorl: the screw-propeller.

112. wind: nautical term = 'to steer'.

Stanza 15

120. shrouds: the rigging.

Stanza 16

126. tell: 'see'.

126. dandled: 'swung idly'.

128. burl: conveys the sense of full, spinning tumult.

Stanza 17

136. towered: the chief sister among the five nuns drowned was reported by *The Times* as being 'a gaunt woman 6ft high'.

Stanza 18

137–8. Ah, touched . . . Are you!: Hopkins addresses his own heart, imagined as moved to both tears and joy at the nun's experience.

141. O unteachably after evil etc.: *after* has verbal force: though the heart seeks wilfully after evil, it is still the means for expressing truth.

142. madrigal: 'sweetly lyrical'. The mystery of the tragic experience begins to centre on the reported action and words of the main nun.

143. Never-eldering revel etc.: the 'never-ageing joy' (as *youth* would see it) of the *river* of blood activated by the heart – an image for the unlooked-for-joy (*glee*) that the tragedy contains.

Stanza 19

147. hawling: the form combines 'hauling' and 'brawling'.

148. sloggering: 'pounding'.

149. she that weather: 'she in that weather . . .', by analogy with 'that day'.

150. fetch: 'resource' or 'expedient'.

Stanza 20

154. coifèd: referring to the head-dress of the sisters' order.

155. double a desperate name!: the name of the country that had persecuted the nuns, as of the ship in which they were drowned.

157. two of a town etc.: Hopkins remarks on the co-existence of good and evil. St Gertrude, the thirteenth-century nun and mystic lived in a convent near Eisleben, the birthplace of Martin Luther. The latter is described as the *beast of the waste wood* because of his rôle as one of the main leaders of the Reformation, whose effects all Jesuits were pledged to reverse.

Stanza 21

165. Orion: the constellation named after the great hunter.

166. unchancelling: a reference to the part of a church (the chancel) where the altar stands, and which is associated with sanctuary. The nuns had been in that sense 'unchancelled'. But a reference to God 'flushing out' the individual soul (cf. stanzas 8 and 9).

168. scroll-leaved flowers etc.: the *storm flakes* were, from Heaven's point of view, emblematic of the value of the suffering undergone by the nuns.

Stanza 22

169. Five! etc.: the number of nuns is emblematic of the number of wounds suffered by Christ. The word *finding* here might be rendered as 'emblem' = the device by which we 'find' the reality (hence also *cipher*). The word *sake* = the revelation of the irreducible uniqueness of Christ as a person.

171. Mark etc.: 'Notice that the emblem (*mark*) represents simultaneously a human nature and that nature's divine significance (*the word of it*): both *Sacrificed*.'

173. But he scores it etc.: 'But Christ marks the same wounds in blood (*in scarlet*) on those whom he has ordained beforehand as his dearest loved ones – the mark (*Stigma*), *signal*, and five-leaved sign (*cinquefoil token*) with which he designates the fleece of the *lamb* for slaughter and reddens the *rose-flake*' (red rose = traditional Christian emblem of martyrdom).

Stanza 23

177. father Francis etc.: St Francis of Assisi, founder of the nuns' order. His body carried the stigmata, the five wounds of Christ – the symbolic pattern (*Lovescape*) of His crucifixion. The *seal of his seraph-arrival* refers to a vision St Francis had of a flaming seraph from heaven carrying in him the image of man crucified.

Stanza 24

199. the throng that catches etc.: both 'catching their breath' and 'catching at something for safety'.

201. The cross to her: '*(holding) the cross to her*'.

201. christens her wild-worst best: transforms the tragedy by recognising Christ's presence in it.

Stanza 25

203. arch and original Breath: Greek αρχή = first cause, Holy Spirit (see Genesis 2:7).

204. Is it love in her etc.: 'Is it that she actually wished to undergo death as Christ had done?' Hopkins begins to ask what the nun's calling on Christ actually meant.

206. else-minded then etc.: 'in that case, Christ's disciples were very differently minded when they feared drowning' (see Matthew 8:25).

208. Or is it that she cried for the crown etc.: 'Or is it that she desired the reward (the *crown*) of martyrdom rather than the death itself; but all the more urgently because of the pain of the occasion?'

Stanza 26

210. For how etc.: an extended image for the contrast in the sudden access of joy after suffering. It is like a mist drifting away to reveal blue skies and the dappled freshness of spring; and later the different beauty of the sky at night.

216. What by your measure etc.: the reader is asked what his image would be for the *treasure* of Heaven – as yet unseen and unimaginable despite his *hearing* what words attempt to say.

Stanza 27

218. it was not these: i.e. neither the desire for death nor the desire for Christ's crown of martyrdom as suggested in stanza 25 above.

219. The jading and jar etc.: 'It is the tiredness and injury suffered at the ordinary hands of life and time that makes the self-pitying heart desire release, not the more dramatic threat of danger.'

222. then further etc.: 'then again, the attraction of Christ's Passion is more comfortingly contemplated in the quietness of prayer (than in the middle of an actual emergency)'.

224. Other, I gather etc.: 'I conclude that her motive in saying what she did was a different one.'

Stanza 28

226. But how shall I . . . etc.: the broken syntax evokes the difficulty of giving the explanation of what really did happen to the nun at that crucial point. It also parallels the panic of the actual scene.

229. There then! etc.: the insistence of the catalogue of names for Christ has the force almost of suggesting that He literally appeared to the nun aboard ship. The crucial word is *Ipse* – 'the man himself'.

Stanza 29

235. single eye!: unique and decisive in its interpretation of the event.

236. unshapeable shock night: the horror had no shape or meaning except through the nun's way of responding to it.

238. Wording it etc.: the nun's words are an 'interpretation' of the fact that all things 'express' Christ (they *are word of* Him) and are given significance only by Him (*worded by*).

240. Simon Peter of a soul: with the strength of the spiritual rock on which the church is founded (see Matthew 16:18).

241. Tarpeïan-fast: the Tarpeïan rock was a cliff on the Capitoline hill outside Rome.

Stanza 30

244. What was the feast etc.: the day following the tragedy (8

December was the Feast of the Immaculate Conception of Mary.

247. for so conceived etc.: just as Mary herself was immaculately conceived, so also her conception of Christ was immaculate.

248. birth of a brain etc.: the nun's experience of Christ at the point of death was itself a kind of giving birth to Christ. (The words *heard*, *kept*, and *uttered* suggest respectively 'conceived', 'carried', and 'gave birth to'.)

249. Word: vocative, addressed to Christ, in apposition to *Jesu* (ll. 242 and 243).

Stanza 31

251. but pity of the rest etc.: Hopkins at first pities those aboard who died *comfortless*, because *unconfessed*. But he then asserts that the gentle touch of Providence in the nun made her also have the effect of 'startling' others to a realisation of Christ. The *shipwrack*, then, is a *harvest* – both of the unbelieving souls aboard and of those unbelievers who later hear of the nun's experience.

Stanza 32

259. Yore-flood: suggesting both Noah's Deluge (Genesis 7) and the waters of creation (Genesis 1:2).

262. ocean of a motionable mind: the spiritual anarchy of man, like the waters of the world's seas, is curbed and contained by God's mastery.

263. Ground of being, and granite: continuing the image of the sea, supported from below and resisted at its margins.

265. heeds but hides, bodes but abides: God's *sovereignty* is 'concerned, but does not reveal iself, foresees but does not forestall'.

Stanza 33

268. for the lingerer etc.: '(an ark) for the lingerer with a love (that) glides . . .'

269. Lower than death: cf. the Creed – 'He descended into Hell'.

270. A vein: Christ is also a 'link', through prayer, to reach those souls in Hell or Purgatory.

271. the uttermost mark etc.: the syntax is 'this was the ultimate extreme (which) our giant, plunged in the suffering of death but then risen, ... reached in the storm of his strides'.

Stanza 34

274. new born: revealed anew in the nature of the nun's death.

275. Double-naturèd: both human and divine.

277. Miracle-in-Mary-of-flame: a composite noun inscaping the paradox registered separately in the previous line – Christ, though of divine source (*heaven-flung*), was physical (*heart-fleshed*) and nurtured in Mary's womb (*maiden-furled*).

278. Mid-numberèd he: the second of the trinity of Father, Son, and Holy Ghost.

279. Not a dooms-day dazzle etc.: this revelation of Christ is not the blinding light of the Day of Judgment nor the *dark* obscurity of his original birth.

281. let flash to the shire: revealed to a particular area. Hence the emphasis in the next and final stanza on the reconversion of England.

Stanza 35

282. Dame: i.e. the nun.

282. at our door: the stanza makes insistent use of the words *our* and *us*, emphasising the significance of the event for Britain.

284. Remember us in the roads etc.: a reference to the missionary work of the Jesuits in England, the *reward* for which would be to have *Our King back, Oh, upon English souls!*

286. easter: a verb – 'Let Him rise anew in us'.

286. crimson-cresseted: the image is of a 'cresset', a metal basket on a pole, burning oil or pitch.

'The Wreck of the Deutschland' was the first poem worked fully in sprung rhythm. Freedom in the number of syllables per line is underpinned by a regular number of stresses in each eight-line stanza: 2–3–4–3–5–5–4–6, but with the first line changing from two to three stresses in the second part. The poem however does not make use of the extra-metrical feet which Hopkins called 'outriders' and which he used so often later (see note to 'The Windhover', p. 274, and other notes *passim*).

32. Moonrise (19 June 1876) St Beuno's (*p. 40*):
A delicate evocation of a natural sight and its penetrating effect on the poet's consciousness. A manuscript shows Hopkins's intention to rewrite it with one extra stress in the second half of each line.

4. Maenefa: a darkly wooded hill rising directly behind St Beuno's College, with prehistoric burial-mounds (hence *barrow*).
5. cusp: sharp point. One edge of the moon has not faded and appears to 'clasp' the rest of its circle.
5. fluke: literally the arrow-head shape at the two ends of the curved part of an anchor.
5. fanged: dialect verb = 'gripped'.

33. The Silver Jubilee (1876) St Beuno's (*p. 41*):
Written as a contribution to the St Beuno's College celebration of Dr James Brown's twenty-fifth year as the first Roman Catholic Bishop of Shrewsbury, whose diocese included the six counties of North Wales. Hopkins also contributed Welsh and Latin poems. This English poem was set to music and sung at the celebrations.

1. no high-hung bells because it was then forbidden to ring bells in Catholic churches.
7. that but now were shut: i.e. before 1850, when the Roman Catholic hierarchy was re-established for England and Wales.
14. some way spent: the Bishop was sixty-four, and close to retirement.

34. The Woodlark (July 1876) St Beuno's (*p. 41*):
The special character of the woodlark's song had been noted by Hopkins ten years earlier at Oxford (Journal, 3 June 1966): 'The cuckoo singing one side, on the other from the ground and unseen the wood-lark, as I suppose, most sweetly with a song of which the structure is more definite than the skylark's and gives the link with that of the rest of birds' – an entry that also mentions the *oxeye* (daisy flower) of l. 28.

35. Penmaen Pool (August 1876) Barmouth (*p. 43*):
Students from St Beuno's would spend part of the summers at Barmouth (Merionethshire), and row up the Mawddach river to

visit Penmaen Pool and the George Inn, for whose Visitors' Book Hopkins wrote this poem.

7. Cadair cliff: Cadair Idris (2,927 ft) to the South.

9. Dyphwys: Diffwys (2,462 ft) to the North.

10. Giant's stool: Cadair Idris, with a play on 'stool' because *cadair* in Welsh means 'chair'.

12. To halve the bowl: the personified mountains 'share' the *bowl* of the pool, as at a meal.

15. repeated topsyturvy: the landscape is reflected upside-down.

17. Charles's Wain: the seven stars of the Plough, in the Great Bear constellation.

27. raindrop-roundels: interlooped circles caused by rain on the pool's surface.

36. God's Grandeur (February–March 1877) St Beuno's (*p. 44*): God's dynamic presence in and behind His created universe shames industrial man's brute materialism. Contrasted with fallen man's desolating effect on the natural world is the resilient freshness at the heart of nature itself.

1. charged: primarily, made 'electrically' alive – hence the later images *flame, shining, lights, bright*. But also 'charged' in the sense of (a) 'rendered a debt that needs to be redeemed' (cf. the financial connotations of *spent* and *dearest* later); (b) 'challenged with' (see secondary meaning of *foil* below); and (c) 'given responsibility for'.

2. shook foil: 'Shaken goldfoil gives off broad glares like sheet lightning and . . . owing to its zigzag dints and creasings and network of small many cornered facets, a sort of fork lightning too.' The image also suggests a shaken rapier, consonant with meaning (b) for *charged* above.

3. the ooze of oil: *gathers*, *ooze* and *crushed* denote something like olive oil, with suitable anointing connotations. The industrial imagery of the end of the octave, however, also makes us think of industrial oil, the systematic exploitation of which dates from around 1860.

4. reck his rod: 'heed His rod (of authority)'; but also 'heed His cross' (Old English 'rood' = 'cross'). A fusion therefore of the Old and the New Testament view of God.

5. **Generations have trod** etc.: an echo of Keats's 'Ode to a Nightingale' – 'No hungry generations tread thee down'.

12. **springs:** the verb also suggests the noun ('springs' of water); hence the claim (l. 10) that 'There lives the dearest freshness deep down things'.

13. **bent:** literally 'curved'; but also 'misshapen by human touch' or financially 'crooked' (slang).

13. **Holy Ghost:** Genesis 1:2.

The sonnet's standard rhythm (iambic pentameter) is here counterpointed by having freer rhythms mounted upon it.

37. **The Starlight Night** (February 1877) St Beuno's (*p. 45*): 'As we drove home the stars came out thick: I leant back to look at them and my heart opening more than usual praised our Lord to and in whom all that beauty comes home' (Journal entry for 1874). The magical beauty of the starlit sky reminds us that the world is to be 'bought' with the coinage of the Christian faith – with prayer, patience, alms, vows – because more important than its outward splendour is the ultimate reality of Christ behind it.

Throughout the octave, and into the sestet, the images are Hopkin's terrestrial equivalents for the ways in which the starlit sky appears to him – like *fire-folk* or *bright boroughs* etc.

4. **dim woods:** the darker background of the sky itself, against which the stars shine out. (Similarly, the *grey lawns* of the next line, with *grey* perhaps suggesting a dawning sky.)

4. **diamond delves:** plural of obsolete 'delf' = 'pit' or 'mine'.

5. **quickgold:** a coinage by analogy with 'quicksilver'.

6. **whitebeam . . . abeles:** respectively, the Chess Apple and the White Poplar, the white undersides of whose leaves are exposed when fluttered by the wind (*wind-beat*).

9. **Buy then! bid then!:** following on from *purchase* in the previous line, Hopkins develops the metaphor of an auctioneer highlighting the beauty of what he is selling. *What?* ('With what?') is the imagined interjection of the purchaser, enjoined to pay the currency of *Prayer, patience, alms, vows.*

10. **May-mess:** the stars appear like clusters of blossom on the hawthorn or May tree, or on fruit trees in May. *May-mess* also suggests 'Mary-mass,' i.e. a festival for Mary. Cf. 'May is Mary's month' ('The May Magnificat', p. 53).

11. **mealed-with-yellow sallows:** *sallows* are pussy willows, the description suggesting the powdery coating of their yellow flowers.

12. **These are indeed the barn:** the sky and the stars are in fact only the outer face of reality, 'housing' the real treasures within. Apart from the thought of natural produce (*shocks* = 'sheaves' in l. 13: cf. Matthew 13:30), the word *barn* also evokes the poor stable at Bethlehem, housing the infant Christ.

13. **This piece-bright paling:** *paling* is the 'fence' of the sky, brightened piecemeal by the stars which also look like 'pieces of eight'. But *paling* also has adjectival force – growing pale as dawn comes, and also 'paling' in significance in comparison with the real glories behind. These include not only Christ but Mary, physically assumed into Heaven, and the Saints (*hallows*).

Standard sonnet rhythm counterpointed; but both the octave and sestet are 'opened' with a line in sprung rhythm.

38. Spring (May 1877) St Beuno's (*p. 45*):
The rich freshness of the season is seen as a reminder of an Edenic purity and as an equivalent for the same potential in man before it is clouded and soured *with sinning*.

2. **weeds, in wheels:** denoting circular, curling growth.

3. **look little low heavens:** the omission of 'like' saves the phrase from being merely a pretty simile.

4. **rinse and wring:** suggests the cleansing and astringent effect of the bird's song. *Wring* also suggests 'ring'.

5. **like lightnings:** the switch to a visual image emphasises the decisive suddenness of the bird's song, and the plural its repeated and echoed effects.

6. **glassy:** 'sharply lustrous'.

6. **leaves and blooms:** either verbs, or nouns in apposition to *they*.

6. **brush:** 'touch', but also as if 'painting' or 'cleaning' the blue of the sky.

10. **strain:** 'the remaining essence, the surviving part of.' The word also has musical connotations. Stemming from *wring* (l. 4), there is further the sense of a 'taut' uniqueness at maximum performance.

11. **have, get:** Christ is urged to capture and preserve for Himself the spiritual springtime in human beings.

14. **Most ... thy choice** etc.: *most* governs both *choice* and *worthy*: 'innocent youth is the *most choice* ("precious") and the period most worth winning'.

Standard sonnet rhythm but with 'sprung leadings' i.e. strongly stressed opening syllables to lines, challenging the iambic pattern.

39. In the Valley of the Elwy (May 1877) St Beuno's (*p.* 46): Hopkins explained the poem's essential meaning in a letter to Bridges: 'The frame of the sonnet is a rule of three sum *wrong*, thus: As the sweet smell to those kind people so the Welsh landscape is NOT to the Welsh; and then the author and principle [i.e. God] of all four terms is asked to bring the sum right.' He also noted that 'the kind of people of the sonnet were the Watsons of Shooter's Hill, nothing to do with the Elwy'.

5. **cordial air:** the household's *comforting smell* (l. 3).
5. **made those kind people a hood:** the object of *made* is *hood* – a covering as sheltering as a bird's *wing* over a *bevy* of eggs, or *mild nights* over the fresh growing things (*new morsels*) of spring.
8. **of course:** the literal, less casual, meaning of the phrase – 'as a matter of course' and *of right* (l. 8).
11. **Only:** with the force of 'And yet'.
11. **the inmate does not correspond:** the native of Wales seen in terms of an 'inhabitant' (*inmate*) of the remembered house of the octave. He does not *correspond* in the sense of not responding to the beauty, nor *correspond*ing to its loveliness, or *correspond*ing ('making complete') the four terms of the pattern mentioned in Hopkins's letter, namely host-house: native-Wales (cf. 'The Sea and the Skylark'). The criticism is not of the Welsh people, but of the general human inability to be fitting inhabitants of God's world. A more specifically Catholic undertone becomes clear if we consider a poem in Welsh that Hopkins had written the previous year, dedicated to the Bishop of Shrewsbury on the twenty-fifth year of his episcopate (celebrated also in 'The Silver Jubilee' above). In the Welsh poem, Hopkins writes '*Dyn sydd yn unig yn ôl*' ('Only man is tardy'), and in the preface to the poem (also in

Welsh) he speaks of the fact that 'earth and water bear greater witness to the ancient religion of Gwynedd than does man'.

14. Being mighty a master etc.: Hopkins imagines a line of ordinary syntax – 'Being a mighty master, and being a fond father' – and rearranges it to throw more separate emphases on its main parts (*mighty . . . master . . . father . . . fond*).

Standard sonnet rhythm is here both 'sprung and counterpointed' – 'the most delicate and difficult business of all'. Counterpoint broadly respects the standard number of syllables, while Sprung Rhythm departs from it (cf. lines 6 and 14).

40. The Sea and the Skylark (May 1877) Rhyl (*p. 46*):
The setting is Rhyl in North Wales. The theme reinforces that of 'God's Grandeur': the contrast between the endless prelapsarian powers of nature and man's unworthy betrayal of those powers.

2. Trench: 'make a penetrating, decisive noise'.

2. ramps: 'storms' and 'rages' against the shore.

4. moon: under whose influence the tide works.

5. Left hand, off land, I hear the lark ascend: an example of what Hopkins called 'vowelling-off (i.e. changing the vowels), in this case causing them to *ascend*, like the lark, up a scale. The verb *hear* has the next four finite verbs dependent on it (*ascend, whirl, pour, pelt*).

6–8. His rash-fresh re-winded new-skeinèd score etc.: Hopkins imagines the bird's song in visual terms. The headlong and new (*rash-fresh*) song, having been *re-winded* on to a receptacle, is allowed to *whirl* off as from a *winch*. But also present is the idea of 'a skein of silk ribbed by having been tightly wound on a narrow card or a notched holder . . . the laps or folds are the notes or short measures and bars' of the song falling vertically to earth.

10. ring right out: the sounds of the sea and the skylark tell of, and expose, their sordid human opposites. The latter are also excluded, as from a 'circle' of purity.

10. turbid: 'muddily unclear'. The word also appears in Matthew Arnold's 'Dover Beach', an interesting parallel to Hopkins's poem.

12. earth's past prime: the notion of Eden, *past* because earth's freshness is now incomplete, without a corresponding freshness in man.

13–14. Our make and making break etc.: industrial man, 'made' in God's image, seems bent towards not only meaningless death (*last dust*) but also his origins in primordial *slime*.

Standard sonnet rhythm, 'in parts sprung and in others counterpointed'. See note on 'In the Valley of the Elwy' above.

41. The Windhover (May 1877) St Beuno's (*p. 47*):
See the discussion of this sonnet in the Introduction (pp. xxxi ff.) Details not included in that discussion are as follows:

1. minion: 'favourite' or 'darling'.

2–3. riding . . . striding: Cf. the Dauphin's description of his horse in Shakespeare's *Henry V*: '*le cheval volant*, the Pegasus, *qui a les narines de feu!* When I bestride him I soar, I am a *hawk*: he trots the air' (III, 7).

4. rung upon the rein: combines the sense of rising in 'rings' and the technical term ('ring on a rein') for curbing and training horses.

4. wimpling: 'rippling', but also curved and pleated like a nun's head-dress.

7. heart in hiding: suggesting the bird's prey, but also the obscurity of the religious life in its avoidance of exploit and danger.

11. dangerous: an earlier meaning of 'danger' was 'power'.

11. chevalier: in the original sense of 'horseman', addressed both to the *riding* bird and (through it) to the princely Christ.

13. ah my dear: the phrase occurs in George Herbert's poem 'Love', addressed to the crucified Christ.

14. Fall, gall: the two words juxtapose Adam's fall and Christ's painful redemption of it.

The first sonnet completely in sprung rhythm; five stresses per line, but with many 'outriding' syllables. These extra-metrical syllables find their place in a foot with a particularly strong stress, and enforce a short pause irrespective of the main caesura. Hopkins wanted this effect differentiated from that of 'falling paeonic' rhythm (a stress followed by three unstressed syllables) which also occurs here, but which he considered more easily flowing. In manuscript, he marked 'outriding' feet with loops below the line. Thus lines 2 and 3 would scan:

dom of daylight's dauphin, || dapple-dawn-drawn Falcon, | in his riding
of the rolling | level || underneath him | steady air, and striding

42. Pied Beauty (Summer 1877) St Beuno's (*p. 48*):
This central poem of praise is a call to give God glory in
responding to the vivid individuality of all created things. It is
based on a simple paradox: the natural phenomena are chosen
for their 'varying' textures or colours, but they manifest a God
whose spiritual beauty is itself *past change*, unvarying. Compare
'As kingfishers catch fire, dragonflies draw flame' for its concentration on intense, unique detail.

   1. **dappled**: 'variegated.'
   2. **brinded**: 'brindled' – brown streaked with other colour.
   3. **rose-moles**: the circular, red markings on the trout's scales.
   3. **in stipple**: '(all done) *in stipple*', marked with dots rather
than lines.
   5. **plotted and pieced** etc.: in distinct sections, the landscape
is given over to grazing (*fold*, as in 'sheepfold'), or left *fallow*,
or cultivated (hence *plough*).
   7. **counter**: 'different' or 'varied' (cf. counterpane).
   7. **spare**: (like *original*) 'unique'.
   8. **fickle**: 'capable of change'.
   10. **fathers-forth**: this compound verb has the details of the
previous three lines as its objects: 'brings them into being as
contrary manifestations of Himself.'

This variation on the sonnet form is what Hopkins called a
'curtal sonnet'; that is, a reduced form of the usual fourteen
lines. It retains roughly the same proportions as the full sonnet,
reducing 8 + 6 lines to 6 + 4, and adding what Hopkins called
a 'halfline tailpiece', whose rhyming brevity brings the sonnet to
a sharp conclusion. Two other examples are 'Peace' (*p. 65*) and
'Not of all my eyes see, wandering on the world' (*p. 84*).

43. Hurrahing in Harvest (September 1877) St Beuno's (*p. 48*):
A rapturous response to the dynamic presence of God in the
natural world, the sonnet 'was the outcome of half an hour of
extreme enthusiasm as I walked home alone one day from
fishing in the Elwy'.

   1. **barbarous**: literally (from the Latin 'barbarosus') 'bearded'
or 'barbed'. The word also conveys elemental energy –

'pagan', until seen as the holy manifestation of the deeper energy of God behind.

1. **stooks:** bound sheaves of barley or wheat.

2. **wind-walks:** the imagined tracks of winds in the sky.

3. **silk-sack clouds** etc.: Hopkins's Journal shows many examples of minutely observed and illustrated cloud effects. Here *Meal-drift* denotes the colour and texture of grain ground to powder (the Journal describes some clouds as 'meal-white'); and as a phrase analogous with 'snow-drift', it shows the clouds being alternately shaped (*moulded*) and changed (*melted*) by the winds. The analogy with 'snow-drift' remains interestingly alive in those words *moulded* and *melted*.

5. **I walk:** in such a giddily ecstatic poem, the effect is almost of treading those *wind-walks*. See the next note.

6. **Down:** verbally, 'drink'; adverbially, '*I walk . . . down*' (cf. *wind-walks* above).

6. **to glean:** in the sense of 'to gather', extending the harvest images.

7–8. **what looks, what lips** etc.: a contrast with human love which returns 'less real', 'less complete and thorough' replies.

9. **azurous hung hills:** the spaces of sky in between the curved outline of mountains are fancifully seen as, themselves, blue inverted (*hung*) hills. Pursuing the fancy, they are, as it were, God's shoulders *wielding* (i.e. 'holding' and 'carrying') the world.

10. **stallion stalwart, very-violet-sweet:** a mixed sense of the physical strength and metaphysical sweetness of God's energy.

11–14. **but the beholder/Wanting** etc.: it is in the event of being witnessed and responded to that these glories are activated. When that happens, it is as if the human being soars from earth.

Sonnet in sprung rhythm, with 'outriding' feet.

44. The Caged Skylark (1877) St Beuno's (*p. 49*):
A fresh, dynamic treatment of the traditional concept of the soul trapped in the body's cage, the sonnet moves argumentatively towards an assertion of the ultimate freedom of the Resurrection.

1. **scanted:** deprived.

2. **bone-house:** the same phrase ('ban-hus') was a typical compound in Old English verse.

3. **beyond the remembering** etc.: 'having forgotten' the freedom of its natural setting.

4. **This:** 'This (spirit)', a phrase parallel to *That bird*, l. 3.

5. **aloft on turf:** turf was sometimes placed in larks' cages.

5. **or poor low stage:** the world, the venue of man's imprisoned experience.

6. **sweetest spells:** self-deluding songs.

9. **the sweet-fowl, song-fowl:** the bird in its natural, free state.

12–14. **Man's spirit will be flesh-bound** etc.: *at best* refers to man's future, resurrected condition, when the body will still be a reality, but without being an encumbrance – as light and undistressing to the spirit as the touch of a rainbow's foot on meadow-down.

Sonnet in falling paeonic rhythm (i.e. some feet being a stress followed by three unstressed syllables), but also 'sprung' and with 'outriding' feet.

45. **The Lantern out of Doors** (1877) St Beuno's (*p. 49*):
A meditation contrasting the limited way in which man is his brother's keeper with the endless reach of Christ's concern for each individual. The difference is pointed by the contrast between the meaning of *interest* in the second line and its repetition in the twelfth line of the sonnet. Its first use is in the sense of idle curiosity; but its use as *Christ's interest* draws on the financial sequence *rare . . . Rich . . . buys . . . interest . . . ransom.*

4. **wading light:** the side-to-side motion of the carried lantern suggests resisted progress as if the darkness itself were tangible (see again *much-thick and marsh air*, l. 7).

6. **mould:** 'physique'.

8. **buys:** 'removes them from view'.

9–10. **wind/What most I may eye after:** 'that which I may most carefully wind my eye after'. Hopkins admitted to Bridges the oddness of the syntactic effect. He explained, however, that the eye 'winds' in the sense of following its focus of attention – the lantern moving away and swinging from side to side.

12. **Christ minds:** apart from the ordinary meanings (Christ is 'concerned' and 'looks after'), there is the dialect meaning of

minds as 'remembers'. All these meanings contrast with the cliché *out of sight is out of mind* in the previous line.

13. foot follows kind: His own *kind*, as a human being; but *kind* also has adverbial force.

Sonnet in standard rhythm, but with a sprung effect opening line 12 and with line 9 'counterpointed'.

46. The Loss of the Eurydice (April 1878) Chesterfield (*p. 50*): The 'Eurydice', a training ship, was overturned by a squall from land off Ventnor, Isle of Wight, with the loss of all but two aboard. The poem can be compared with 'The Wreck of the Deutschland' in the movement from the actual tragedy to a general concern for the religious condition of England. It is, however, a slighter and less compelling poem than its famous predecessor, and as a result its audacities of inversion and rhyme seem more vulnerable. Hopkins's confessional presence in the first part of 'The Wreck of the Deutschland', and that poem's more forthright aim of justifying the ways of God to men, make it also the more complex of the two poems.

6. furled: buried (under sand and water).

7. flockbells: sheepbells.

16. bole and bloom: the ship and the men (*bole* literally = trunk); the two words also emphasise the indiscriminate loss of men and boys, in images of achieved and potential growth.

23. Boreas: the North Wind.

25. beetling baldbright cloud: darkly lowering, with tinges of light suggesting storm.

27. Hailropes, etc.: the image is of hail and snow swirling and winding before being released.

29. keep: (Carisbrook) castle, Isle of Wight.

32. Boniface Down: chalk down, behind Ventnor.

33. press: technically, as much sail as a ship can carry.

34. royals: the sails on the topmost royal-mast of the ship.

43. she who: i.e. the ship

47. Cheer's death: 'the end of hope'.

50. Right: a personification of Duty, which commands the captain to go down with his ship.

53–6. It is even seen etc.: this stanza's meaning runs, 'Even a selfish opportunist (*time-server*), one who normally avoids responsibility, will in real extremity sacrifice everything and act correctly.'

57. Sydney Fletcher: one of the two survivors.

61. afterdraught: the suction following the ship's sinking.

68. rivelling: literally 'causing to wrinkle': the man has to screw up his face in an attempt to see.

78. strung by duty etc.: an analogy is drawn between the parts of the dead sailor's body combining in the beauty of the whole and the trained discipline of his calling as a seaman.

87. born own: own born.

88. Fast foundering: i.e. in being lost from the Roman Catholic faith.

89–96. I might let bygones be etc.: Hopkins laments England's 'betrayals' of the Roman Catholic faith since the Reformation in the form of ruined, plundered, or unvisited shrines. He might forget these, except that he must deplore the fact that men, holy of body and quickened with life, capable of courage in death, like the members of this very crew, go themselves to ruin and damnation – because they do not die in Christ.

99. The riving off that race: the separation of that race.

101–2. a starlight-wender etc.: there was a time when England was so intimate with God's truth and grace that a pilgrim on his way to the shrine of the Virgin Mary at Walsingham would call the guiding Milky Way, Walsingham Way.

103. And one . . .: Hopkins explained that this curtailed reference was to Duns Scotus, the champion of the Immaculate Conception.

106. Wept, wife etc.: '(O well) wept, wife; (O well) wept, sweetheart who would like to have been a wife'.

107. them: i.e. the dead sailors.

111–16. Holiest, loveliest etc.: these are the supposed prayers of a bereaved mother, wife, or sweetheart.

112. Save my hero etc.: Hopkins explained that the line meant 'hero of a Saviour, be the saviour of my hero'.

114. at the awful overtaking: at the Last Judgment. The main verbs in this stanza are past-tense imperatives (see first note to 'Henry Purcell', p. 283).

117–20. Not that hell etc.: 'Not that redemption is possible for those in hell; but for souls who only *seem* to be lost, renewed prayer will bring eternal forgiveness.'

A poem in sprung rhythm, with three stresses in the third line of each stanza and four in the others.

47. The May Magnificat (May 1878) Stonyhurst (*p. 53*):
'My soul magnifies the Lord': Mary's affirmation of praise on learning that the child she has conceived is Jesus lies behind this poem of praise to Mary herself. Hopkins was at the time teaching classics at Stonyhurst College, where it was a tradition to hang such verses near the statue of the Virgin. Of the feasts associated with her, the one which makes May her month seems arbitrary. Hopkins stresses the obvious suitability of May as the month of natural growth (stanzas 1–7), which reminds us of Mary's fruitfulness and praise (stanza 8), but also says that the month recalls the same to Mary herself.

5. Candlemas: February, celebrating Mary's presentation of the child Christ to the priest Simeon in the Temple (Luke 2:26), Jewish law indicating that this would have been at a certain period after birth.

5. Lady Day: Feast of the Annunciation, celebrating Mary's conception of Christ by the Spirit, and fixed by the Church exactly nine months before 25 December. The dates for this and Candlemas therefore *follow reason*.

21. bugle blue eggs: the colour is compared to that of the bugle (*ajuga reptans*), a woodland plant which blossoms in May.

31–2. How she did in her stored etc.: 'How she did magnify the Lord stored in her.'

39. thorp: Old English word for field or village.

41. azuring-over greybell: the bluebell, initially greyish, slowly turning blue (*azuring over*) as it opens.

46–7. Tells Mary her mirth etc.: 'Tells Mary to remember her mirth in the period before Christ's birth and her exultation (her Magnificat, or song of praise).'

A 'sprung' treatment of the Horatian stanza form, with four stresses in each line of the first couplet and three in each of the second.

48. 'Denis' (March 1879) (*p. 55*):

3. three-heeled timber: a wooden arrow with three flights.

4. gold: the bull's-eye of the target (the *navel* of l. 5, where *butt* means the target itself).

49. 'The furl of fresh-leaved dogrose down' (March 1879) (*p. 55*):

3. Had swarthed: 'had made dark-hued'.

50. 'He mightbe slow' (March 1879) (*p. 56*):
The subject may be the Arthur of the poem on Denis above.

2. feck: obsolete Scots = 'worth' or 'value'. The fact that the word is a noun may be why Hopkins finally cancelled the phrase *Not feck at first*.

51. 'What being in rank-old nature' (June 1879) (*p. 56*):
Possibly written in response to a piece of music by a composer like Purcell.

52. Binsey Poplars (March 1879) Oxford (*p. 57*):
Binsey (Godstow) is an area of Oxford. The felling of the aspens (poplars) which lined the river there symbolised painfully for Hopkins man's destruction of the unique inscapes of nature.

1. dear: indicating not only delight, but also their preciousness as things which are ruined only at great cost.
1. airy cages: the outlines of the trees suggest tremulous structures within which the sunlight is *quelled* or *quenched* in the sense of being contained.
4. following folded rank: growing in linear sequence along the bends ('folds') of the river.
6. dandled: as if the aspens playfully swing their shadows.
6. sandalled: connoting the obvious silence of the shadows, but also possibly their interwoven visual effects.
14. sleek and seeing ball: the *eye* of the next line.
21. únselve: destroy the unrepeatable, *especial* identity of.

Indentation emphasises exactly the variation from six down to two stresses per line.

53. Duns Scotus's Oxford (March 1879) Oxford (*p. 58*):
This tribute to Duns Scotus's influence on Hopkins's way of looking at the world takes advantage of the fact that Scotus studied, and subsequently lectured, at Oxford. The city's sub-urban development in the second half of the last century is

contrasted with the rural beauty beyond it, and Hopkins
laments the passing of the time when country and town had
been in a more balanced and complementary relationship. But
he still breathes the same air, and can haunt the same places, as
the thirteenth-century philosopher who, for Hopkins, penetrated
to the essential nature of reality and the ways in which man
perceives it.

2. rook-racked: Hopkins realistically includes the more rau-
cous noise of rooks in his catalogue of the sounds of the city.

4. encounter: semantically, the word suggests the meeting of
opposites; but see next note.

4. coped and poisèd powers: the features of town and country
set each other off in a complementary balance.

5. base and brickish skirt: Hopkins lamented the fringes of
red-brick suburban buildings developing in his time and
which changed the direct meeting of the *grey beauty* of the
city with the green country around it.

5. sours: (which) sours.

8. keeping: the sense of natural 'congruity' of the rural
surroundings.

11. most sways my spirits to peace: Hopkins was grateful for
Duns Scotus's example in justifying the role of the senses in
our experience of reality.

12. realty: reality

12. rarest-veinèd unraveller: Scotus's philosophy was
renowned for its detailed and precise discriminations in
describing the nature of experience.

13. Italy: referring to St Thomas Aquinas, the thirteenth-
century philosopher, whose works are more orthodoxly central to the Catholic Church; *rival* because he devalued the
knowledge that comes to man through the senses.

13. Greece: the ultimate source of so much Western philosophy, the country of Plato and Aristotle.

14. fired France for Mary without spot: Scotus lectured in
Paris, and demanded the acceptance of the doctrine of the
Immaculate Conception of Christ's mother. The doctrine was
made central for Catholics only in 1854. This is another sense
in which Scotus *rivalled* Aquinas.

Sonnet in sprung rhythm, with 'outriding' feet.

54. Henry Purcell (April 1879) Oxford (*p. 58*):
Hopkins refers frequently in his correspondence to Henry Purcell (1659–95), organist at Westminster Abbey and the Chapel Royal, and Hopkins's favourite composer 'for personal preference and fellow feeling'. Generally recognised as the greatest English-born composer, Purcell was celebrated for the art of finding exact musical equivalents for the full range of human moods. Characteristically, however, Hopkins celebrates him more for the individuating than the generalising power of his music.

1. **Have fair fallen:** a singular imperative in the past tense, which Hopkins defended by analogy with, for example, 'Have done'. The sense is 'May good fortune have befallen you'.

2. **arch-especial:** distinctive in the utmost sense.

3–4. **with the reversal** etc.: i.e. may the passing years have brought a reversal of the outwardly-imposed sentence under which he lay as one (en)*listed to a heresy* (Protestantism).

5–8. **Not mood in him nor meaning** etc.: what in the music makes the deepest impact on Hopkins is not the mood or meaning etc., which other composers might equally have fostered, but the individuating essence which proclaims the music Purcell's alone.

10. **Have an eye to the sakes of him:** 'I'll look for the distinctive qualities of his genius.'

10. **quaint moonmarks:** Hopkins explained, 'I mean crescent shaped markings on the quill-feathers, either in the colouring of the feather or made by the overlapping of one on another'.

11–14. **so some great stormfowl:** the bird is only preparing for flight, but in the act the impressiveness of his plumage is carried in upon us with a new knowledge and wonder.

12. **plumèd purple-of-thunder:** referring to the bird's colouring.

13. **wuthering:** a North country word describing the noise and movement of wind.

13. **a colossal smile:** a metaphor for the suddenly revealed impressiveness of the plumage.

14. **but meaning motion:** 'only *meaning* to move (into flight).'

A sprung rhythm sonnet in Alexandrines (six stresses per line) with 'outriding' feet.

55. Repeat that, repeat (undated fragment) (*p. 59*):

　5. flushes: cf. 'and thrush/ Through the echoing timber does so rinse and wring/ The ear' ('Spring', *p. 45*).

56. The Candle Indoors (1879) Oxford (*p. 60*):
Though not intended as such at first, this was recognised by the poet as a companion piece to 'The Lantern out of Doors' (*p. 49*). The tendency to want the work of others to be dedicated to God is checked and sobered by the realisation that each person must first of all correct and dedicate himself.

　2. puts blissful back: the candle's light appears to push the darkness back.
　4. Or to-fro tender trambeams truckle at the eye: slender beams of light from the candle appear to advance and recede (as when you half close, and then open, your eyes). *Truckle at* means 'being subject to the influence of'. There is also an indirect comparison of the beams with tram-lines, helped by the more obvious suggestion in *truck(le)*.
　6–8. a-wanting, just for lack/Of answer etc.: 'wanting, and all the more eagerly wanting because there is no answer, that the man or woman there should be working to enlarge God's kingdom and glorify Him'.
　9. Come you indoors etc.: the poet addresses himself from here on, saying that first of all there is much to improve in his own nature, where he has authority and can act on his desire to glorify God.
　12. beam-blind: cf. Christ's words 'Or how wilt thou say to thy brother, let me pull the mote out of thine eye; and behold a beam is in thine own eye. Thou hypocrite, first cast out the beam out of thine own eye . . .' (Matthew 7:4).
　12–13. yet to a fault/In a neighbour deft-handed: 'yet very quick to point out a fault in someone else'.
　13. that liar: that hypocrite referred to in Christ's words above.
　14. spendsavour salt: cf. Matthew 5:13 – Christ calls his disciples the salt of the earth, and adds that when salt has lost its savour it is good for nothing but to be 'cast out'.

Standard sonnet rhythm counterpointed.

57. The Handsome Heart (1879) Oxford (*p. 60*):
Written during Hopkins's year as a priest at St Aloysius's Church in Oxford. The child's gracious answer came as a reply to Hopkins's offer to reward him and a friend for having helped Hopkins in the sacristy during Holy Week. In a letter, Hopkins explained that by the term 'handsome heart' he means beauty of character.

   3. still plied and pressed: i.e. for a different answer.
   4. poised: 'confident'.
   5. carriers: carrier pigeons.
   6–8. Doff darkness etc.: 'pay no heed to darkness'. The pigeon's homing instinct is a metaphor for the child's instinctively correct reply. In both, natural instinct is as good as long years of training.
   9. Mannerly-hearted!: with a heart that knows good conduct.
   9. more than handsome face: Hopkins placed beauty of character (the 'handsome heart') higher than beauty of mind, just as that was higher than beauty of body (*handsome face*).
   10. or muse of mounting vein: 'poetic inspiration': again a lesser thing than the 'handsome heart'.
   12–13. Of heaven what boon etc.: 'What favour or gift can I ask of heaven for you, that has not already been granted!'
   13–14. Only . . . O on that path etc.: he prays only that the child should continue always in the same path.
   14. brace sterner that strain: 'consolidate the firmness of that tendency and effort (*strain*)' which keeps him on the right course.'

Standard sonnet rhythm counterpointed.

58. 'How all's to one thing wrought' (June 1879) (*p. 61*):
A characteristic theme: what W. B. Yeats called the choice between 'perfection of the life or of the work'. Before any questions of merely artistic merit, Hopkins wants to know what or whom the artist *serves or not/Serves and what side he takes.*

59. Cheery Beggar (summer 1879) Oxford (*p. 62*):
Hopkins was assistant priest of St Aloysius church, St Giles, Oxford.

   1. Mágdalen: Magdalen College. The area east beyond Magdalen Bridge is called the *Plain*.

3. falls of rain: a letter of February 1879 to his mother notes the sudden change from heavy rain to fine weather.

4. fineflour: though Bridges mis-transcribed it as 'fineflower', the reference is to the pollen wafted from the stamens (*gold-nails*) of flowers.

60. The Bugler's First Communion (July 1897) Oxford (*p. 62*)
During Hopkins's period of nearly a year as a priest in Oxford, he assumed extra duties as Chaplain to the nearby Cowley Barracks, *over the hill* from north Oxford. The occasion of a bugler boy from the barracks coming to his first communion at Hopkins's church enables the poet to celebrate not only the nature of the Eucharist, but the 'martial' nature of the communicant's loyalty to Christ and, indirectly, Hopkins's own role as Jesuit priest.

5–6. after a boon etc.: 'in quest of a blessing he had asked for when I was recently there (at the barracks)'.

10. how fain I of feet: 'how speedily glad I was'.

11. his youngster: i.e. Christ's

12. Low-latched in leaf-light housel etc.: the Roman Catholic belief that Christ is actually present in the Communion wafer (for which *housel* is an archaic word).

13. There!: marking the actual offering of the wafer.

13–16. and your sweetest sendings etc.: the syntax is 'may the sweetest gifts sent by you, divine heavens, befall him by this Communion'. The gifts are then listed: a brave heart, loving Christ; a true tongue without boast or reproach; a vital, handsome chastity.

17–18. angel-warder etc.: a guardian-angel is enjoined to 'disperse [*squander*] the black armies from hell [that] sally to molest him'.

20. Dress his days etc.: a line evocative of the deft, elegant and cool discipline of a religiously committed life.

22. limber: lithe, agile.

25. tread tufts of consolation: in a precarious avoidance of depression and despair.

28. Christ's royal ration: the bread and wine of the Communion.

29–30. not all so strains/Us: 'not all those things which so tenses us to a heightened appreciation.'

30. fretted: delicately varied.

31. sweeter ending: Paradise.

33. that sealing sacred ointment!: the ointment which dedicated and anointed the priest's hands at his original ordination.

34. what bans off bad: 'what fends off evil'.

37–40. whose least me quickenings lift etc.: '(those sweet hopes) whose slightest stirrings raise me to joy'. Those hopes are of seeing a modern (*our day*) knight (*Galahad*) devoted to God alone. The *brow and bead of being* (l. 39) evokes the beads of blood-like sweat of Christ's agony in the garden of Gethsemane: the ultimate example of self-sacrifice.

40–4. this child's drift etc.: the bugler's career, as a soldier, is already divinely determined. Hopkins therefore does not see this as a threat (*disaster*, l. 42) to the bugler's Christian role, yet, though *bound home*, might he not wander and backslide? Leaving things to God, Hopkins lays that fear by.

45–7. Recorded only etc.: 'As long as this is recorded . . .' – that Hopkins has voiced prayers which, if unheard, would shake (*brandle*) impenetrable (*adamantine*) heaven.

48. Forward-like, but however etc.: the syntax of the final line can be followed thus: 'But yet (this fear) is premature (*forward-like*), and it is most likely that favourable heaven heard these (*pleas*)'.

The poem is in sprung rhythm, with 'overreaving' (i.e. the scansion running on from line to line). 'Outriding' (i.e. extrametrical) syllables occur in the third foot of the last line in each stanza.

61 Morning, Midday, and Evening Sacrifice (August 1879) Oxford (*p. 64*):
The freshness of youth, the strength of maturity, and the ripe wisdom of age are seen as the gifts which the three stages of man's life must give to God.

1. die-away: denoting the gently merging colours of youth's complexion.

2. wimpled: curved.

6. fuming: the *freshness* is like the smoke from incense rising to God's glory.

8. thew: muscle.

9. Tower: 'grow proudly' (Nature's command).

17. **In silk-ash kept from cooling**: the silky ash around a wood fire is an image for the grey hairs underneath which the mind is still warmly active.

21. **Your offering, with despatch, of**: 'Come, your offer of all this (the matured mind), and without delay either' [Hopkins's paraphrase].

62. Andromeda (August 1879) Oxford (*p. 65*):
In Greek legend, Andromeda was the daughter of Cepheus, king of the Ethiopians. Her mother, Cassiopeia, had offended the Mereids (sea-maidens) with the result that Poseidon sent a sea-monster to ravage the country. The monster could be placated only by the sacrifice of Andromeda, bound to a rock. Perseus, the son of Zeus, rescued and married her. Hopkins uses Andromeda's plight as a symbol of the Church beset by her enemies on earth, with Perseus representing Christ, the Church's spouse, rescuing His bride. This allegorical usefulness overrode Hopkins's usual objections to what he considered the triviality of classical mythology.

1. **Time's Andromeda**: the Church throughout, and in, time.
2–3. **With not her either beauty's equal** etc.: 'unequalled in both her beauty and her injury'.
7. **A wilder beast from West**: of the many dangers Hopkins felt in his time were threatening the true Church as he conceived it, he was probably here thinking of the new rational, liberalising developments in theology. The extremity of his imagery can be compared to his description of Luther, the father of the Protestant Reformation, as the 'beast of the waste wood' in 'The Wreck of the Deutschland' (stanza 20).
9. **Her Perseus linger** etc.: '(Will) her Perseus linger . . . ?', a denying question.
11. **forsaken that she seems**: 'despite the fact that she seems forsaken'.
13–14. **then to alight disarming** etc.: the objects of *disarming* are *thongs* and *fangs* (the thongs tying Andromeda, and the fangs of the monster).
13. **no one dreams**: i.e. 'unexpectedly'.
14. **With Gorgon's gear and barebill**: Perseus was returning from killing the Gorgon Medusa, carrying her head; *barebill* = sword.

Sonnet in standard rhythm, but counterpointed by Hopkins's avowed attempt at 'a more Miltonic plainness and severity'.

63. Peace (1879) Oxford (*p. 65*):
A poem which anticipates Hopkins's later contemplations on the nature of Christian patience and resilience in 'Patience, hard thing! the hard thing but to pray . . .' and 'My own heart let me more have pity on . . .', and their opposites in the form of the 'sonnets of desolation' of the Irish period.

> **2. under be:** the inversion makes *under* more a part of the verb 'be' than an adverb; cf. 'understand'.
> **4. To own my heart:** inversion of 'To my own heart': he will not lie to his own heart. But the inversion creates another meaning: he will not lie in order to appear to be in independent control of (*to own*) his emotions.
> **5. piecemeal peace:** 'intermittent peace'.
> **5. pure peace:** *pure* not only in the sense of 'unadulterated', but also 'total', 'nothing but' peace.
> **6. wars:** inner, spiritual conflicts.
> **6. the death of it:** i.e. 'of peace itself'.
> **7. reaving Peace:** not a vocative addressed to Peace, but a present-participial phrase: 'since my Lord "plunders" or "carries off" Peace, He should leave at least some good to take its place'.
> **8. Patience:** not peace itself, but an intermediary condition necessary for it. The basic meaning of *patience* as 'the acceptance of suffering' is relevant – hence the adjective *exquisite* ('acute', 'keen').
> **9. plumes to Peace:** the notion of 'gaining a covering' and 'growing naturally'. By comparison, Patience is something barer and more unaccommodated.
> **11. brood and sit:** a Biblical reference to the Spirit (Genesis 1:2) brooding on the surface of the waters, hatching the Creation itself. This is the sense in which peace *comes with work to do*.

This is a 'curtal sonnet': see notes on 'Pied Beauty' (*p. 48*). The metre is 'standard Alexandrines' (six iambic feet per line).

64. At the Wedding March (October 1879) Bedford Leigh, Lancashire (*p. 66*): The priest prays inwardly for the future of a pair he has just joined in marriage.

1. **hang your head:** 'decorate (with *honour*), as with a garland'.

3. **lissome:** gracefully lithe.

3. **scions:** literally, young shoots from parent plant: offspring.

6. **déeper than divined:** deeper than you could have imagined.

7–8. **dear charity,/ . . . fast bind:** cf. Colossians 3.

10. **I to him turn:** to God or Christ, who makes the bond of marriage extend beyond time; hence *immortal years*.

The poem is in sprung rhythm, with four stresses to a line.

65 Felix Randal (April 1880) Liverpool (*p.* 67):
The subject was a blacksmith (*farrier*), probably one of Hopkins's parishioners at Leigh in Lancashire, where the poet was priest for three months at the end of 1879. The poem was, however, written at Liverpool where Hopkins found his priestly duties less rewarding. He measures God's gift of grace in the Eucharist (in which each man is as a receptive child) against the tribute also due to the blacksmith's former physical strength, before 'sickness broke him'.

3. **till time when:** 'till the time came when . . .'

5. **Sickness broke him:** with the slight suggestion of animal power being curbed. Cf. note on *powerful amidst peers* below.

6. **a heavenlier heart:** a heart directed more towards heavenly things.

7. **our sweet reprieve and ransom:** the salvation offered through the Holy Communion.

8. **all road ever:** colloquial Lancashire expression meaning 'in whatever way'.

9. **us too it endears:** this is essentially a priest's poem: illness not only 'draws affection' from the priest, but makes his role as priest 'precious'.

11. **child:** the parishioner's spiritual relationship to the priest.

12. **How far from then forethought of** etc.: 'How far were your years of active life from any forethought of their cessation in sickness and death.'

13. **random:** suggests both the cluttered untidiness of the forge and the random sparks from the fire. Architecturally, the term denotes rough stonework.

13. **powerful amidst peers:** his *peers* could be either the other

blacksmiths or the horses themselves, matching his *big-boned* stature.

14. fettle: as a verb, dialect: 'to condition and trim'.

14. sandal: horseshoe.

A poem in sprung rhythm, with six stresses to a line and many 'outriding' feet.

66. Brothers (August 1880) Hampstead (*p. 67*):
Hopkins had the example of Wordsworth's simple poems in mind here – the delight in an unpretentious anecdote and the way in which it reveals primary human emotions of moral value. The incident occurred during Hopkins's period as sub-minister at Mount St Mary's College, Chesterfield.

5. Shrovetide the period when penitents were 'shriven' (cleansed) of sin, in readiness for the Lenten fast which directly followed.

15. By meanwhiles: 'in short, unnoticed periods'.

18. lost in Jack: unselfconsciously possessed by the expectation of his brother's entry on stage.

38. framed in fault: 'given a distorted shape by man's Original Sin'.

39. there's salt: i.e. to heal Nature's wounds.

The poem is in sprung rhythm, with three stresses to a line, and with no 'overreaving' (i.e. no metrical continuation from line to line).

67. Spring and Fall (September 1880) Lydiate, Lancashire (*p. 69*):
Not founded on any real incident, nor on any real child or place, the poem articulates the universal theme of transience, linked to that of human growth from innocence to experience. Hopkins's time at Liverpool, where the poem was written, was often marked by depression and despair. Human failings, and desolating work in sordid industrial conditions, gain an indirect and impersonal expression in this address 'to a young child'. At the same time, it could have taken its inspiration from the painting 'Autumn Leaves' by Millais, Hopkins's favourite artist.

2. Goldengrove: a fairly common place-name throughout Britain.

2. unleaving: i.e., shedding its leaves in autumn.

6. It will come to such sights colder: 'it will come colder (less emotionally) to such sights', but also 'it will come to such colder sights than this'. Both meanings emphasise the poem's claim that it is not nature's death that we really mourn.

8. wanwood: the coinage suggests forests dead and colourless.

8. leafmeal: *meal* evokes the brown-golden colour of the fallen leaves, while the coinage is by analogy with 'piecemeal', i.e. 'fallen leaf-by-leaf'.

9. And yet you *will* weep and know why: the *yet* is in contradiction of *nor spare a sigh* (l. 7). The child will in future years know that what she mourns is human mortality.

10–12. Now no matter, child, the name etc: to *name* the real sources of grief would be of no significance to the child at present because, though they are the sources (*springs*) of all grief, these intimations of human mortality come at present from non-verbal levels of understanding – those of the *heart* and spirit (*ghost*).

14. blight: suitably with its original sense of organic disease.

A poem in sprung rhythm, with four stresses to a line. In this shorter measure, Hopkins thought it important that a falling rhythm at the end of one line should be followed by a 'sprung head' (i.e. a stressed first syllable) in the next.

68. Inversnaid (September 1881) (*p. 69*):
Hopkins had briefly visited Inversnaid, near Loch Lomond in Scotland, and the poem is poetry of place in the linguistic as well as the visual sense. It also drew, however, on images stored in much earlier notebooks. The poem expresses a general, deep-seated respect for natural wildness out of the reach of society's influence, which alone is really desolating. In a letter to Bridges he expressed fears of 'the decline of wild nature'.

1. burn: (Scots) stream.

3. In coop and in comb: respectively, the convex and concave 'rib' effects of water running over stones.

4. Flutes: 'makes grooves in': its subject is *burn*, its object *the fleece of his foam*.

5. windpuff-bonnet of fáwn-fróth: the light vapour caused by the descent of a waterfall into a pool.

6. twindles: combining the sense of 'twists' and 'dwindles'.

9. Degged: (Lancashire dialect) 'sprinkled'.

10. **groins of the braes:** the depressions between hillsides, carved or followed by the stream.

11. **heathpacks:** heather clumps.

11. **flitches:** tufts.

12. **beadbonny ash:** the adjective could refer to the purplish, almost knobbly clusters of the ordinary ash tree's flowers, or to the bright scarlet berries of the Mountain Ash.

69. 'As kingfishers catch fire, dragonflies draw flame' (1881) (*p. 70*):

This sonnet is one of the most forthright expressions of Hopkins's belief in what Duns Scotus called 'haecceitas' – the individual and unique 'thisness' of every item in the created world. Every action or effect is the manifestation of unique inner selfhood. Christian man finds his context in such a world, but the poem implies that there is an even greater value ('I say more . . .', l. 9) in man's self-revelation because that is a conscious act, and Hopkins keeps the diction of real value – *more, just, grace, Christ, lovely* – for the description of man in the sestet.

1. **catch fire . . . draw flame:** by reflecting the sunlight.

2. **tumbled over rim in roundy wells:** the absence of commas gives these words the force of a single compound adjective describing *stones* in l. 3.

3. **tucked:** 'plucked'.

4. **Bow:** denoting the bell's shape.

6. **that being indoors each one dwells:** 'that *being* which dwells indoors in each single thing'.

7. **Selves – goes itself:** 'registers its individual identity'; *goes* also has the force of 'speaks' or 'utters' (cf. *goes Death on drum*, 'The Wreck of the Deutschland' st. 11).

8. *for that I came:* reminiscent of Christ's words 'I came that you might have life . . .' (John 10:10).

9. **justices:** 'manifests the inner justness of his nature'.

10. **Keeps gráce: etc.:** 'pays due regard to grace' – which in turn *keeps all his goings graces*.

11. **Acts:** like *plays* in the next line, not in the sense of 'acting out' a part, but 'expressing the reality of'. Elsewhere Hopkins wrote, 'It is as if a man said: That is Christ playing at me and me playing at Christ, only that it is no play but truth; that is Christ *being me* and me being Christ.'

13–14. **Lovely in limbs** etc.: Christ's beauty is made attractive to God by its manifestation through the limbs, the eyes and the features of other men.

A sonnet in sprung rhythm, with five stresses to a line.

70. **Ribblesdale** (1882) Stonyhurst (*p. 70*):
In September 1882 Hopkins began a spell of teaching at Stony-hurst College, near Blackburn in Lancashire, a public school staffed almost entirely by Jesuits. He had previously spent three years there studying philosophy (1869–72) and it was a place which much impressed him with its beautiful moorland scenery. But the later period at Stonyhurst was marked by ailments and depression – a background, to some degree, to this poem's contrast between God's created beauties and man's grudging and ruinous response. A Latin epigraph from Paul's epistle to the Romans (8:19–20), in the manuscripts of the poem speaks of future freedom from man-and-nature's fallen bondage; but Hopkins's sonnet still ends darkly.

1. **with leavès throng:** a Lancashire use of *throng* as adjective ('crowded with').
2. **louchèd:** Hopkins explained that he meant 'slouched' or 'slouching'.
4. **That canst but only be** etc.: nature praises God by 'being' rather than consciously 'doing' – but it is at least an eternal praise.
5–6. **strong/Thy plea:** i.e. nature's deserved right to God's attention.
6–7. **who dealt . . . down:** who 'created'; and 'sustains' (*nay does now deal*).
7. **reel:** 'meander'.
8. **and o'er gives all:** 'and gives everything over (*to rack or wrong*)'.
9–10. **And what is earth's eye** etc.: earth's unconscious praise can be made sensitive, articulate, and felt only in man.
10. **dogged:** 'grimly persistent'.
12. **To thriftless reave:** 'to plunder wastefully'.
13–14. **this bids wear/Earth** etc.: this blind selfishness in man bids earth wear an expression of care etc.

The standard sonnet rhythm is very markedly counterpointed.

71. A Trio of Triolets (March 1883) Stonyhurst (*p. 71*):
The triolets were published in *The Stonyhurst Magazine* (the magazine of Stonyhurst College) vol. 1, no. 9 (March 1883), p. 162.

72. The Leaden Echo and the Golden Echo (finished October 1882) Stonyhurst (*p. 72*):
The poem was planned as a chorus in Hopkins's unfinished drama, 'St Winefred's Well', started in October 1879. According to a legend of the later middle-ages, St Winefred was a niece of St Beuno's. Her head was cut off by a chieftain's son, Caradoc, whose sexual advances she had resisted. Beuno restored the head to her body, and where the head had fallen (at Holywell, near St Beuno's College) there appeared a spring of healing water. King Henry VII's mother, Lady Margaret Beaufort, had the well enclosed by a stone building, and it remains a place of pilgrimage. Here, a despairing meditation on the transience of beauty is countered by the notion that beauty, to be preserved, must be selflessly sacrificed to *God, beauty's self and beauty's giver*.

The Leaden Echo
1. **bow or brooch** etc.: the catalogue stresses beauty as something that can be physically preserved or lost, and also emphasises a feminine context (*bow, braid, lace* etc.).
3–4. **Ó is there no frowning ... Dówn?:** the last two words go together, i.e. *frowning down* the wrinkles, 'smoothing them out'.
4. **messengers:** i.e. the advance signs of age. Cf. George Herbert's poem 'The Forerunners'.
8. **wisdom is early to despair:** wisdom is the early acceptance of the fact that beauty vanishes.

The Golden Echo
17. **Spare!:** i.e. 'leave off!, listen!'
26. **wimpled-water-dimpled:** 'dimpled like wimpled water'. The phrase describes *face*.
27. **fleece of beauty:** Hopkins explained that *fleece* should convey the sense of velvet texture.
28. **Never fleets móre:** this verb has, as its composite subject, the catalogue which begins with *whatever's prized* in line 24.
34. **beauty-in-the-ghost:** 'beauty of the spirit'.

35. beauty's self and beauty's giver: physical beauty has its identity and reality, and its source, in the fuller beauty of God.

37. hair of the head, numbered: an allusion to Matthew 10:30 and Luke 7:7.

38–41. what we had lighthanded left etc.: the image informing these lines is that of a seed carelessly thrown into dull earth (*surly ... mould*): it will have germinated and grown, unbeknown to us on *this side* of the grave, while producing a copious harvest on that other side, in heaven. There is a reference in the word *hundredfold* to Christ's words in Matthew 19:29.

42. care-coiled: 'disturbed by care'.

42. so fagged, so fashed, so cogged: 'so exhausted, so careworn, so deluded'; *fashed* is a Scots dialect word and *cogged* an archaic word, with implications of the fraudulent manipulation of dice in gambling.

45. Far with fonder a care: 'with a far fonder care'.

Hopkins's delight in 'sprung' movement is in one sense given freer rein here, without keeping to a patterned number of stresses per line; but the long lines put even more to the test his claim that 'everything is weighed and timed in them'.

73. *from* **St Winefred's Well** (October 1879–April 1885) (*p. 74*):
'St Winefred's Well' is the unfinished play for which 'The Leaden Echo and the Golden Echo' (see previous note) was intended as a Chorus. Hopkins meant the play 'to be short, say in 3 or even 2 acts; the characters few' (letter to Bridges, 8 October 1879).

74. The Blessed Virgin compared to the Air we Breathe (May 1883) Stonyhurst (*p. 80*):
Written as a 'Maypiece' in honour of the Virgin Mary, according to the custom at Stonyhurst (cf. 'The May Magnificat'), this poem's extended comparison is reminiscent of the intellectually sustained conceits of seventeenth-century 'Metaphysical' verse. Just as the air sustains life and moderates the heat of the sun, so the Virgin is a medium for man's spiritual life and a mediator of God's glory and power.

4. **Girdles:** 'encircles'.

5. **frailest-flixed:** 'delicately fleeced'.

7. **riddles:** 'inter-penetrates'.

16. **Minds me:** 'reminds me'.

22. **But mothers each new grace:** grace, the source of holiness, is God's gift, but mediated through Mary.

24. **Mary Immaculate:** Hopkins believed Mary herself to have been born by Immaculate Conception: a dogma made central for Roman Catholics by papal proclamation in 1854.

25. **Merely a woman:** 'only' but also 'completely' a woman.

36-7. **the same/Is Mary:** i.e. mercy *is* Mary.

40-1. **let dispense/Her prayers:** i.e. 'let her prayers dispense . . .'.

43. **The sweet alms' self is her:** Mary is not only the giver, but the gift itself (of mercy).

48. **ghostly good:** 'spiritual benefit'.

51-2. **Laying . . ./The deathdance:** terminating or mitigating the physical tendency towards death.

53-4. **Yet no part but . . .:** Mary plays her *part* (l. 49), but in reality this is Christ's saving role that is enacted.

56-72. **He does take fresh and fresh** etc.: Christ's physical birth is in the past, but he is spiritually and endlessly reborn now in each man. *Nazareth* and *Bethlem* denote the places of Christ's conception and birth. Meditation upon Biblical scenes, for their renewing spiritual energies, was central to Jesuits as part of the Ignatian spiritual exercises.

79-80. **sapphire-shot,/Charged, steepèd:** *sapphire* qualifies all these three adjectives for *sky*.

80-1. **will not/Stain light:** from here to the end of the verse-paragraph is developed the analogous fact that the blueness of the air enhances rather than obscures the colours and definition of other things, and of sunlight itself. It similarly mitigates the glare of the sun. Without it, the sun would blind and create a surrounding blackness against which other stars would also be harshly visible.

103. **So God was god of old:** the harsh sun has been an analogy for the Old Testament conception of God, now contrasted with the tenderer New Testament Nativity.

106. **daystar:** the sun, used thus as image for Christ in 2 Peter 1:19.

119. **froward**: perverse.

The poem is in sprung rhythm, with three stresses to a line.

75. 'The times are nightfall' (1885) (*p. 83*):
A sonnet lacking its last three lines, and possibly related to 'Spelt from Sibyl's Leaves' (*p. 91*).

76. 'Not of all my eyes see, wandering on the world' (1885) (*p. 84*):
In this form, the earlier of two versions, the poem is another curtal sonnet. (See notes on 'Pied Beauty', *p. 275*)

7. **tabour**: 'tap lightly', as on a drum.
9. **Mells**: 'mixes'.

77. 'To seem the stranger lies my lot, my life' (1885) (*p. 84*):
Hopkins's conversion had meant alienation from family and from Anglican England. His move to Ireland now brought literal separation. His mood here reflects physical as well as spiritual tiredness – which might have been his fate even outside Ireland – but the patriotic note struck in this sonnet reflects also his complex experience of the Irish political situation at that time. The Irish Jesuits supported Irish Home Rule, a thing which Hopkins could only with difficulty do because of his deep love for England, his hopes in any case for England's reconversion to Roman Catholicism, and his natural respect for authority.

3. **are in Christ not near**: his family was staunchly Anglican, and had resisted and deeply lamented his conversion to Catholicism. The phrase ironically borrows the conventional mode of address in correspondence between professional Catholics – 'Dear Father in Christ' etc. For his expression of the alienation of those closest to him, cf. John Clare's lines from the poem 'I am', which Hopkins had copied into his journal in the summer of 1865, twenty years before the present poem: 'And e'en the dearest – that I loved the best – / Are strange – nay, rather stranger than the rest'. Newman's *Apologia Pro Vita Sua* (1864), one of the main influences on Hopkins's conversion, had also stressed this alienation from one's family ('You may think how lonely I am') and quoted the Latin version of Psalms 45:10 – 'forget also thine own people, and thy father's house'.
7. **were I pleading**: i.e. about the tragedy of the Irish situation.

Hopkins's English patriotism did not exclude a real sorrow at England's neglect and mismanagement of Ireland.

8. but by where wars are rife: 'where only conflicts multiply'.

9–10. a third/Remove: already removed from his family and from England, he feels alienated also from the Catholic Church in Ireland over the Home Rule question.

11–13. Only what word/Wisest etc.: the force of *only* is 'except that . . .'.

14. leaves me a lonely began: *began* as a noun ('one who only began, and did not finish') is possibly by analogy with the horse-racing term, 'an also-ran'.

Standard sonnet rhythm (i.e. iambic pentameter), but very heavily counterpointed in the second half of the octave.

78. 'I wake and feel the fell of dark, not day' (1885) (*p. 85*):

1. the fell of dark: as a noun, *fell* = the hairy skin of an animal. But the word also has the adjectival force of 'fierce, terrible' and the verbal force of 'fall' ('the fall of dark', 'the dark which fell').

4. And more must: he must experience more horror until literal or spiritual daylight come.

7–8. cries like dead letters etc.: literally, letters that cannot be delivered or returned because of inadequate directions.

10. my taste was me: the language of the sestet registers the spiritual desolation as an unrelieved neurotic awareness of the egotistic, physical self.

11. Bones built in me etc.: '*Bones built* (the curse) *in me, flesh filled* (the curse), *blood brimmed the curse*'.

12. Selfyeast of spirit etc.: the notion that the spirit should leaven or transform the *dull dough* of physical existence; but, being embroiled in a total selfness, it only *sours*.

14. but worse: the predicament of those who, without belief, are really damned or *lost*.

Standard sonnet rhythm (i.e. iambic pentatmeter), but with freely dramatic concentration of stresses at times.

79. 'Strike, churl; hurl cheerless wind' (May 1885) Dublin (*p. 86*):
A wry echo of King Lear's language in the storm is used of May weather in Dublin that he described in a letter to his mother (17

May 1885): '. . . at least it is winter in Ireland. I still have a fire. The hail today lay long like pailfuls of coarse rice'.

80. 'No worst, there is none. Pitched past pitch of grief (1885) (*p. 86*):

1. **No worst:** one cannot call an experience the *worst* when, always, even worse experiences succeed.

1. **Pitched past pitch of grief:** *pitch* combines 'being thrown', blackness, and the experience of a highly-strung consciousness.

2. **schooled at forepangs:** the *pangs* (pains) 'learn' their power from previous ones (*forepangs*).

3. **Comforter:** addressed to the Holy Ghost.

5. **herds-long:** driven and crowded endlessly together.

8. **fell:** Fury shouts its aim of being both 'swift' and 'terrible'.

8. **force:** 'perforce'.

9–10. **cliffs of fall/Frightful:** an image which – with the later ones of storm, poor shelter and sleep – seems to distil the experience of Shakespeare's *King Lear*. Cf. Gloucester thinking himself at Dover cliffs in that play (IV, vi).

13–14. **a comfort** etc.: the vulnerable comfort of painful life not being endless, of sleep closing each cruel day.

Standard sonnet rhythm (i.e. iambic pentameter), but with strong sprung rhythm effects.

81. To what serves Mortal Beauty? (August 1885) (*p. 87*):
The poem places human physical beauty in relation, on the one hand, to the dangers that can vulgarise it (its temptations to lustful feelings and to vain self-regard), and on the other to its nature as God's gift and the medium of a more important spiritual and inner beauty. These can be compared to similar discriminations in the poem 'The Handsome Heart' (*p. 60*).

1. **dangerous:** in the sense of exciting only physical passion.

2. **the O-seal-that-so feature:** the beauty that would make one want to capture and preserve (*seal*) it for all time, as in art.

2–3. **flung prouder form/Than Purcell tune** etc.: the difference between the self-regarding display of beauty and the unself-conscious (but unique) identity expressed in Purcell's music. For the latter, see the sonnet 'Henry Purcell' (*p. 58*).

3. **See: it does this:** the poem begins to answer its opening question.

3–4. **keeps warm/Men's wits to the things that are:** keeps men's understanding alive to the most important realities, to genuine spiritual 'being'.

4–5. **a glance/Master more may:** 'may bring about more (than *gaze*)'. Inner identity 'glances' or *flashes* (l. 11). Similarly, it calls for deft alertness rather than the fuller *gaze* demanded by physical beauty alone.

6–8. **Those lovely lads** etc.: the reference is to some British boys seen at a Roman slave-market by Pope Gregory I (*c*. 590–604 A.D.). Their beauty prompted him to send Augustine (later St Augustine of Canterbury) to win England to Christianity.

10. **love's worthiest, were all known:** 'the things that are worthiest of love, taking into account inner as well as outer realities'.

11. **selves:** 'inner identities'.

12–13. **own,/Home at heart,** etc.: 'recognize, in your own heart, that (physical beauty) is the sweet gift of heaven'.

14. **wish that though, wish all,** etc.: 'wish for that beautiful person, and for all humans, the better beauty of God's grace'.

A sonnet in alexandrines (six stresses per line) but with its standard rhythm very heavily stressed: Hopkins placed markings over juxtaposed syllables, indicating that they had equal stress in recitation although only one carried the 'metrical' stress.

82. **'Not, I'll not, carrion comfort, Despair, not feast on thee'** (1885) (*p. 87*):

1. **carrion comfort:** Despair seen as dead emotion, off which the poet would dangerously feed.

5. **O thou terrible:** spoken to God.

5. **rude on me:** adverbial phrase (*rudely on me*) governing the verb *rock* in next line.

6. **lionlimb:** cf. Job 10:16.

7. **darksome:** 'gloomy'.

7. **fan:** the image is of winnowing, with a scoop used to throw the grain against the wind, thus separating it from the chaff.

10. **coil:** 'bustle', 'confusion'.

10. **I kissed the rod:** the rod of God's authority, but also the

'rood' (cross) of Christ's sacrifice. Cf. 'I took of vine a cross-barred rod or rood' ('The Half-way House, p. 18).

12. **The hero:** Christ.

13. **That night, that year:** cf. *'But where I say/Hours I mean years, mean life'* ('I wake and feel the fell of dark, not day', p. 85).

83. 'Yes. Why do we all, seeing of a soldier, bless him?' (August 1885) Clongowes (*p. 88*):

Our respect for soldiers and sailors springs from our hope that the disciplined valour of their calling is also true of their character. As usual, the subject appeals to the spiritually militant nature of Hopkins's Jesuit training, and leads also to a picture of Christ as the King of manly struggle.

2. **redcoats:** British soldiers uniforms were red.

2. **tars:** obsolete colloquial term for 'sailors'.

3. **Here it is:** 'this is the answer'.

4. **proud:** refers to the heart which *calls the calling manly*.

8. **And scarlet wear** etc.: '(And fain will find) scarlet wear (to) express the spirit of war there'.

10. **reeve:** 'to pass through and secure'.

10. **There he bides:** i.e. in Heaven.

13. **So God-made-flesh does too:** just as man's best actions emulate Christ, so Incarnate God-in-Christ acted, and would act, fully as a man.

14. **Were I come o'er again:** i.e. were He to become man on earth again: *it should be this* same pattern he would follow.

A sonnet in alexandrines (six stresses per line), heavily stressed – with additional strong stresses not counting metrically.

84. 'Thee, God, I come from, to thee go' (1885) (*p. 89*):

In the Dublin period that saw the writing of the 'terrible sonnets' these stanzas seem oddly thin. Compare, for example, the phrase 'acknowledging thy stress' (l. 6) with the fleshed-out terror of the 'terrible sonnets' or the opening of 'The Wreck of the Deutschland' of ten years earlier. Equally formulaic are the lines that were meant to be incorporated in this unfinished poem: 'Jesus Christ sacrificed/ On the cross ... // Moulded, he, in maiden's womb,/ Lived and died and from the tomb/ Rose in power and is our/Judge that comes to deal our doom'.

85. 'Patience, hard thing! the hard thing but to pray' (1885) (*p. 89*):
Rule 8 'for the Discernment of Spirits' in St Ignatius Loyola's exercises advised as follows: 'Let him who is in desolation strive to remain in patience, which is the virtue contrary to the troubles which harass him; and let him think that he will shortly be consoled, making diligent efforts against the desolation'. This and the next sonnet movingly mix such doctrinal advice with the common-sense that tells us all to draw back from unnecessary self-torment.

1–4. **but to pray** etc.: it is hard 'even to pray for' Patience, as the next three lines explain: because the prayer should really involve an acceptance of the things which give Patience its real meaning (*war, wounds, weary times* and *tasks* etc.).
5. **and, these away:** cf. Shakespeare Sonnet 97 – 'And, thou away, the very birds are mute' – and Hopkins's own poem 'The Half-way House': 'it is evening now and Thou away' (p. 18).
10. **to bruise them dearer:** *dearer* (archaic) = 'more grievously'.
14. **combs:** honeycombs.

Standard sonnet rhythm, but with marked counterpointing at times.

86. 'My own heart let me more have pity on' (1885) (*p. 90*):
5–8. **I cast for comfort** etc.: '*I cast for comfort I can no more get/By groping round my comfortless* (world), *than blind/Eyes in their dark* (world) *can* (find) *day or thirst can find etc.*' The last reference seems an echo of Coleridge's 'The Rime of the Ancient Mariner': 'water, water every where,/Nor any drop to drink'.
9. **poor Jackself:** his own common self.
11–12. **let joy size** etc.: 'let joy grow and strengthen at a time and occasion to be determined by God'.
12–13. **whose smile/'s not wrung:** 'whose favour is not to be forced'.
13–14. **as skies/Betweenpie mountains:** *Betweenpie* is a verb – 'as skies dapple the space between two mountains'.
14. **lights:** its subject is God's *smile* (l. 12).

The standard sonnet rhythm of the octave is much less discernible in the sestet.

87. To his Watch, (undated) (*p. 91*):

7. **One spell and well that one:** the idea that we must use *well* our *one spell* on earth.

88. Spelt from Sibyl's Leaves (1884–85) (*p. 91*):
Just as the Sibyl deciphered the judgment of the gods from natural signs, Hopkins here prefigures God's judgment in a description of evening first obliterating and then transforming the world as usually seen by day. It brings in a new order which emphasises, in its *black* and *white*, the clear understanding of 'wrong' and 'right' by which man is urged to live.

1. **earthless:** because as if dissolving the material world, and being of a different order of reality from it.

1. **equal:** in one sense, *equal* to the task of transformation.

1. **attuneable:** capable of 'harmonising' two different dimensions.

3–4. **Her fond yellow hornlight** etc.: the rays of the sun, *wound to the west* at sunset, give way to the *hoarlight* of the period before the stars appear (hence *hollow*); but both *waste* in the sense of fading and giving way to the different light when the stars do appear.

4–5. **earliest stars, earlstars** etc.: the earliest stars then give way to the appearance of the full constellations (*stars principal*) which *overbend* or dominate, revealing the face of heaven – *fire-featuring* it.

5–7. **her being has unbound** etc.: the *being* of earth is its unique 'dappled' variety: this is now dissolving, merging and losing separate identity. The dialect word *throughther* (l. 6) = 'through each other'.

7. **Heart, you round me right:** the obsolete verb *round* = 'warn' or 'whisper'.

9. **beakleaved boughs:** because the leaves are silhouetted like beaks against the sky.

9. **damask:** 'mark with patterns'.

10–14. **Óur tale, O óur oracle!** etc.: Hopkins remarks the lesson implicit in a scene which has changed the world to black and white. The final lines of the poem can be loosely paraphrased: 'Let life, once past, wind off all her once varied patterns on to two spools; let her divide and pen that variety in two flocks representing in the end only two things – right and wrong; let her pay attention only to these two divisions; let her be aware of a world to come where these are the only two divisions which count; let her be aware of a punishment that will take the form of an eternal life lived only with the tormented self, divorced from God.'

Hopkins called this 'the longest sonnet ever made'. It is in sprung rhythm, with eight stresses to a line.

89. On the Portrait of Two Beautiful Young People (Christmas 1886) Monasterevan (*p. 92*):
Hopkins was on a few days' holiday over Christmas and New Year at Monasterevan House in County Kildare where he saw this painting of a boy and girl, relatives of his hosts. The poem is an elegy – 'in Gray's elegy metre,' Hopkins said, 'severe, no experiments'. The theme is how time compromises both innocence and beauty. The poem focuses on, or reflects indirectly, images in the actual painting – for example, the fruit and vines surrounding the two faces (ll. 3–4), the girl's ringlet (l. 12), the girl's 'leaning' towards her brother (l. 13), while *His looks . . . fall directly forth on life* (ll. 15–16).

8. **all heft:** 'all effort' – forecasting the 'effort', *hope*, and *hazard* still to come.

12. **Barrow:** the river running through Monasterevan.

24. **One once that was found wanting:** Matthew 19: 16–24.

29. **eye:** used as a verb = 'see'.

90. Harry Ploughman (September 1887) Dromore (*p. 93*):
Conceived at the same time as the more overtly political 'Tom's Garland'. They were regarded by Hopkins as companion pieces, celebrating respectively a rural and an urban labourer. Hopkins on reflection considered both poems technically over-wrought, but emphasised the importance of reading-aloud for an understanding of them. Harry Ploughman is realised purely in terms of physique and the physical effort that his work entails – though not reductively, and not without a firm ennobling power in the imagery.

1–2. **with a broth of goldish flue** etc.: *flue*, literally fluff of cotton, depicts the light hair on his arms.

2. scooped flank: the slim waist, as if hollowed-out.

2–3. lank/Rope-over thigh: lean, with taut over-lying muscles.

3. knee-nave: knee-cap, *nave* meaning literally 'hub of a wheel'.

5–6. fall to;/Stand at stress: these are the main verbs of the one sentence so far. All the parts of Harry's body are depicted as *one crew* awaiting orders for action, *steered* by the alertness of the man's eye.

6. barrowy: 'bulging' (from 'barrow' = mound).

7. onewhere curded, onewhere sucked or sank: the muscles (as already described) in some places are bulging or knotted (*curded*), in others tensely drawn in.

9. beechbole: trunk of a beech tree.

9–10. finds his . . . rank/And features, in flesh: the main verbs of the sentence, whose subject is *each limb's barrowy brawn* (l. 6). The words *features, in flesh* mean that the muscles 'manifest physically' what work they have to do.

13. quail: Harry's body pliantly moves with, and yields to, the strong, uneven movement (*the wallowing*) of the plough.

14. crossbridle: his *curls* cross and tangle in the wind.

15. wind-lilylocks-laced: his white hair (*lilylocks*) blown into an elaborate pattern by the wind (*wind . . . laced*). This insetting of a word between parts of a compound word is called tmesis, but its potential would have been highlighted by Hopkins learning about the Welsh poetic device called 'trychiad' (see Introduction, p. xlvi–xlvii).

16. Churlsgrace: the peasant's ability (Old English 'churl' = peasant).

16. child of Amansstrength: the *churlsgrace* is the product of 'a man's strength'. The phrase *Amansstrength* has a kind of mythic resonance.

16–19. how it hangs or hurls/Them etc.: *it* refers to churlsgrace; *them* refers to the *furls* or 'furrows': 'See how his peasant accomplishment suspends or hurls the furrows in a fountaining, partly glittering action, with the plough and cold furrows underneath, and with his feet racing with and along the furrows, strapped in thick, strong, wrinkled leather.'

The metre is sprung rhythm, with five 'official' stresses to a line, but also with extra-metrical stresses and 'hurried' and 'outriding' feet.

91. Tom's Garland (September 1887) Dromore (*p. 94*):
A companion piece to 'Harry Ploughman' (*p. 93*). Its theme is
the view of the commonwealth or well-ordered society as being
like a single body, with a proper station and function to each
part, the lowliest taking its pride from 'the honour that belongs
to the whole'. Hopkins's explanation to Bridges refers to St
Paul, Plato, and Hobbes as authority for such a view. One also
remembers Menenius's speech to the plebeians in Shakespeare's
Coriolanus (I, i), and many other individual images are also
borrowed from that play. For Hopkins, social anarchy is not
the result of low status but of people finding no place at all in
the body-politic.

The following is a paraphrase of the poem's development:

> Tom – his boots garlanded with squat and surly steel (nails);
> then sturdy Dick, Tom's fellow-labourer, fallow or idle now
> after work, sets aside his pick and strides homewards, striking
> sparks from the ground with his boots. Tom, a navvy at ease
> with the world, thinks now only of supper and bed. His is a
> low lot but (being one who need never feel hunger, who is
> seldom sick, seldomer heartsore, who treads invulnerably
> through the thousands of thorns that thoughts can be) he
> swings or dismisses it as a light matter. 'I waste no time
> thinking of the Commonweal! I would lack high status even
> in a state where all had bread: What! belonging to a well-
> ordered country is itself honour enough in all of us – whether
> one is the lordly head, encircled by the stars, or the mighty
> foot that disfigures the mother-earth'. But there are those who
> are given no satisfaction in either mind or bodily strength;
> who neither carry the dangerous adornment of wealth nor
> labour safely at the lower levels; cast out from the glory of
> life, and its comfort, from everything; with no individuality
> or place in the world's general good; devoid of both wealth
> and honest labour; anxiety, however, they do have a share in
> – and this, when it becomes Despair, makes them lazy curs;
> when it becomes Rage, it makes them something worse,
> human wolves; and their packs infest the age.

This 'caudal' or 'caudated' sonnet has two 'codas' or additions
to the usual fourteen lines: the lines beginning 'Undenizened ...'

and those beginning 'In both . . .' See also 'That Nature is a Heraclitean Fire' (p. 97).

Standard sonnet rhythm (iambic pentameter), but with 'hurried' feet crowding up to four syllables into the time of one.

92. Epithalamion (1888) Dublin (p. 95):
An epithalamion (literally, 'at the bridal-chamber') is a poem in praise of a bride and groom. This was meant for the marriage of Hopkins's brother Everard, married April 1888. But it remained unfinished and Everard and his bride Amy never received it. It was written in a 'Royal University of Ireland' answer-book, probably while Hopkins was invigilating examinations. The imagined landscape, however, is still English, witness the southern *dean* ('dell' or 'valley'), the *clough* ('ravine') and *cleave* ('cleft') of l. 4.

36. **coffer:** the box-like stone basin of the pool.
37. **selfquainèd:** from 'quoin', the angle or corner in a wall.

93. 'The sea took pity: it interposed with doom' (p. 97):
An undated fragment, in pencil, found amongst the poet's posthumous papers.

94. That Nature is a Heraclitean Fire and of the comfort of the Resurrection (July 1888) (p. 97):
The philosophy of Heraclitus (fl. 500 BC) held that all constituents of the material world were variants of the one crucial element of fire. The world was therefore characterised by conditions of perpetual unrest, flux and movement. The sense of permanence in anything was an illusion. The true condition was one of an eternal strife between opposites, never one of complete 'being' but of eternal 'becoming'. Hopkins agrees with the Greek philosopher in seeing the tensions and opposites of a dynamically varied universe, but then turns to celebrate man's ultimately different position in the order of things, as one guaranteed definite immortality through Christ's resurrection.

1-2. **Cloud-puffball** etc.: the first two lines describe the appearance and movement of clouds, always of particular visual interest for Hopkins.
1. **chevy:** 'scamper' or 'chase',
3. **Down roughcast, . . . whitewash:** the reference is to differently surfaced walls on which sunlight and shadows play.

4. Shivelights: light thrown in shafted, fragmented patterns.

4. shadowtackle: shadows thrown by the elm's leaves and branches in the pattern of a ship's sail tackle.

4. lace, lance, and pair: verbs, suggesting the recurrent inter-weaving, and inter-penetration of the shadows.

5. ropes: the verb suggests the wind's own imagined shape and also its effect on things.

6. rutpeel: possibly the ridged, strip effects of dried mud in the ruts.

6. parches: the subject of this verb is *the bright wind* (l. 5).

7. Squandering ooze: the object of *parches*. The casually spread mud is dried by the wind, first to a kind of *dough*, then to a *crust*, and then to *dust*.

7–9. stanches, starches etc.: again, the subject of these verbs is *the bright wind* (l. 5) which 'dries out' the many layers and the footprints which *treadmire toil* has impressed (*footfretted*) in the mud.

9. nature's bonfire: i.e. the process seen, in Heraclitean terms, as the eternal flux of growth and decay, light and shade.

[For the next six-and-a-half lines Hopkins follows Heraclitus in seeing man, too, as simply part of this process. But already the resistance is there to seeing man so reductively. These lines emphasise the tragedy when man's unique spiritual individuality is thought of as coming to a complete end:]

10. clearest-selvèd spark: man is unique because it is only in him that individuality is consciously present.

11. firedint: the mark or impression made by each man's unique selfhood and identity.

12. Both: i.e. both the physical individual himself and his reality as impressed on others, and on the world.

14. disseveral: '*dis*tinct' and '*sever*ed'.

16. Enough!: on turning from a Heraclitean train of thought, Hopkins's words (*joyless*, *dejection*) remind us obliquely that Heraclitus was known as the weeping philosopher.

20. residuary worm: i.e. the worm which consumes what 'remains' of man.

21. at a trumpet crash: refers to I Corinthians 15: 51–52 – 'we shall all be changed, in a moment, in the twinkling of an eye, at the last trump'.

23. Jack: common man.

23. **potsherd:** fragment of broken pottery.

23. **patch:** (archaic) 'a fool'.

This is a 'caudal' or 'caudated' sonnet, with three extra 'codas' of three lines each being added to the usual fourteen-line pattern (see also 'Tom's Garland', *p. 94*). The poem is in sprung rhythm, with many 'outriding' feet. Apart from the short ones, the lines have consistently six stresses each.

95. In honour of St Alphonsus Rodriguez (1888) Dublin (*p. 98*):

Alphonsus Rodriguez had been for forty years hall-porter at the College of Palma in Majorca. His description, in the sonnet's dedication, as 'Laybrother of the Society of Jesus' means that he would have accepted vows of poverty, obedience and chastity, but without being a priest. The poem was 'written to order on the occasion of the first feast since his canonization proper', and gives to a life of quiet service and inner victory the tribute usually reserved for more obvious, outward conquest.

4. **forge:** in the sense that the glory is marked visibly in the *gashed flesh* and *galled shield* of the warrior.

5. **On Christ they do:** similar strokes that *gashed* or *galled* Christ's body left on Him the stigmata, or five wounds, of the crucifixion.

6–7. **But be the war within** etc.: 'but if the war is within'; the verb 'be' governs the next two clauses as well.

8. **hurtle:** the noise of violent activity.

9–10. **hews** etc.: a contrast is established between the more obvious large-scale shaping of geography and the imperceptible growth – the *trickling increment* (l. 10) – of organic things like violets and trees.

12. **conquest:** in the form of St Alphonsus's selfless dedication and his conquest over 'evil spirits' which tormented him (according to a letter from Hopkins to Bridges).

A sonnet in standard rhythm, but with some extra-metrical stresses and elisions.

96. 'Thou are indeed just, Lord, if I contend' (March 1889) (*p. 99*):

Written only some three months before the poet's death. Hopkins had come to consider his five years in Ireland as 'wasted' in terms of creative results. Private retreat notes of January 1888 had contained the remark 'All my undertakings miscarry: I am like a straining eunuch'. The tone of the sonnet is a mixture of humble pleading and outraged disappointment. The Latin epigraph is from the lament of Jeremiah (12:1) and has its English equivalent in the first three lines of the poem.

7. sots and thralls of lust: drunkards and slaves to lust.

9. brakes: thickets.

11. fretty chervil: a wild herb with finely divided (*fretty*) parsley-like leaves.

13. wakes: i.e. 'comes to life'.

14. Mine etc.: the force of *mine* is presumably to be dispersed throughout the line: '*My* lord, lord of *my* life, send *my* roots rain.'

The standard sonnet rhythm of the iambic pentameter should be read (Hopkins urged) '*adagio molto* and with great stress'.

97. 'The shepherd's brow, fronting forked lightning, owns' (April 1889) (*p. 99*):
Compared to the awe-inspiring and heroic glory of God's sphere of action, man is seen as puny, awkward and trivial. The sonnet's strident cynicism made Bridges think it did not merit inclusion among the 'last serious poems'. He included it amongst the 'Fragments'. But its manuscript history shows a complete poem, seriously worked at, and its realistic appraisal of man's basic nature, when not transformed by God's grace, is one which also underlies Hopkins's other, more idealistic poems.

1. fronting: 'facing'.

1. owns: 'acknowledges'.

3. Angels fall: the fate of the fallen angels connect with the *lightning* image of the first line: 'I beheld Satan as lightning fall from heaven' (Luke, 10:18).

7. *memento mori*: used as a noun, it means 'a reminder of death': literally 'remember that you must die'.

9. voids: 'excretes'.

10. blazoned in however bold the name: 'however gloriously named or renowned'.

11. Man Jack: in Hopkins, 'Jack' denotes the ordinary, limited man.

11. **hussy:** 'worthless woman'.

12. **die these deaths** etc.: 'suffer the torments of this realisation, and feed the *flame* of idealism'.

13. **That ...** etc.: he breaks off, finding suddenly hopeless even the earnest piety of his own complaint against man. Instead, an image of life's vanities, distorted like reflections in a spoon, comes to his mind.

13–14. **tame/My tempests there** etc.: the acceptance of life's grotesque nature 'tames' both his own idealistic strivings and his *fussy* complaints.

A sonnet in standard rhythm, but insistently counterpointed.

98. To R. B. (April 1889) (*p. 100*):

The title is a dedication to Robert Bridges, and the poem an account of a feeling of creative deadlock. The sense of spiritual failure, against a background often of physical collapse, marked the final years of Hopkins's career in Ireland. Here, the desolation is also claimed to affect the poet's creative powers. But it is an irony, peculiar to art in many forms, that such negative experience can be expressed with an imaginative power that belies that negativity. Just as the 'terrible sonnets' achieve triumphant form while expressing desolating trauma, the present sonnet is good poetry saying that good poetry is not possible.

1–4. **The fine delight** etc.: the flash of inspiration or feeling which, though brief in itself, prompts creative thought and plants the seed of that which will become the poem.

5–8. **Nine months she then** etc.: *she* = the mind, seen as pregnant with the poems (*wears*, *bears*) and finally raising and tending its offspring (*cares* and *combs*). The mind is thus the widow of the first inspiration, which 'fathered' the poem and then disappeared. But now her aim and work have been happily determined. This is the normal fruitful process which the sestet of the present sonnet claims is no longer possible in Hopkins's case.

9. **Sweet fire the sire of muse:** i.e. the *fine delight that fathers thought* of line 1.

A sonnet in standard rhythm, but with some 'hurried' feet.

SUGGESTIONS FOR FURTHER READING

The Texts:

Poetry

Catherine Phillips (ed.), *Gerard Manley Hopkins*, 'Oxford Authors' series (Oxford University Press, 1986). W. H. Gardner and N. H. MacKenzie (eds), *The Poems of Gerard Manley Hopkins*, 4th edition (Oxford University Press, 1967, 1984).

Prose

Claude Colleer Abbott (ed.), *The Letters of Gerard Manley Hopkins to Robert Bridges* (Oxford University Press, 1955), *The Correspondence of Gerard Manley Hopkins and R. W. Dixon* (Oxford University Press, 1956) and *Further Letters of Gerard Manley Hopkins* (Oxford University Press, 1956).

Humphry House and Graham Storey (eds.), *The Journals and Papers of Gerard Manley Hopkins* (Oxford University Press, 1959).

Christopher Devlin S.J. (ed.), *The Sermons and Devotional Writings of Gerard Manley Hopkins* (Oxford University Press, 1959).

Biographical:

The fullest and most authoritative biographies are:

Robert Bernard Martin, *Gerard Manley Hopkins: A Very Private Life* (HarperCollins, 1991);

Norman White, *Hopkins: A Literary Biography* (Oxford University Press, 1992).

Other studies with a strong biographical emphasis are:

Alfred Thomas S. J., *Hopkins the Jesuit: The Years of Training* (Oxford University Press, 1969);

R. K. R. Thornton, *All My Eyes See: The Visual World of Gerard Manley Hopkins* (Coelfrith Press, 1975);

Bernard Bergonzi, *Gerard Manley Hopkins*, 'Masters of World Literature' series (Macmillan, 1977);

Paddy Kitchen, *Gerard Manley Hopkins* (Hamish Hamilton, 1978).

Norman White, *Gerard Manley Hopkins in Wales* (Seren, 1998).

Bibliographies:

Edward H. Cohen, *Works and Criticism of Gerard Manley Hopkins: A Comprehensive Bibliography* (Washington, 1969).

Tom Dunne, *Gerard Manley Hopkins: A Comprehensive Bibliography* [to 1970–1] (Oxford University Press, 1976).

Commentaries:

Donald McChesney, *A Hopkins Commentary* (University of London Press, 1968).

Peter Milward S. J., *A Commentary on Gerard Manley Hopkins' 'Wreck of the Deutschland'* (Tokyo, 1969) and *A Commentary on the Sonnets of Gerard Manley Hopkins* (Tokyo, 1969).

Paul Mariani, *A Commentary on the Complete Poems of Gerard Manley Hopkins* (Cornell, 1969).

Norman H. MacKenzie, *A Reader's Guide to Gerard Manley Hopkins* (Thames and Hudson, 1981).

Criticism (selections from essays and volumes):

The Kenyon Critics, *Gerard Manley Hopkins: A Critical Symposium* (Burns and Oates, 1945).

Norman Weyand S. J. (ed.), *Immortal Diamond: Studies in Gerard Manley Hopkins* [essays by fellow-Jesuits] (Sheed and Ward, 1949).

Geoffrey Hartman (ed.), *A Collection of Critical Essays*, 'Twentieth Century Views' series (Prentice-Hall, 1966).

Margaret Bottrall (ed.), *Gerard Manley Hopkins: Poems*, 'Casebook' series (Macmillan, 1975).

Gerald Roberts (ed.), *Gerard Manley Hopkins*, 'The Critical Heritage' series (Routledge, 1987).

Criticism (individual essays and volumes):

Alan Heuser, *The Shaping of Gerard Manley Hopkins* (Oxford University Press, 1958).

Todd K. Bender, *Gerard Manley Hopkins: The Classical Background and Critical Reception of his Work* (Baltimore, 1966).

Elizabeth W. Schneider, *The Dragon in the Gate* (Berkeley, 1968).

Barbara Hardy, 'Forms and Feelings in the Sonnets of Gerard Manley Hopkins', the First Annual Lecture, The Hopkins Society, London (1970). Reprinted in Hardy's *The Advantage of Lyric* (Indiana University Press, 1977).

Robert O. Preyer, ' "The Fine Delight that Fathers Thought": Gerard Manley Hopkins and the Romantic Survival' in Malcolm Bradbury and David Palmer (eds.), *Victorian Poetry*, 'Stratford-upon-Avon Studies' series (Edward Arnold, 1972).

C. Küper, *Walisische Traditionen in der Dichtung von Gerard Manley Hopkins* (Bonn, 1973).

Seamus Heaney, 'The Fire i' the Flint: Reflections on the Poetry of Gerard Manley Hopkins', in Heaney's *Preoccupations* (Faber, 1980).

Graham Storey, *A Preface to Hopkins*, 'Preface Books' series (Longman, 1981).

Helen Vendler, 'Gerard Manley Hopkins and Sprung Rhythm', in Vendler's *The Breaking of Style* (Harvard University Press, 1995).

NOTE ON THE TEXT

The text for the poetry is that of *The Poems of Gerard Manley Hopkins*, edited by W. H. Gardner and N. H. Mackenzie, Oxford University Press, 4th edn, 1967. The present volume, however, does not compartmentalise early, major, unfinished or translated poems. In a selection, this has the advantage of bringing together, in chronological order, an integrated sampling of the best poems in each kind and each condition. The present edition also returns poems that were not given a title by Hopkins himself to their untitled form.

The text of the letters is that of *The Letters of Gerard Manley Hopkins to Robert Bridges* and *Further Letters of Gerard Manley Hopkins*, both edited by C. C. Abbott, Oxford University Press, 1955 and 1956 respectively. The text of the devotional writings is that of *The Sermons and Devotional Writings of Gerard Manley Hopkins*, edited by Christopher Devlin S. J., Oxford University Press, 1959.

ACKNOWLEDGEMENTS

For the always pleasurable advantage of discussion of Hopkins's work over many years, the editor is indebted especially to the following: Dorothy Bednarowska, Beatrice Batson and the staff and students of the English Department of Wheaton College, Illinois, Charlotte Otten and the staff and students of the English Department of Calvin College, Michigan, John Wain, Jason Walford Davies and Damian Walford Davies. He would also like to record his appreciation of the expert editorial guidance of Hilary Laurie and Kate Shearman at Everyman.

Work for this edition has also benefited from invitations to the editor to take various aspects of Hopkins as his subjects for the following lectures: the lecture on Hopkins for the international Graduate Summer School, Exeter College, Oxford; the Reichel Lecture, University of Wales, Bangor; the Helen-Louise McGuffie Lecture, Bethany College, West Virginia; the Gwyn Jones Lecture of the Arts Council of Wales; the annual lecture of the North Wales Music Festival and the Workers' Educational Association; and the annual lecture of the Hopkins Society.

The editor and publishers wish to thank the following for permission to use copyright material:

Artellus Ltd on behalf of the Estate of the author for an article by Anthony Burgess reprinted in the *Irish Times*, 14th October, 1989; British Broadcasting Corporation for extracts from BBC Radio 3 programme, *How Meet Beauty: A Broadcast Symposium* (1977); and permission from Elspeth Barker on behalf of George Barker, John Fuller on behalf of Roy Fuller, David Higham Associates on behalf of Elizabeth Jennings, Christopher Ricks, Hallam Tennyson, The Principal Master on behalf of the Society of Jesus for Rev. Alfred Thomas, and William Wain on behalf of John Wain for their contributions to the discussion; Carcanet Press for an extract from Donald Davie, *Purity of*

Diction in English Verse (1952); Curtis Brown Ltd, London, on behalf of the Estate of the author for material from John Wain, *Essays on Literature and Ideas* (1966), Copyright © the Estate of John Wain; Faber and Faber Ltd for material from T. S. Eliot, *After Strange Gods* (1934); and with Farrar Straus & Giroux, Inc for material from Seamus Heaney, *Preoccupations: Selected Prose 1968–78* (1980), Copyright © 1980 by Seamus Heaney; and an extract from John Berryman, 'No 377' from *His Toy, His Dream, His Rest* (1969), Copyright © 1969 by John Berryman, renewed 1977 by Kate Donahue Berryman; David Higham Associates on behalf of the Estate of the author for material from Geoffrey Grigson, *Gerard Manley Hopkins* (1955), Writers and Their Work series, No. 59, published for the British Council and the National Book League, Longman; Robin Leavis for an extract from F. R. Leavis, *New Bearings in English Poetry*, Chatto & Windus (1982); Angelo Longo Editore for material by Ernest Ferlita s j from P. Bottalla, G. Marra and F. Marucci, eds, *Gerard Manley Hopkins: Tradition and Innovation* (1990); New Welsh Review for 'Walford Davies interviews John Wain', *New Welsh Review*, 7 (1989–90); Oxford University Press for material from Christopher Ricks, *Essays in Appreciation* (1966); and on behalf of the Society for Jesus for poems from W. H. Gardner and N. H. MacKenzie, eds, *The Poems of Gerard Manley Hopkins* (4th edition 1967); and material from Humphrey House and Graham Storey, eds, *The Journals and Papers of Gerard Manley Hopkins* (1959), Claude Colleer Abbott, ed., *Further Letters of GMH* (2nd edition 1956), Claude Colleer Abbott, ed., *The Letters of GMH to Robert Bridges* (1955) and Christopher Devlin, ed., *The Sermons and Devotional Writings of GMH* (1959); The Society of Authors as the Literary Representatives of the Estate of the author for material from a review by John Middleton Murry in *The Atheneum*, June 1919.

Every effort has been made to trace the copyright holders, but, if any have been inadvertently overlooked, the publishers will be pleased to make the necessary arrangements at the first opportunity.

INDEX OF TITLES AND FIRST LINES
(POETRY)

(First lines within inverted commas)

'A bugler boy from barrack (it is over the hill' 62
'Ah child, no Persian-perfect art!' 27
Alchemist in the City, The 14
'All slumbered whom our rud red tiles' 29
'Although the letter said' 9
Andromeda 65
'As a dare-gale skylark scanted in a dull cage' 49
'As Devonshire letters, earlier in the year' 15
'As kingfishers catch fire, dragonflies draw flame' 70
A Trio of Triolets 71
At the Wedding March 66

'Beyond Magdalen and by the Bridge, on a place called there the
Plain' 62
Binsey Poplars 57
Blessed Virgin compared to the Air we Breathe, The 80
Brothers 67
Bugler's First Communion, The 62
'But tell me, child, your choice; what shall I buy' 60

Caged Skylark, The 49
Candle Indoors, The 60
Cheery Beggar 62
'Cloud-puffball, torn tufts, tossed pillows flaunt forth, then chevy
on an air—' 97
Complaint, A 19

'Denis, whose motionable, alert, most vaulting wit' 55
Duns Scotus's Oxford 58

'Earnest, earthless, equal, attunable, vaulty, voluminous . . .
stupendous' 91
'Earth, sweet Earth, sweet landscape, with leavès throng' 70

'Elected Silence, sing to me'   23
Elopement, The   29
Epithalamion   95
Escorial, The   3

Felix Randal   67
'Felix Randal the farrier, O is he dead then? my duty all ended'   67
'Forward she leans, with hollowing back, stock-still'   12
' "From nine o'clock till morning light" '   22

'Glory be to God for dappled things—'   48
God's Grandeur   44
'God, though to Thee our psalm we raise'   24
'God with honour hang your head'   66

Habit of Perfection, The   23
Half-way House, The   18
Handsome Heart, The   60
'Hard as hurdle arms, with a broth of goldish flue'   93
'Hark, hearer, hear what I do; lend a thought now, make believe'   95
Harry Ploughman   93
'Have fair fallen, O fair, fair have fallen, so dear'   58
Heaven-Haven   9
'He mightbe slow and something feckless first'   56
Henry Purcell   58
'Honour is flashed off exploit, so we say'   98
Horace: Odi profanum volgus et arceo   28
Horace: Persicos odi, puer, apparatus   27
'How all's to one thing wrought!'   61
'How lovely the elder brother's'   67
'How to kéep – is there any ány, is there none such'   72
Hurrahing in Harvest   48

'I awoke in the Midsummer not-to-call night, in the white and
   the walk of the morning'   40
'I bear a basket lined with grass'   26
'I caught this morning morning's minion, king—'   47
'I had a dream. A Wondrous thing'   8
'I have desired to go'   9
'I must hunt down the prize'   10
In honour of St Alphonsus Rodriguez   98
'In the lodges of the perishable souls'   17
In the Valley of the Elwy   46

Inversnaid   69
Io   12
'I remember a house where all were good'   46
'I thought that you would have written: my birthday came and
    went'   19
'It was a hard thing to undo this knot'   10
'I wake and feel the fell of dark, not day'   85

Lantern out of Doors, The   49
Leaden Echo and the Golden Echo, The   72
'Let me be to Thee as the circling bird'   18
Lines for a Picture of St Dorothea   26
'Look at the stars! look, look up at the skies!'   45
Loss of the Eurydice, The   50
'Love I was shewn upon the mountain-side'   18

'Margaret, are you grieving'   69
'May is Mary's month, and I'   53
May Magnificat, The   53
'Miss Story's character! too much you ask'   11
'Moonless darkness stands between'   20
Moonrise   40
Morning, Midday, and Evening Sacrifice   64
'Mortal my mate, bearing my rock-a-heart'   91
'My aspens dear, whose airy cages quelled'   57
'My own heart let me more have pity on'   90
'My prayers must meet a brazen heaven'   17
'Myself unholy, from myself unholy'   16
'My window shows the travelling clouds'   14

New Readings   9
Nightingale, The   22
Nondum   24
' "No news in the Times to-day" '   71
'Nothing is so beautiful as Spring—'   45
'Not, I'll not, carrion comfort, Despair, not feast on thee'   87
'Not of all my eyes see, wandering on the world'   84
'No worst, there is none. Pitched past pitch of grief'   86
'Now Time's Andromeda on this rock rude'   65

'O I admire and sorrow! The heart's eye grieves'   92
'On ear and ear two noises too old to end'   46
On the Portrait of Two Beautiful Young People   92

'Patience, hard thing! the hard thing but to pray'   89
Peace   65
Penmaen Pool   43
Pied Beauty   48

'Repeat that, repeat'   59
Ribblesdale   70

Sea and the Skylark, The   46
'See how Spring opens with disabling cold'   16
Shakspere   17
Silver Jubilee, The   41
'Some candle clear burns somewhere I come by'   60
'Sometimes a lantern moves along the night'   49
Spelt from Sibyl's Leaves   91
Spring   45
Spring and Death   8
Spring and Fall   69
Starlight Night, The   45
'Strike, churl; hurl, cheerless wind, then'   86
St Winefred's Well   74
'Summer ends now; now, barbarous in beauty, the stooks rise'   48

'Teevo cheevo cheevio chee'   41
That nature is a Heraclitean Fire and of the comfort of the
    Resurrection   97
'The boughs, the boughs are bare enough'   7
' "The child is father to the man" '   72
'The dappled die-away'   64
'The earth and heaven, so little known'   20
'Thee, God, I come from, to thee go'   89
'The Eurydice – it concerned thee, O Lord'   50
'The fine delight that fathers thought; the strong'   100
'The furl of fresh-leaved dogrose down'   55
'There is a massy pile above the waste'   3
'The sea took pity: it interposed with doom'   97
'The shepherd's brow, fronting forked lightning, owns'   99
'The stars were packed so close that night'   21
'The times are nightfall, look, their light grows less'   83
'The world is charged with the grandeur of God'   44
'This darksome burn, horseback brown'   69
'Thou art indeed just, Lord, if I contend'   99

'Though no high-hung bells or din'   41
'Thou mastering me'   31
To his Watch   91
'Tom – garlanded with squat and surly steel'   94
Tom's Garland   94
To Oxford ('As Devonshire letters, earlier in the year')   15
To Oxford ('New-dated from the terms that reappear')   13
To Oxford ('Thus, I come underneath this chapel-side')   13
To R. B.   100
'To seem the stranger lies my lot, my life'   84
'Towery city and branchy between towers'   58
To what serves Mortal Beauty?   87
'To what serves mortal beauty – dangerous; does set danc—'   87
'Tread back—and back, the lewd and lay!—'   28

'What being in rank-old nature should earlier have that breath
    been'   56
'What is it, Gwen, my girl? why do you hover and haunt me?'   74
'When will you ever, Peace, wild wooddove, shy wings shut'   65
'"When you ask for Cockle's Pills"'   71
'Who long for rest, who look for pleasure'   43
'Why should their foolish bands, their hopeless hearses'   10
'Wild air, world-mothering air'   80
Windhover, The   47
Winter with the Gulf Stream   7
Woodlark, The   41
Wreck of the Deutschland, The   31

'Yes. Why do we all, seeing of a soldier, bless him?'   88